HERE COMES...

DAREDEVIL

DAREDEVIL BY MARK WAID VOL. 3. Contains material originally published in magazine form as DAREDEVIL #11-15, AVENGING SPIDER-MAN #6 and THE PUNISHER #10. First printing 2012. Hardcover ISBN# 978-0-7851-6100-4. Softcover ISBN# 978-0-7851-6101-1. Published by MARVEL WORLDWIDE, INC., a subsidiary of MARVEL ENTERTAINMENT, LLC. OFFICE OF PUBLICATION: 135 West 50th Street, New York, NY 10020. Copyright © 2012 Marvel Characters, Inc. All rights reserved. Hardcover: $19.99 per copy in the U.S. and $21.99 in Canada (GST #R127032852). Softcover: $16.99 per copy in the U.S. and $18.99 in Canada (GST #R127032852). Canadian Agreement #40668537. All characters featured in this issue and the distinctive names and likenesses thereof, and all related indicia are trademarks of Marvel Characters, Inc. No similarity between any of the names, characters, persons, and/or institutions in this magazine with those of any living or dead person or institution is intended, and any such similarity which may exist is purely coincidental. **Printed in the U.S.A.** ALAN FINE, EVP - Office of the President, Marvel Worldwide, Inc. and EVP & CMO Marvel Characters B.V.; DAN BUCKLEY, Publisher & President - Print, Animation & Digital Divisions; JOE QUESADA, Chief Creative Officer; TOM BREVOORT, SVP of Publishing; DAVID BOGART, SVP of Operations & Procurement, Publishing; RUWAN JAYATILLEKE, SVP & Associate Publisher, Publishing; C.B. CEBULSKI, SVP of Creator & Content Development; DAVID GABRIEL, SVP of Publishing Sales & Circulation; MICHAEL PASCIULLO, SVP of Brand Planning & Communications; JIM O'KEEFE, VP of Operations & Logistics; DAN CARR, Executive Director of Publishing Technology; SUSAN CRESPI, Editorial Operations Manager; ALEX MORALES, Publishing Operations Manager; STAN LEE, Chairman Emeritus. For information regarding advertising in Marvel Comics or on Marvel.com, please contact Niza Disla, Director of Marvel Partnerships, at ndisla@marvel.com. For Marvel subscription inquiries, please call 800-217-9158. **Manufactured between 7/23/2012 and 9/3/2012 (hardcover), and 7/23/2012 and 3/4/2013 (softcover), by R.R. DONNELLEY, INC., SALEM, VA, USA.**

10 9 8 7 6 5 4 3 2 1

WRITERS
MARK WAID
(AVENGING SPIDER-MAN #6 & DAREDEVIL #11-15)
GREG RUCKA
(AVENGING SPIDER-MAN #6 & PUNISHER #10)

AVENGING SPIDER-MAN #6, PUNISHER #10 & DAREDEVIL #11
ARTIST
MARCO CHECCHETTO
COLOR ARTIST
MATT HOLLINGSWORTH

DAREDEVIL #12 & #14-15
ARTIST
CHRIS SAMNEE
COLOR ARTIST
JAVIER RODRIGUEZ

DAREDEVIL #13
PENCILER
KHOI PHAM
INKER
TOM PALMER
COLOR ARTIST
JAVIER RODRIGUEZ

LETTERER
VC'S JOE CARAMAGNA
COVER ARTISTS
STEVE McNIVEN, MARK MORALES & MARTE GRACIA
(AVENGING SPIDER-MAN #6)
MARCO CHECCHETTO
(PUNISHER #10)
MARCOS MARTIN
(DAREDEVIL #11)
PAOLO RIVERA
(DAREDEVIL #12 & #14-15)
AND **KHOI PHAM & JAVIER RODRIGUEZ**
(DAREDEVIL #13)

ASSISTANT EDITOR
ELLIE PYLE
EDITOR
STEPHEN WACKER

COLLECTION EDITOR & DESIGN *CORY LEVINE* • ASSISTANT EDITORS *ALEX STARBUCK* & *NELSON RIBEIRO*
EDITORS, SPECIAL PROJECTS *JENNIFER GRÜNWALD* & *MARK D. BEAZLEY*
SENIOR EDITOR, SPECIAL PROJECTS *JEFF YOUNGQUIST* • SENIOR VICE PRESIDENT OF SALES *DAVID GABRIEL*
SVP OF BRAND PLANNING & COMMUNICATIONS *MICHAEL PASCIULLO*

EDITOR IN CHIEF *AXEL ALONSO* • CHIEF CREATIVE OFFICER *JOE QUESADA*
PUBLISHER *DAN BUCKLEY* • EXECUTIVE PRODUCER *ALAN FINE*

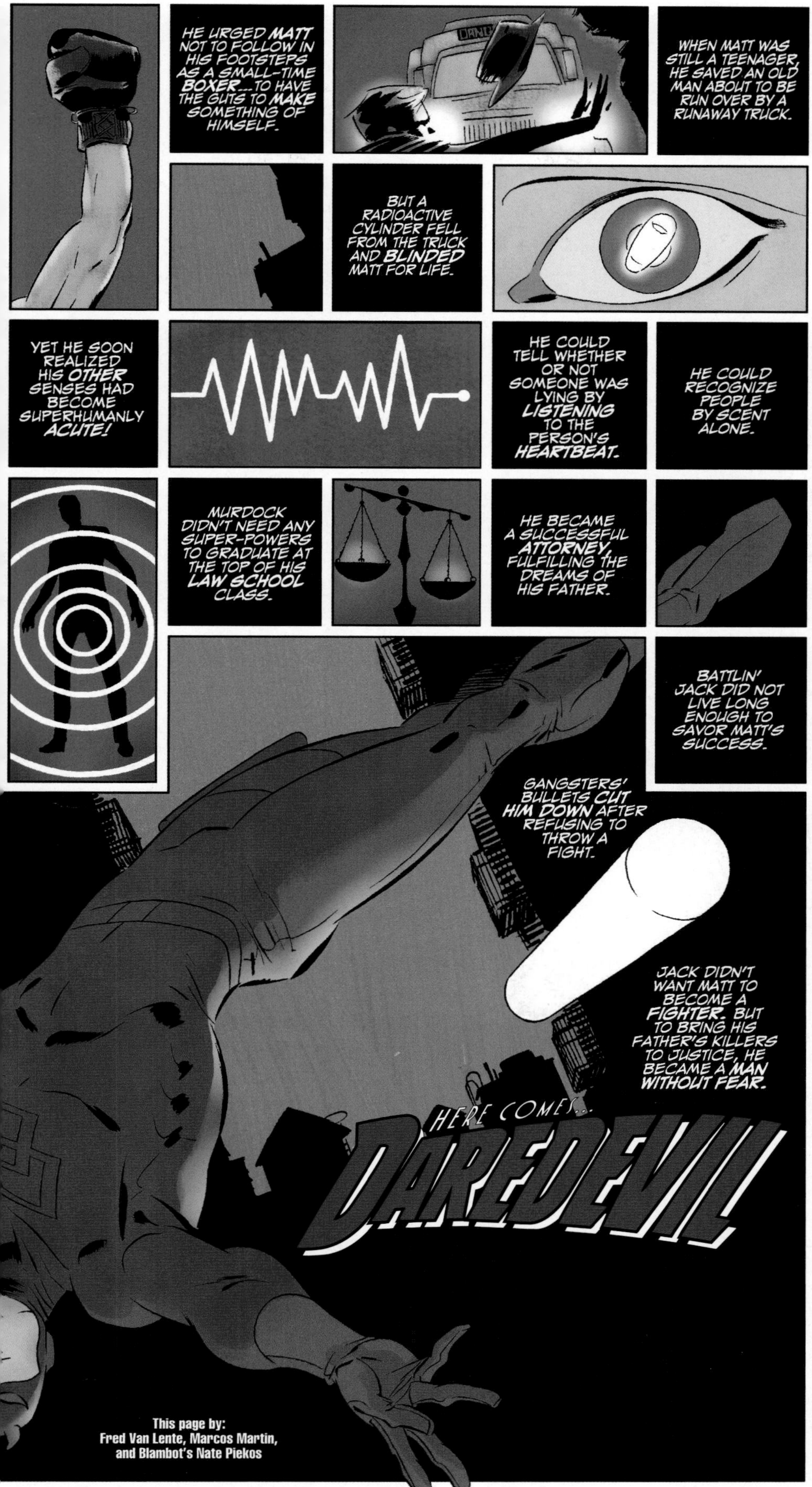
HE URGED MATT NOT TO FOLLOW IN HIS FOOTSTEPS AS A SMALL-TIME BOXER...TO HAVE THE GUTS TO MAKE SOMETHING OF HIMSELF.
WHEN MATT WAS STILL A TEENAGER, HE SAVED AN OLD MAN ABOUT TO BE RUN OVER BY A RUNAWAY TRUCK.
BUT A RADIOACTIVE CYLINDER FELL FROM THE TRUCK AND BLINDED MATT FOR LIFE.
YET HE SOON REALIZED HIS OTHER SENSES HAD BECOME SUPERHUMANLY ACUTE!
HE COULD TELL WHETHER OR NOT SOMEONE WAS LYING BY LISTENING TO THE PERSON'S HEARTBEAT.
HE COULD RECOGNIZE PEOPLE BY SCENT ALONE.
MURDOCK DIDN'T NEED ANY SUPER-POWERS TO GRADUATE AT THE TOP OF HIS LAW SCHOOL CLASS.
HE BECAME A SUCCESSFUL ATTORNEY, FULFILLING THE DREAMS OF HIS FATHER.
BATTLIN' JACK DID NOT LIVE LONG ENOUGH TO SAVOR MATT'S SUCCESS.
GANGSTERS' BULLETS CUT HIM DOWN AFTER REFUSING TO THROW A FIGHT.
JACK DIDN'T WANT MATT TO BECOME A FIGHTER. BUT TO BRING HIS FATHER'S KILLERS TO JUSTICE, HE BECAME A MAN WITHOUT FEAR.
HERE COMES...
DAREDEVIL!
This page by:
Fred Van Lente, Marcos Martin, and Blambot's Nate Piekos

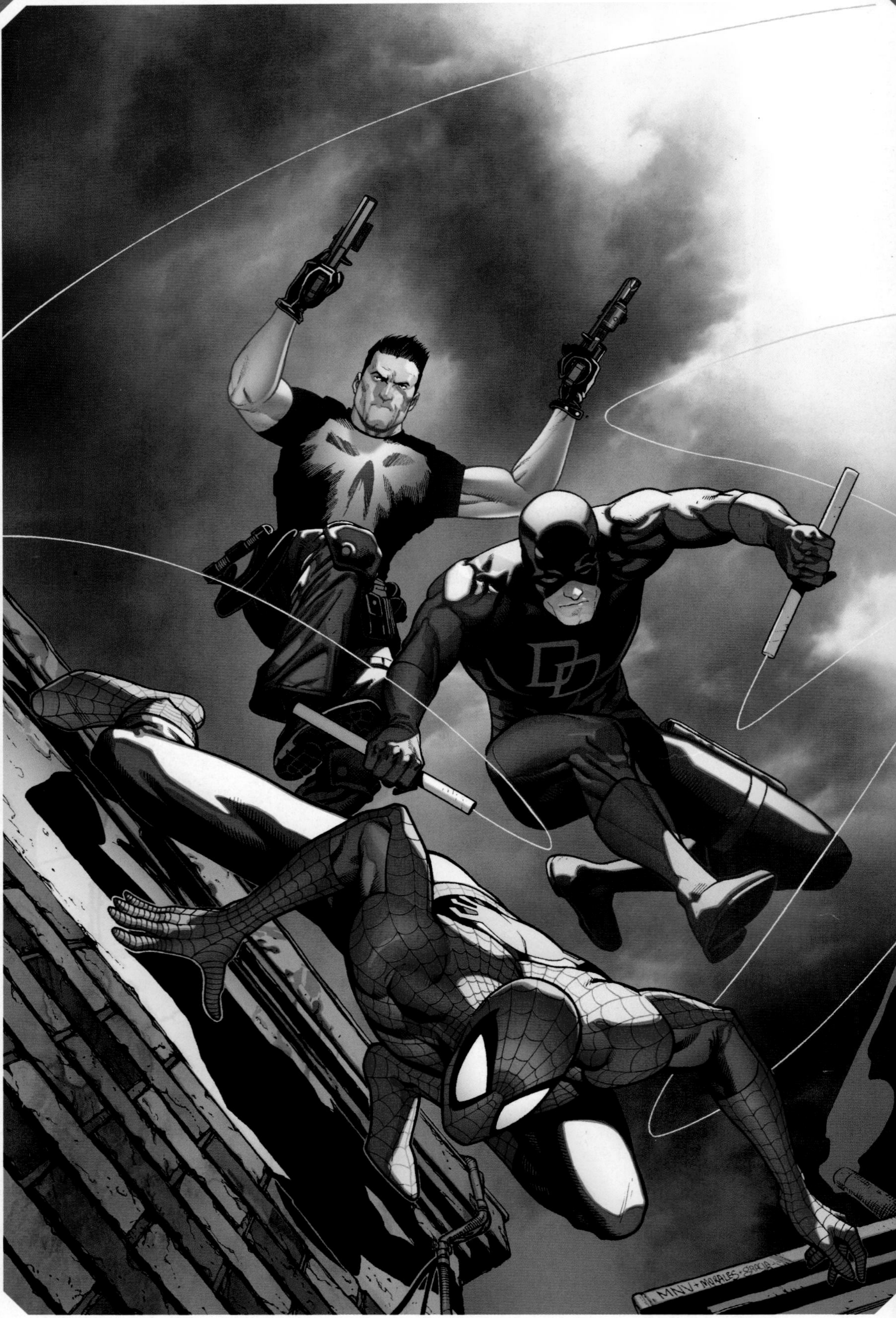

AVENGING SPIDER-MAN #6

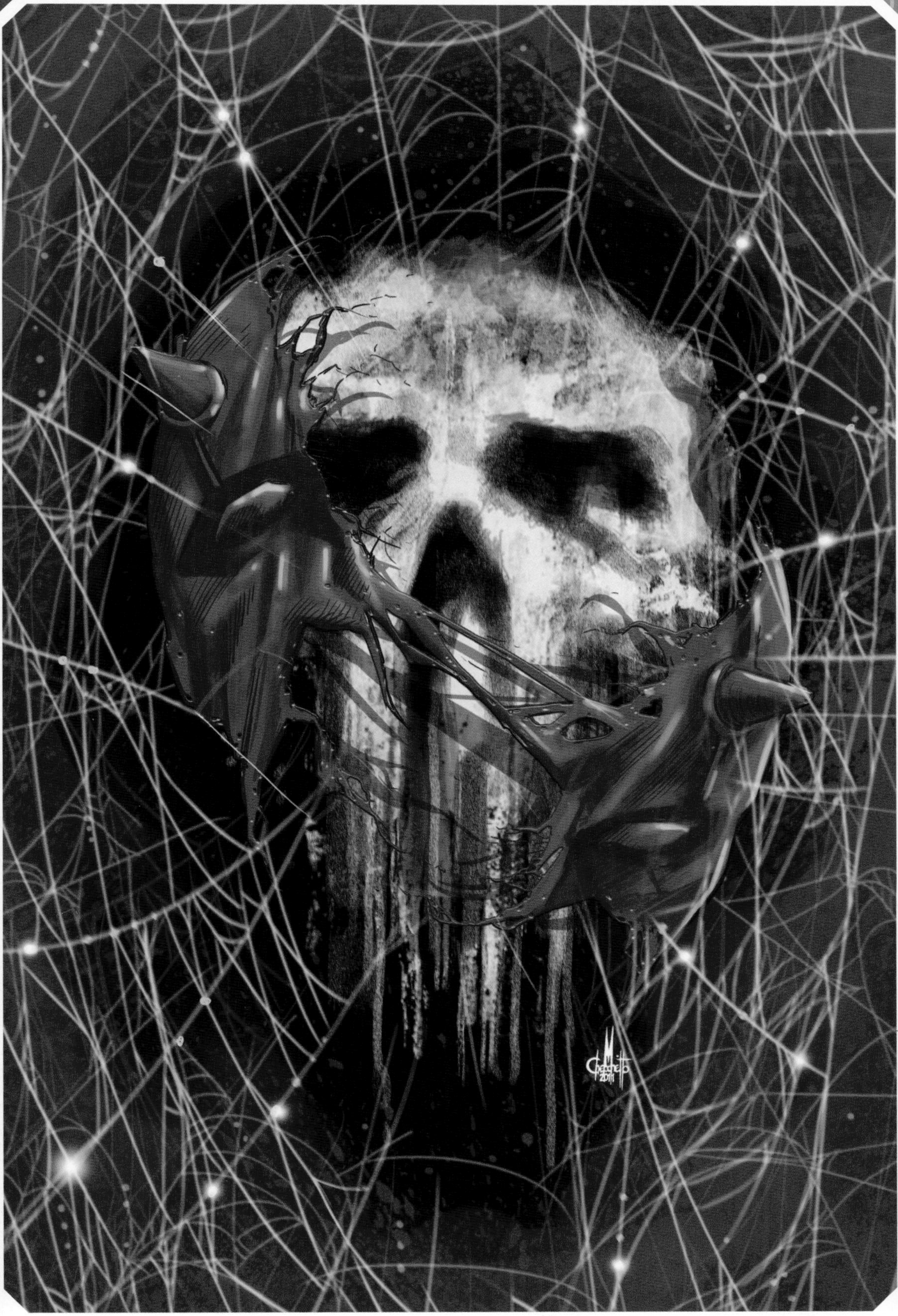

AVENGING SPIDER-MAN #6 **VARIANT BY MARCO CHECCHETTO**

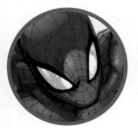

While attending a demonstration in radiology, high school student Peter Parker was bitten by a spider which had accidentally been exposed to radioactive rays. Through a miracle of science, Peter soon found that he had gained the spider's powers...and had, in effect, become a human spider! With great power and great responsibility, he's the...

AVENGING SPIDER-MAN

HERE COMES... DAREDEVIL

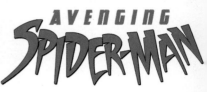

When Matt Murdock was a teenager he saved a man from being hit by a truck but a radioactive cylinder fell from the truck, and blinded Matt for life. He soon discovered his other senses had been enhanced to superhuman levels and his sight had been replaced by a new 360-degree radar sense! He became a lawyer, but also the Man Without Fear!

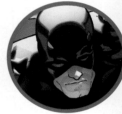

Frank Castle was a decorated Marine Corps officer who served his country above and beyond the call of duty in time of war. He returned from battle to the arms of his wife and children, only to have them stolen away in a brutal act of random, savage violence. Frank Castle died with his family. Now, all he has is his desire for vengeance and his need to punish the wicked. Simply, he is...

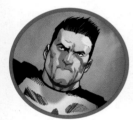

THE PUNISHER

AVENGING SPIDER-MAN

PREVIOUSLY...

Daredevil came into possession of The Omega Drive which is full of information about A.I.M., Hydra, Black Spectre, Agence Byzantine, and the Secret Empire. Now everyone wants it, including the Punisher.

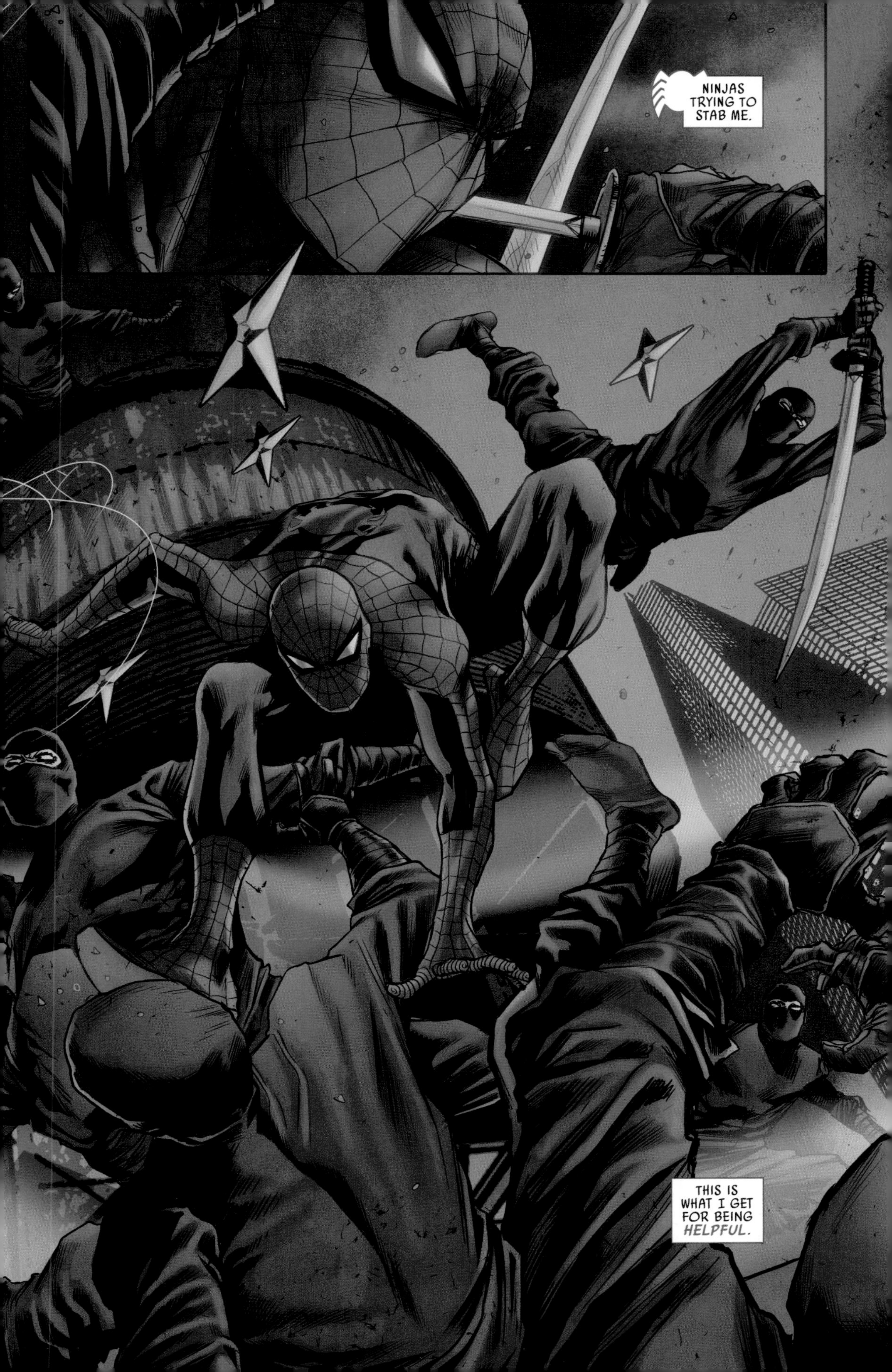
NINJAS TRYING TO STAB ME.
THIS IS WHAT I GET FOR BEING *HELPFUL*.

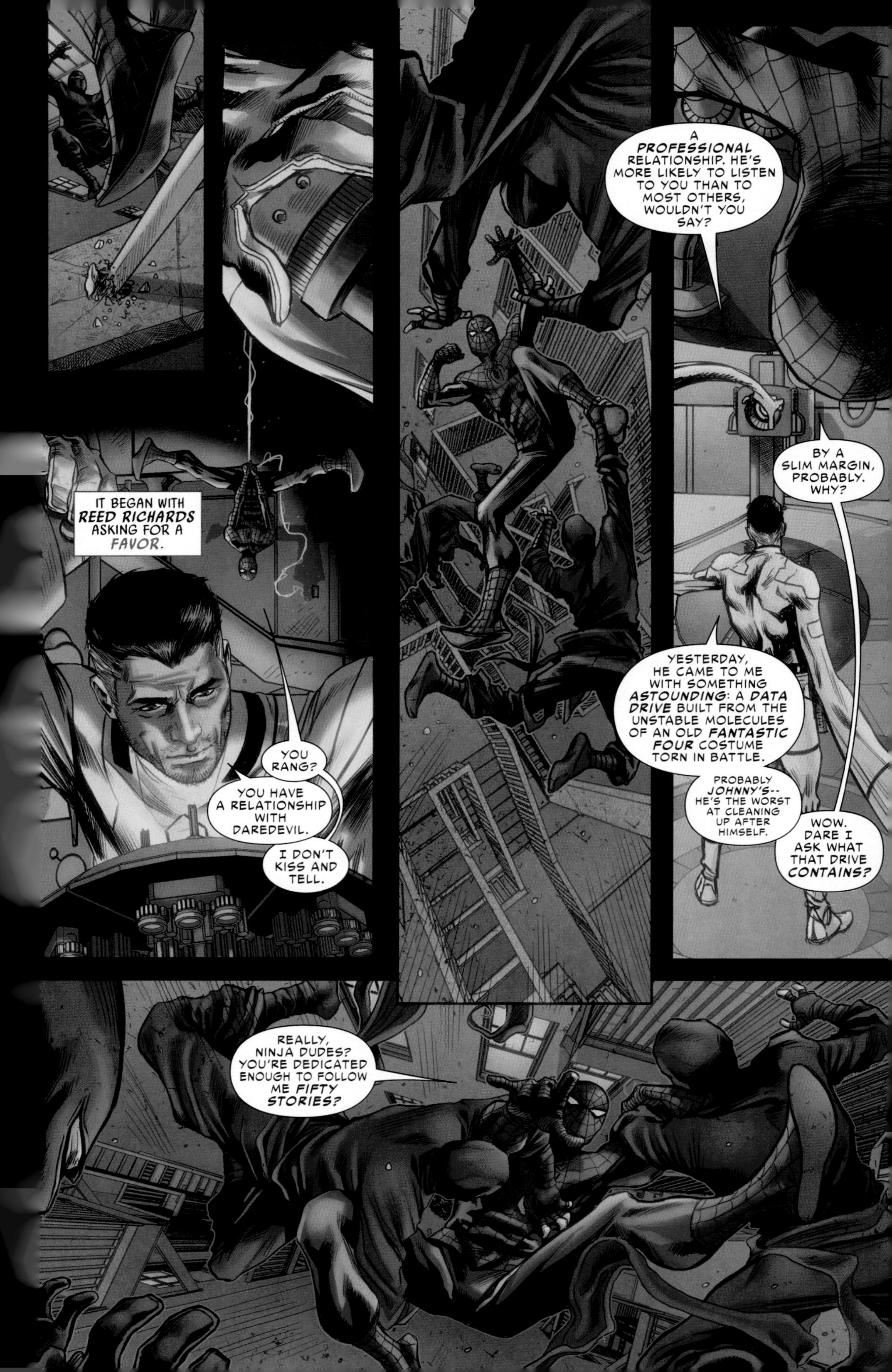
IT BEGAN WITH REED RICHARDS ASKING FOR A FAVOR.
YOU RANG?
YOU HAVE A RELATIONSHIP WITH DAREDEVIL.
I DON'T KISS AND TELL.
A PROFESSIONAL RELATIONSHIP. HE'S MORE LIKELY TO LISTEN TO YOU THAN TO MOST OTHERS, WOULDN'T YOU SAY?
BY A SLIM MARGIN, PROBABLY. WHY?
YESTERDAY, HE CAME TO ME WITH SOMETHING ASTOUNDING: A DATA DRIVE BUILT FROM THE UNSTABLE MOLECULES OF AN OLD FANTASTIC FOUR COSTUME TORN IN BATTLE.
PROBABLY JOHNNY'S-- HE'S THE WORST AT CLEANING UP AFTER HIMSELF.
WOW. DARE I ASK WHAT THAT DRIVE CONTAINS?
REALLY, NINJA DUDES? YOU'RE DEDICATED ENOUGH TO FOLLOW ME FIFTY STORIES?

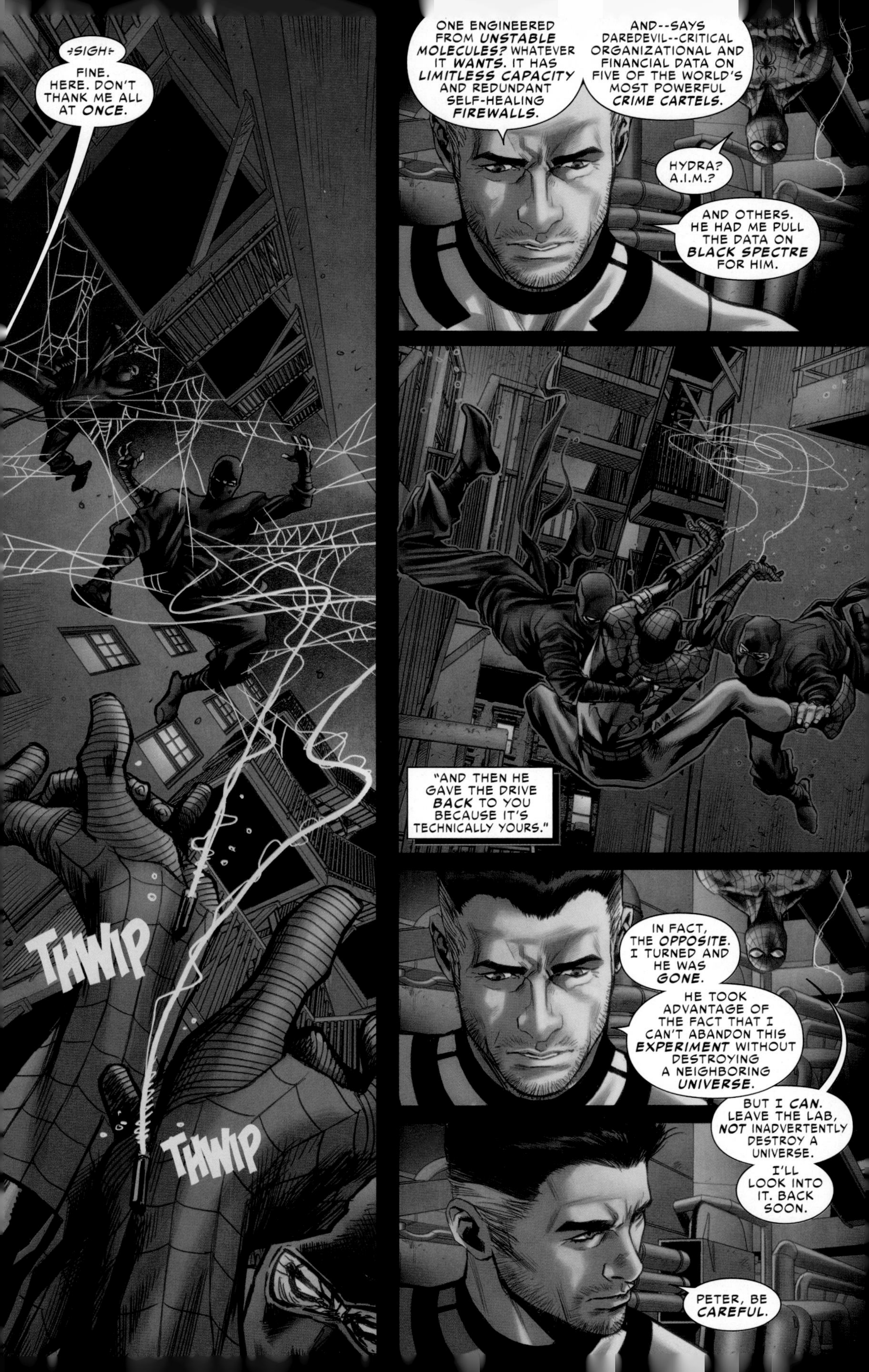

SIGH
FINE. HERE. DON'T THANK ME ALL AT ONCE.
THWIP
THWIP
ONE ENGINEERED FROM UNSTABLE MOLECULES? WHATEVER IT WANTS. IT HAS LIMITLESS CAPACITY AND REDUNDANT SELF-HEALING FIREWALLS.
AND--SAYS DAREDEVIL--CRITICAL ORGANIZATIONAL AND FINANCIAL DATA ON FIVE OF THE WORLD'S MOST POWERFUL CRIME CARTELS.
HYDRA? A.I.M.?
AND OTHERS. HE HAD ME PULL THE DATA ON BLACK SPECTRE FOR HIM.
"AND THEN HE GAVE THE DRIVE BACK TO YOU BECAUSE IT'S TECHNICALLY YOURS."
IN FACT, THE OPPOSITE. I TURNED AND HE WAS GONE.
HE TOOK ADVANTAGE OF THE FACT THAT I CAN'T ABANDON THIS EXPERIMENT WITHOUT DESTROYING A NEIGHBORING UNIVERSE.
BUT I CAN. LEAVE THE LAB, NOT INADVERTENTLY DESTROY A UNIVERSE.
I'LL LOOK INTO IT. BACK SOON.
PETER, BE CAREFUL.

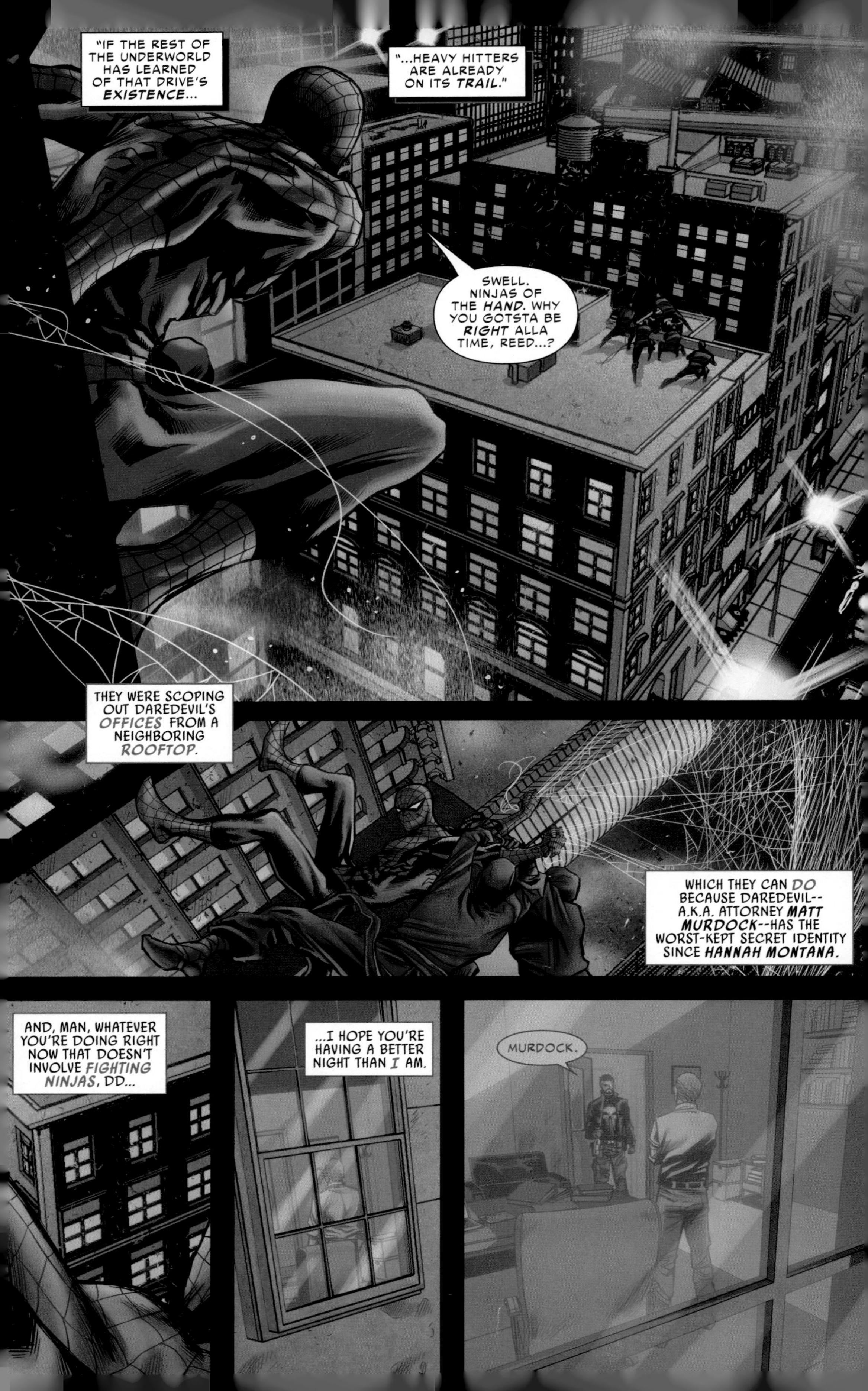
"IF THE REST OF THE UNDERWORLD HAS LEARNED OF THAT DRIVE'S *EXISTENCE*...
"...HEAVY HITTERS ARE ALREADY ON ITS *TRAIL*."
SWELL. NINJAS OF THE *HAND*. WHY YOU GOTSTA BE *RIGHT* ALLA TIME, REED...?
THEY WERE SCOPING OUT DAREDEVIL'S *OFFICES* FROM A NEIGHBORING *ROOFTOP*.
WHICH THEY CAN *DO* BECAUSE DAREDEVIL--A.K.A. ATTORNEY *MATT MURDOCK*--HAS THE WORST-KEPT SECRET IDENTITY SINCE *HANNAH MONTANA*.
AND, MAN, WHATEVER YOU'RE DOING RIGHT NOW THAT DOESN'T INVOLVE *FIGHTING NINJAS*, DD...
...I HOPE YOU'RE HAVING A BETTER NIGHT THAN *I* AM.
MURDOCK.

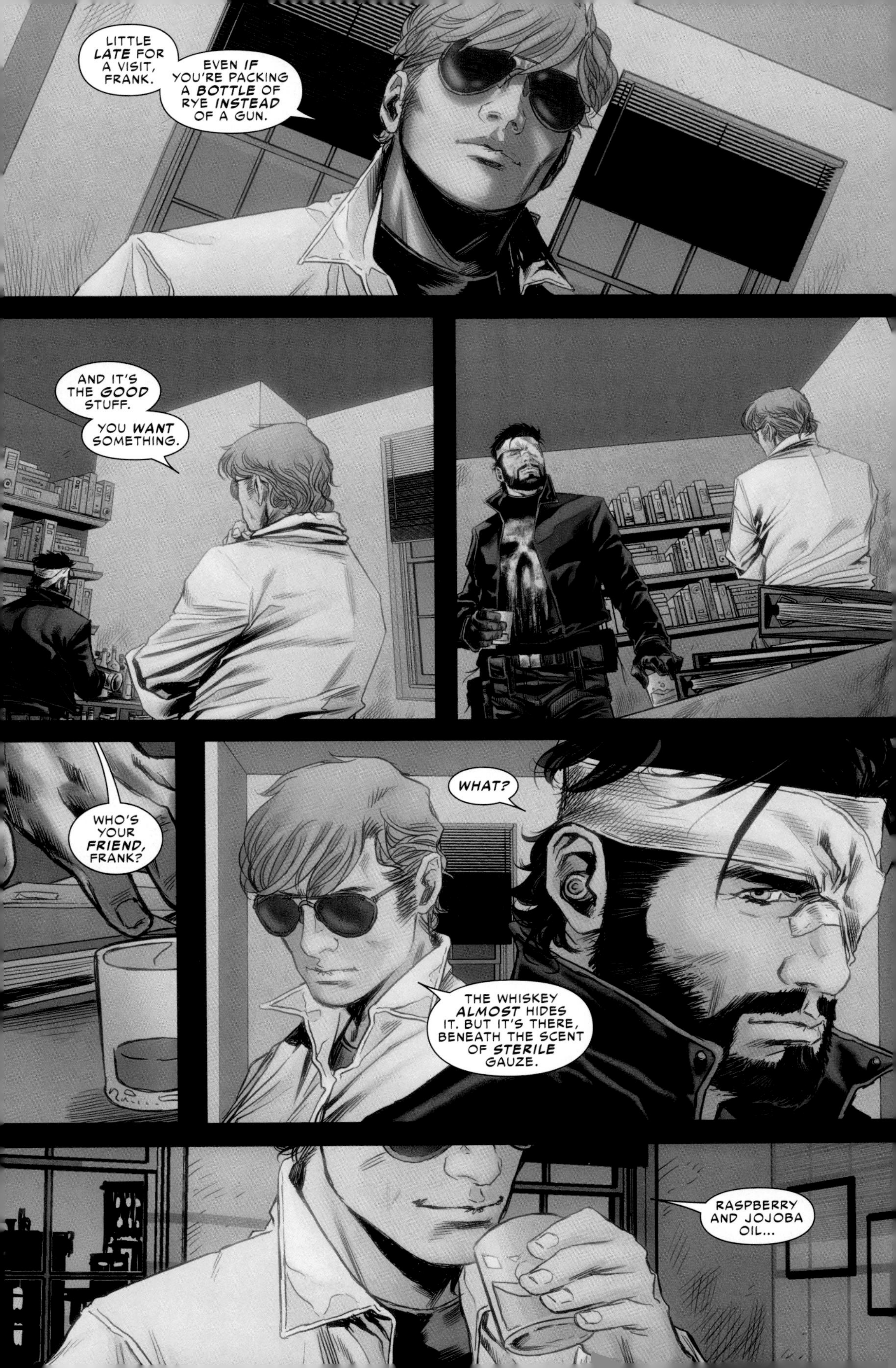
LITTLE LATE FOR A VISIT, FRANK.
EVEN IF YOU'RE PACKING A BOTTLE OF RYE INSTEAD OF A GUN.
AND IT'S THE GOOD STUFF.
YOU WANT SOMETHING.
WHO'S YOUR FRIEND, FRANK?
WHAT?
THE WHISKEY ALMOST HIDES IT. BUT IT'S THERE, BENEATH THE SCENT OF STERILE GAUZE.
RASPBERRY AND JOJOBA OIL...

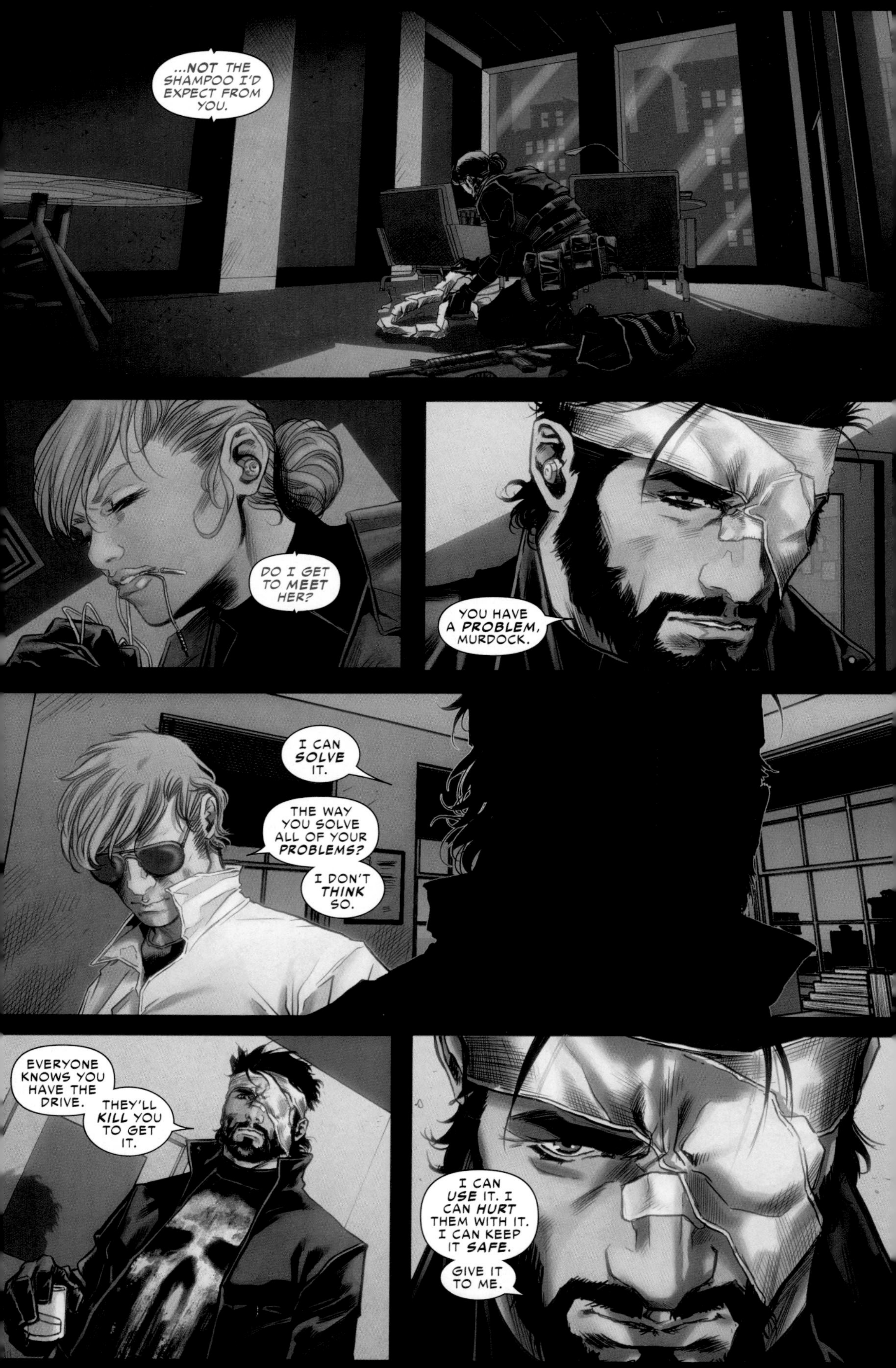
...NOT THE SHAMPOO I'D EXPECT FROM YOU.
DO I GET TO MEET HER?
YOU HAVE A PROBLEM, MURDOCK.
I CAN SOLVE IT.
THE WAY YOU SOLVE ALL OF YOUR PROBLEMS?
I DON'T THINK SO.
EVERYONE KNOWS YOU HAVE THE DRIVE.
THEY'LL KILL YOU TO GET IT.
I CAN USE IT. I CAN HURT THEM WITH IT. I CAN KEEP IT SAFE.
GIVE IT TO ME.

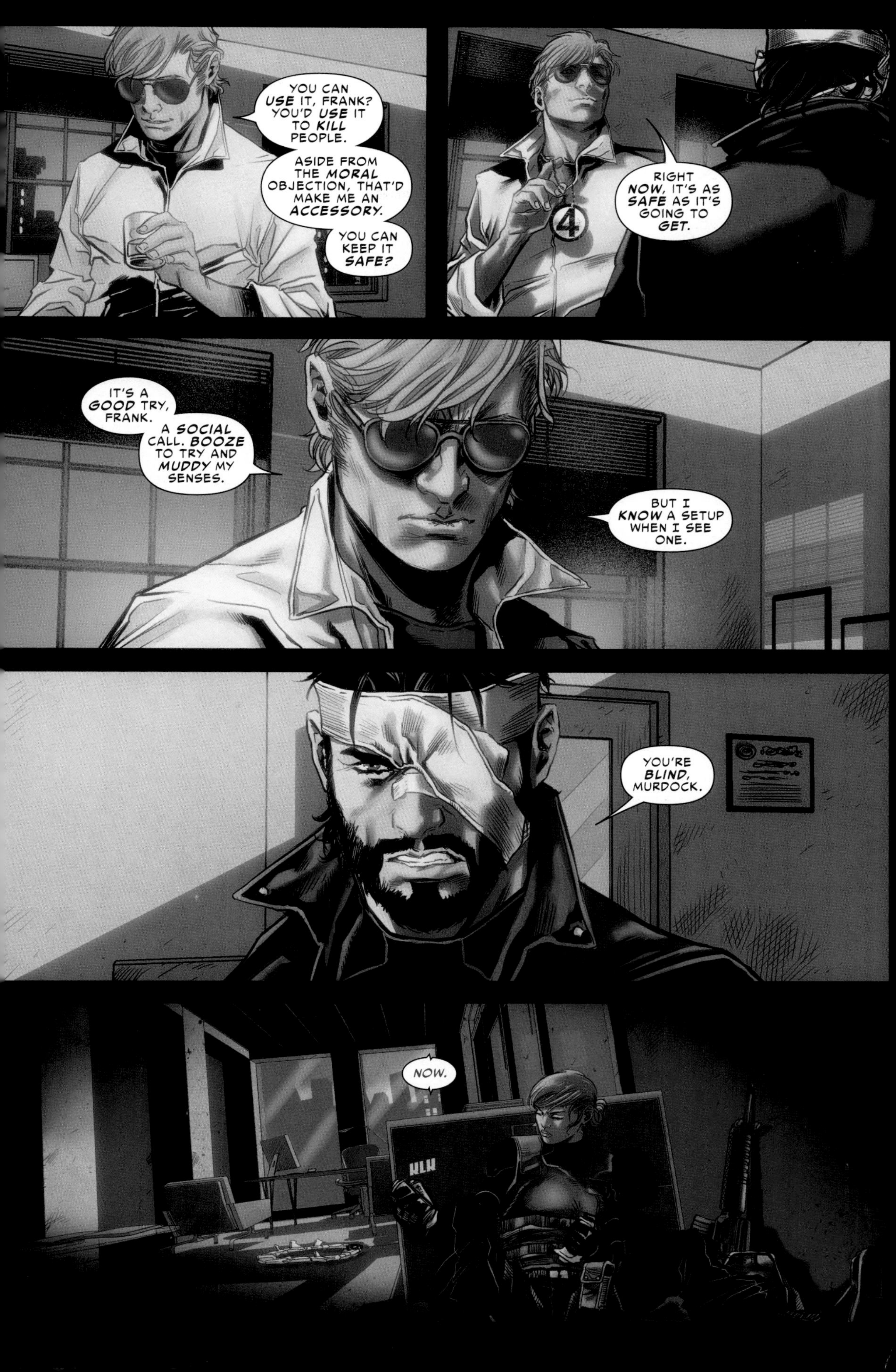
YOU CAN USE IT, FRANK? YOU'D USE IT TO KILL PEOPLE.
ASIDE FROM THE MORAL OBJECTION, THAT'D MAKE ME AN ACCESSORY.
YOU CAN KEEP IT SAFE?
RIGHT NOW, IT'S AS SAFE AS IT'S GOING TO GET.
IT'S A GOOD TRY, FRANK.
A SOCIAL CALL. BOOZE TO TRY AND MUDDY MY SENSES.
BUT I KNOW A SETUP WHEN I SEE ONE.
YOU'RE BLIND, MURDOCK.
NOW.

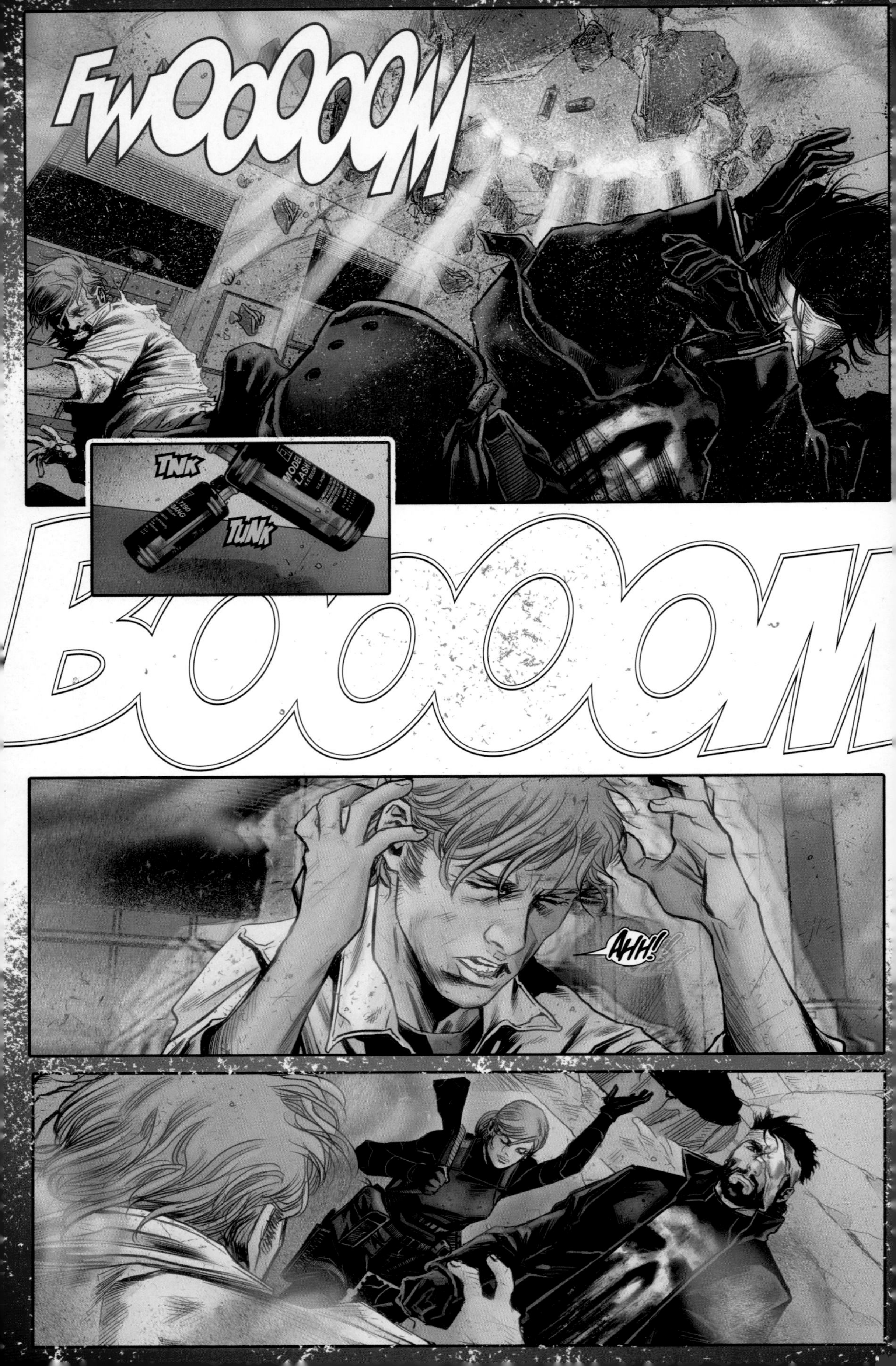
FWOOOOM
TNK
TUNK
BOOOOM
AHH!

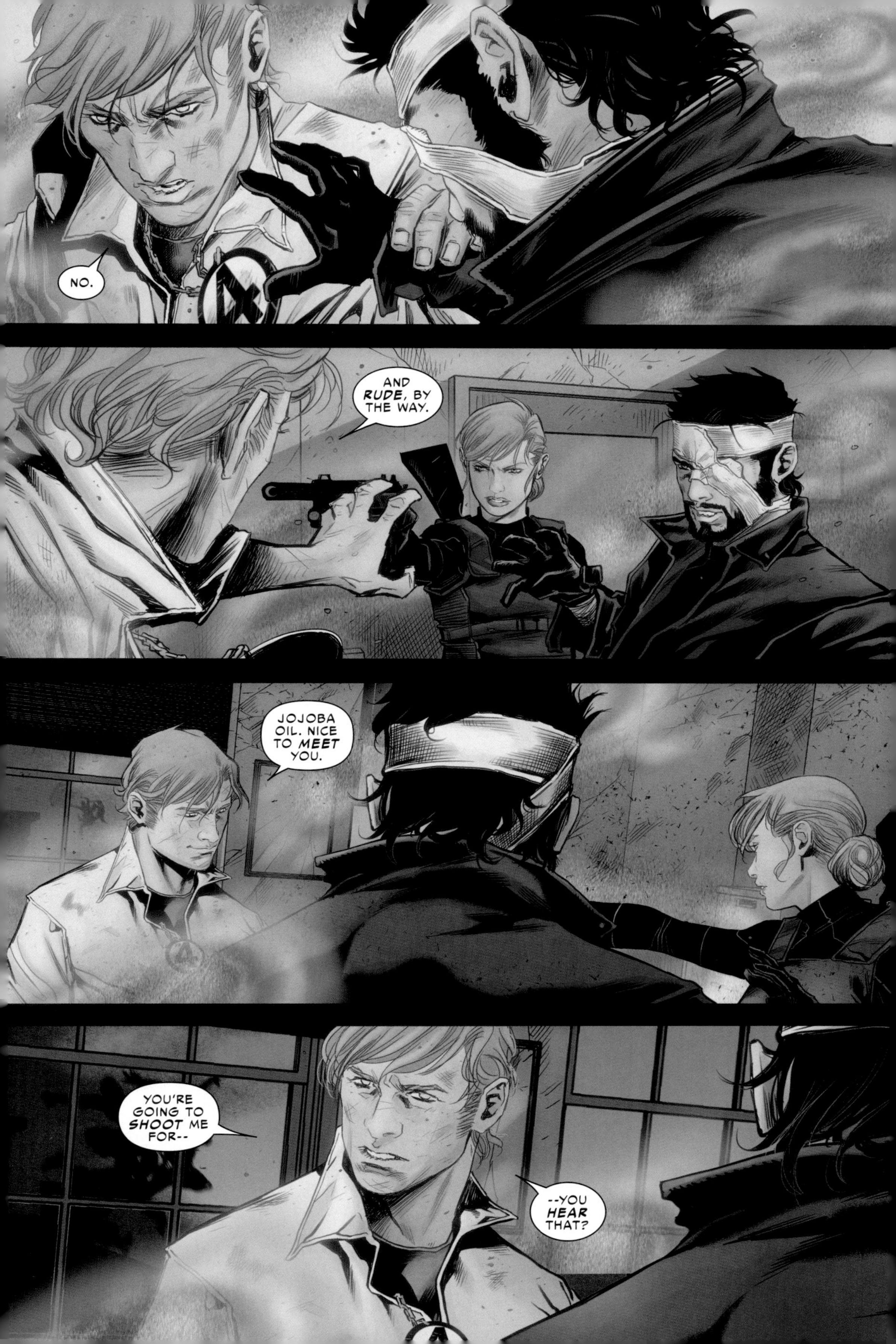
NO.
AND RUDE, BY THE WAY.
JOJOBA OIL. NICE TO MEET YOU.
YOU'RE GOING TO SHOOT ME FOR--
--YOU HEAR THAT?

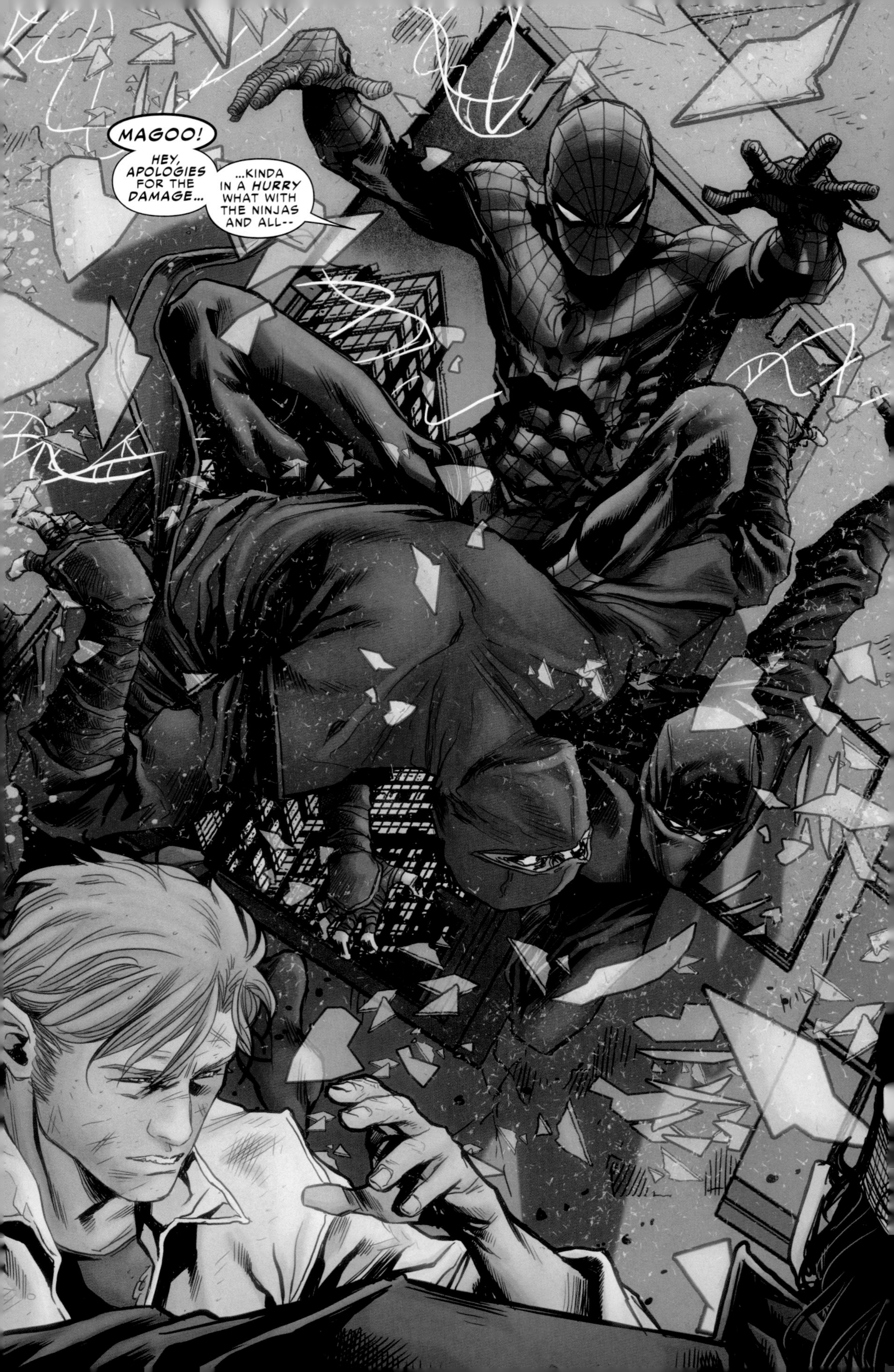
MAGOO!
HEY, APOLOGIES FOR THE DAMAGE...
...KINDA IN A HURRY WHAT WITH THE NINJAS AND ALL--

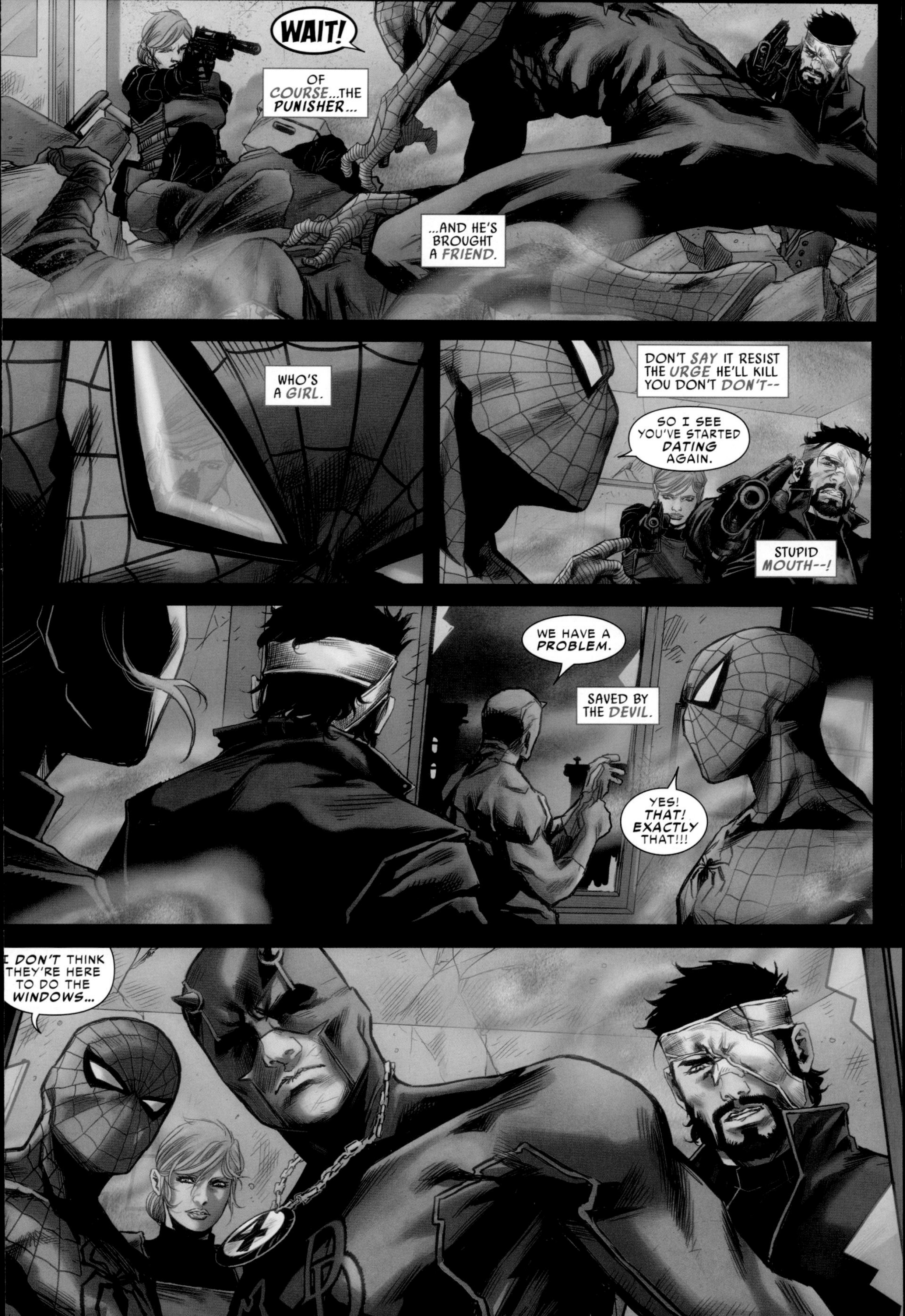

WAIT!
OF COURSE...THE PUNISHER...
...AND HE'S BROUGHT A FRIEND.
WHO'S A GIRL.
DON'T SAY IT RESIST THE URGE HE'LL KILL YOU DON'T DON'T--
SO I SEE YOU'VE STARTED DATING AGAIN.
STUPID MOUTH--!
WE HAVE A PROBLEM.
SAVED BY THE DEVIL.
YES! THAT! EXACTLY THAT!!!
I DON'T THINK THEY'RE HERE TO DO THE WINDOWS...

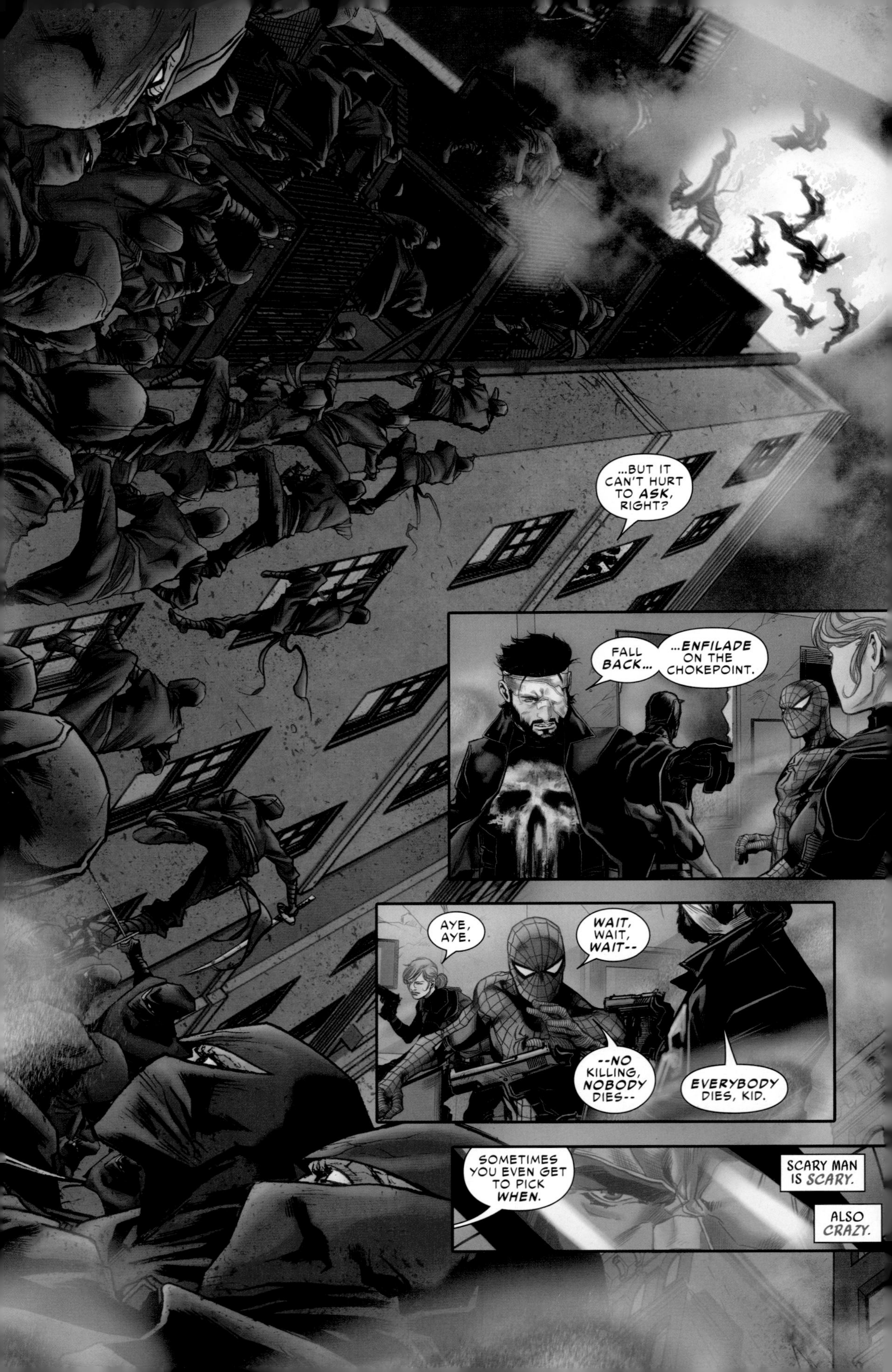

...BUT IT CAN'T HURT TO ASK, RIGHT?
FALL BACK...
...ENFILADE ON THE CHOKEPOINT.
AYE, AYE.
WAIT, WAIT, WAIT--
--NO KILLING, NOBODY DIES--
EVERYBODY DIES, KID.
SOMETIMES YOU EVEN GET TO PICK WHEN.
SCARY MAN IS SCARY.
ALSO CRAZY.

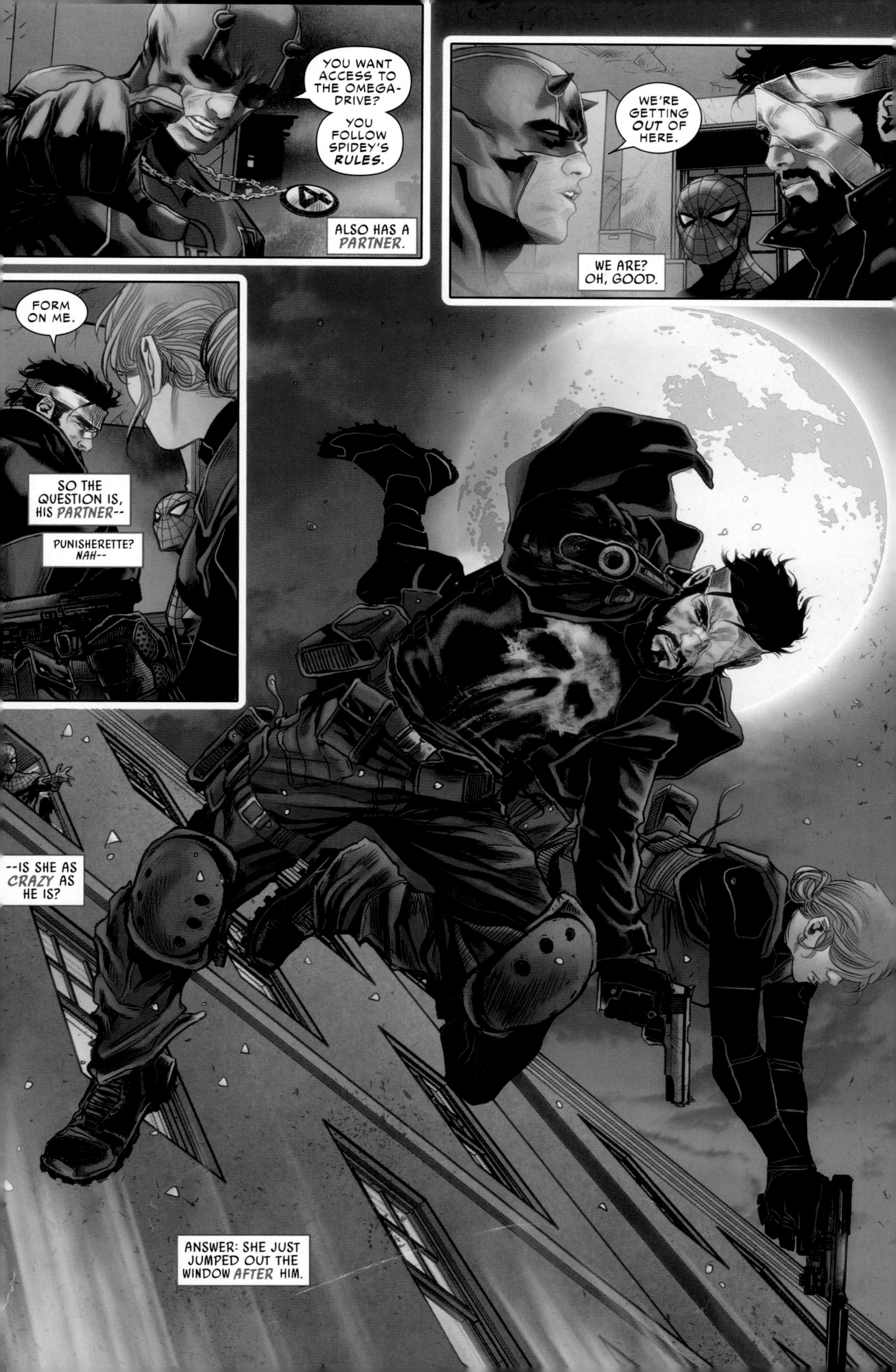

YOU WANT ACCESS TO THE OMEGA-DRIVE?
YOU FOLLOW SPIDEY'S RULES.
ALSO HAS A PARTNER.
WE'RE GETTING OUT OF HERE.
WE ARE? OH, GOOD.
FORM ON ME.
SO THE QUESTION IS, HIS PARTNER--
PUNISHERETTE? NAH--
--IS SHE AS CRAZY AS HE IS?
ANSWER: SHE JUST JUMPED OUT THE WINDOW AFTER HIM.

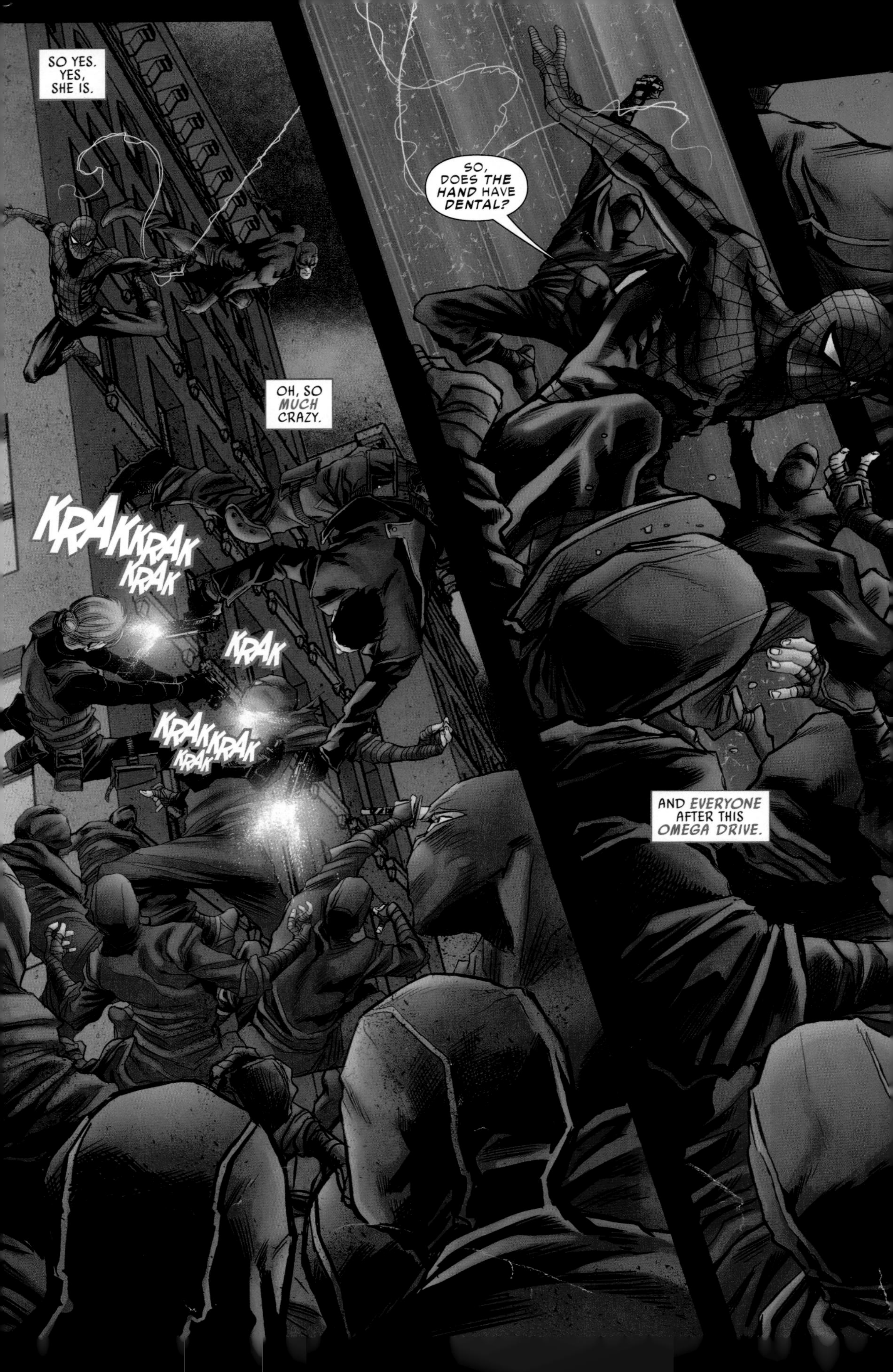
SO YES. YES, SHE IS.
OH, SO MUCH CRAZY.
KRAKKRAK KRAK
KRAK
KRAKKRAK KRAK
SO, DOES THE HAND HAVE DENTAL?
AND EVERYONE AFTER THIS OMEGA DRIVE.

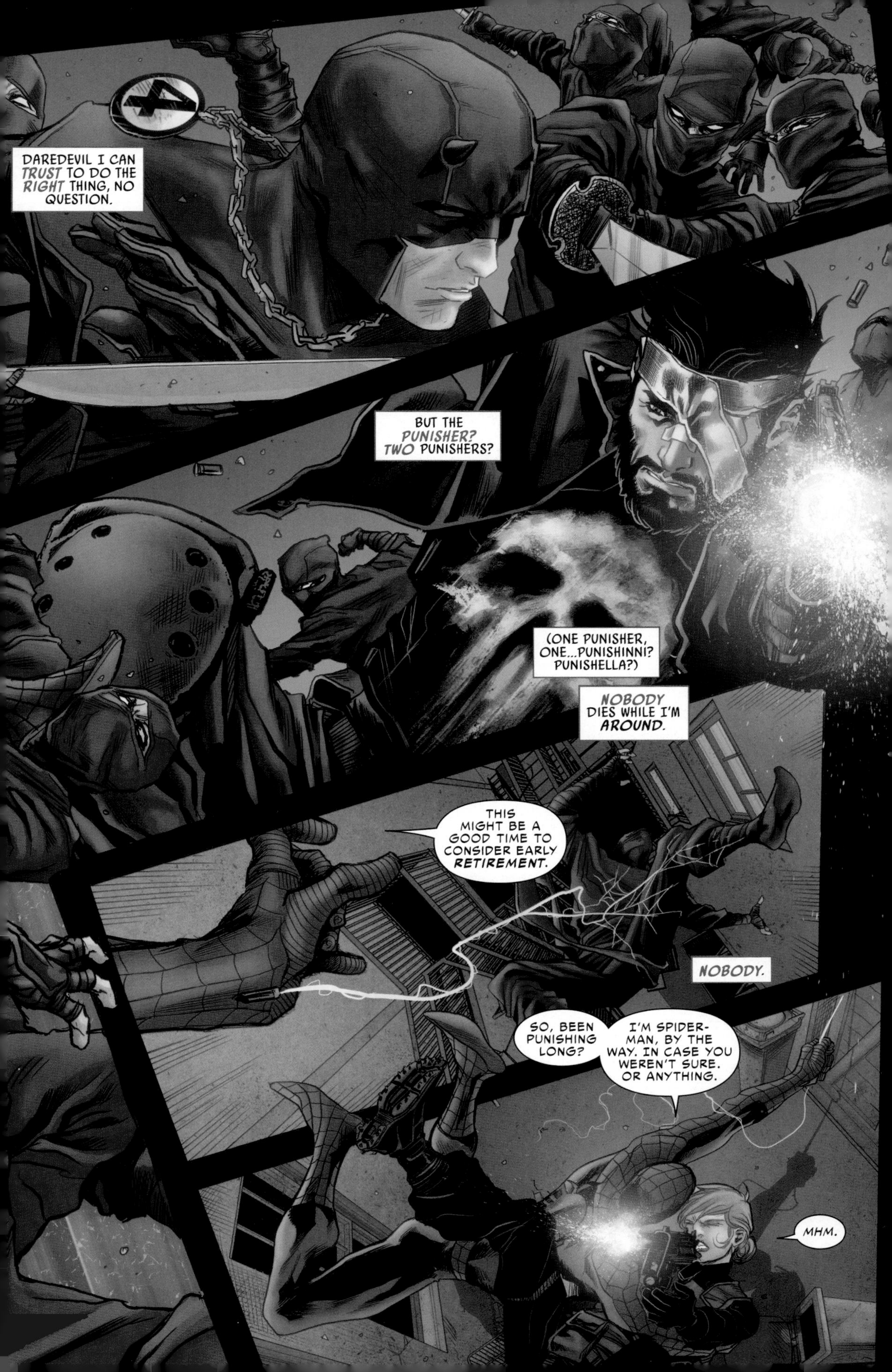
DAREDEVIL I CAN TRUST TO DO THE RIGHT THING, NO QUESTION.
BUT THE PUNISHER? TWO PUNISHERS?
(ONE PUNISHER, ONE...PUNISHINNI? PUNISHELLA?)
NOBODY DIES WHILE I'M AROUND.
THIS MIGHT BE A GOOD TIME TO CONSIDER EARLY RETIREMENT.
NOBODY.
SO, BEEN PUNISHING LONG?
I'M SPIDER-MAN, BY THE WAY. IN CASE YOU WEREN'T SURE. OR ANYTHING.
MHM.

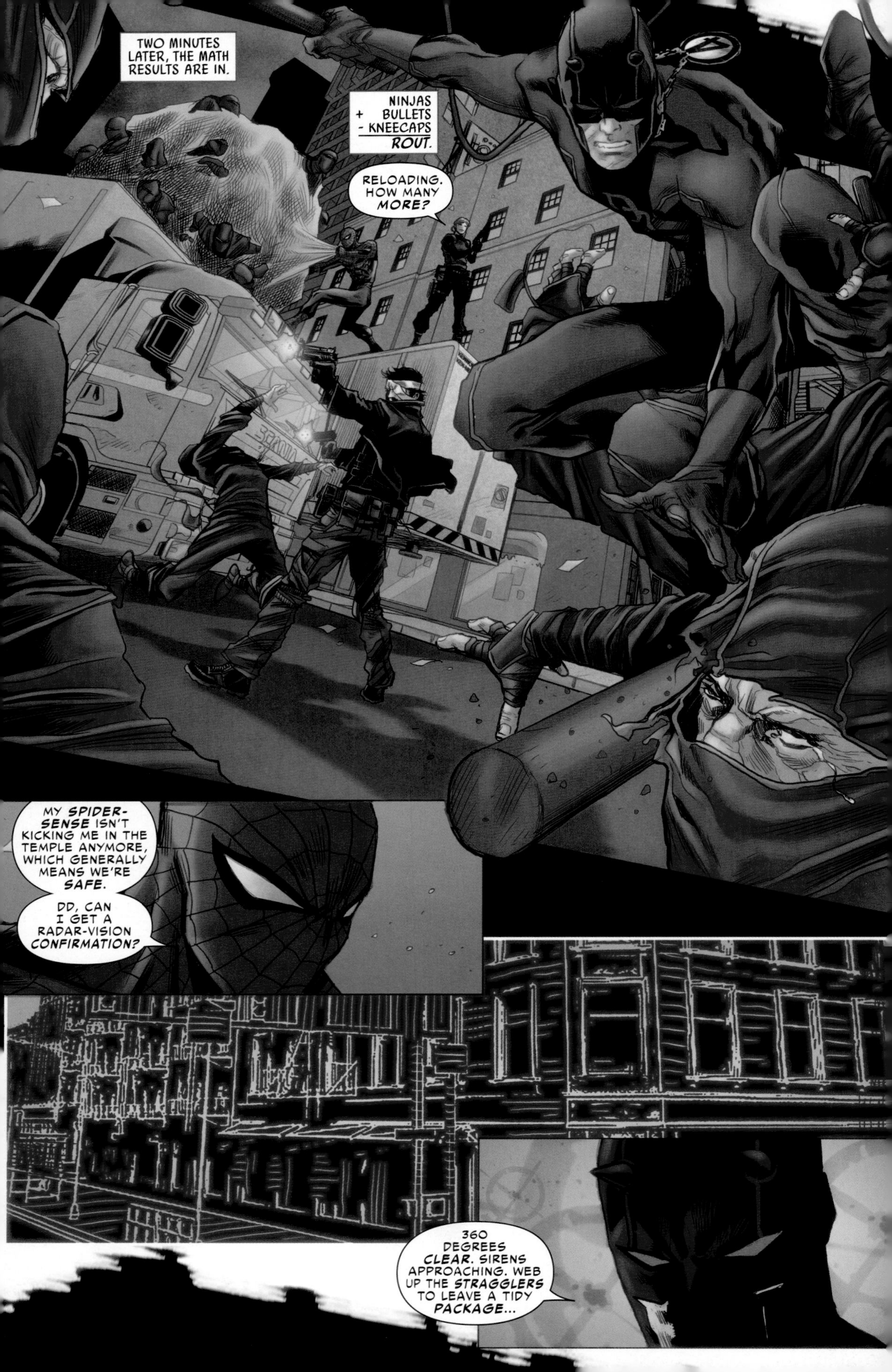
TWO MINUTES LATER, THE MATH RESULTS ARE IN.
NINJAS + BULLETS - KNEECAPS ROUT.
RELOADING. HOW MANY MORE?
MY SPIDER-SENSE ISN'T KICKING ME IN THE TEMPLE ANYMORE, WHICH GENERALLY MEANS WE'RE SAFE.
DD, CAN I GET A RADAR-VISION CONFIRMATION?
360 DEGREES CLEAR. SIRENS APPROACHING. WEB UP THE STRAGGLERS TO LEAVE A TIDY PACKAGE...

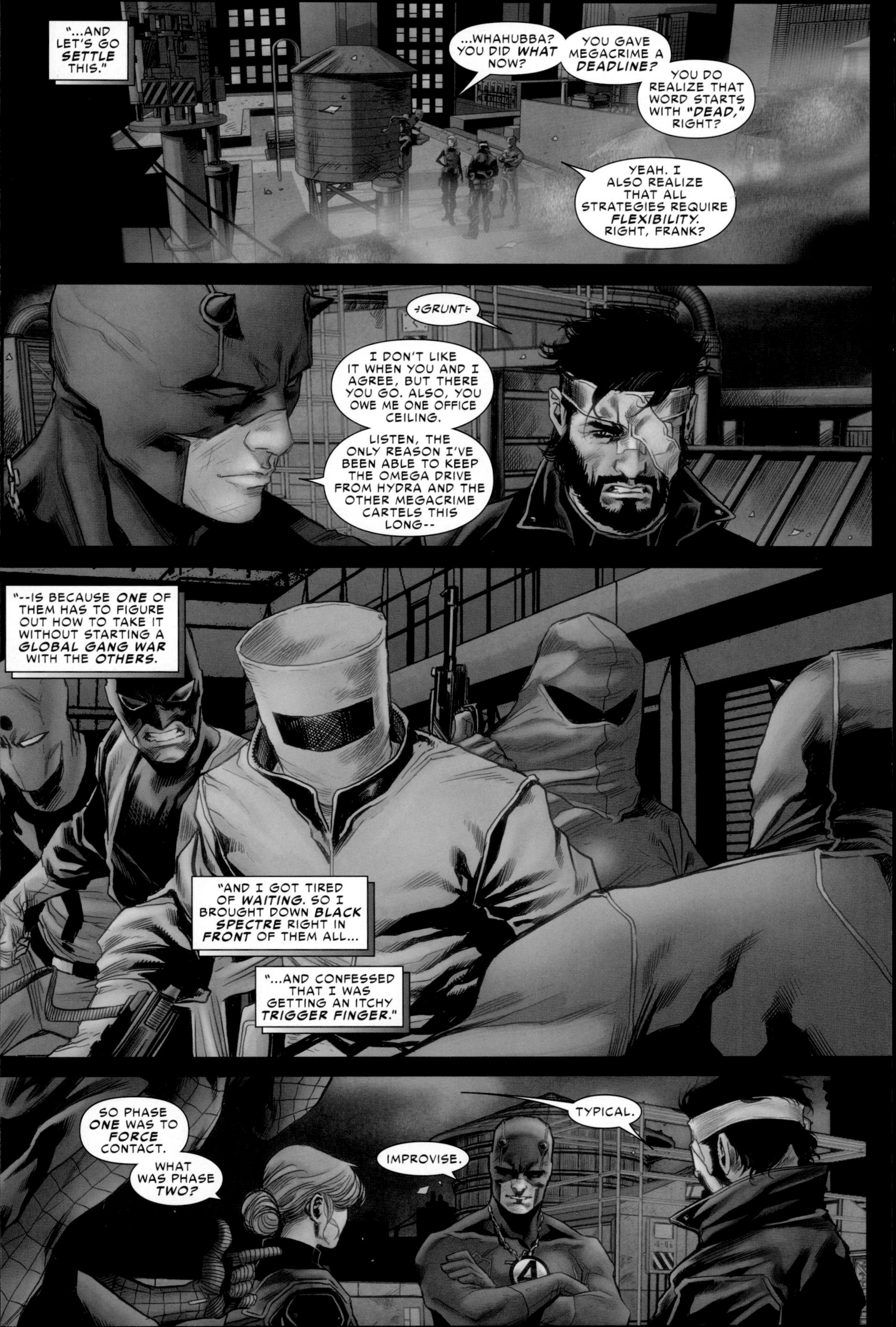
"...AND LET'S GO SETTLE THIS."
...WHAHUBBA? YOU DID WHAT NOW?
YOU GAVE MEGACRIME A DEADLINE?
YOU DO REALIZE THAT WORD STARTS WITH "DEAD," RIGHT?
YEAH. I ALSO REALIZE THAT ALL STRATEGIES REQUIRE FLEXIBILITY. RIGHT, FRANK?
GRUNT
I DON'T LIKE IT WHEN YOU AND I AGREE, BUT THERE YOU GO. ALSO, YOU OWE ME ONE OFFICE CEILING.
LISTEN, THE ONLY REASON I'VE BEEN ABLE TO KEEP THE OMEGA DRIVE FROM HYDRA AND THE OTHER MEGACRIME CARTELS THIS LONG--
"--IS BECAUSE ONE OF THEM HAS TO FIGURE OUT HOW TO TAKE IT WITHOUT STARTING A GLOBAL GANG WAR WITH THE OTHERS.
"AND I GOT TIRED OF WAITING. SO I BROUGHT DOWN BLACK SPECTRE RIGHT IN FRONT OF THEM ALL...
"...AND CONFESSED THAT I WAS GETTING AN ITCHY TRIGGER FINGER."
SO PHASE ONE WAS TO FORCE CONTACT.
WHAT WAS PHASE TWO?
TYPICAL.
IMPROVISE.

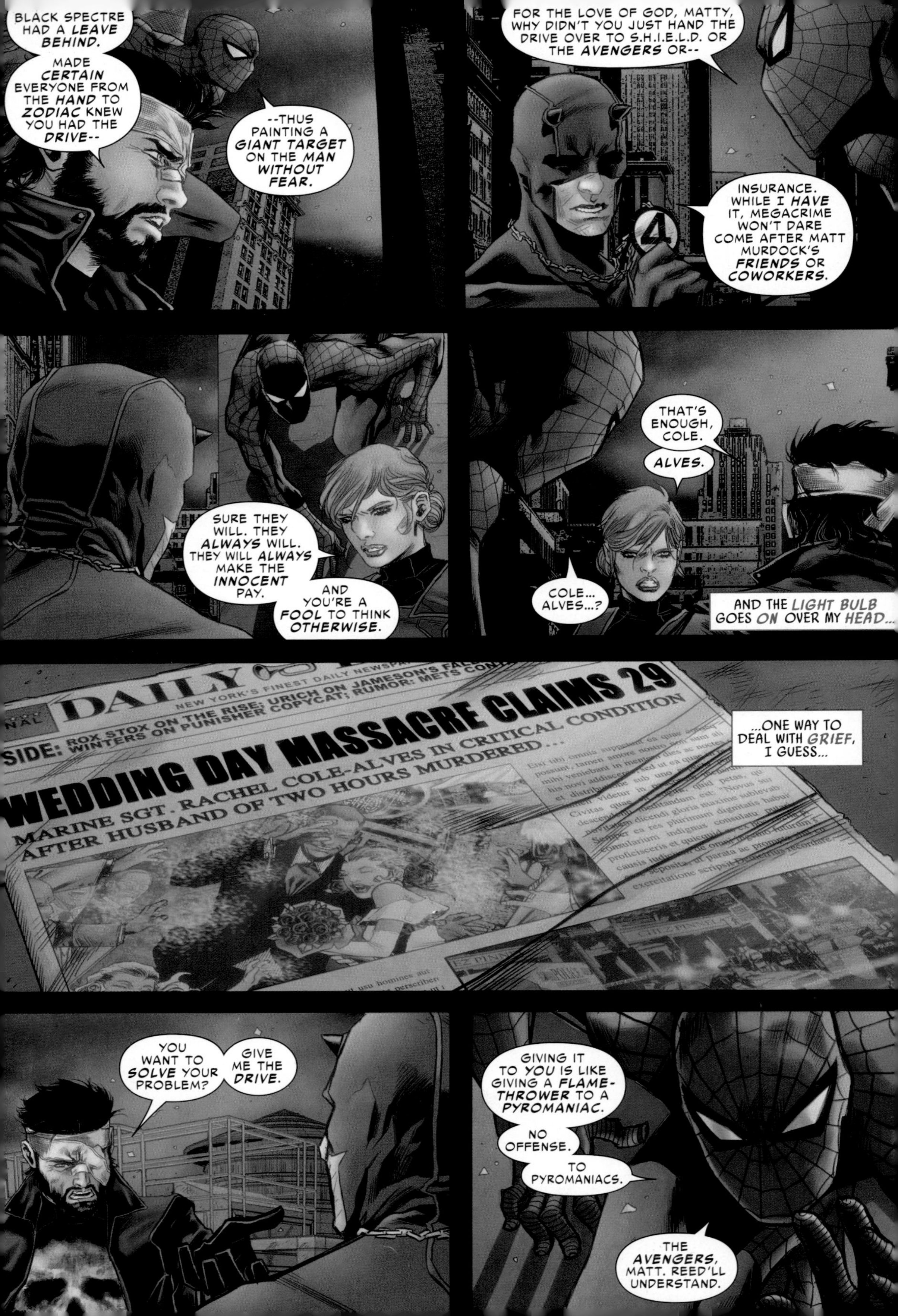
BLACK SPECTRE HAD A LEAVE BEHIND.
MADE CERTAIN EVERYONE FROM THE HAND TO ZODIAC KNEW YOU HAD THE DRIVE--
--THUS PAINTING A GIANT TARGET ON THE MAN WITHOUT FEAR.
FOR THE LOVE OF GOD, MATTY, WHY DIDN'T YOU JUST HAND THE DRIVE OVER TO S.H.I.E.L.D. OR THE AVENGERS OR--
INSURANCE. WHILE I HAVE IT, MEGACRIME WON'T DARE COME AFTER MATT MURDOCK'S FRIENDS OR COWORKERS.
SURE THEY WILL. THEY ALWAYS WILL. THEY WILL ALWAYS MAKE THE INNOCENT PAY.
AND YOU'RE A FOOL TO THINK OTHERWISE.
THAT'S ENOUGH, COLE.
ALVES.
COLE... ALVES...?
AND THE LIGHT BULB GOES ON OVER MY HEAD...
DAILY
NEW YORK'S FINEST DAILY NEWSPAPER
ROX STOX ON THE RISE: URICH ON JAMESON'S FALL
WINTERS ON PUNISHER COPYCAT; RUMOR: METS CON
WEDDING DAY MASSACRE CLAIMS 29
MARINE SGT. RACHEL COLE-ALVES IN CRITICAL CONDITION AFTER HUSBAND OF TWO HOURS MURDERED...
...ONE WAY TO DEAL WITH GRIEF, I GUESS...
YOU WANT TO SOLVE YOUR PROBLEM?
GIVE ME THE DRIVE.
GIVING IT TO YOU IS LIKE GIVING A FLAME-THROWER TO A PYROMANIAC.
NO OFFENSE.
TO PYROMANIACS.
THE AVENGERS, MATT. REED'LL UNDERSTAND.

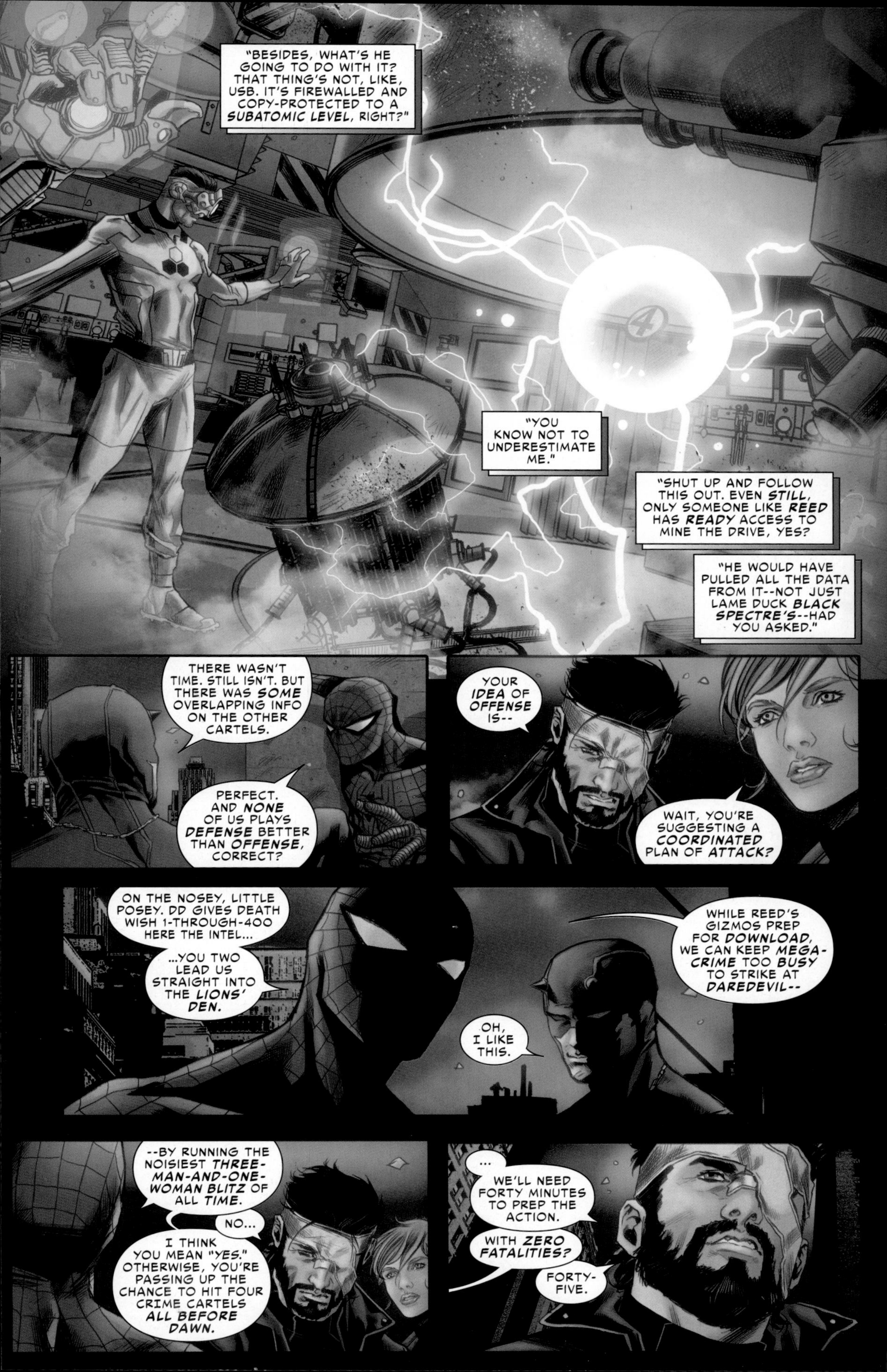
"BESIDES, WHAT'S HE GOING TO DO WITH IT? THAT THING'S NOT, LIKE, USB. IT'S FIREWALLED AND COPY-PROTECTED TO A SUBATOMIC LEVEL, RIGHT?"
"YOU KNOW NOT TO UNDERESTIMATE ME."
"SHUT UP AND FOLLOW THIS OUT. EVEN STILL, ONLY SOMEONE LIKE REED HAS READY ACCESS TO MINE THE DRIVE, YES?
"HE WOULD HAVE PULLED ALL THE DATA FROM IT--NOT JUST LAME DUCK BLACK SPECTRE'S--HAD YOU ASKED."
THERE WASN'T TIME. STILL ISN'T. BUT THERE WAS SOME OVERLAPPING INFO ON THE OTHER CARTELS.
PERFECT. AND NONE OF US PLAYS DEFENSE BETTER THAN OFFENSE, CORRECT?
YOUR IDEA OF OFFENSE IS--
WAIT, YOU'RE SUGGESTING A COORDINATED PLAN OF ATTACK?
ON THE NOSEY, LITTLE POSEY. DD GIVES DEATH WISH 1-THROUGH-400 HERE THE INTEL...
...YOU TWO LEAD US STRAIGHT INTO THE LIONS' DEN.
WHILE REED'S GIZMOS PREP FOR DOWNLOAD, WE CAN KEEP MEGA-CRIME TOO BUSY TO STRIKE AT DAREDEVIL--
OH, I LIKE THIS.
--BY RUNNING THE NOISIEST THREE-MAN-AND-ONE-WOMAN BLITZ OF ALL TIME.
NO...
I THINK YOU MEAN "YES." OTHERWISE, YOU'RE PASSING UP THE CHANCE TO HIT FOUR CRIME CARTELS ALL BEFORE DAWN.
...
WE'LL NEED FORTY MINUTES TO PREP THE ACTION.
WITH ZERO FATALITIES?
FORTY-FIVE.

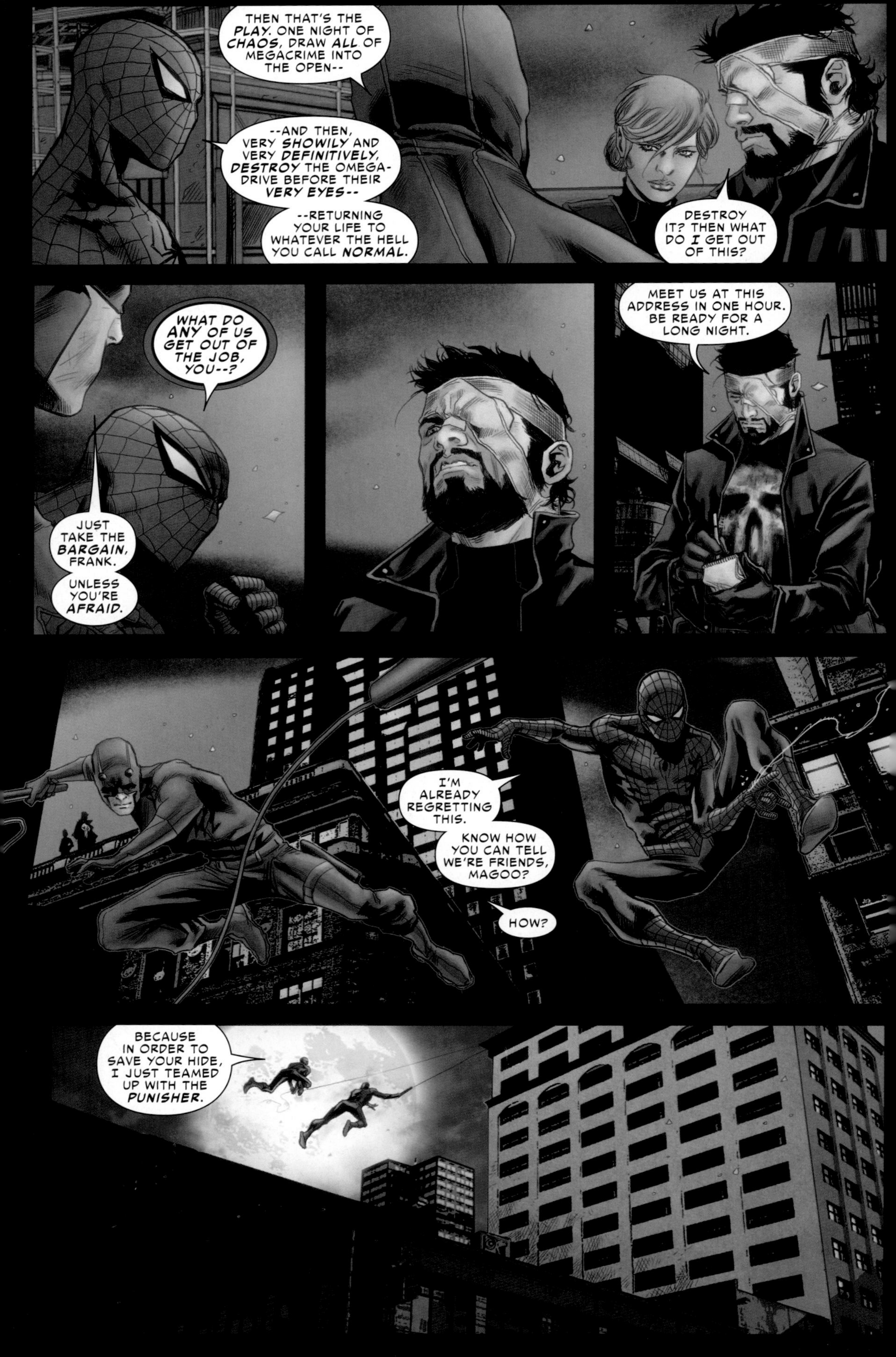
THEN THAT'S THE PLAY. ONE NIGHT OF CHAOS, DRAW ALL OF MEGACRIME INTO THE OPEN--
--AND THEN, VERY SHOWILY AND VERY DEFINITIVELY, DESTROY THE OMEGA-DRIVE BEFORE THEIR VERY EYES--
--RETURNING YOUR LIFE TO WHATEVER THE HELL YOU CALL NORMAL.
DESTROY IT? THEN WHAT DO I GET OUT OF THIS?
WHAT DO ANY OF US GET OUT OF THE JOB, YOU--?
JUST TAKE THE BARGAIN, FRANK.
UNLESS YOU'RE AFRAID.
MEET US AT THIS ADDRESS IN ONE HOUR. BE READY FOR A LONG NIGHT.
I'M ALREADY REGRETTING THIS.
KNOW HOW YOU CAN TELL WE'RE FRIENDS, MAGOO?
HOW?
BECAUSE IN ORDER TO SAVE YOUR HIDE, I JUST TEAMED UP WITH THE PUNISHER.

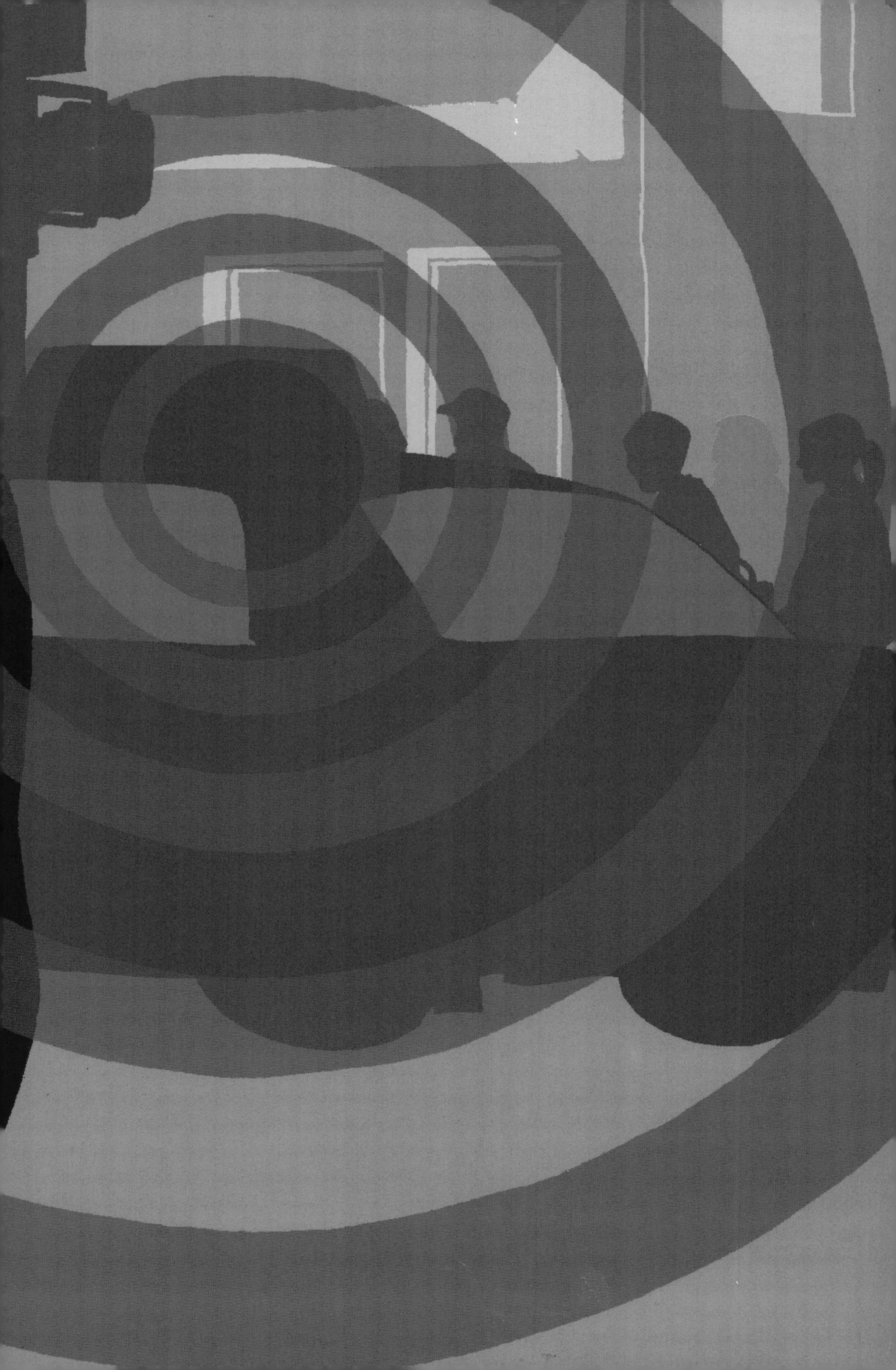

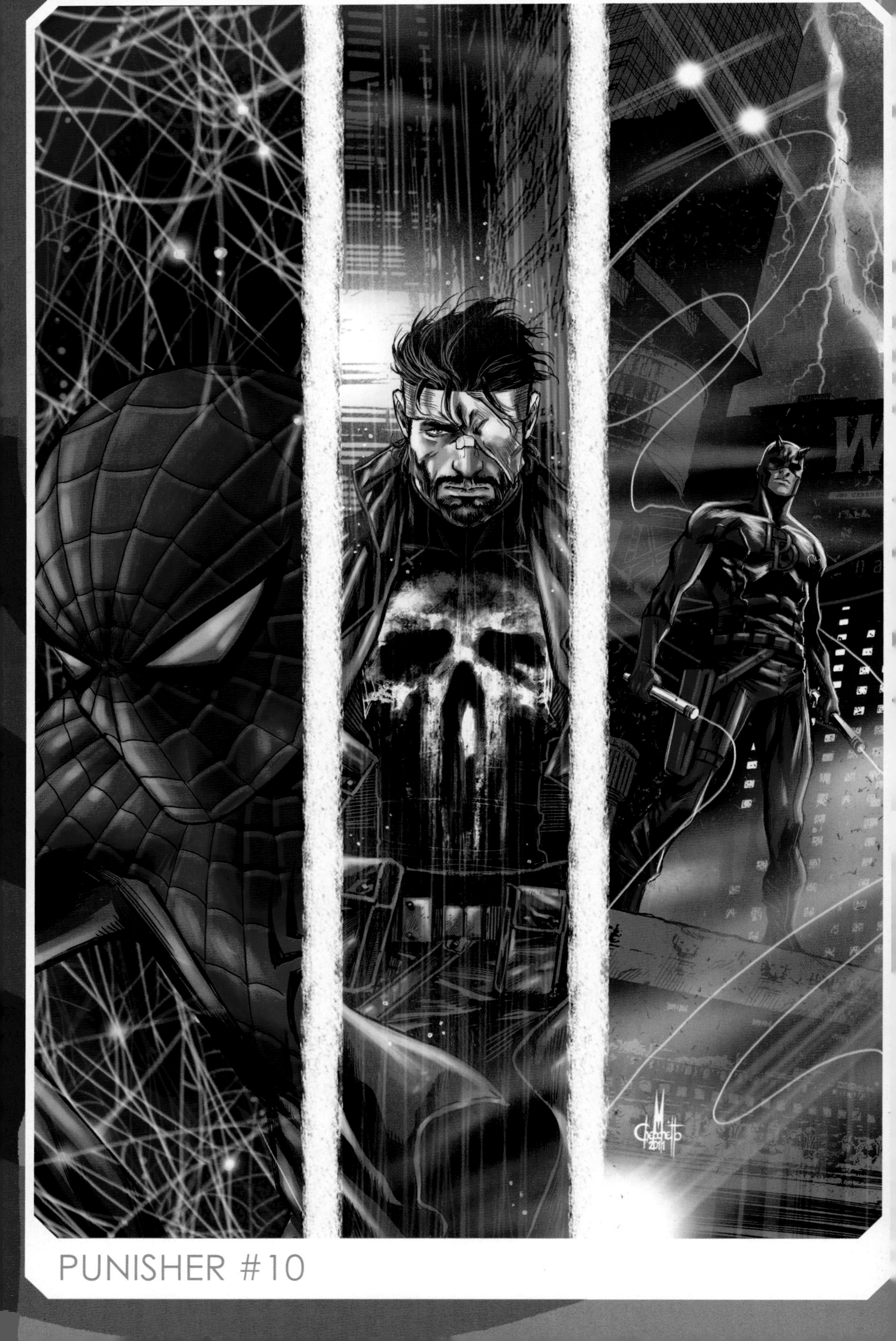

PUNISHER #10

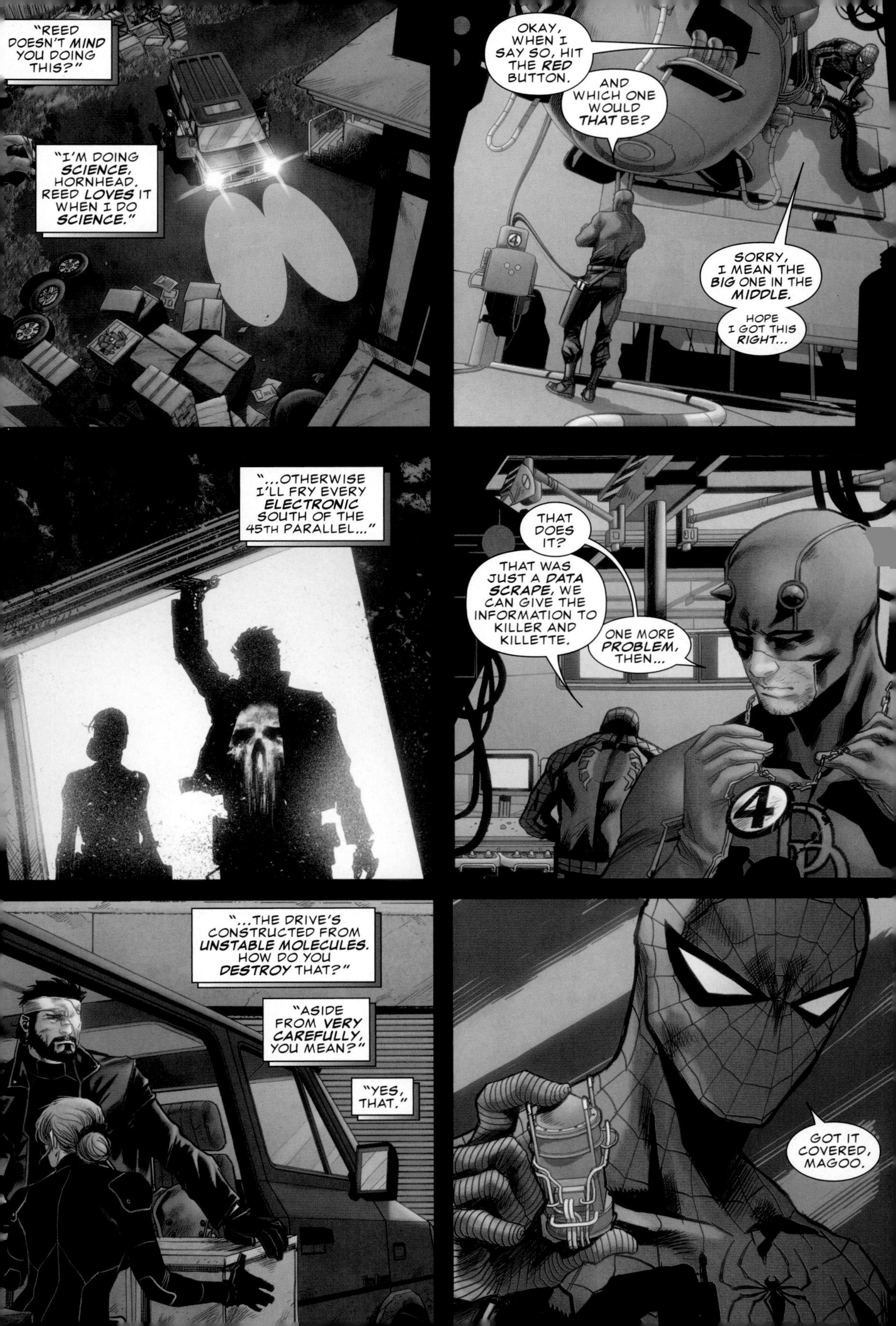
"REED DOESN'T MIND YOU DOING THIS?"
"I'M DOING SCIENCE, HORNHEAD. REED LOVES IT WHEN I DO SCIENCE."
OKAY, WHEN I SAY SO, HIT THE RED BUTTON.
AND WHICH ONE WOULD THAT BE?
SORRY, I MEAN THE BIG ONE IN THE MIDDLE.
HOPE I GOT THIS RIGHT...
"...OTHERWISE I'LL FRY EVERY ELECTRONIC SOUTH OF THE 45TH PARALLEL..."
THAT DOES IT?
THAT WAS JUST A DATA SCRAPE, WE CAN GIVE THE INFORMATION TO KILLER AND KILLETTE.
ONE MORE PROBLEM, THEN...
"...THE DRIVE'S CONSTRUCTED FROM UNSTABLE MOLECULES. HOW DO YOU DESTROY THAT?"
"ASIDE FROM VERY CAREFULLY, YOU MEAN?"
"YES, THAT."
GOT IT COVERED, MAGOO.

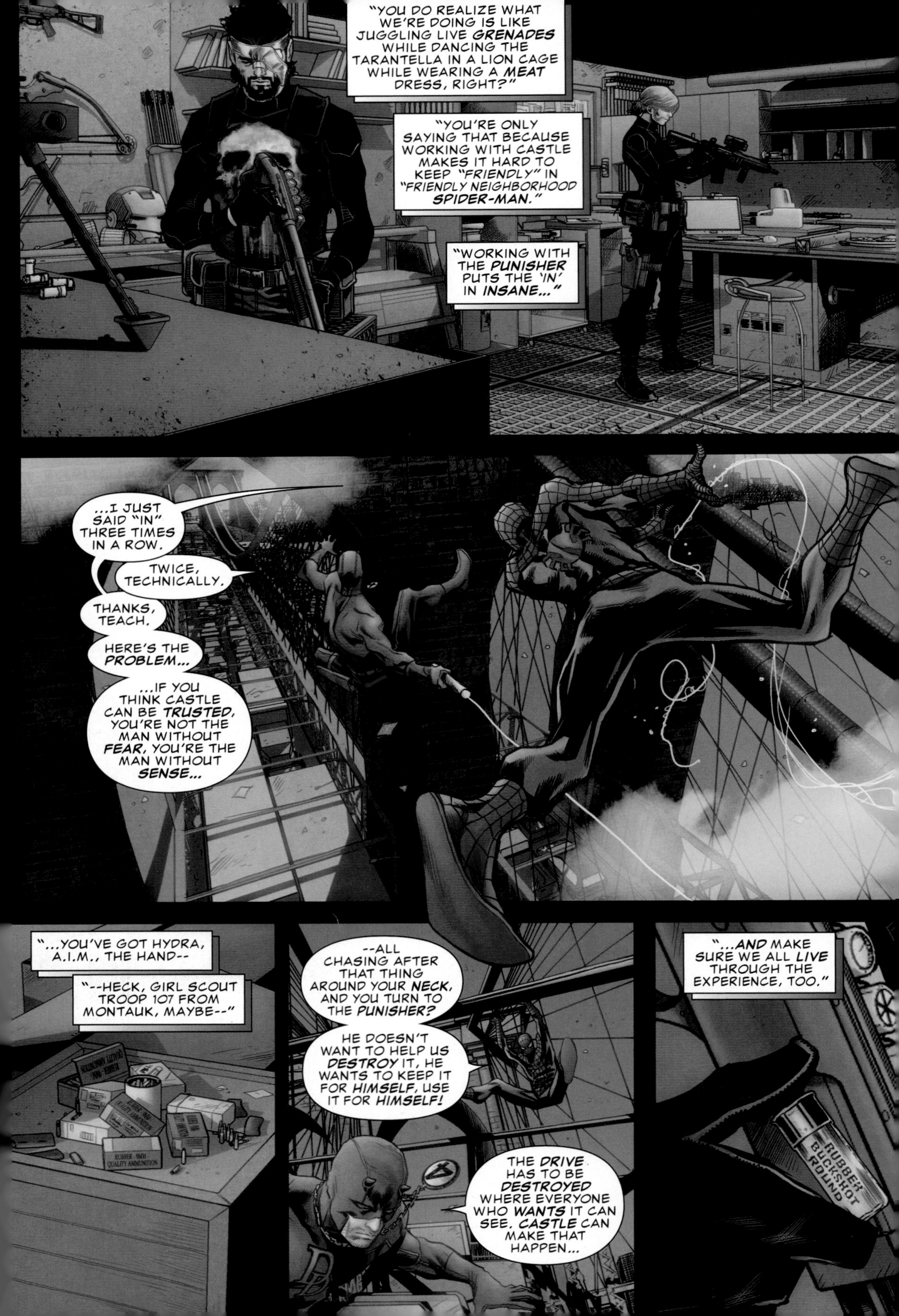
"YOU DO REALIZE WHAT WE'RE DOING IS LIKE JUGGLING LIVE GRENADES WHILE DANCING THE TARANTELLA IN A LION CAGE WHILE WEARING A MEAT DRESS, RIGHT?"
"YOU'RE ONLY SAYING THAT BECAUSE WORKING WITH CASTLE MAKES IT HARD TO KEEP "FRIENDLY" IN "FRIENDLY NEIGHBORHOOD SPIDER-MAN."
"WORKING WITH THE PUNISHER PUTS THE 'IN' IN INSANE..."
...I JUST SAID "IN" THREE TIMES IN A ROW.
TWICE, TECHNICALLY.
THANKS, TEACH.
HERE'S THE PROBLEM...
...IF YOU THINK CASTLE CAN BE TRUSTED, YOU'RE NOT THE MAN WITHOUT FEAR, YOU'RE THE MAN WITHOUT SENSE...
"...YOU'VE GOT HYDRA, A.I.M., THE HAND--
"--HECK, GIRL SCOUT TROOP 107 FROM MONTAUK, MAYBE--"
RUBBER 9MM QUALITY AMMUNITION
--ALL CHASING AFTER THAT THING AROUND YOUR NECK, AND YOU TURN TO THE PUNISHER?
HE DOESN'T WANT TO HELP US DESTROY IT, HE WANTS TO KEEP IT FOR HIMSELF, USE IT FOR HIMSELF!
THE DRIVE HAS TO BE DESTROYED WHERE EVERYONE WHO WANTS IT CAN SEE. CASTLE CAN MAKE THAT HAPPEN...
"...AND MAKE SURE WE ALL LIVE THROUGH THE EXPERIENCE, TOO."
RUBBER BUCKSHOT ROUND

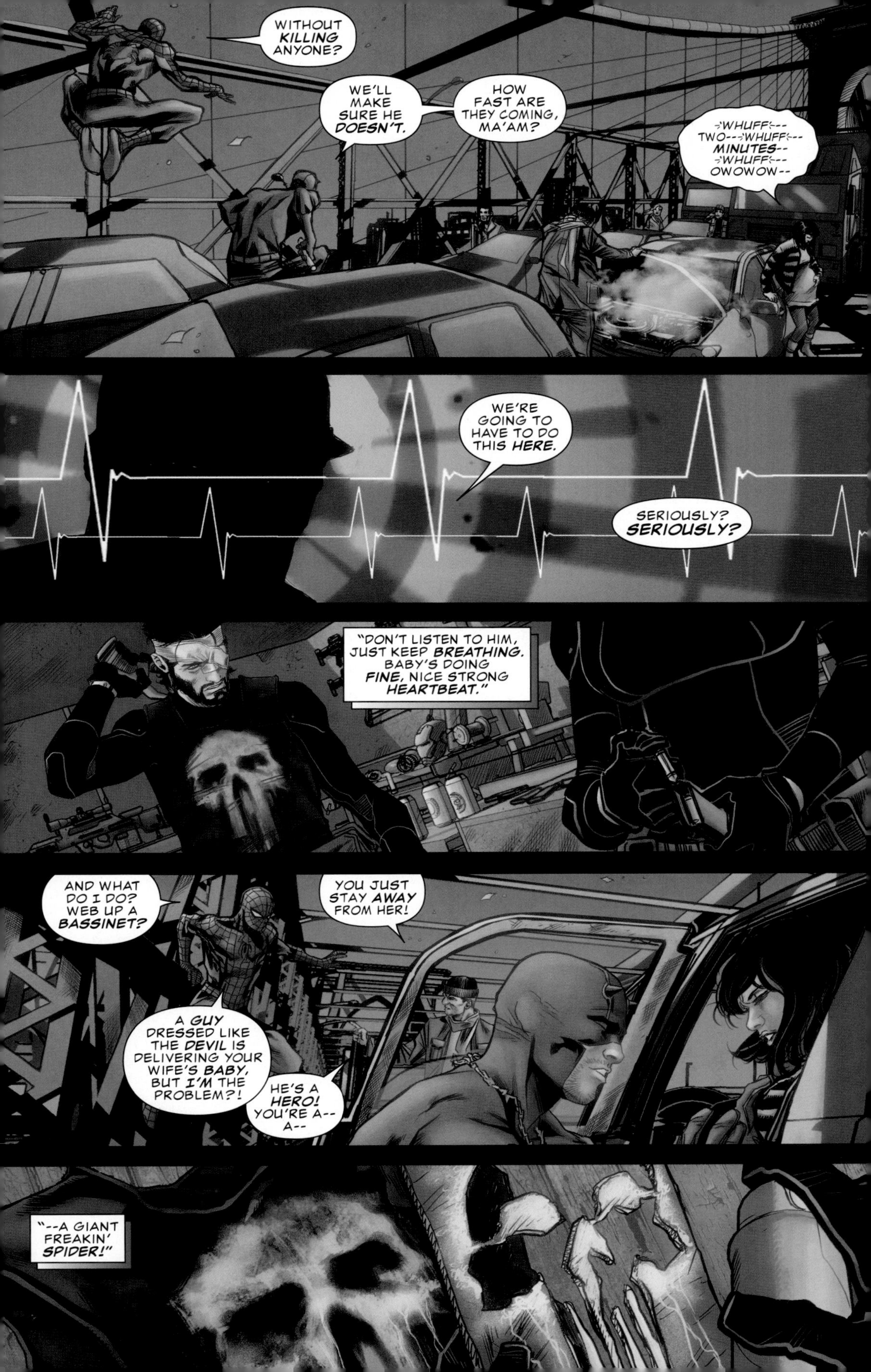
WITHOUT KILLING ANYONE?
WE'LL MAKE SURE HE DOESN'T.
HOW FAST ARE THEY COMING, MA'AM?
WHUFF-- TWO-- WHUFF-- MINUTES-- WHUFF-- OWOWOW--
WE'RE GOING TO HAVE TO DO THIS HERE.
SERIOUSLY? SERIOUSLY?
"DON'T LISTEN TO HIM, JUST KEEP BREATHING. BABY'S DOING FINE, NICE STRONG HEARTBEAT."
AND WHAT DO I DO? WEB UP A BASSINET?
YOU JUST STAY AWAY FROM HER!
A GUY DRESSED LIKE THE DEVIL IS DELIVERING YOUR WIFE'S BABY, BUT I'M THE PROBLEM?!
HE'S A HERO! YOU'RE A-- A--
"--A GIANT FREAKIN' SPIDER!"

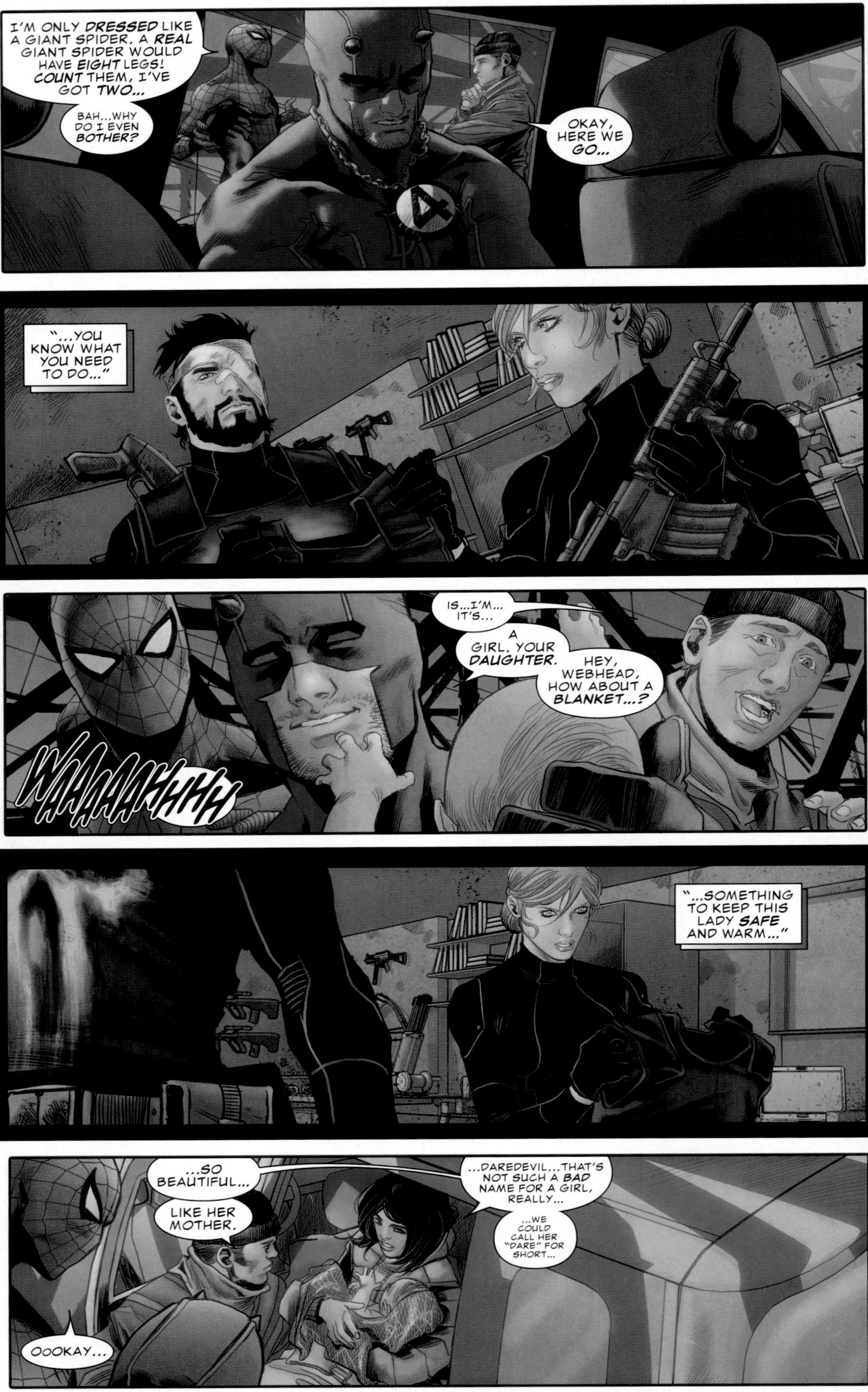

I'M ONLY DRESSED LIKE A GIANT SPIDER. A REAL GIANT SPIDER WOULD HAVE EIGHT LEGS! COUNT THEM, I'VE GOT TWO...
BAH...WHY DO I EVEN BOTHER?
OKAY, HERE WE GO...
"...YOU KNOW WHAT YOU NEED TO DO..."
IS...I'M... IT'S...
A GIRL. YOUR DAUGHTER.
HEY, WEBHEAD, HOW ABOUT A BLANKET...?
WAAAAAHHHH
"...SOMETHING TO KEEP THIS LADY SAFE AND WARM..."
...SO BEAUTIFUL...
LIKE HER MOTHER.
...DAREDEVIL...THAT'S NOT SUCH A BAD NAME FOR A GIRL, REALLY...
...WE COULD CALL HER "DARE" FOR SHORT...
OOOKAY...

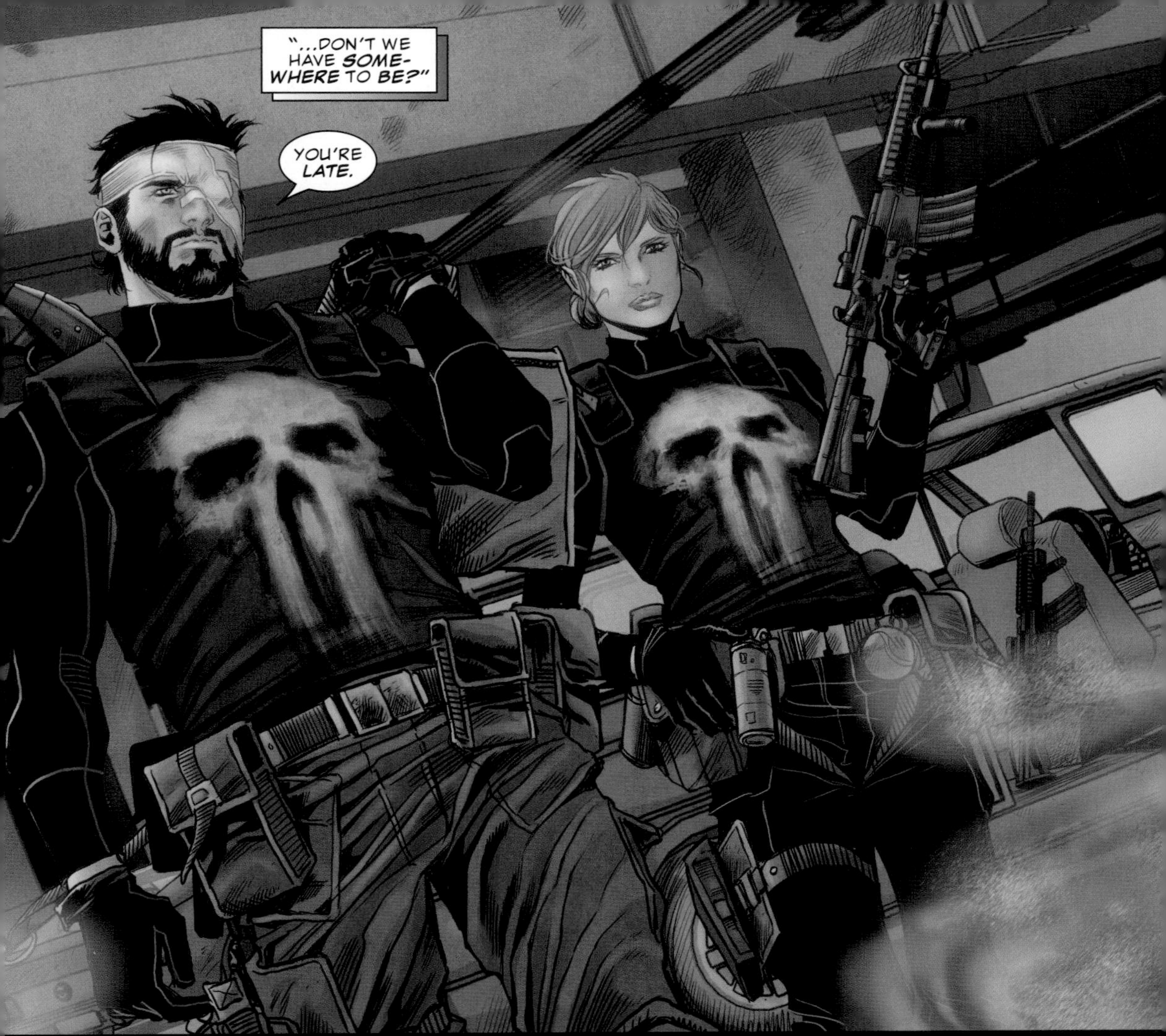
"...DON'T WE HAVE SOME-WHERE TO BE?"
YOU'RE LATE.

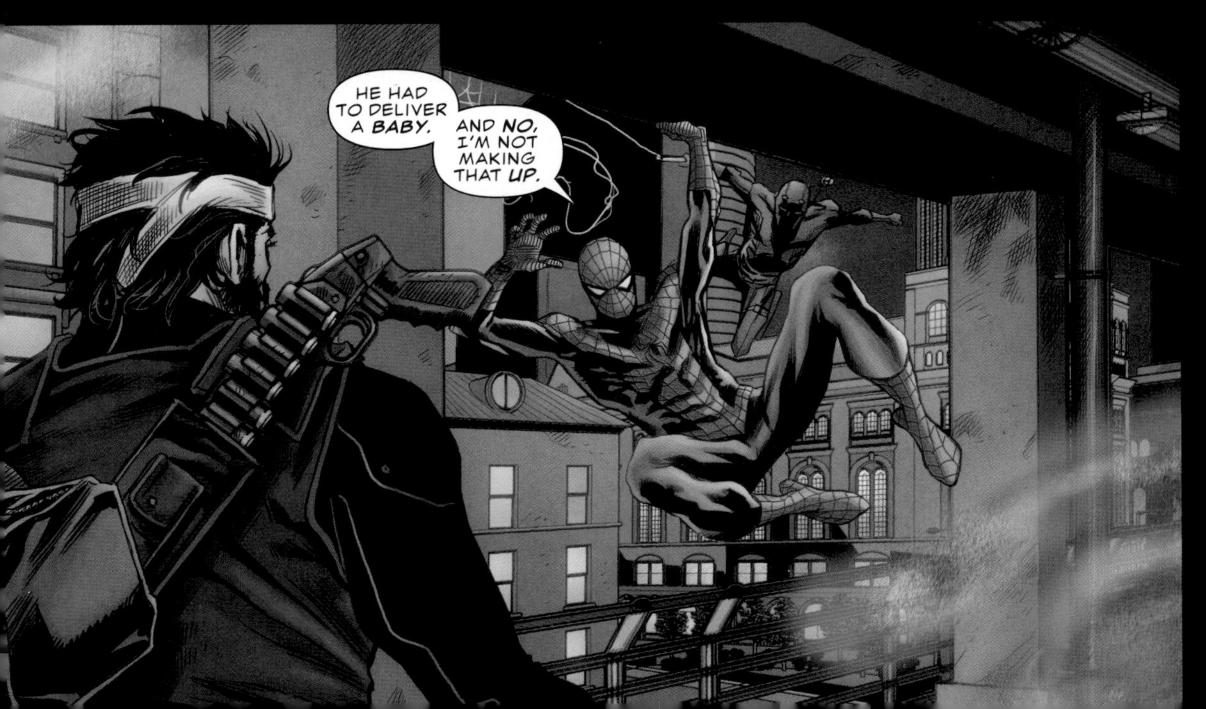
HE HAD TO DELIVER A BABY.
AND NO, I'M NOT MAKING THAT UP.

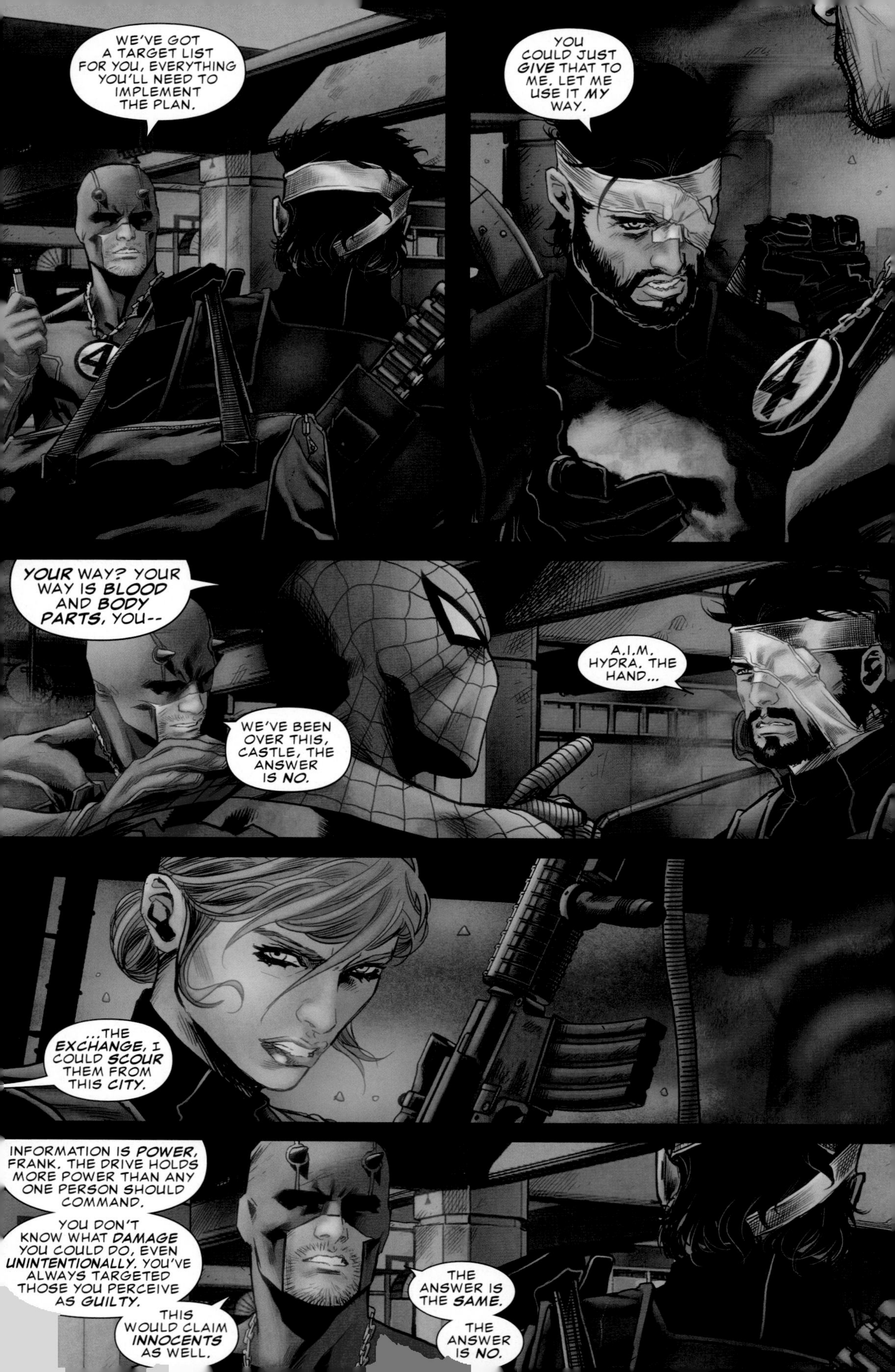
WE'VE GOT A TARGET LIST FOR YOU, EVERYTHING YOU'LL NEED TO IMPLEMENT THE PLAN.
YOU COULD JUST GIVE THAT TO ME. LET ME USE IT MY WAY.
YOUR WAY? YOUR WAY IS BLOOD AND BODY PARTS, YOU--
WE'VE BEEN OVER THIS, CASTLE, THE ANSWER IS NO.
A.I.M. HYDRA. THE HAND...
...THE EXCHANGE, I COULD SCOUR THEM FROM THIS CITY.
INFORMATION IS POWER, FRANK. THE DRIVE HOLDS MORE POWER THAN ANY ONE PERSON SHOULD COMMAND.
YOU DON'T KNOW WHAT DAMAGE YOU COULD DO, EVEN UNINTENTIONALLY. YOU'VE ALWAYS TARGETED THOSE YOU PERCEIVE AS GUILTY.
THIS WOULD CLAIM INNOCENTS AS WELL.
THE ANSWER IS THE SAME.
THE ANSWER IS NO.

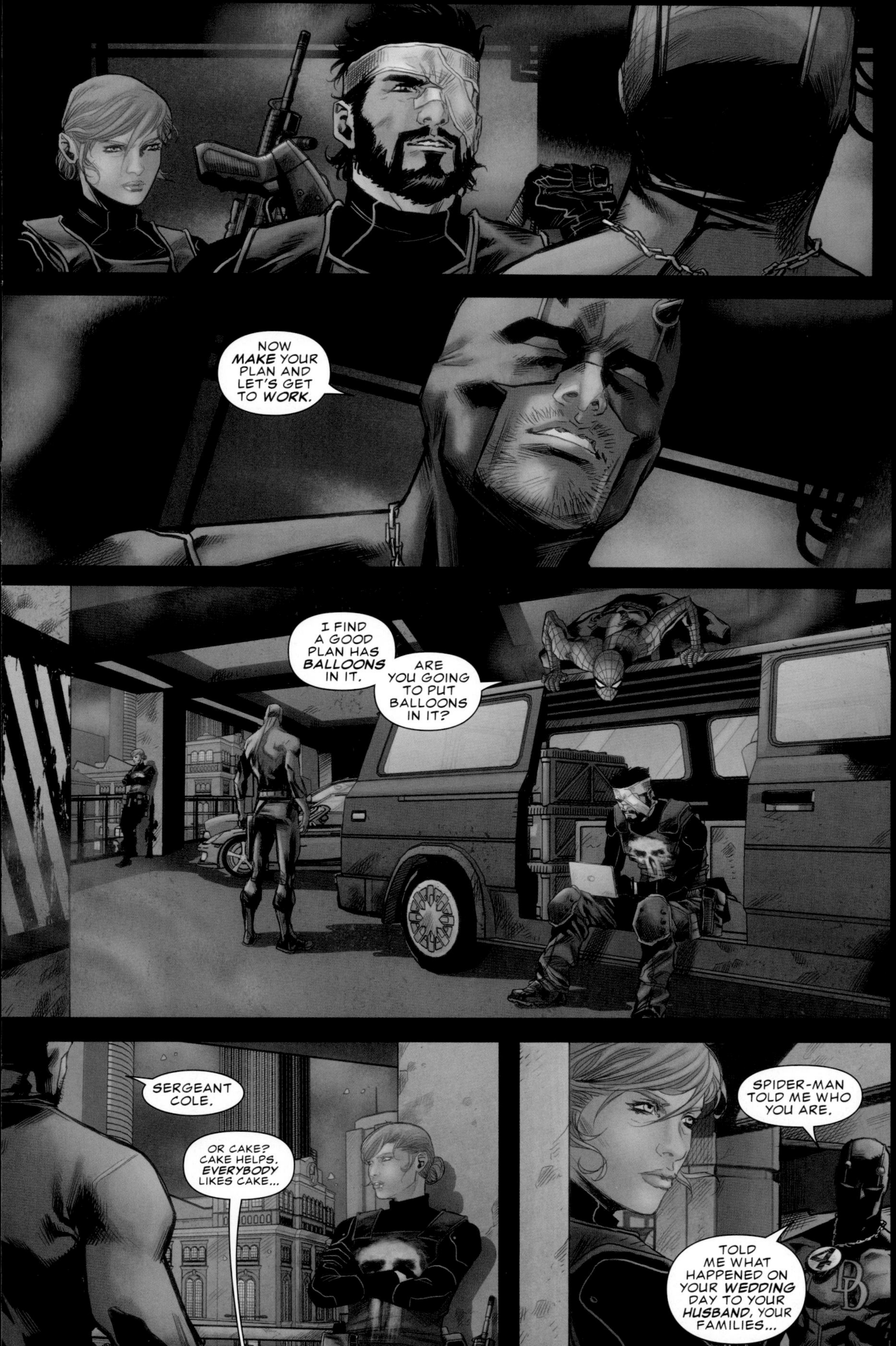
NOW MAKE YOUR PLAN AND LET'S GET TO WORK.
I FIND A GOOD PLAN HAS BALLOONS IN IT.
ARE YOU GOING TO PUT BALLOONS IN IT?
OR CAKE? CAKE HELPS. EVERYBODY LIKES CAKE...
SERGEANT COLE.
SPIDER-MAN TOLD ME WHO YOU ARE.
TOLD ME WHAT HAPPENED ON YOUR WEDDING DAY TO YOUR HUSBAND, YOUR FAMILIES...

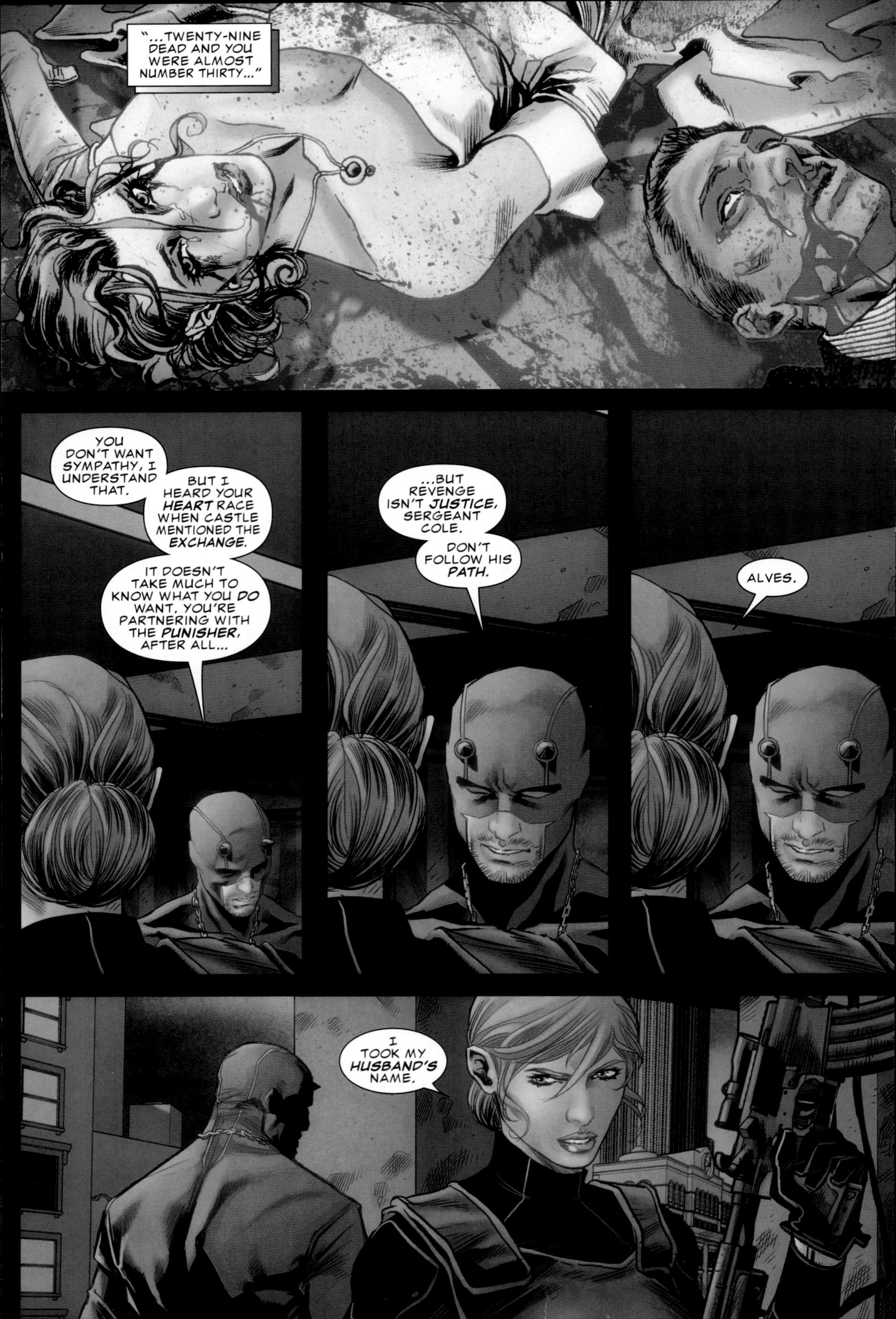
"...TWENTY-NINE DEAD AND YOU WERE ALMOST NUMBER THIRTY..."
YOU DON'T WANT SYMPATHY, I UNDERSTAND THAT.
BUT I HEARD YOUR **HEART** RACE WHEN CASTLE MENTIONED THE **EXCHANGE**.
IT DOESN'T TAKE MUCH TO KNOW WHAT YOU **DO** WANT. YOU'RE PARTNERING WITH THE **PUNISHER**, AFTER ALL...
...BUT REVENGE ISN'T **JUSTICE**, SERGEANT COLE.
DON'T FOLLOW HIS **PATH**.
ALVES.
I TOOK MY **HUSBAND'S** NAME.

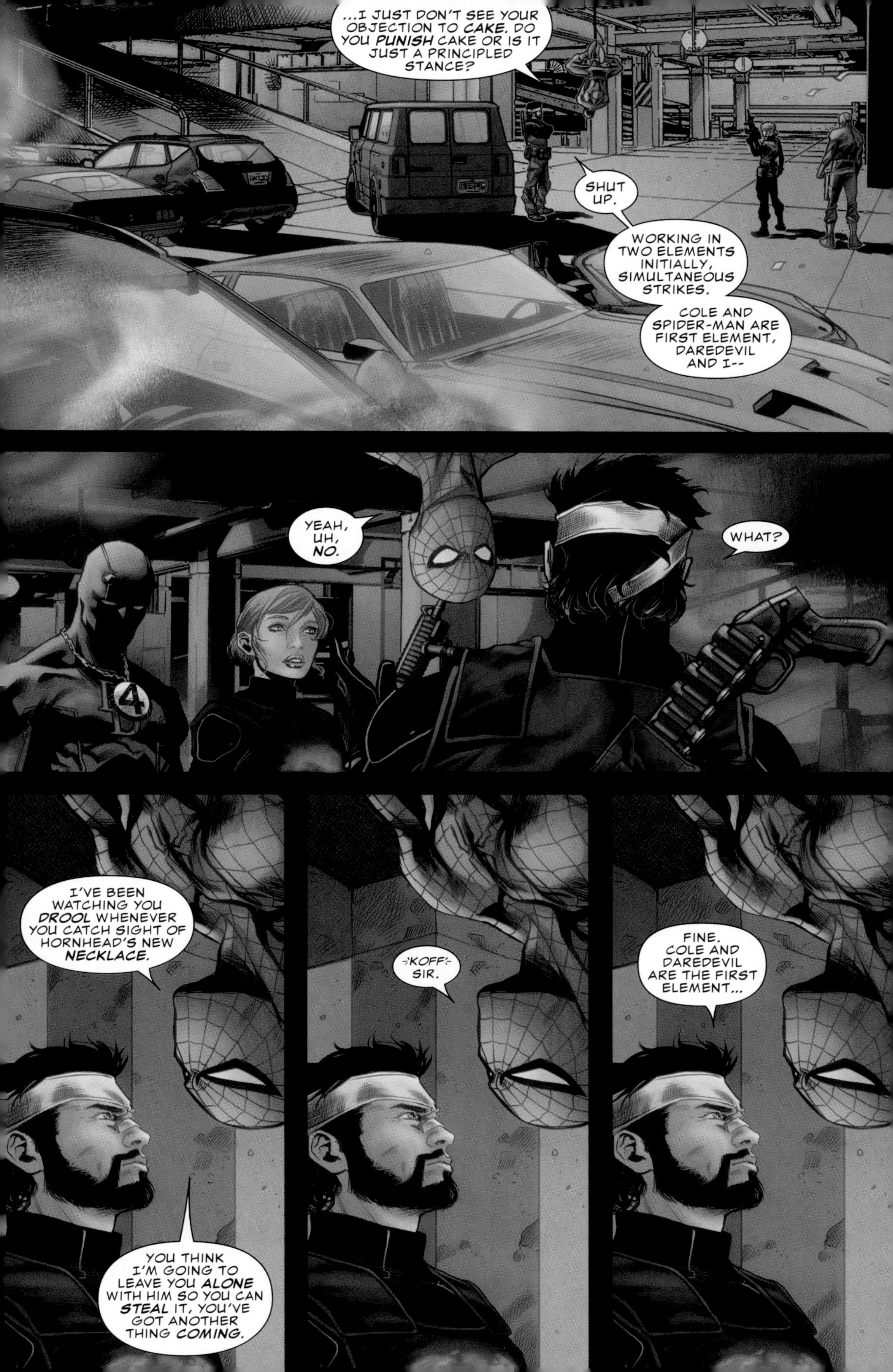
...I JUST DON'T SEE YOUR OBJECTION TO CAKE. DO YOU PUNISH CAKE OR IS IT JUST A PRINCIPLED STANCE?
SHUT UP.
WORKING IN TWO ELEMENTS INITIALLY, SIMULTANEOUS STRIKES.
COLE AND SPIDER-MAN ARE FIRST ELEMENT, DAREDEVIL AND I--
YEAH, UH, NO.
WHAT?
I'VE BEEN WATCHING YOU DROOL WHENEVER YOU CATCH SIGHT OF HORNHEAD'S NEW NECKLACE.
YOU THINK I'M GOING TO LEAVE YOU ALONE WITH HIM SO YOU CAN STEAL IT, YOU'VE GOT ANOTHER THING COMING.
KOFF SIR.
FINE. COLE AND DAREDEVIL ARE THE FIRST ELEMENT...

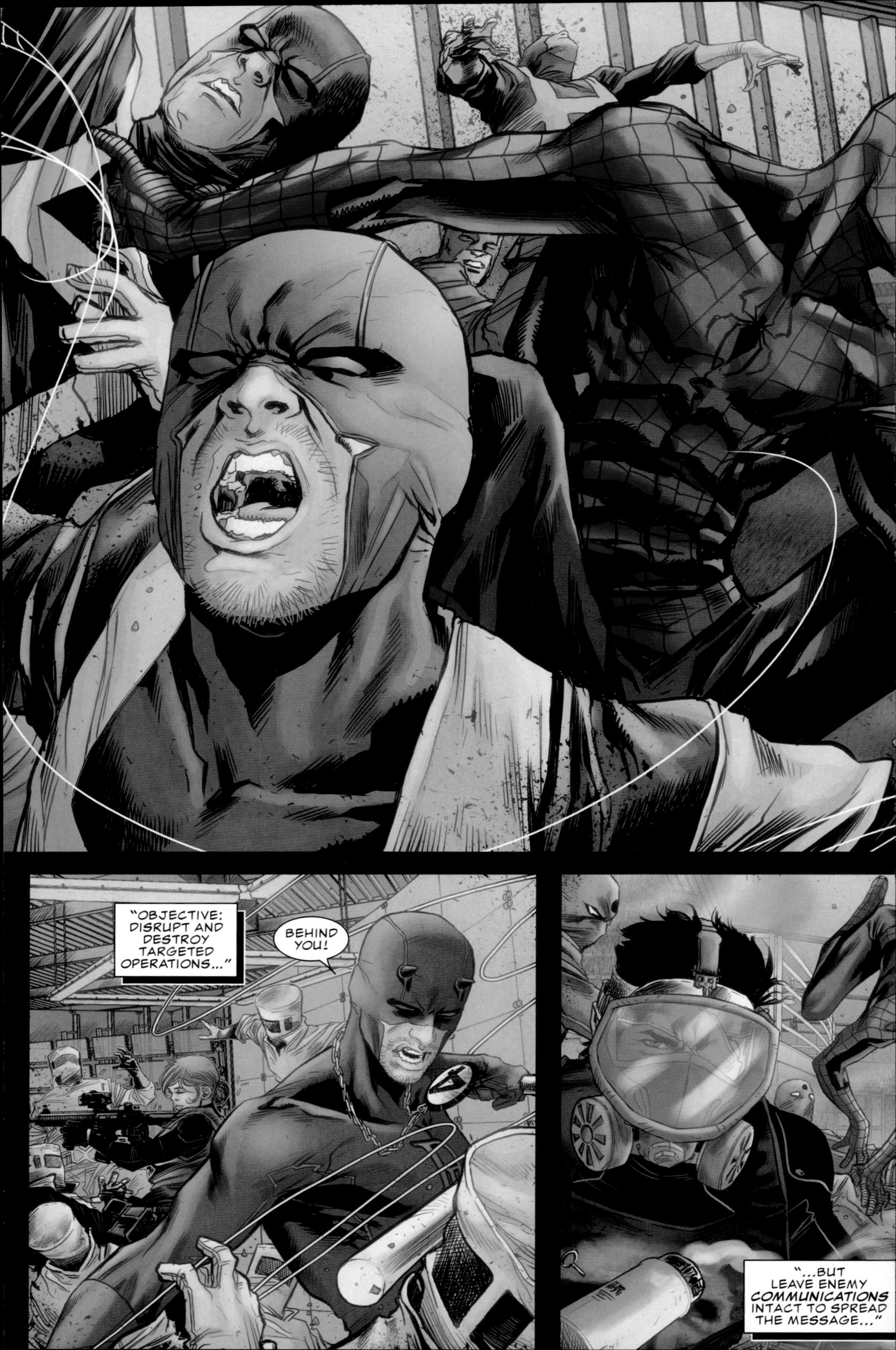

"OBJECTIVE: DISRUPT AND DESTROY TARGETED OPERATIONS..."
BEHIND YOU!
"...BUT LEAVE ENEMY COMMUNICATIONS INTACT TO SPREAD THE MESSAGE..."

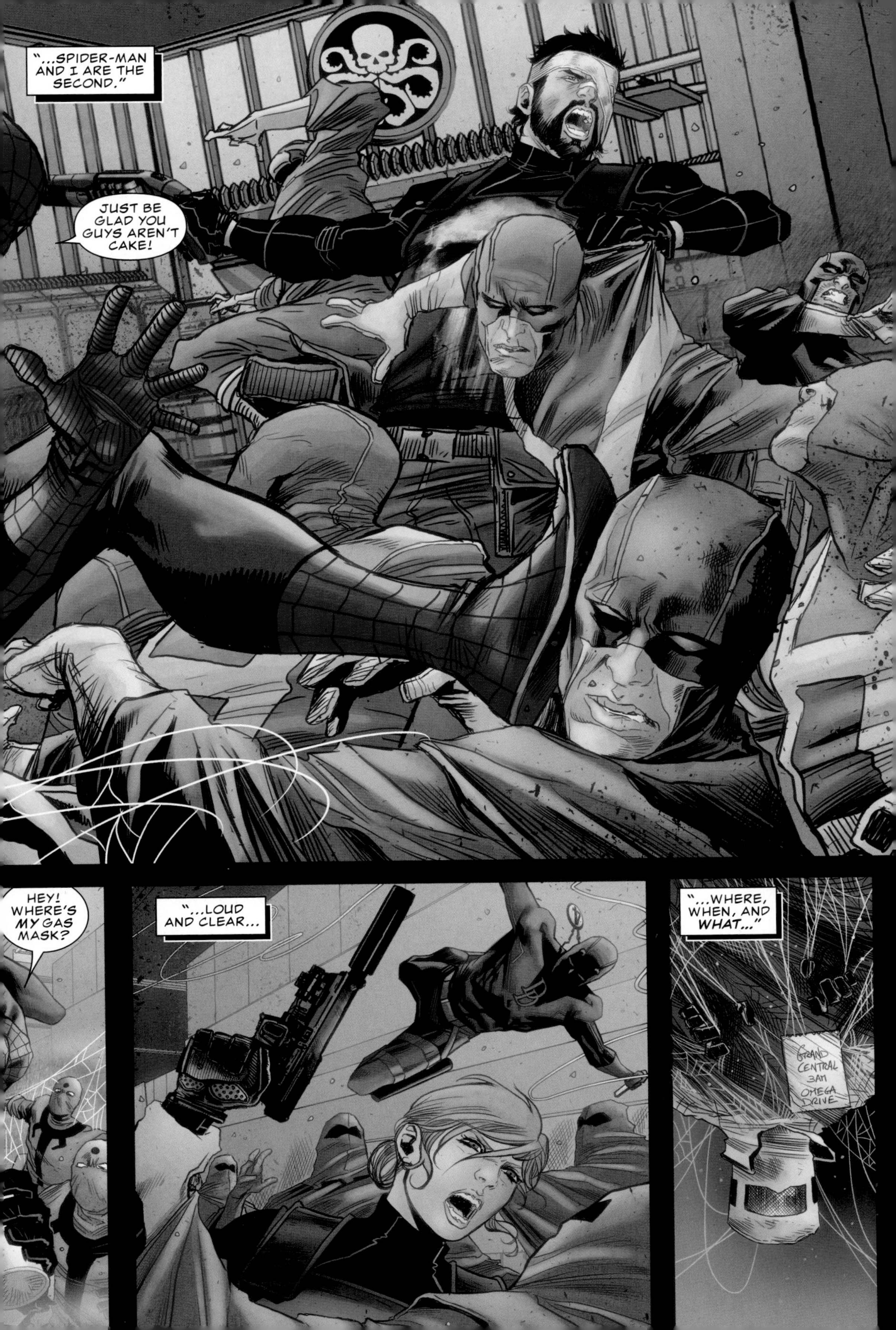

"...SPIDER-MAN AND I ARE THE SECOND."
JUST BE GLAD YOU GUYS AREN'T CAKE!
HEY! WHERE'S MY GAS MASK?
"...LOUD AND CLEAR...
"...WHERE, WHEN, AND WHAT..."
GRAND CENTRAL 3AM OMEGA DRIVE

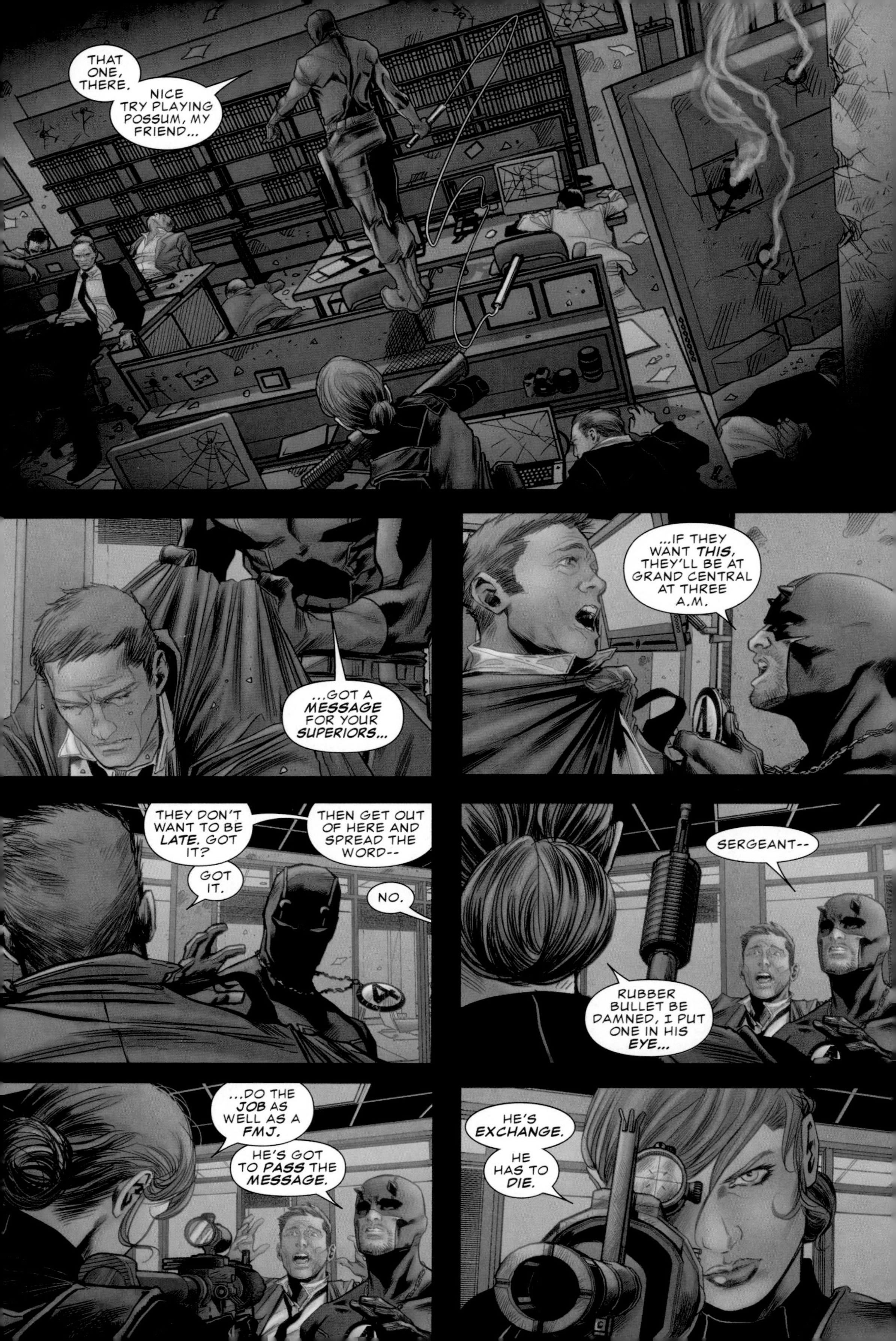
THAT ONE, THERE.
NICE TRY PLAYING POSSUM, MY FRIEND...
...GOT A MESSAGE FOR YOUR SUPERIORS...
...IF THEY WANT THIS, THEY'LL BE AT GRAND CENTRAL AT THREE A.M.
THEY DON'T WANT TO BE LATE. GOT IT?
GOT IT.
THEN GET OUT OF HERE AND SPREAD THE WORD--
NO.
SERGEANT--
RUBBER BULLET BE DAMNED, I PUT ONE IN HIS EYE...
...DO THE JOB AS WELL AS A FMJ.
HE'S GOT TO PASS THE MESSAGE.
HE'S EXCHANGE.
HE HAS TO DIE.

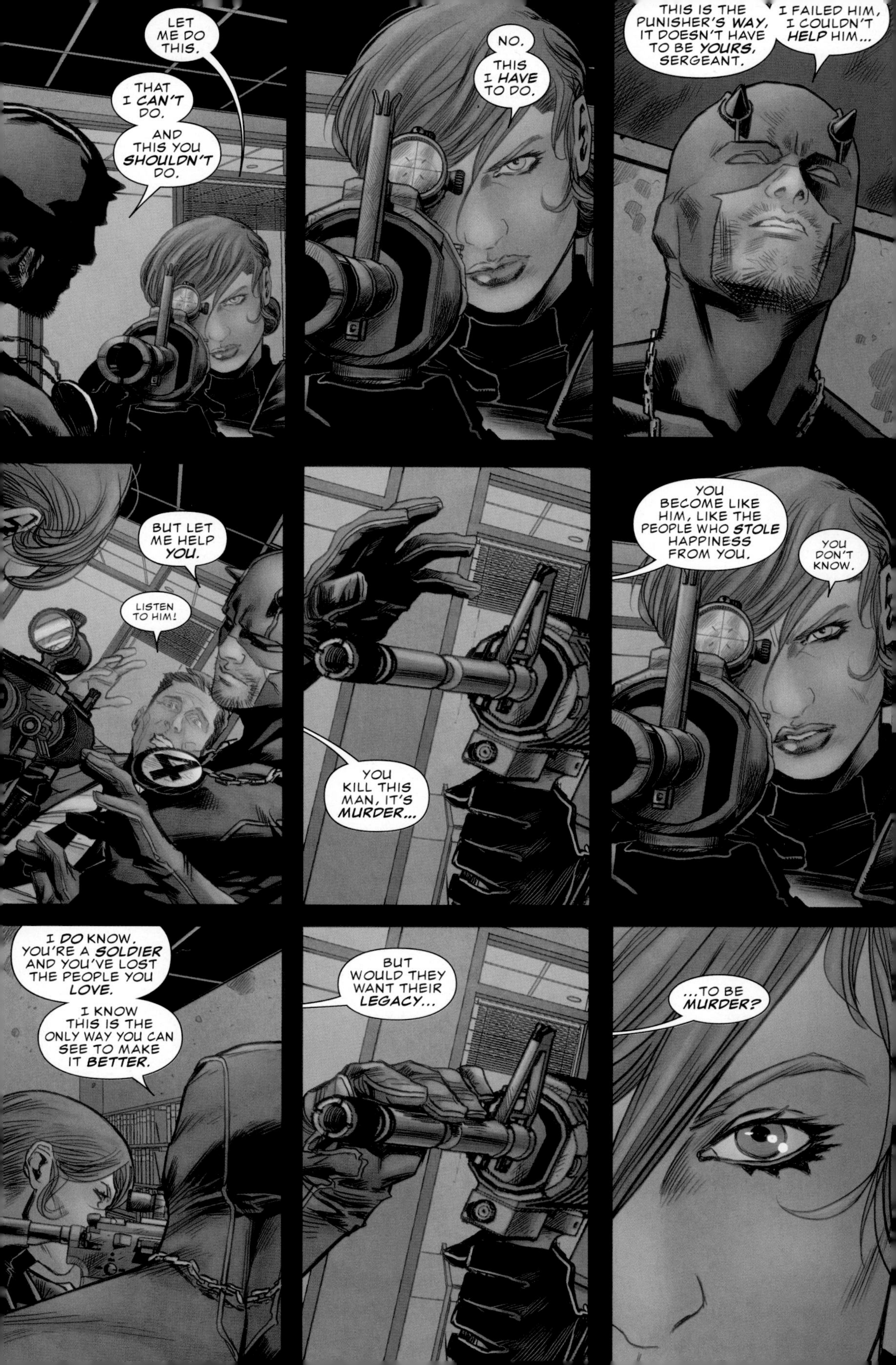
LET ME DO THIS.
THAT I CAN'T DO.
AND THIS YOU SHOULDN'T DO.
NO.
THIS I HAVE TO DO.
THIS IS THE PUNISHER'S WAY, IT DOESN'T HAVE TO BE YOURS, SERGEANT.
I FAILED HIM, I COULDN'T HELP HIM...
BUT LET ME HELP YOU.
LISTEN TO HIM!
YOU KILL THIS MAN, IT'S MURDER...
YOU BECOME LIKE HIM, LIKE THE PEOPLE WHO STOLE HAPPINESS FROM YOU.
YOU DON'T KNOW.
I DO KNOW. YOU'RE A SOLDIER AND YOU'VE LOST THE PEOPLE YOU LOVE.
I KNOW THIS IS THE ONLY WAY YOU CAN SEE TO MAKE IT BETTER.
BUT WOULD THEY WANT THEIR LEGACY...
...TO BE MURDER?

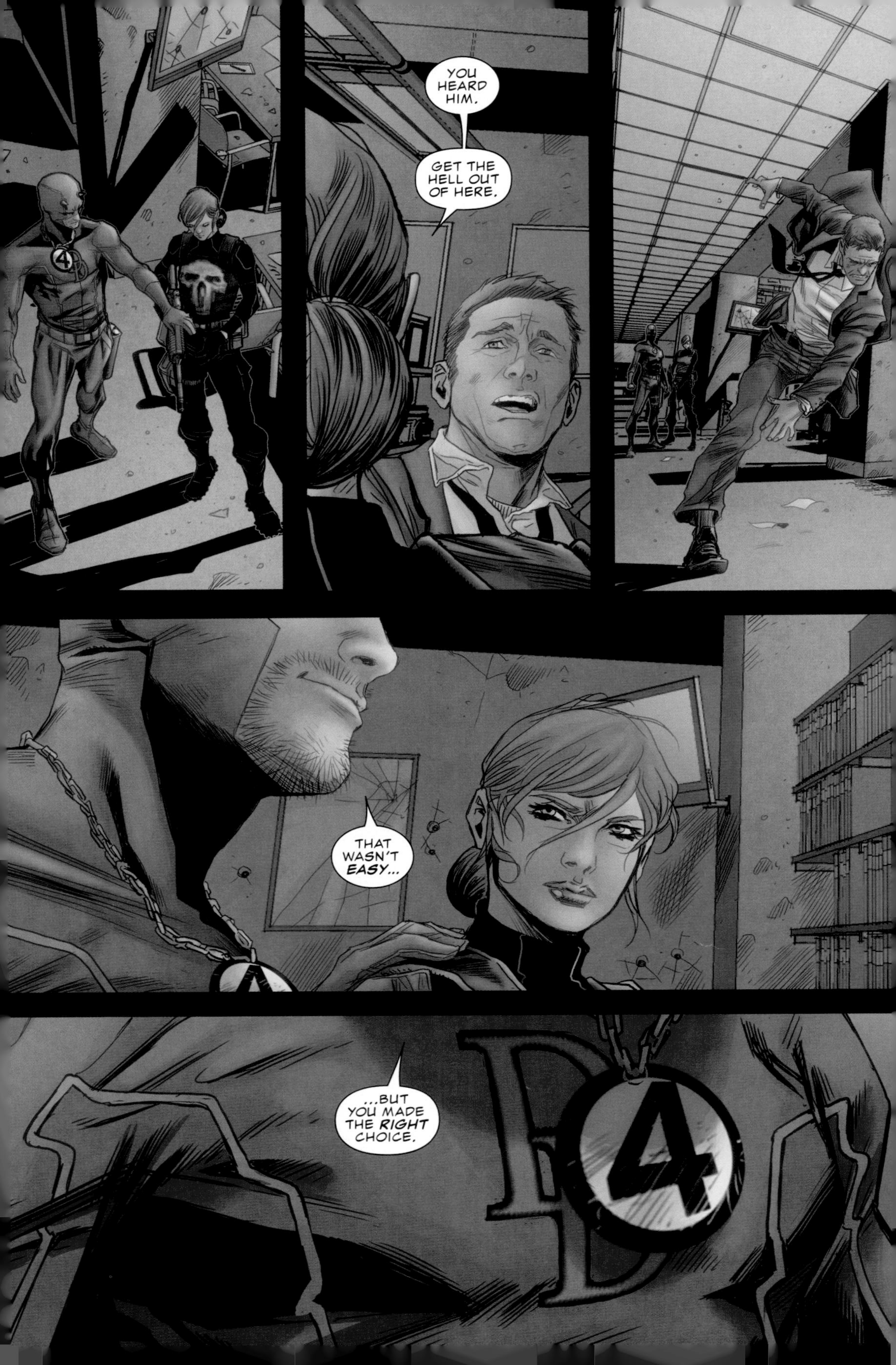
YOU HEARD HIM.
GET THE HELL OUT OF HERE.
THAT WASN'T EASY...
...BUT YOU MADE THE RIGHT CHOICE.

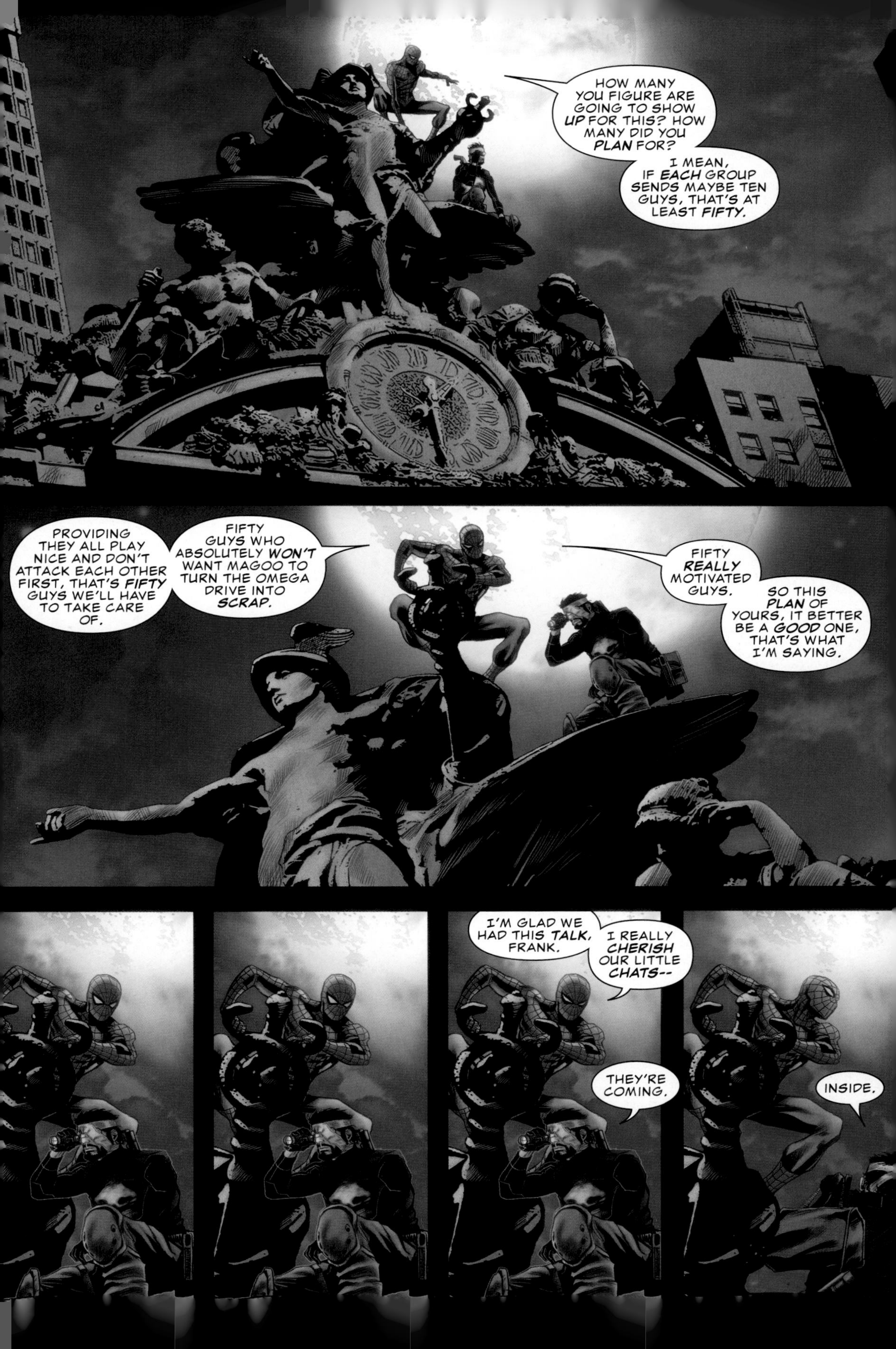
HOW MANY YOU FIGURE ARE GOING TO SHOW UP FOR THIS? HOW MANY DID YOU PLAN FOR?
I MEAN, IF EACH GROUP SENDS MAYBE TEN GUYS, THAT'S AT LEAST FIFTY.
PROVIDING THEY ALL PLAY NICE AND DON'T ATTACK EACH OTHER FIRST, THAT'S FIFTY GUYS WE'LL HAVE TO TAKE CARE OF.
FIFTY GUYS WHO ABSOLUTELY WON'T WANT MAGOO TO TURN THE OMEGA DRIVE INTO SCRAP.
FIFTY REALLY MOTIVATED GUYS.
SO THIS PLAN OF YOURS, IT BETTER BE A GOOD ONE, THAT'S WHAT I'M SAYING.
I'M GLAD WE HAD THIS TALK, FRANK.
I REALLY CHERISH OUR LITTLE CHATS--
THEY'RE COMING.
INSIDE.

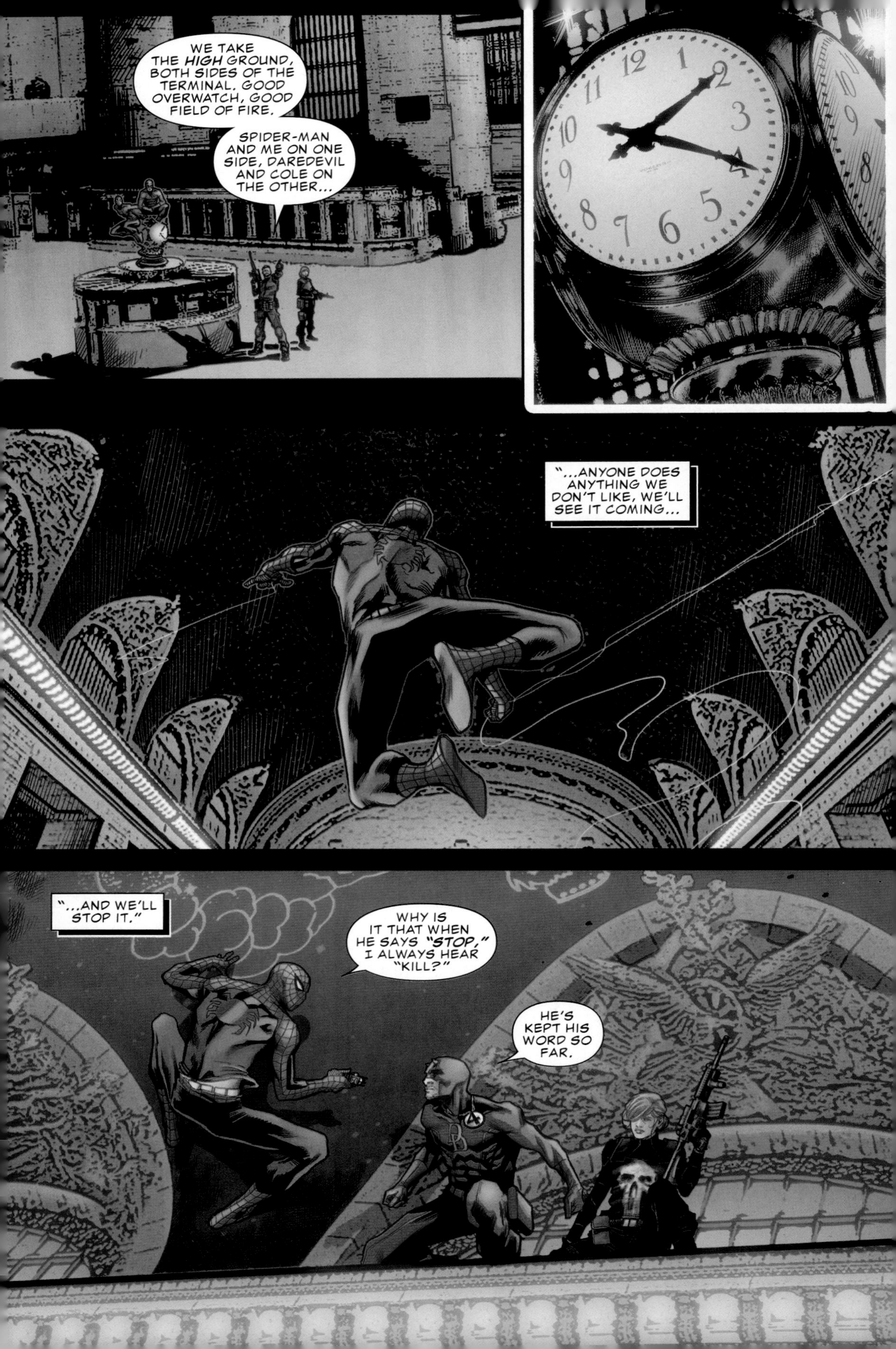
WE TAKE THE HIGH GROUND, BOTH SIDES OF THE TERMINAL. GOOD OVERWATCH, GOOD FIELD OF FIRE.
SPIDER-MAN AND ME ON ONE SIDE, DAREDEVIL AND COLE ON THE OTHER...
"...ANYONE DOES ANYTHING WE DON'T LIKE, WE'LL SEE IT COMING...
"...AND WE'LL STOP IT."
WHY IS IT THAT WHEN HE SAYS "STOP," I ALWAYS HEAR "KILL?"
HE'S KEPT HIS WORD SO FAR.

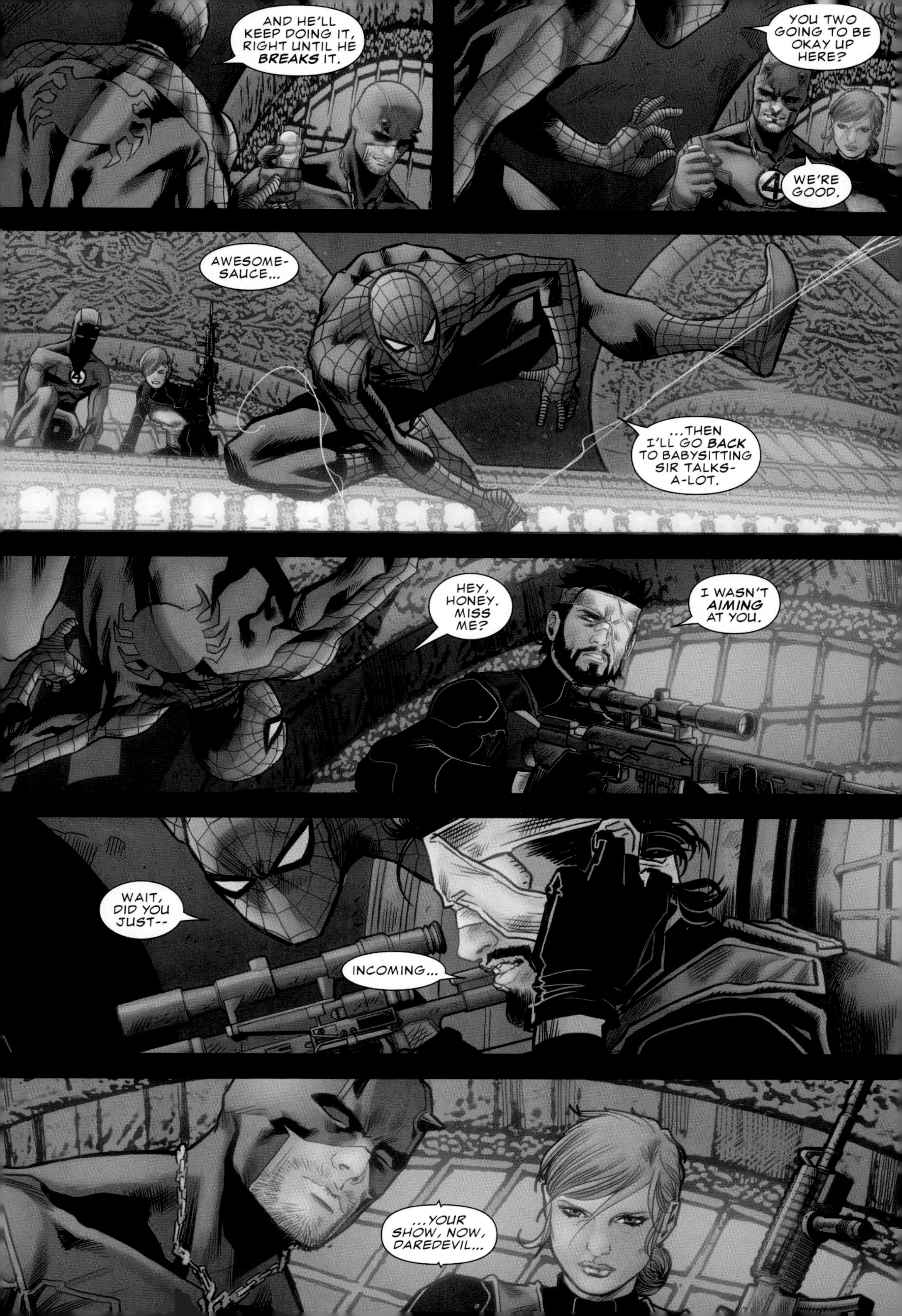
AND HE'LL KEEP DOING IT, RIGHT UNTIL HE BREAKS IT.
YOU TWO GOING TO BE OKAY UP HERE?
WE'RE GOOD.
AWESOME-SAUCE...
...THEN I'LL GO BACK TO BABYSITTING SIR TALKS-A-LOT.
HEY, HONEY. MISS ME?
I WASN'T AIMING AT YOU.
WAIT, DID YOU JUST--
INCOMING...
...YOUR SHOW, NOW, DAREDEVIL...

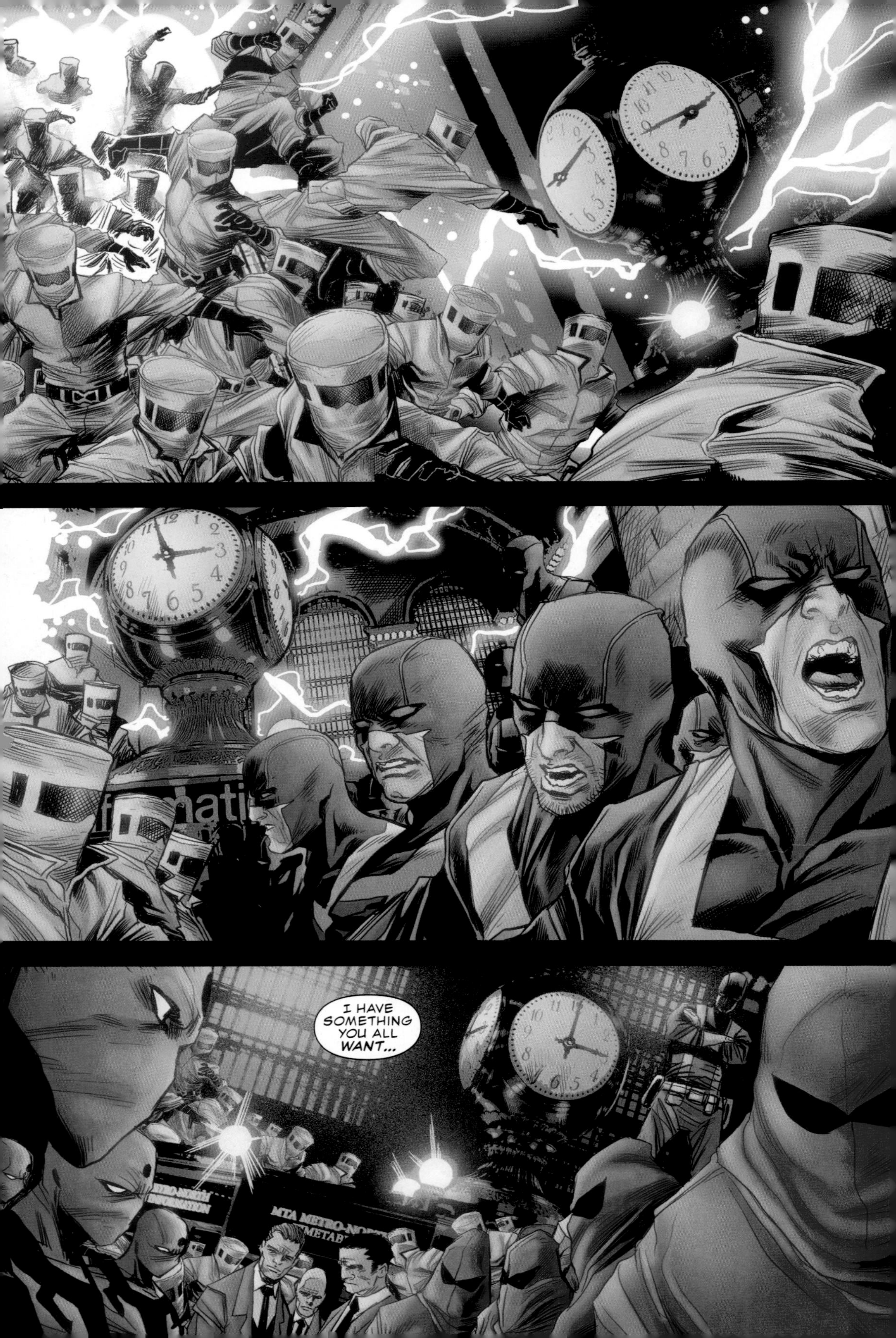
I HAVE SOMETHING YOU ALL WANT...

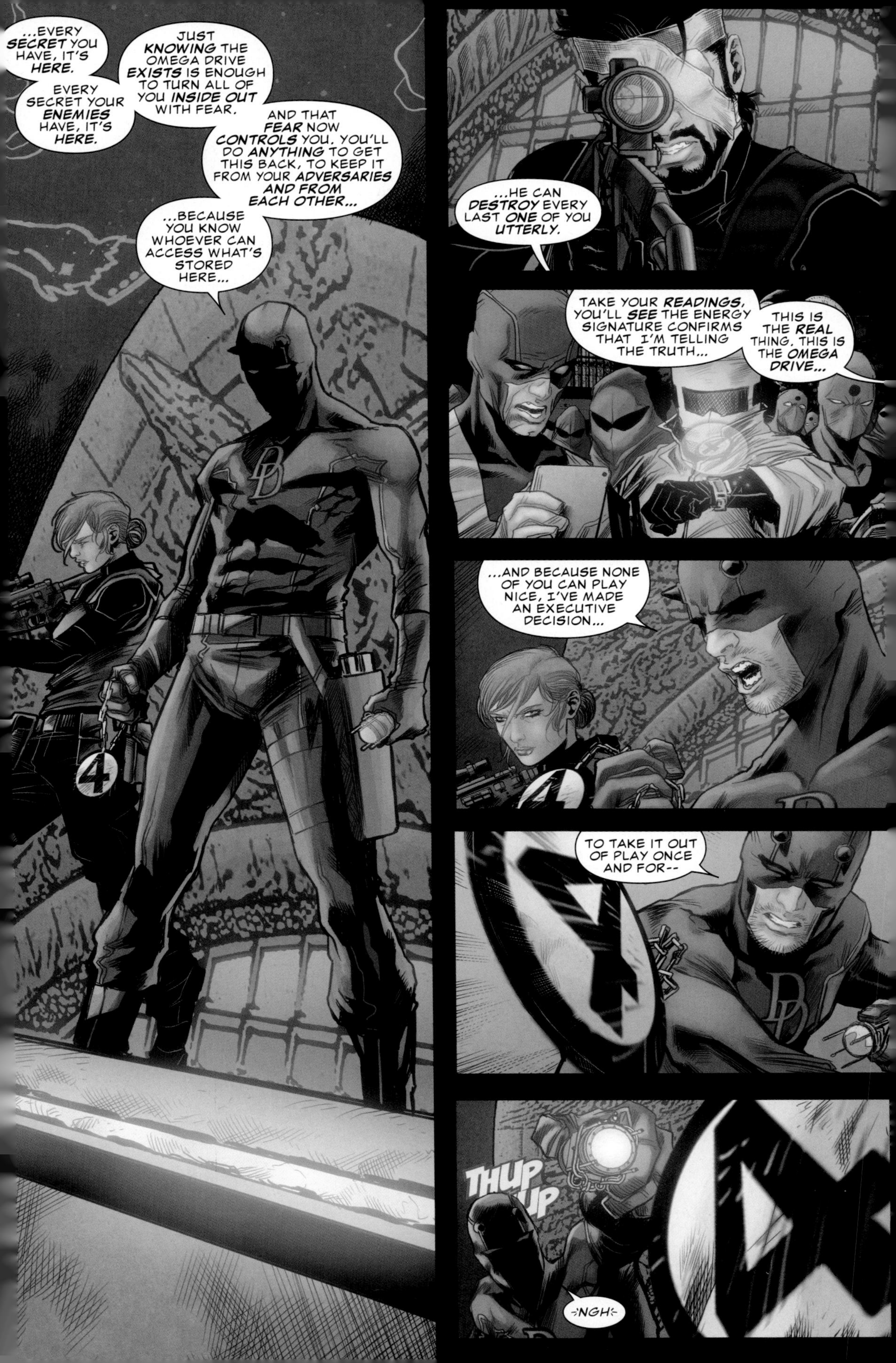
...EVERY SECRET YOU HAVE, IT'S HERE.
EVERY SECRET YOUR ENEMIES HAVE, IT'S HERE.
JUST KNOWING THE OMEGA DRIVE EXISTS IS ENOUGH TO TURN ALL OF YOU INSIDE OUT WITH FEAR.
AND THAT FEAR NOW CONTROLS YOU. YOU'LL DO ANYTHING TO GET THIS BACK, TO KEEP IT FROM YOUR ADVERSARIES AND FROM EACH OTHER...
...BECAUSE YOU KNOW WHOEVER CAN ACCESS WHAT'S STORED HERE...
...HE CAN DESTROY EVERY LAST ONE OF YOU UTTERLY.
TAKE YOUR READINGS. YOU'LL SEE THE ENERGY SIGNATURE CONFIRMS THAT I'M TELLING THE TRUTH...
THIS IS THE REAL THING. THIS IS THE OMEGA DRIVE...
...AND BECAUSE NONE OF YOU CAN PLAY NICE, I'VE MADE AN EXECUTIVE DECISION...
TO TAKE IT OUT OF PLAY ONCE AND FOR--
THUP
NGH

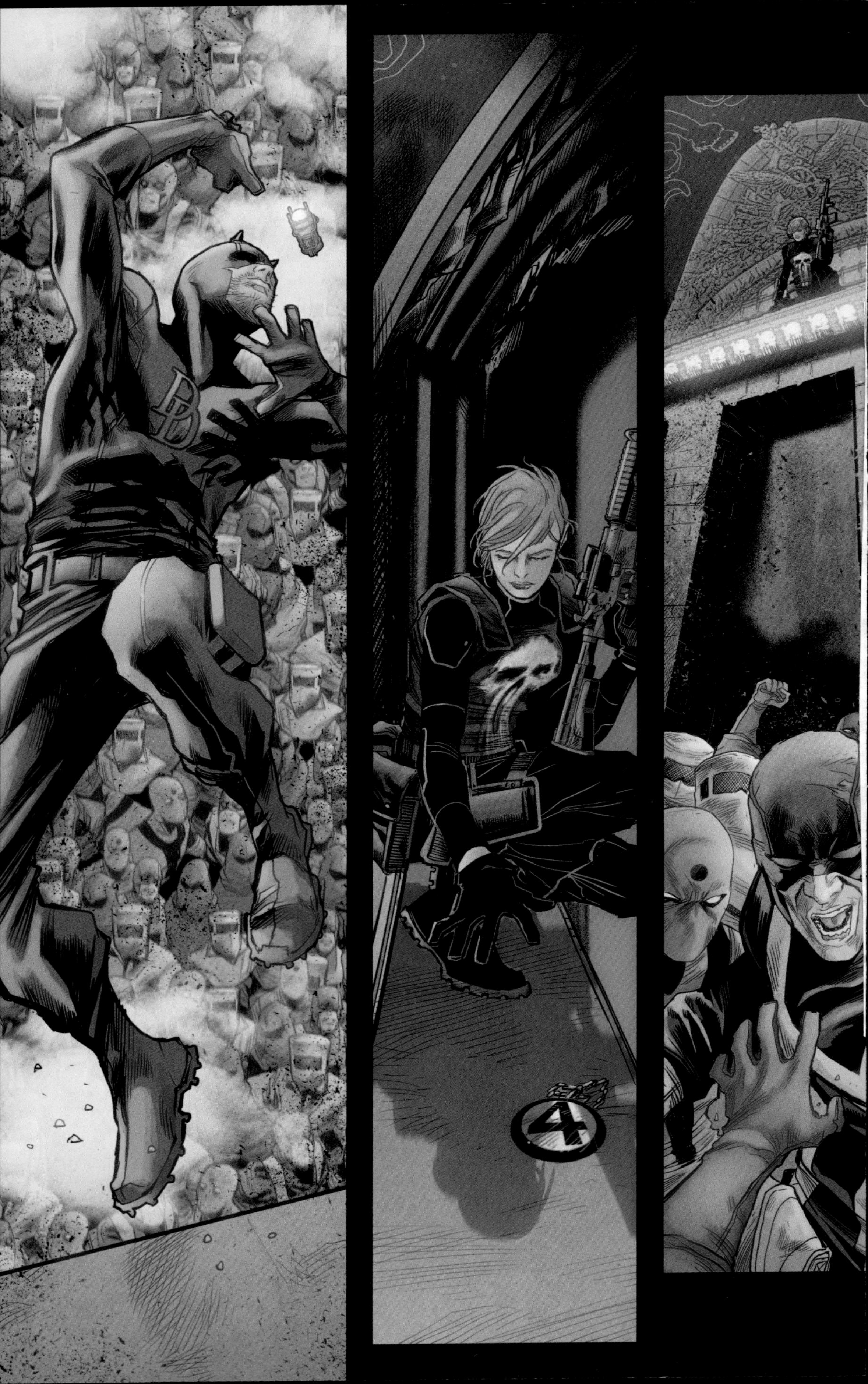

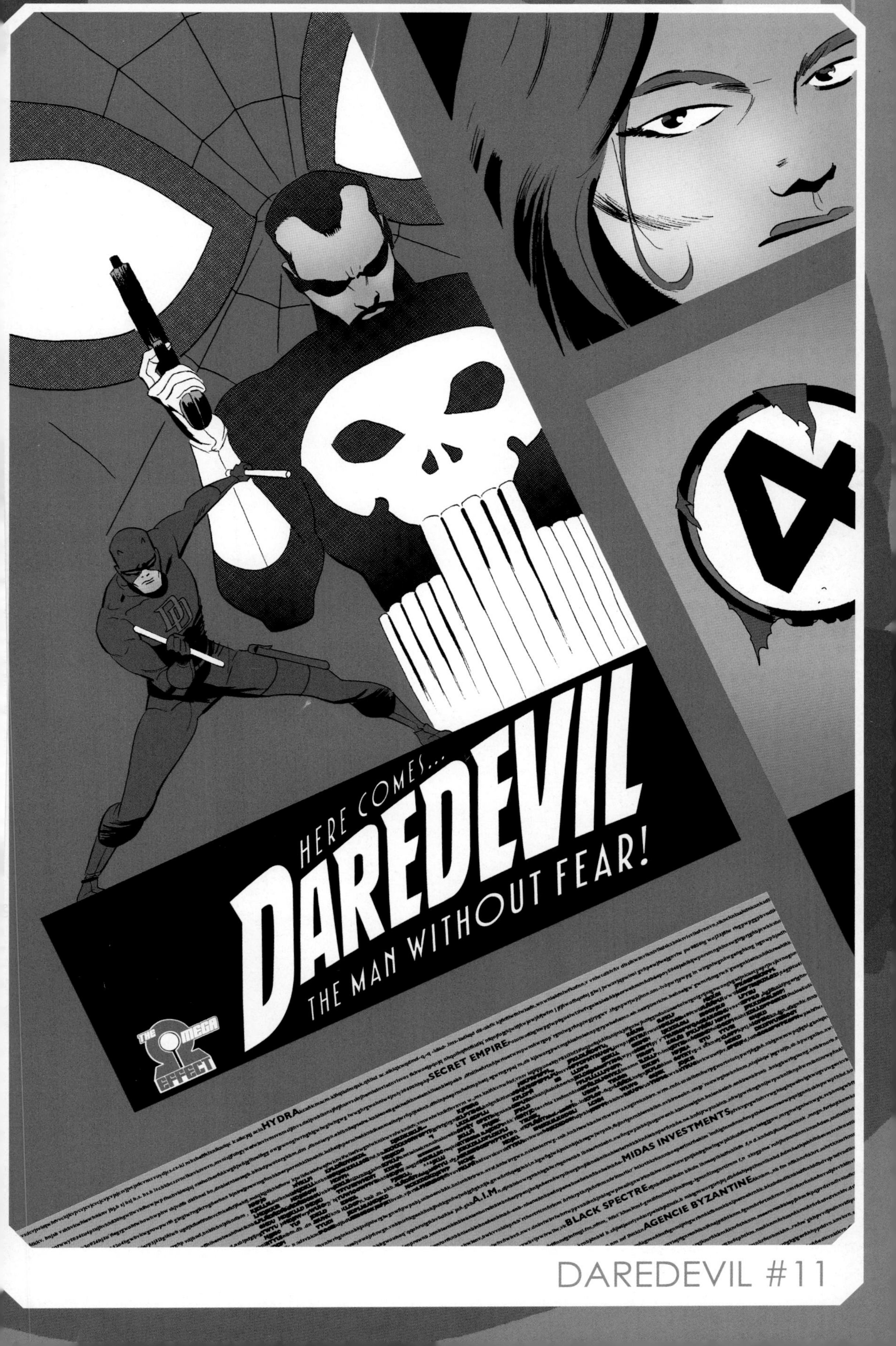
HERE COMES...
DAREDEVIL
THE MAN WITHOUT FEAR!
THE OMEGA EFFECT
SECRET EMPIRE
HYDRA
A.I.M.
MIDAS INVESTMENTS
BLACK SPECTRE
AGENCIE BYZANTINE

DAREDEVIL #11

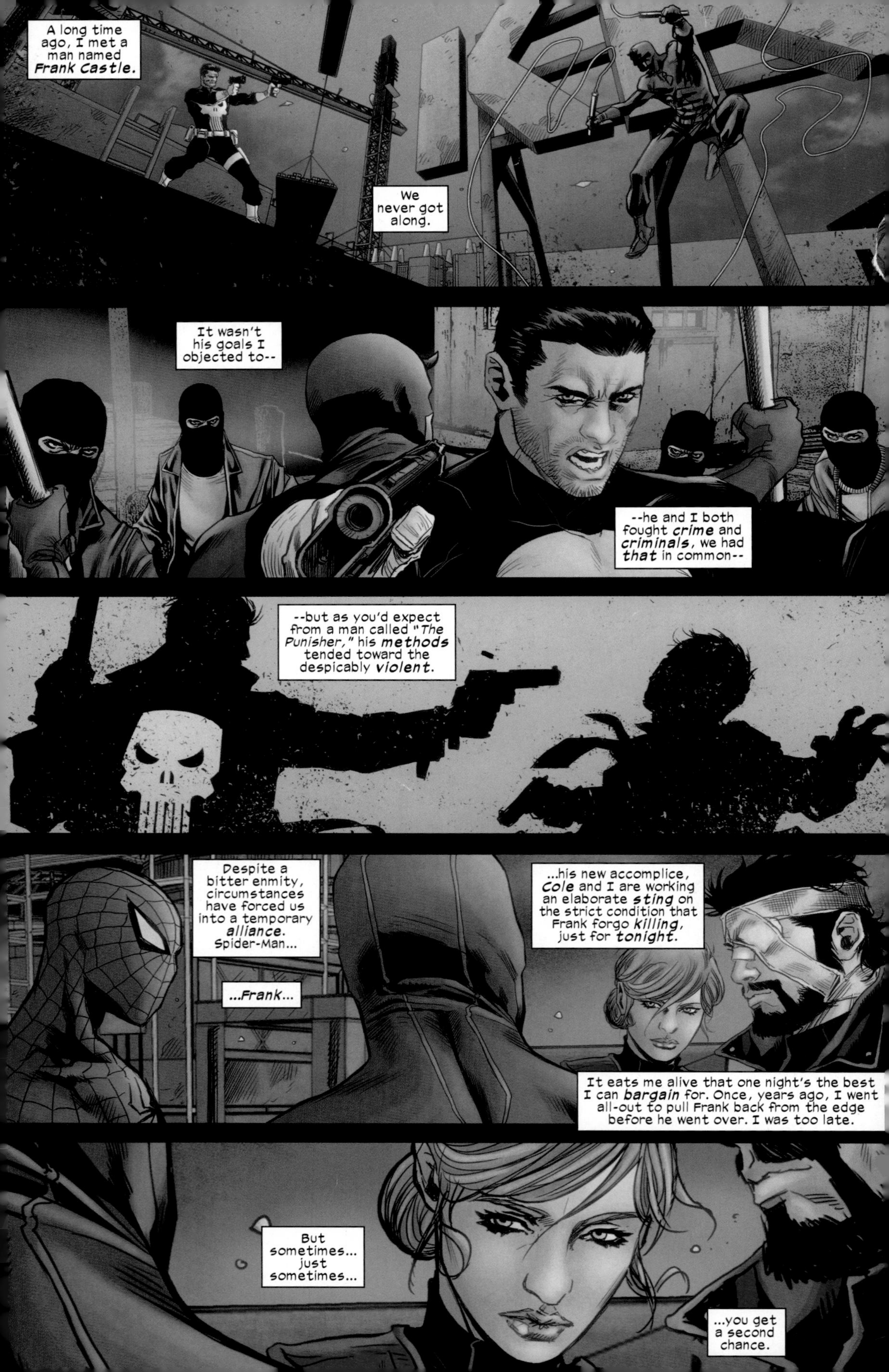

A long time ago, I met a man named *Frank Castle.*
We never got along.
It wasn't his goals I objected to--
--he and I both fought *crime* and *criminals*, we had *that* in common--
--but as you'd expect from a man called "*The Punisher*," his *methods* tended toward the despicably *violent*.
Despite a bitter enmity, circumstances have forced us into a temporary *alliance*. Spider-Man...
...*Frank*...
...his new accomplice, *Cole* and I are working an elaborate *sting* on the strict condition that Frank forgo *killing*, just for *tonight*.
It eats me alive that one night's the best I can *bargain* for. Once, years ago, I went all-out to pull Frank back from the edge before he went over. I was too late.
But sometimes... just sometimes...
...you get a second chance.

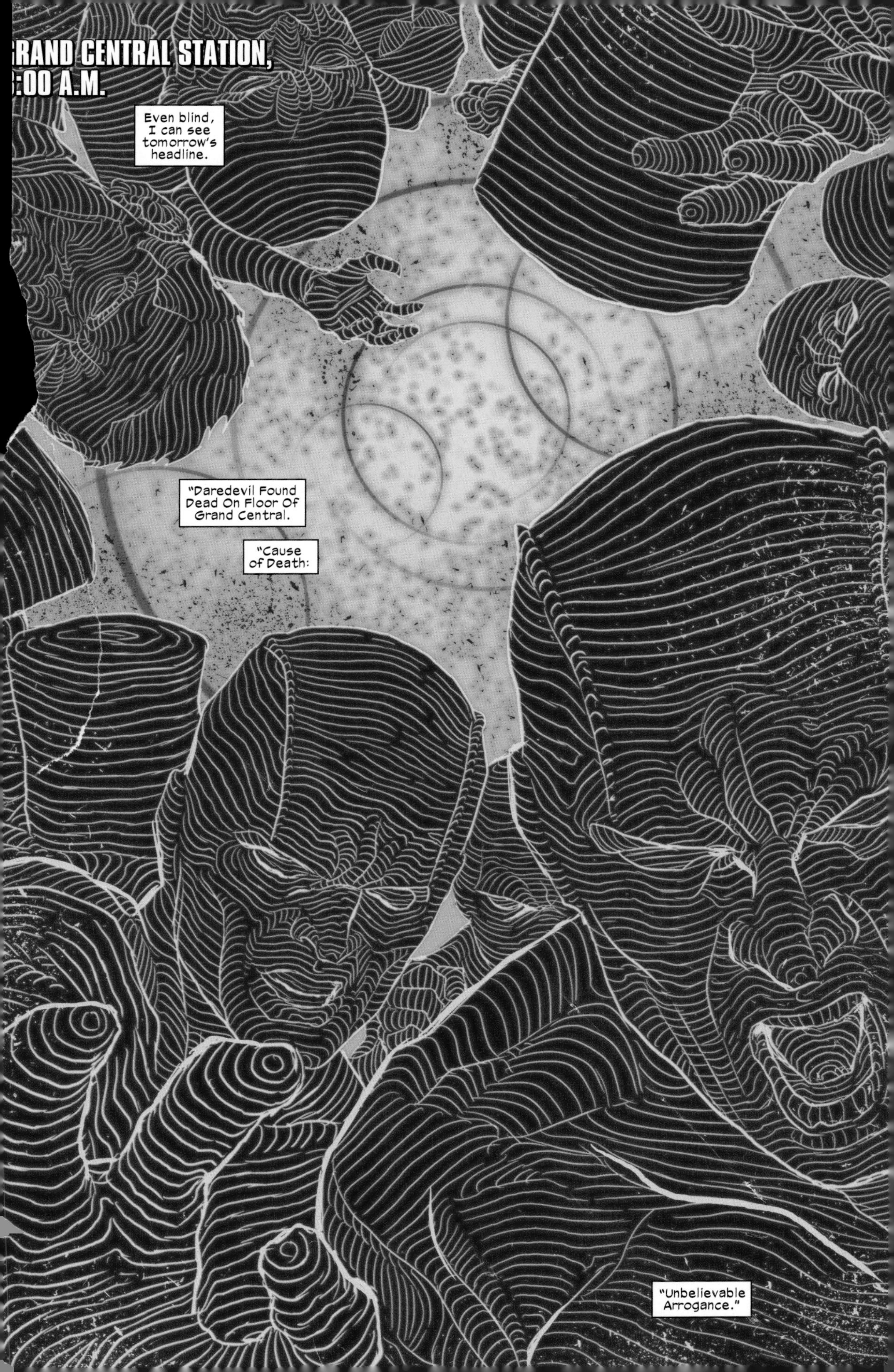
RAND CENTRAL STATION,
:00 A.M.
Even blind, I can see tomorrow's headline.
"Daredevil Found Dead On Floor Of Grand Central.
"Cause of Death:
"Unbelievable Arrogance."

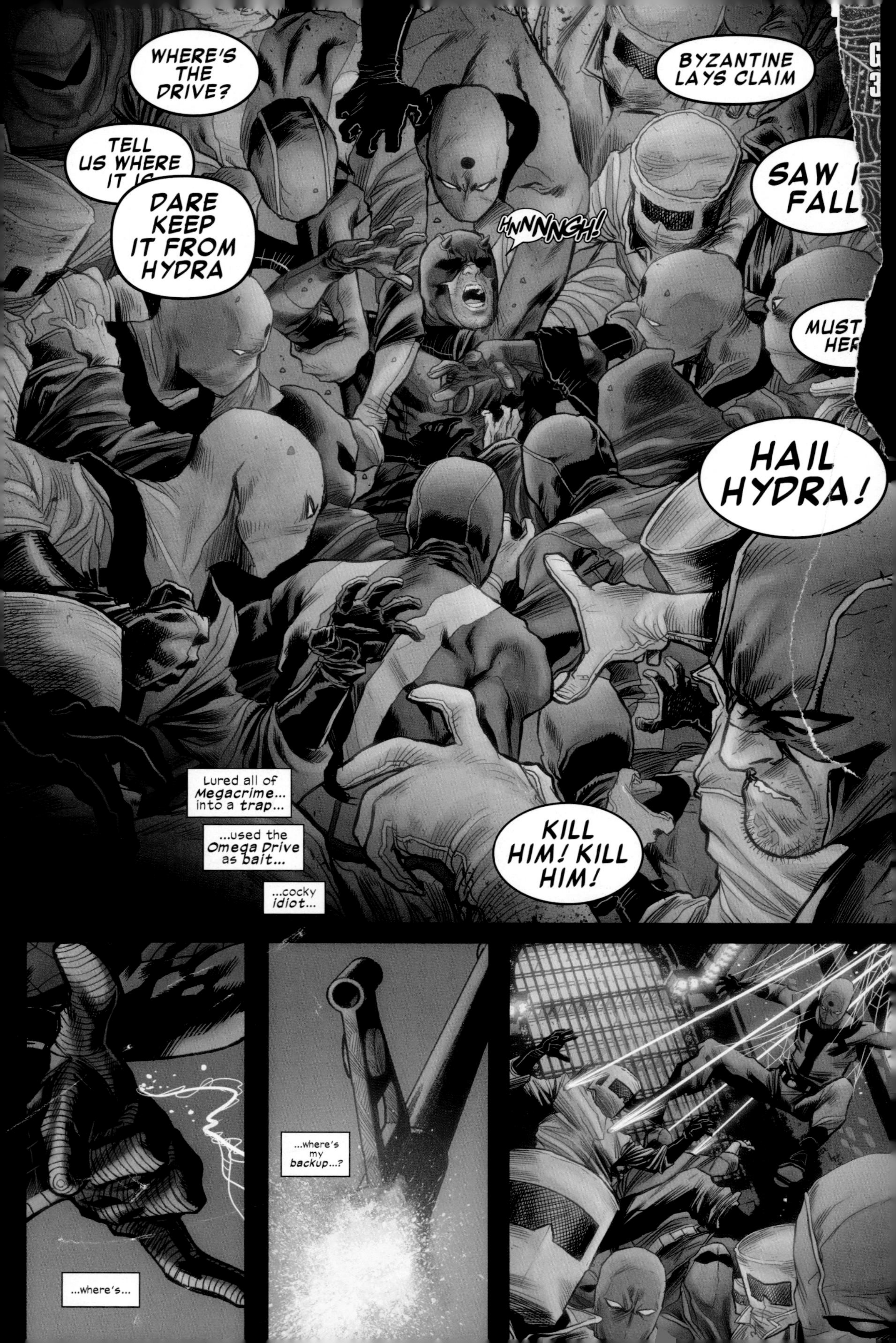
WHERE'S THE DRIVE?
TELL US WHERE IT
DARE KEEP IT FROM HYDRA
HNNNNGH!
BYZANTINE LAYS CLAIM
SAW
FALL
MUST
HER
HAIL HYDRA!
Lured all of Megacrime... into a trap...
...used the Omega Drive as bait...
...cocky idiot...
KILL HIM! KILL HIM!
...where's...
...where's my backup...?

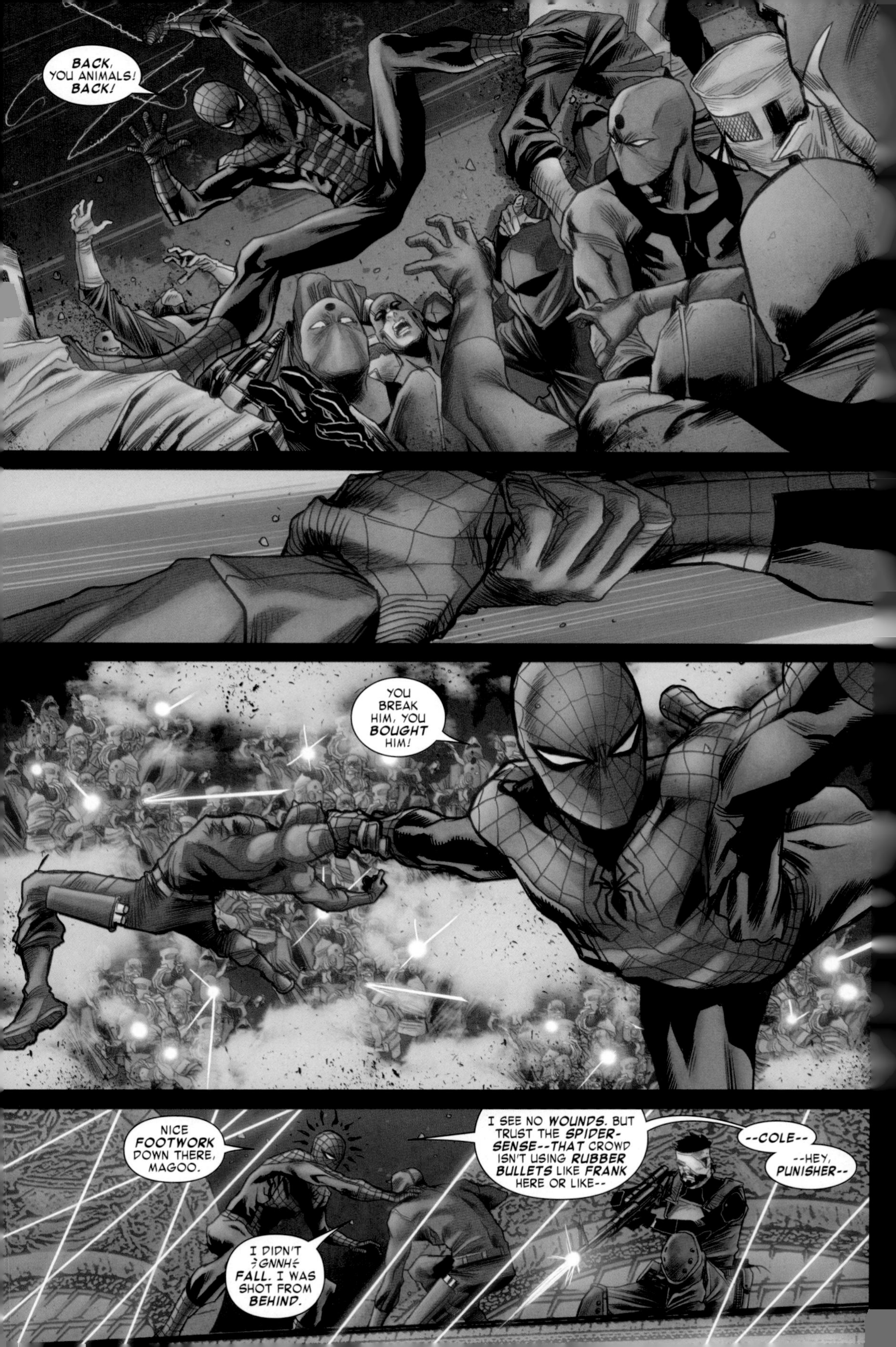
BACK, YOU ANIMALS! BACK!
YOU BREAK HIM, YOU BOUGHT HIM!
NICE FOOTWORK DOWN THERE, MAGOO.
I DIDN'T GNNH FALL. I WAS SHOT FROM BEHIND.
I SEE NO WOUNDS. BUT TRUST THE SPIDER-SENSE--THAT CROWD ISN'T USING RUBBER BULLETS LIKE FRANK HERE OR LIKE--
--COLE--
--HEY, PUNISHER--

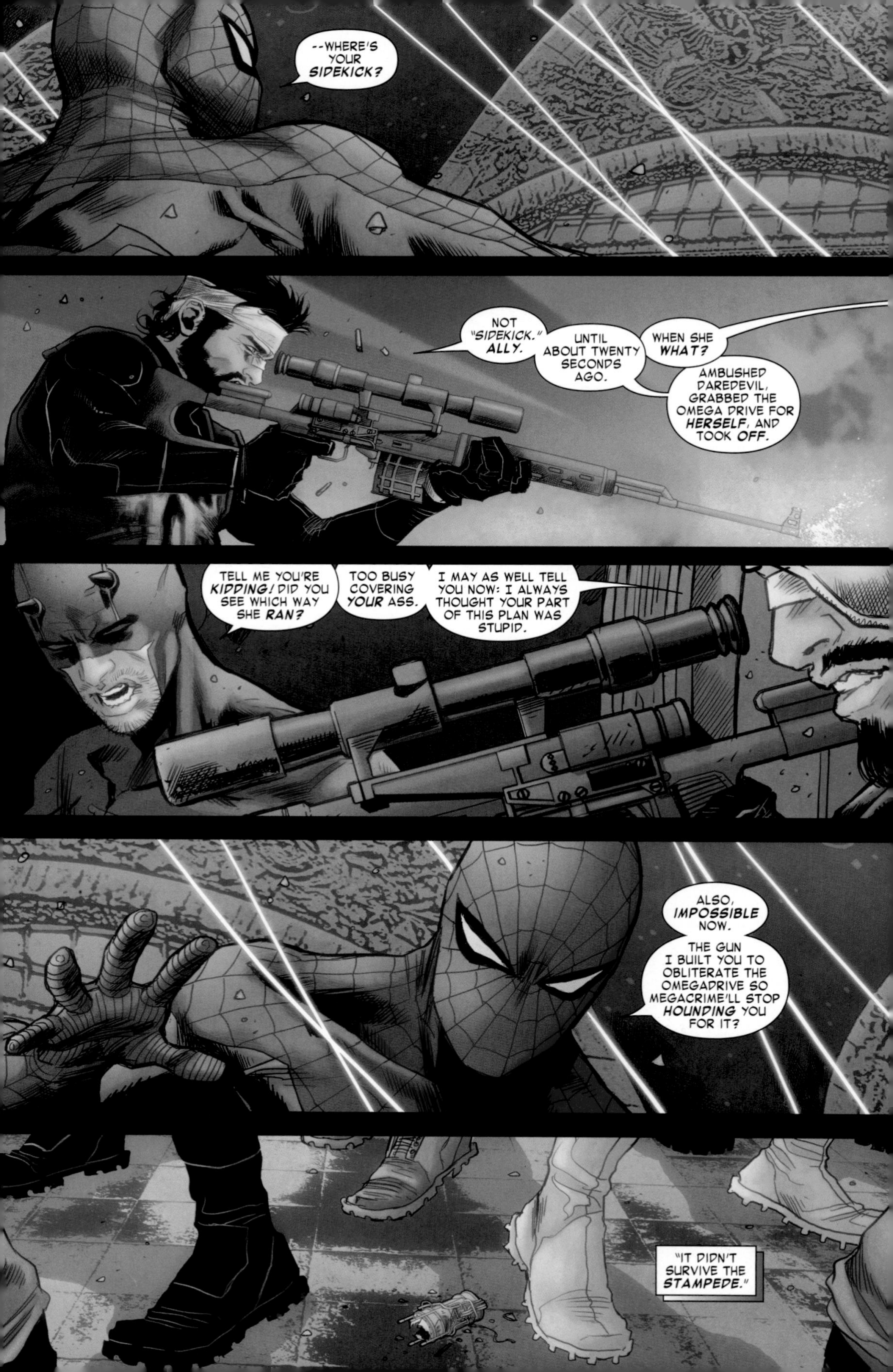
--WHERE'S YOUR *SIDEKICK?*
NOT "*SIDEKICK.*" ***ALLY.***
UNTIL ABOUT TWENTY SECONDS AGO.
WHEN SHE ***WHAT?***
AMBUSHED DAREDEVIL, GRABBED THE OMEGA DRIVE FOR ***HERSELF***, AND TOOK ***OFF.***
TELL ME YOU'RE ***KIDDING!*** DID YOU SEE WHICH WAY SHE ***RAN?***
TOO BUSY COVERING ***YOUR*** ASS.
I MAY AS WELL TELL YOU NOW: I ALWAYS THOUGHT YOUR PART OF THIS PLAN WAS STUPID.
ALSO, ***IMPOSSIBLE*** NOW.
THE GUN I BUILT YOU TO OBLITERATE THE OMEGADRIVE SO MEGACRIME'LL STOP ***HOUNDING*** YOU FOR IT?
"IT DIDN'T SURVIVE THE ***STAMPEDE.***"

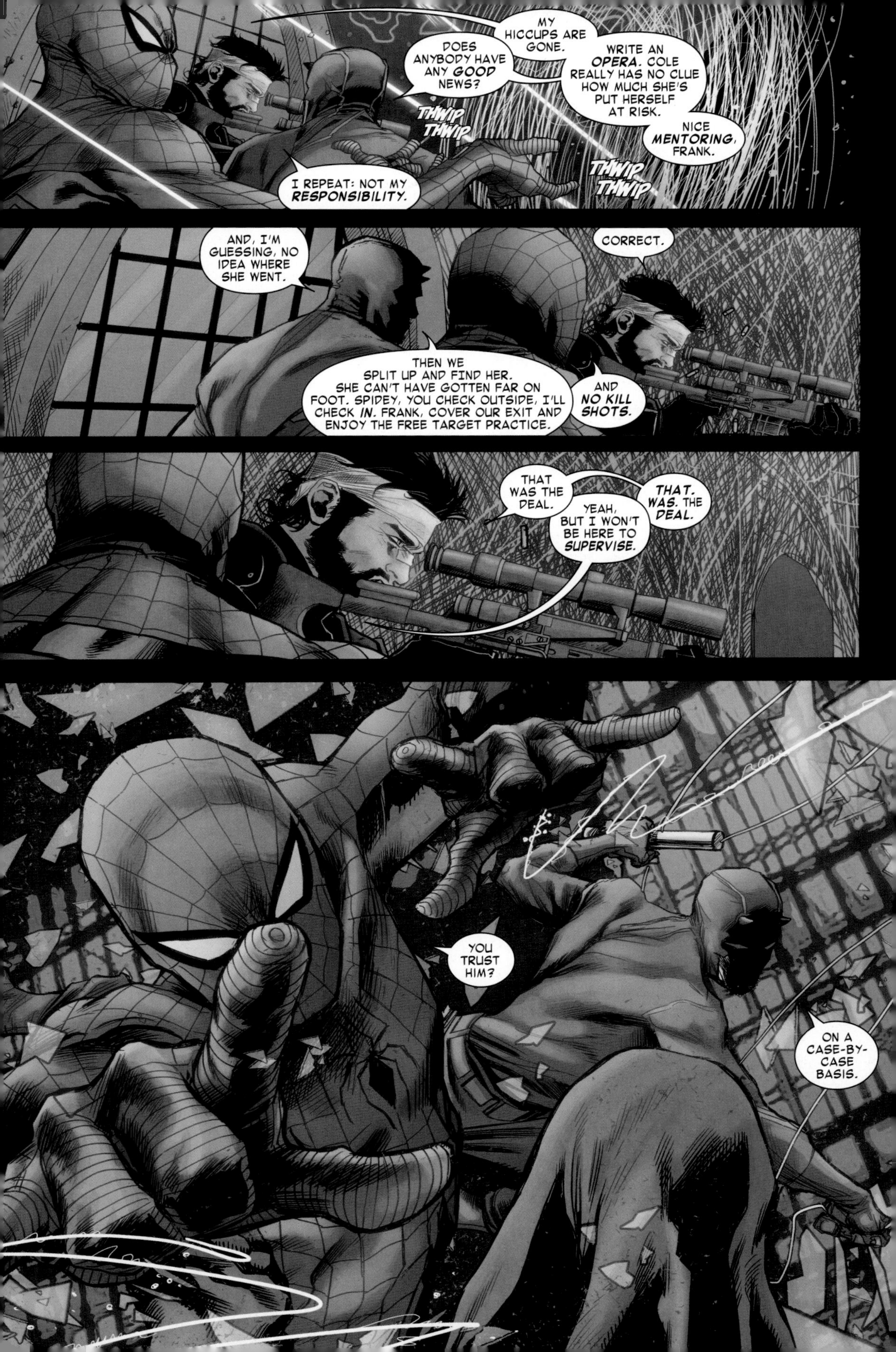
DOES ANYBODY HAVE ANY GOOD NEWS?
MY HICCUPS ARE GONE.
WRITE AN OPERA. COLE REALLY HAS NO CLUE HOW MUCH SHE'S PUT HERSELF AT RISK.
THWIP THWIP
NICE MENTORING, FRANK.
I REPEAT: NOT MY RESPONSIBILITY.
THWIP THWIP
AND, I'M GUESSING, NO IDEA WHERE SHE WENT.
CORRECT.
THEN WE SPLIT UP AND FIND HER. SHE CAN'T HAVE GOTTEN FAR ON FOOT. SPIDEY, YOU CHECK OUTSIDE, I'LL CHECK IN. FRANK, COVER OUR EXIT AND ENJOY THE FREE TARGET PRACTICE.
AND NO KILL SHOTS.
THAT WAS THE DEAL.
YEAH, BUT I WON'T BE HERE TO SUPERVISE.
THAT. WAS. THE DEAL.
YOU TRUST HIM?
ON A CASE-BY-CASE BASIS.

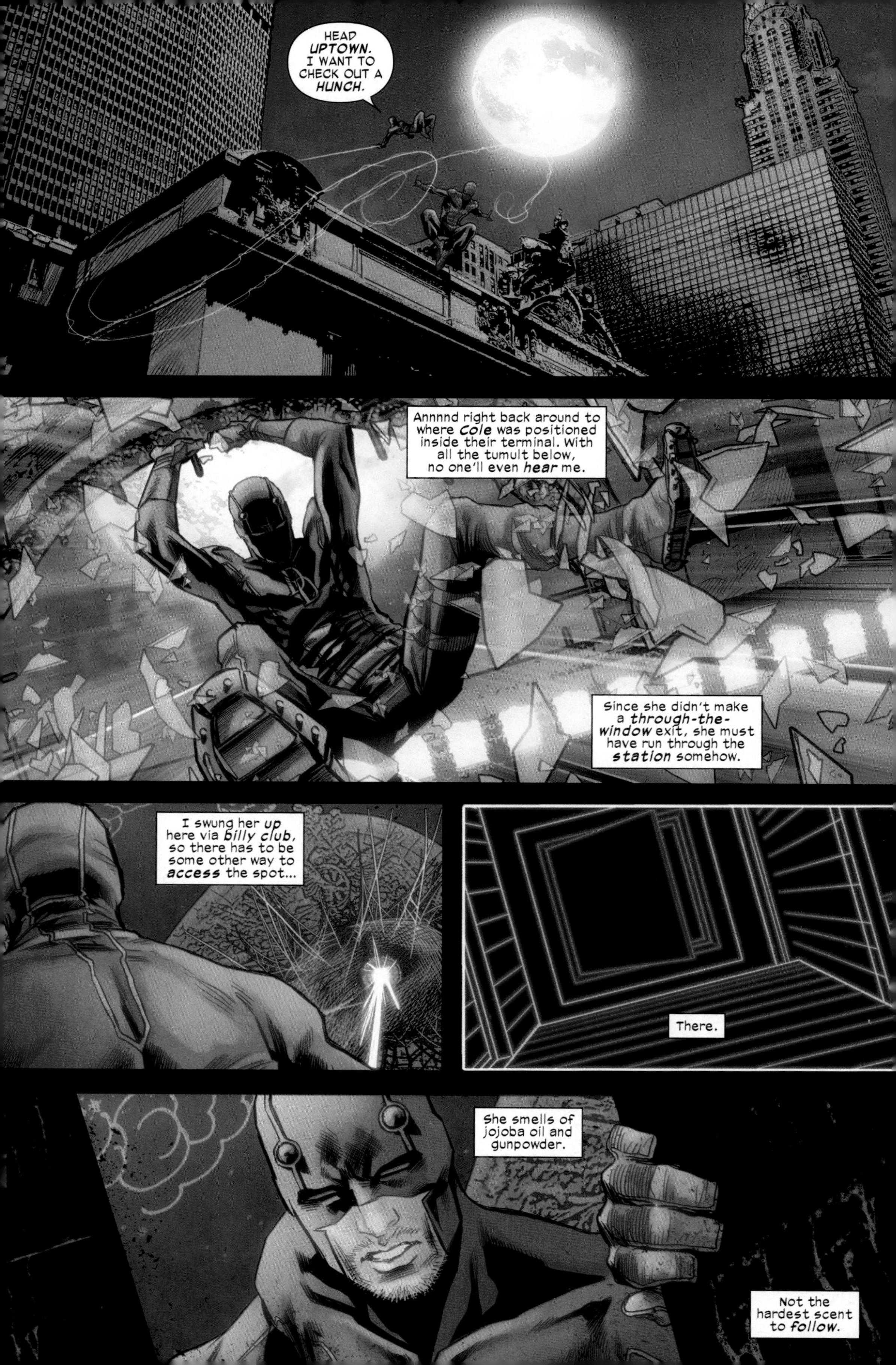
HEAD UPTOWN. I WANT TO CHECK OUT A HUNCH.
Annnnd right back around to where Cole was positioned inside their terminal. With all the tumult below, no one'll even hear me.
Since she didn't make a through-the-window exit, she must have run through the station somehow.
I swung her up here via billy club, so there has to be some other way to access the spot...
There.
She smells of jojoba oil and gunpowder.
Not the hardest scent to follow.

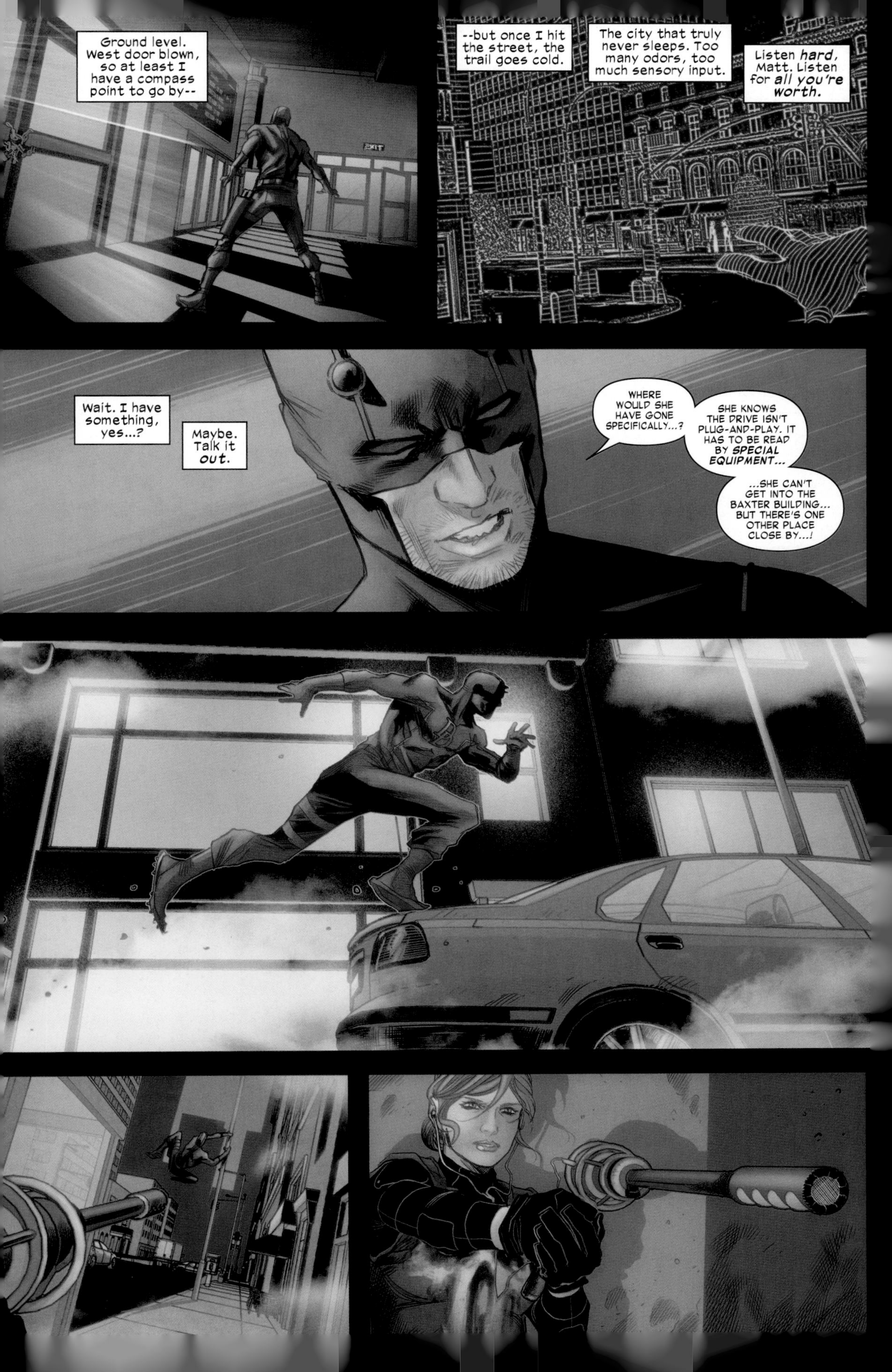
Ground level. West door blown, so at least I have a compass point to go by--
EXIT
--but once I hit the street, the trail goes cold.
The city that truly never sleeps. Too many odors, too much sensory input.
Listen *hard*, Matt. Listen for *all you're worth.*
Wait. I have something, yes...?
Maybe. Talk it *out*.
WHERE WOULD SHE HAVE GONE SPECIFICALLY...?
SHE KNOWS THE DRIVE ISN'T PLUG-AND-PLAY. IT HAS TO BE READ BY ***SPECIAL EQUIPMENT...***
...SHE CAN'T GET INTO THE BAXTER BUILDING... BUT THERE'S ONE OTHER PLACE CLOSE BY...!

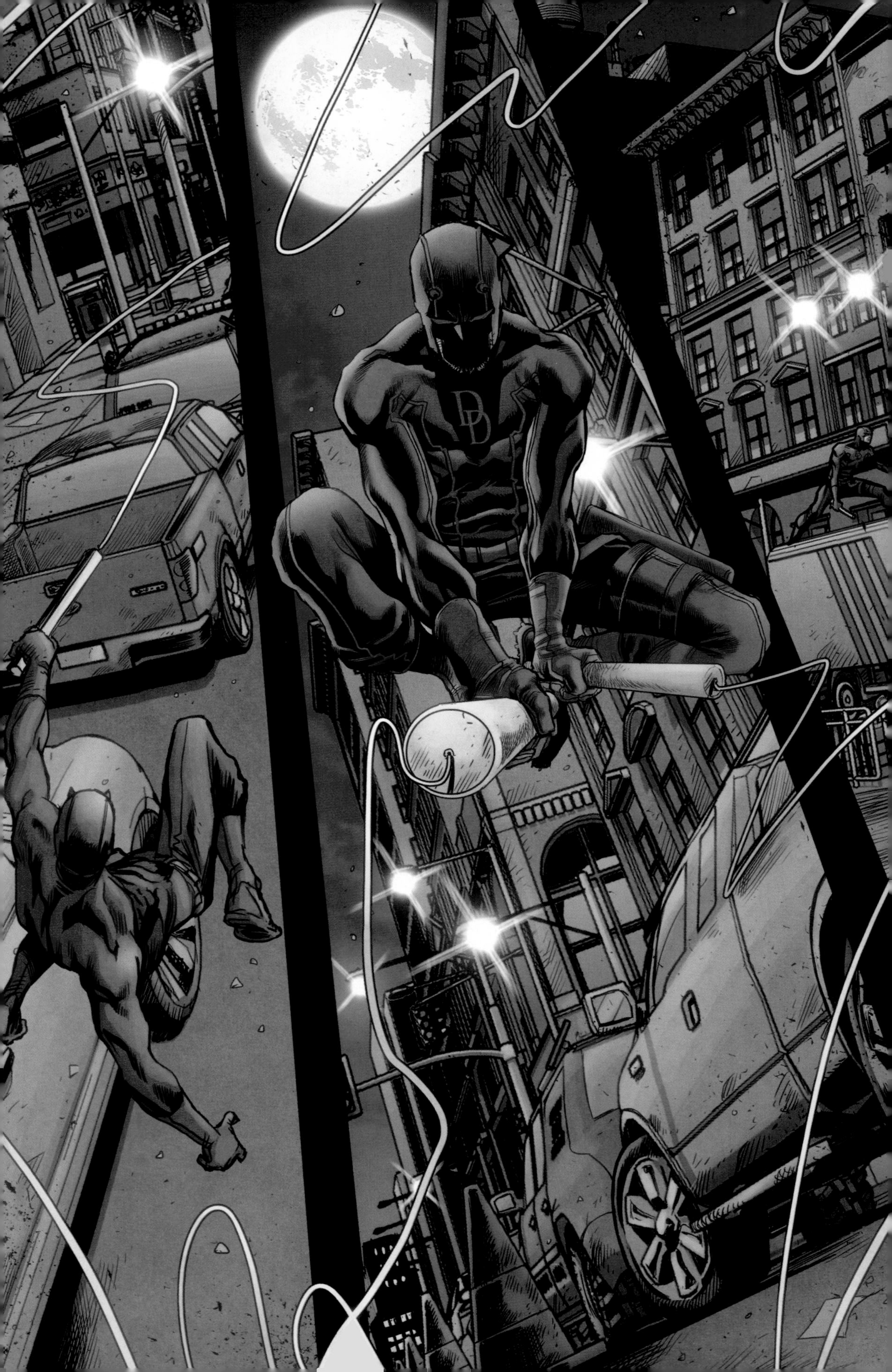

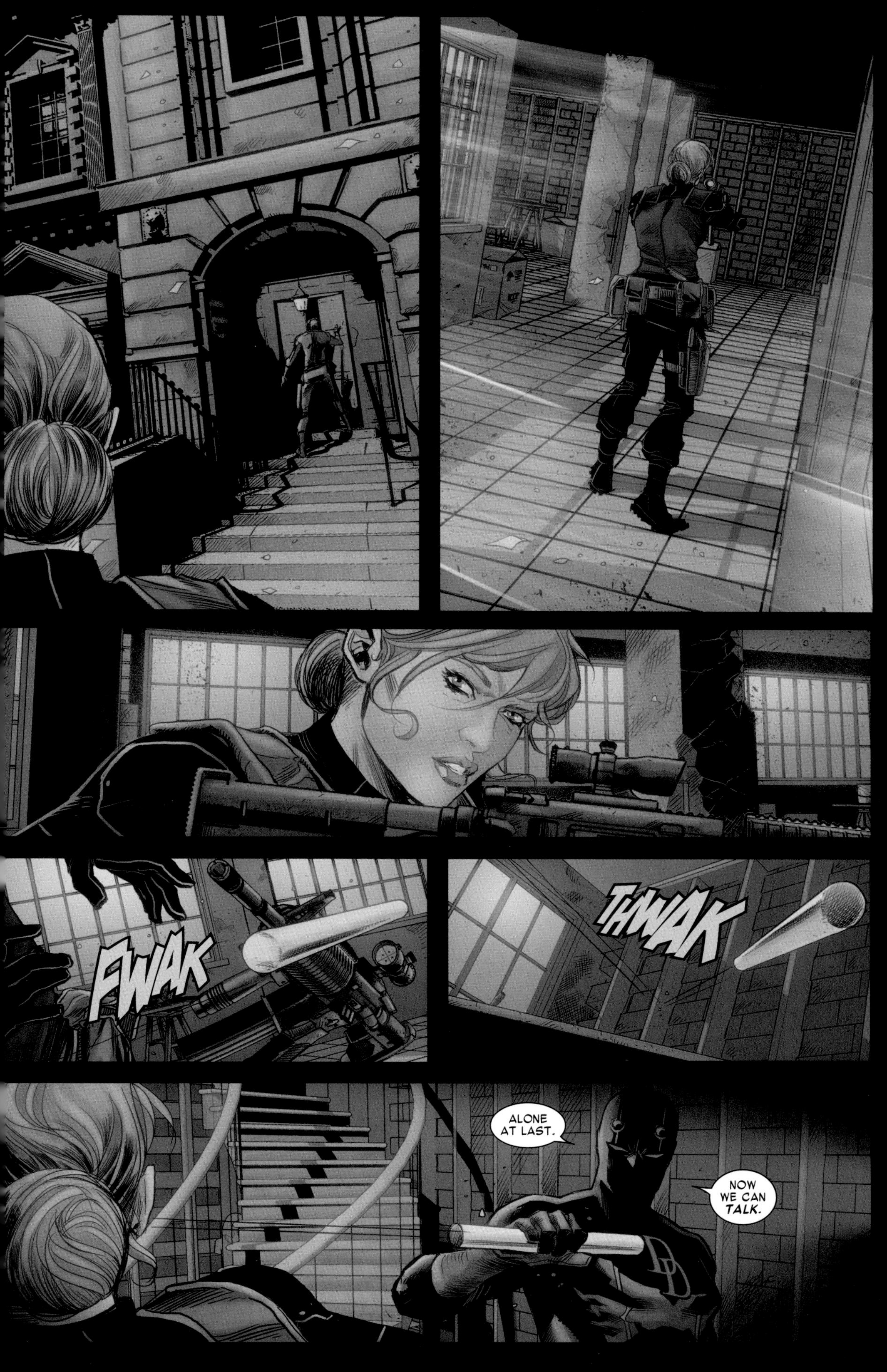
FWAK
THWAK
ALONE AT LAST.
NOW WE CAN TALK.

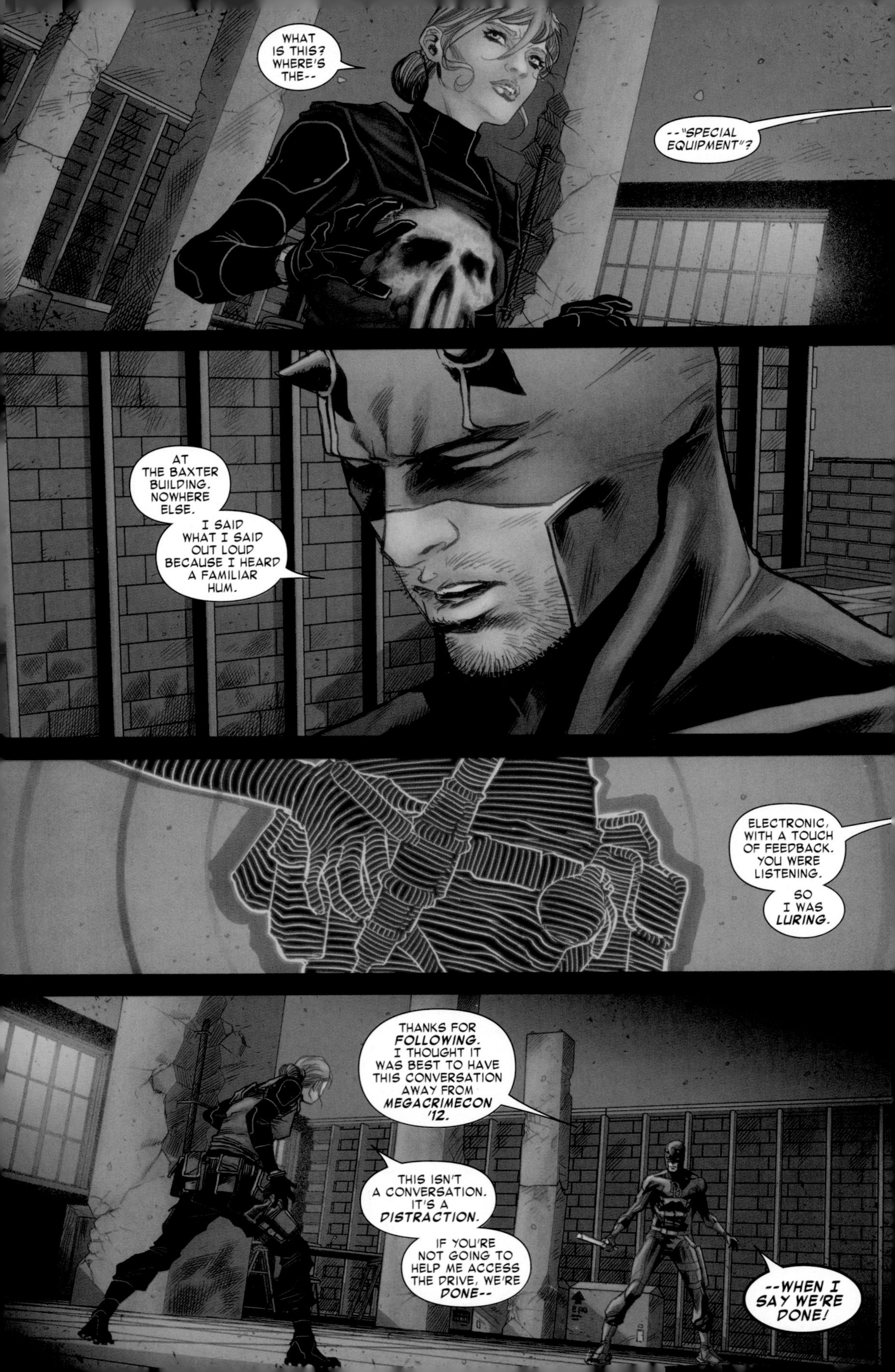

WHAT IS THIS? WHERE'S THE--
--"SPECIAL EQUIPMENT"?
AT THE BAXTER BUILDING. NOWHERE ELSE.
I SAID WHAT I SAID OUT LOUD BECAUSE I HEARD A FAMILIAR HUM.
ELECTRONIC, WITH A TOUCH OF FEEDBACK. YOU WERE LISTENING.
SO I WAS *LURING.*
THANKS FOR *FOLLOWING.* I THOUGHT IT WAS BEST TO HAVE THIS CONVERSATION AWAY FROM *MEGACRIMECON '12.*
THIS ISN'T A CONVERSATION. IT'S A *DISTRACTION.*
IF YOU'RE NOT GOING TO HELP ME ACCESS THE DRIVE, WE'RE *DONE--*
--WHEN I SAY WE'RE DONE!

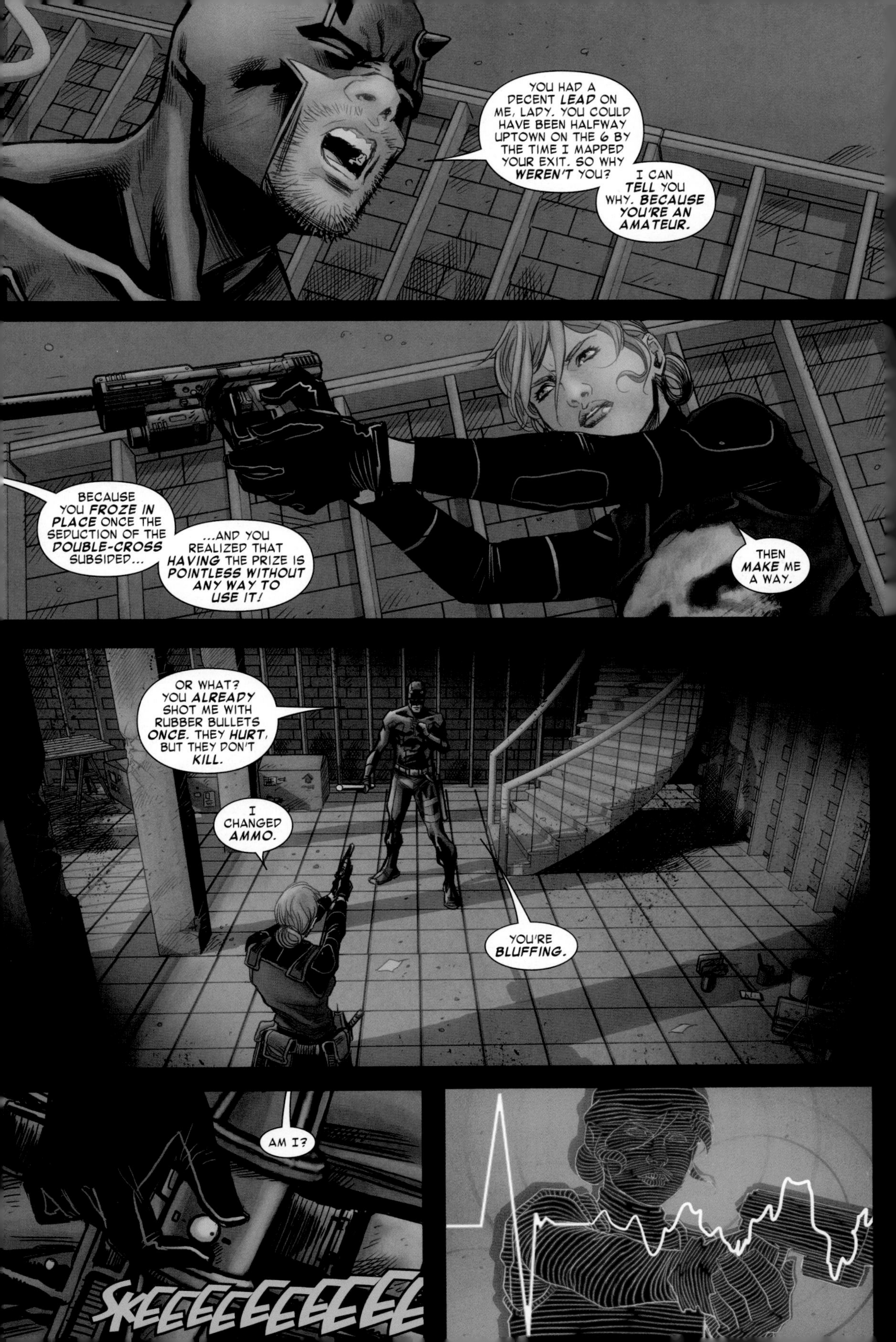
YOU HAD A DECENT LEAD ON ME, LADY. YOU COULD HAVE BEEN HALFWAY UPTOWN ON THE 6 BY THE TIME I MAPPED YOUR EXIT. SO WHY WEREN'T YOU?
I CAN TELL YOU WHY. BECAUSE YOU'RE AN AMATEUR.
BECAUSE YOU FROZE IN PLACE ONCE THE SEDUCTION OF THE DOUBLE-CROSS SUBSIDED...
...AND YOU REALIZED THAT HAVING THE PRIZE IS POINTLESS WITHOUT ANY WAY TO USE IT!
THEN MAKE ME A WAY.
OR WHAT? YOU ALREADY SHOT ME WITH RUBBER BULLETS ONCE. THEY HURT, BUT THEY DON'T KILL.
I CHANGED AMMO.
YOU'RE BLUFFING.
AM I?
SKEEEEEEEEEEE

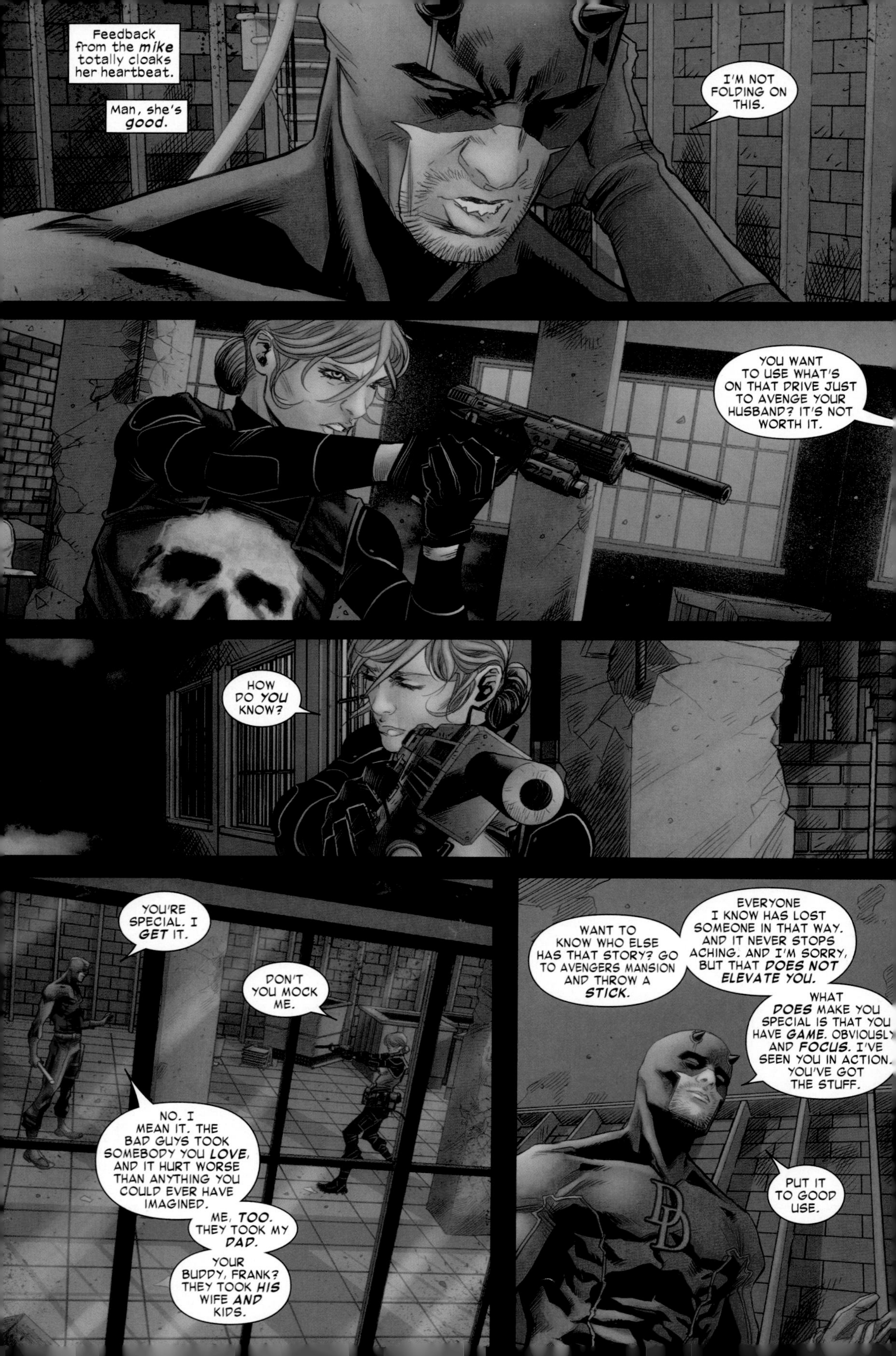
Feedback from the *mike* totally cloaks her heartbeat.
Man, she's *good*.
I'M NOT FOLDING ON THIS.
YOU WANT TO USE WHAT'S ON THAT DRIVE JUST TO AVENGE YOUR HUSBAND? IT'S NOT WORTH IT.
HOW DO *YOU* KNOW?
YOU'RE SPECIAL. I *GET* IT.
DON'T YOU MOCK ME.
NO. I MEAN IT. THE BAD GUYS TOOK SOMEBODY YOU *LOVE*, AND IT HURT WORSE THAN ANYTHING YOU COULD EVER HAVE IMAGINED.
ME, *TOO*. THEY TOOK MY *DAD*.
YOUR BUDDY, FRANK? THEY TOOK *HIS* WIFE *AND* KIDS.
WANT TO KNOW WHO ELSE HAS THAT STORY? GO TO AVENGERS MANSION AND THROW A *STICK*.
EVERYONE I KNOW HAS LOST SOMEONE IN THAT WAY. AND IT NEVER STOPS ACHING. AND I'M SORRY, BUT THAT *DOES NOT ELEVATE YOU.*
WHAT *DOES* MAKE YOU SPECIAL IS THAT YOU HAVE *GAME*. OBVIOUSLY AND *FOCUS*. I'VE SEEN YOU IN ACTION. YOU'VE GOT THE STUFF.
PUT IT TO GOOD USE.

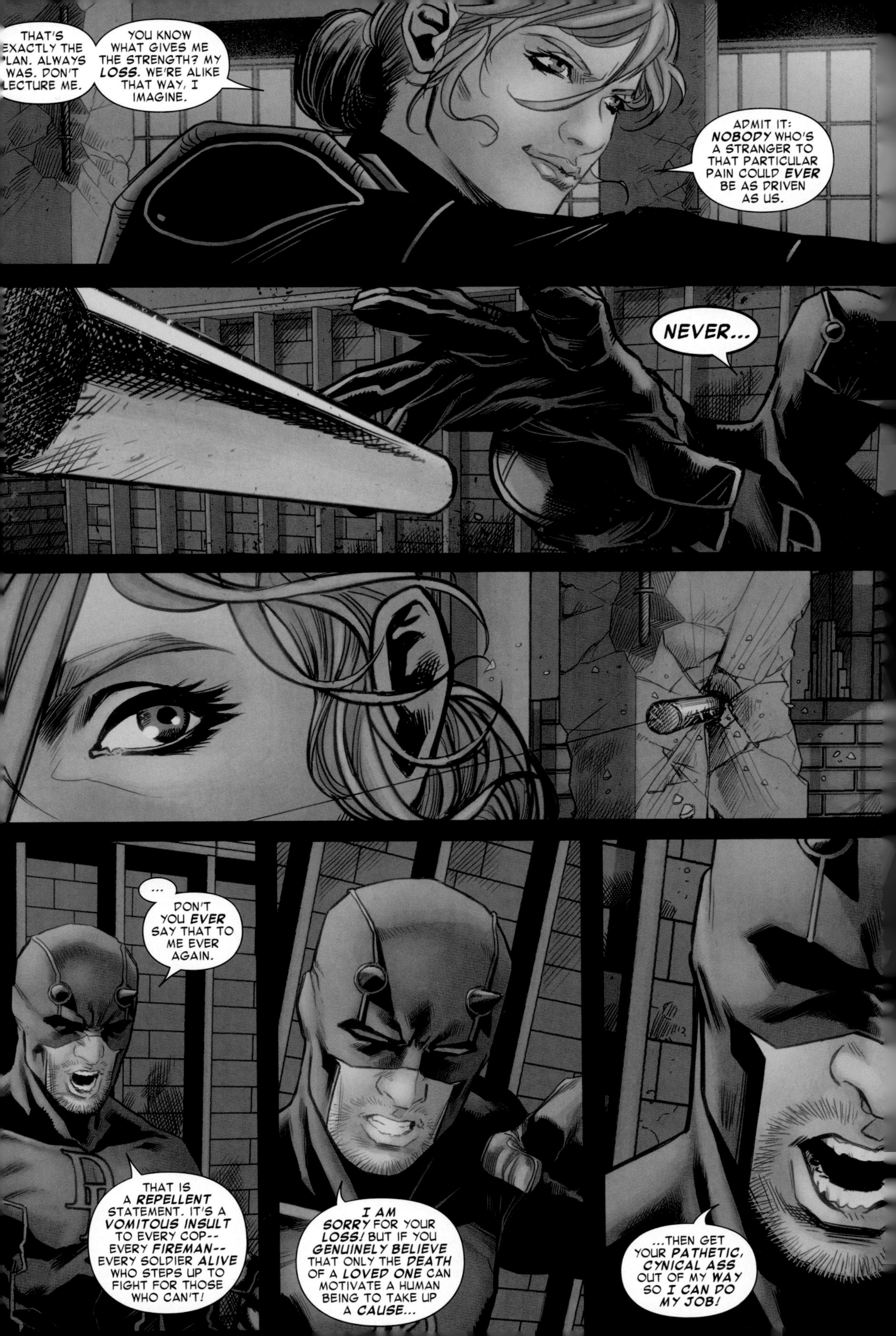
THAT'S EXACTLY THE PLAN. ALWAYS WAS. DON'T LECTURE ME.
YOU KNOW WHAT GIVES ME THE STRENGTH? MY LOSS. WE'RE ALIKE THAT WAY, I IMAGINE.
ADMIT IT: NOBODY WHO'S A STRANGER TO THAT PARTICULAR PAIN COULD EVER BE AS DRIVEN AS US.
NEVER...
... DON'T YOU EVER SAY THAT TO ME EVER AGAIN.
THAT IS A REPELLENT STATEMENT. IT'S A VOMITOUS INSULT TO EVERY COP-- EVERY FIREMAN-- EVERY SOLDIER ALIVE WHO STEPS UP TO FIGHT FOR THOSE WHO CAN'T!
I AM SORRY FOR YOUR LOSS! BUT IF YOU GENUINELY BELIEVE THAT ONLY THE DEATH OF A LOVED ONE CAN MOTIVATE A HUMAN BEING TO TAKE UP A CAUSE...
...THEN GET YOUR PATHETIC, CYNICAL ASS OUT OF MY WAY SO I CAN DO MY JOB!

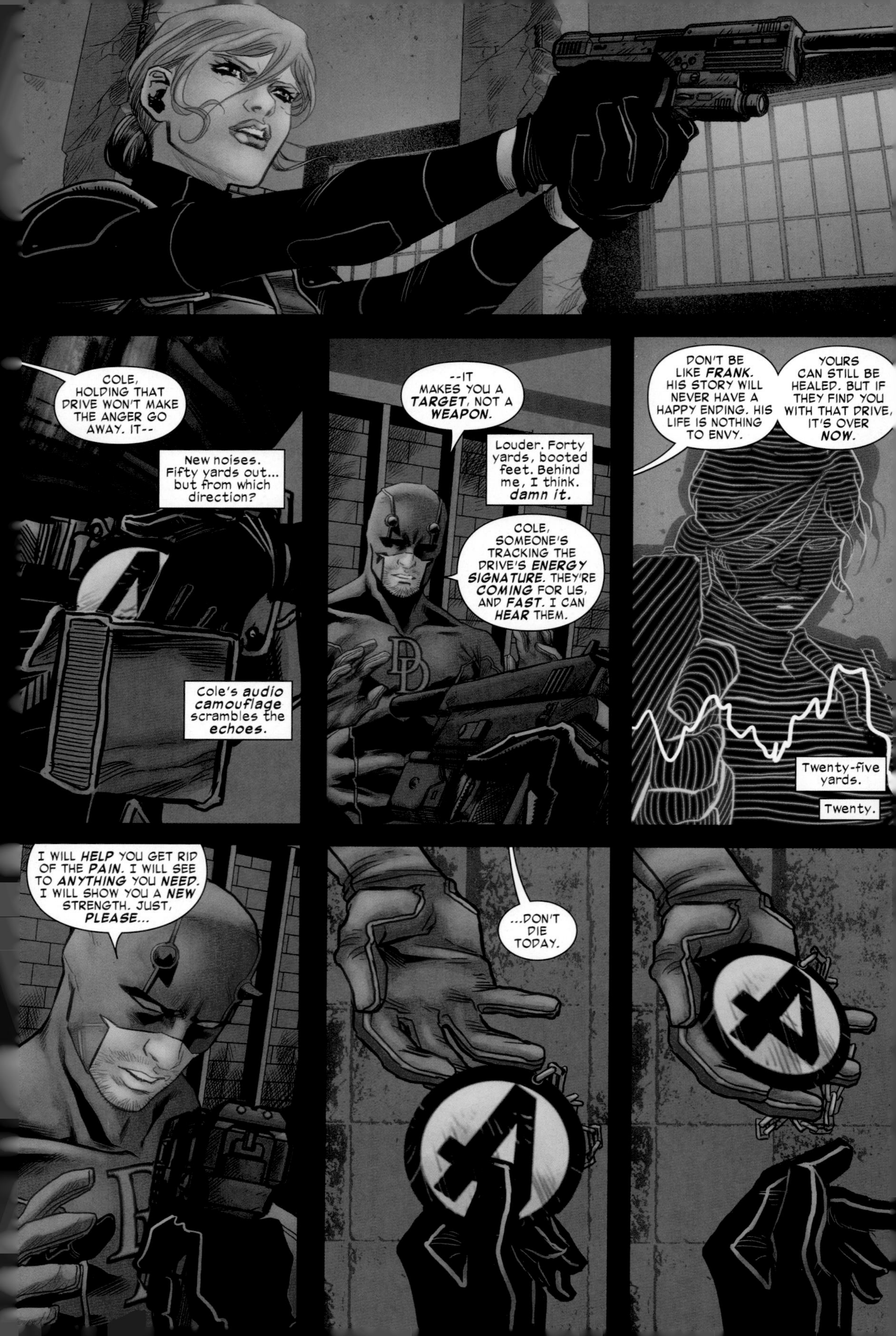
COLE, HOLDING THAT DRIVE WON'T MAKE THE ANGER GO AWAY. IT--
New noises. Fifty yards out... but from which direction?
Cole's audio camouflage scrambles the echoes.
--IT MAKES YOU A TARGET, NOT A WEAPON.
Louder. Forty yards, booted feet. Behind me, I think. damn it.
COLE, SOMEONE'S TRACKING THE DRIVE'S ENERGY SIGNATURE. THEY'RE COMING FOR US, AND FAST. I CAN HEAR THEM.
DON'T BE LIKE FRANK. HIS STORY WILL NEVER HAVE A HAPPY ENDING. HIS LIFE IS NOTHING TO ENVY.
YOURS CAN STILL BE HEALED. BUT IF THEY FIND YOU WITH THAT DRIVE, IT'S OVER NOW.
Twenty-five yards.
Twenty.
I WILL HELP YOU GET RID OF THE PAIN. I WILL SEE TO ANYTHING YOU NEED. I WILL SHOW YOU A NEW STRENGTH. JUST, PLEASE...
...DON'T DIE TODAY.

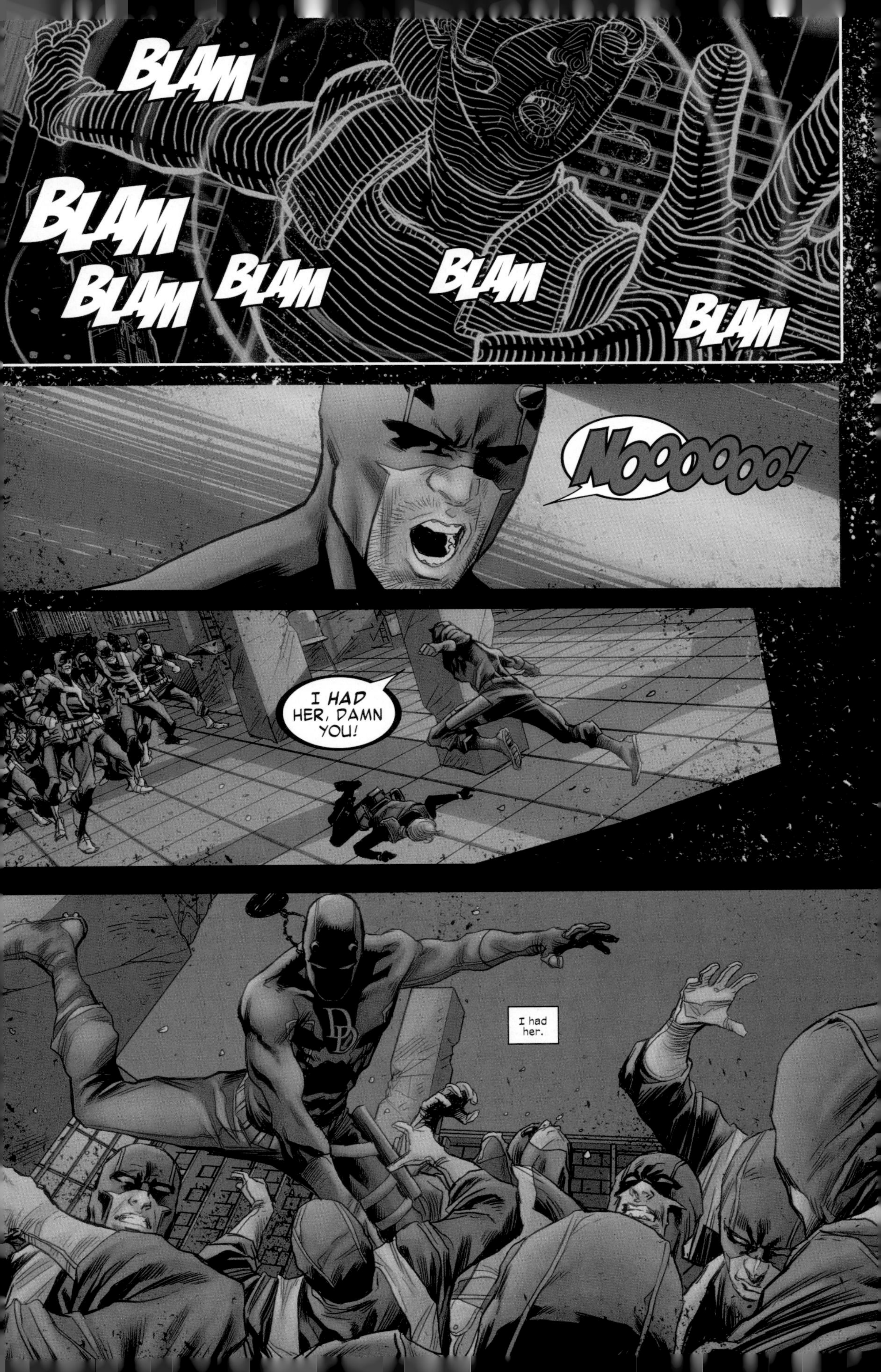
BLAM
BLAM
BLAM
BLAM
BLAM
BLAM
NOOOOOO!
I HAD HER, DAMN YOU!
I had her.

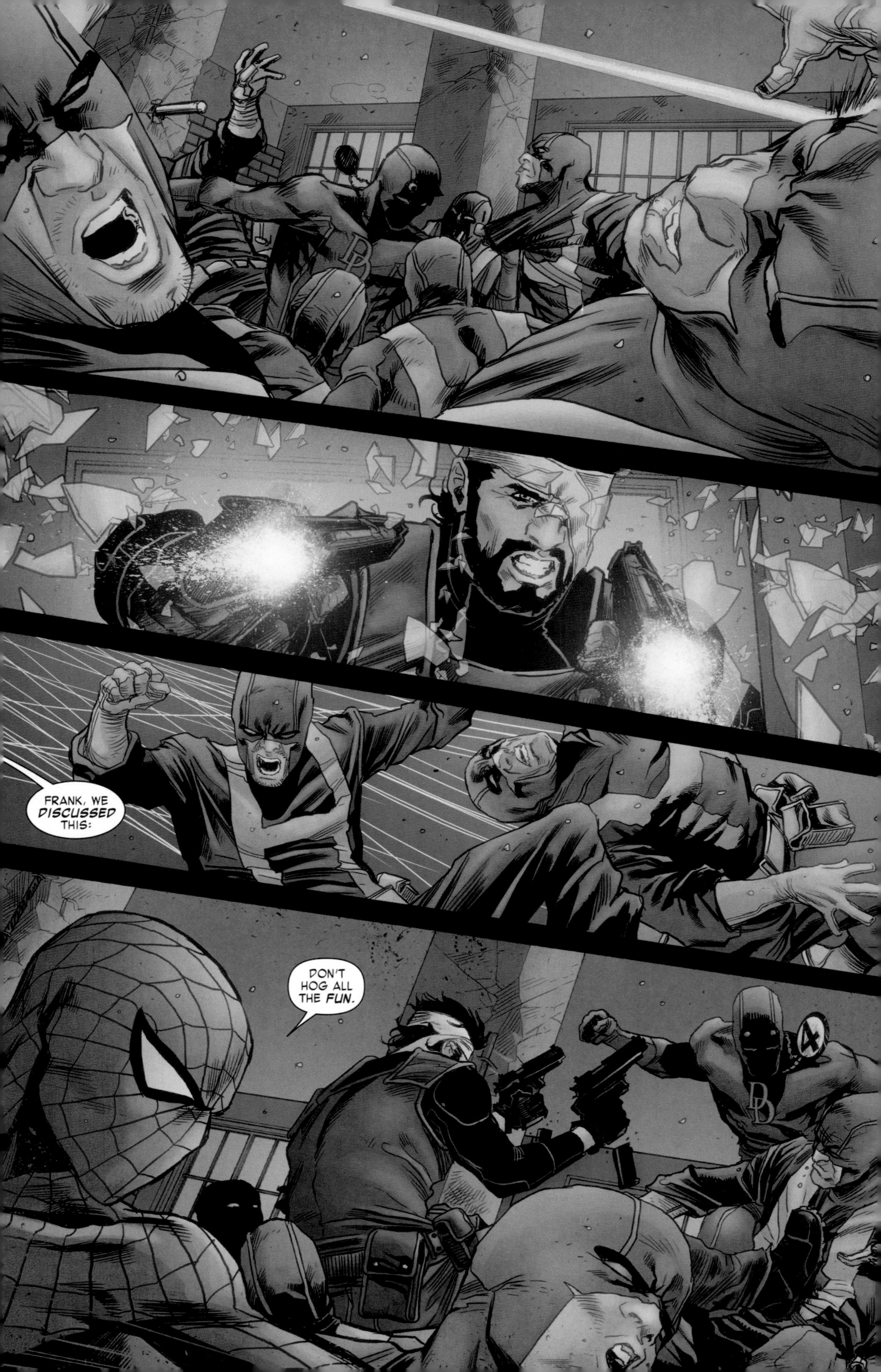
FRANK, WE *DISCUSSED* THIS:
DON'T HOG ALL THE *FUN*.

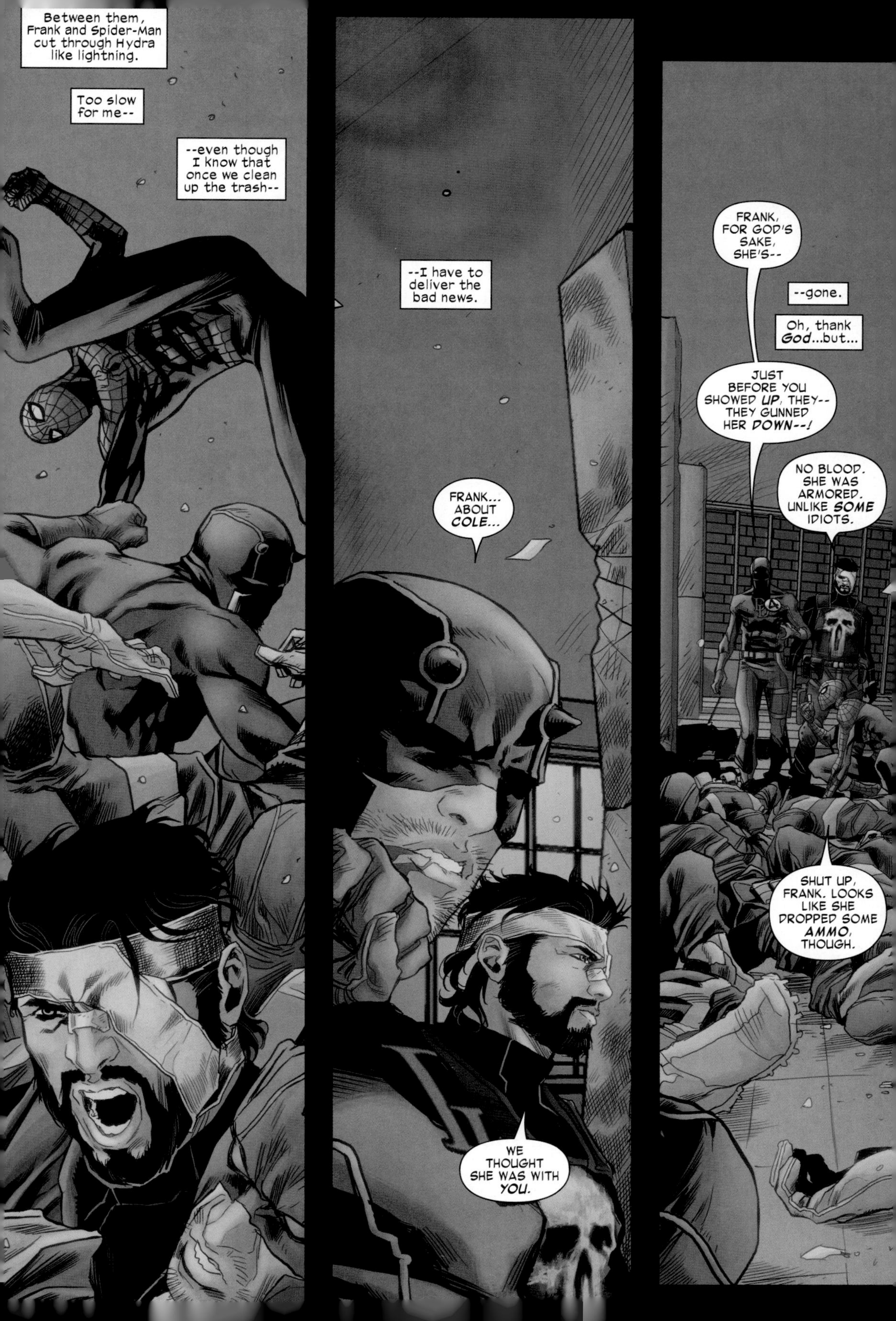
Between them, Frank and Spider-Man cut through Hydra like lightning.
Too slow for me--
--even though I know that once we clean up the trash--
--I have to deliver the bad news.
FRANK... ABOUT COLE...
WE THOUGHT SHE WAS WITH YOU.
FRANK, FOR GOD'S SAKE, SHE'S--
--gone.
Oh, thank God...but...
JUST BEFORE YOU SHOWED UP, THEY--THEY GUNNED HER DOWN--!
NO BLOOD. SHE WAS ARMORED. UNLIKE SOME IDIOTS.
SHUT UP, FRANK. LOOKS LIKE SHE DROPPED SOME AMMO, THOUGH.

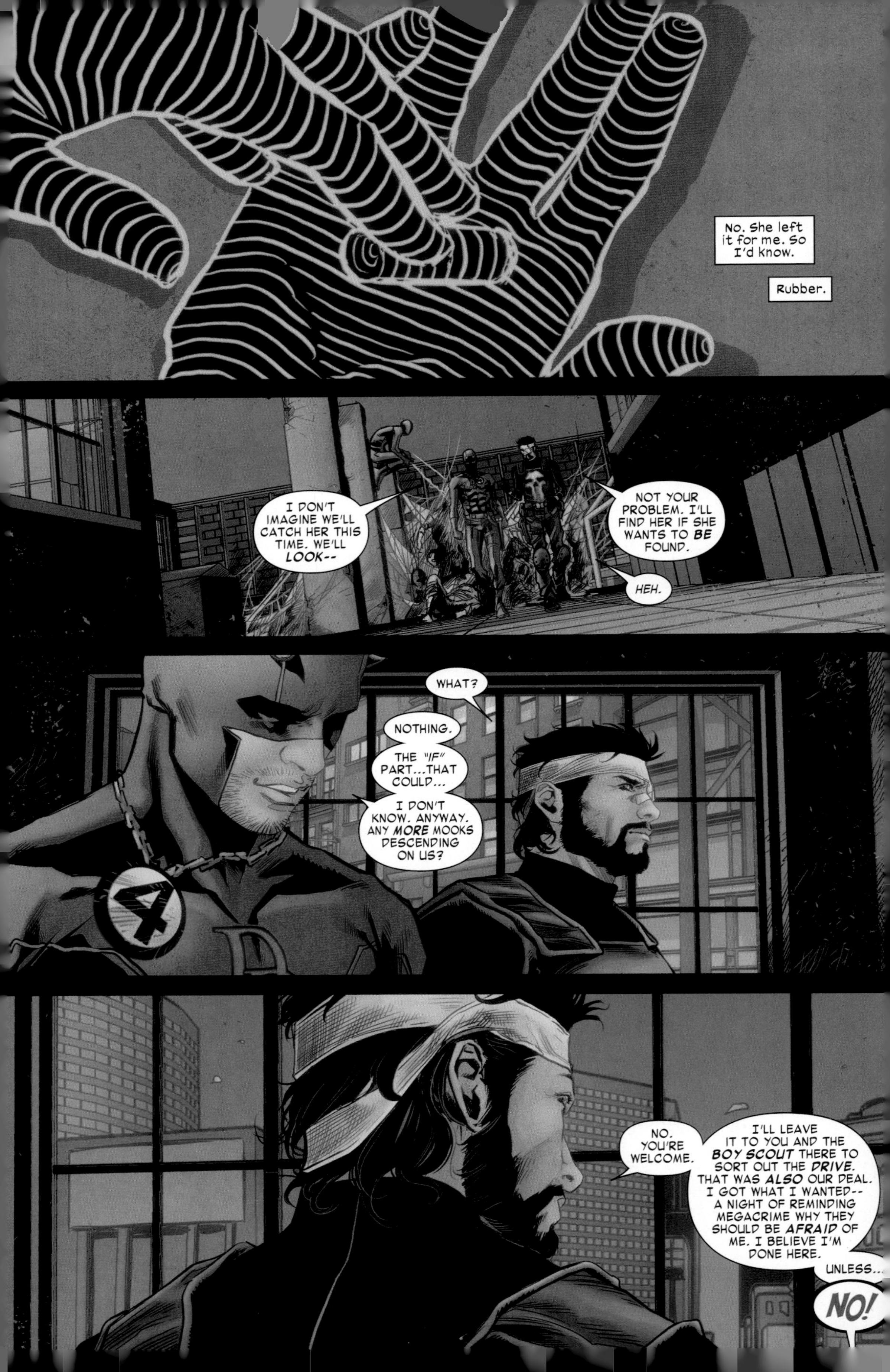
No. She left it for me. So I'd know.
Rubber.
I DON'T IMAGINE WE'LL CATCH HER THIS TIME. WE'LL LOOK--
NOT YOUR PROBLEM. I'LL FIND HER IF SHE WANTS TO BE FOUND.
HEH.
WHAT?
NOTHING.
THE "IF" PART...THAT COULD...
I DON'T KNOW. ANYWAY. ANY MORE MOOKS DESCENDING ON US?
NO. YOU'RE WELCOME.
I'LL LEAVE IT TO YOU AND THE BOY SCOUT THERE TO SORT OUT THE DRIVE. THAT WAS ALSO OUR DEAL. I GOT WHAT I WANTED-- A NIGHT OF REMINDING MEGACRIME WHY THEY SHOULD BE AFRAID OF ME. I BELIEVE I'M DONE HERE.
UNLESS...
NO!

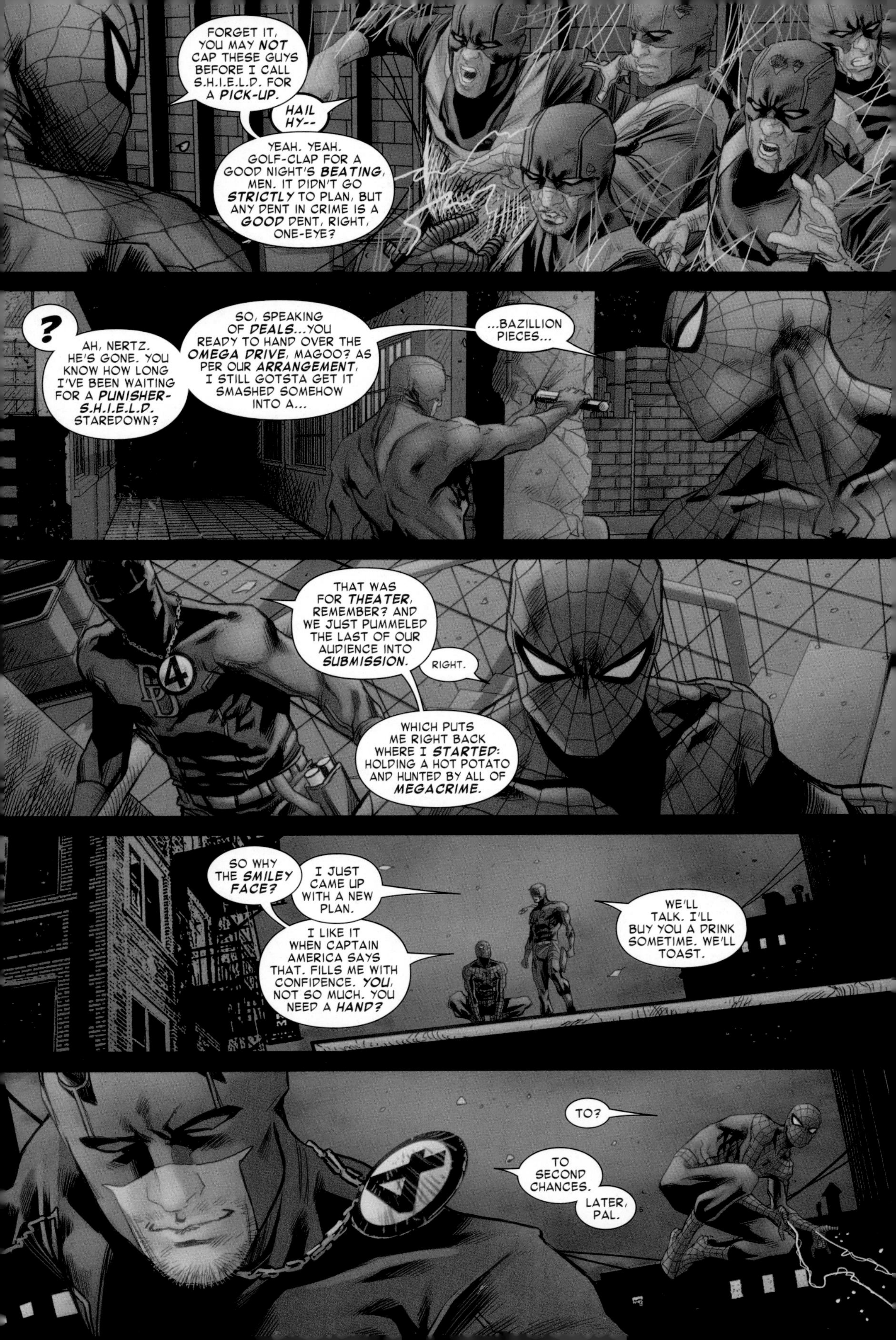
FORGET IT, YOU MAY NOT CAP THESE GUYS BEFORE I CALL S.H.I.E.L.D. FOR A PICK-UP.
HAIL HY--
YEAH. YEAH. GOLF-CLAP FOR A GOOD NIGHT'S BEATING, MEN. IT DIDN'T GO STRICTLY TO PLAN, BUT ANY DENT IN CRIME IS A GOOD DENT, RIGHT, ONE-EYE?
?
AH, NERTZ. HE'S GONE. YOU KNOW HOW LONG I'VE BEEN WAITING FOR A PUNISHER-S.H.I.E.L.D. STAREDOWN?
SO, SPEAKING OF DEALS...YOU READY TO HAND OVER THE OMEGA DRIVE, MAGOO? AS PER OUR ARRANGEMENT, I STILL GOTSTA GET IT SMASHED SOMEHOW INTO A...
...BAZILLION PIECES...
THAT WAS FOR THEATER, REMEMBER? AND WE JUST PUMMELED THE LAST OF OUR AUDIENCE INTO SUBMISSION.
RIGHT.
WHICH PUTS ME RIGHT BACK WHERE I STARTED: HOLDING A HOT POTATO AND HUNTED BY ALL OF MEGACRIME.
SO WHY THE SMILEY FACE?
I JUST CAME UP WITH A NEW PLAN.
I LIKE IT WHEN CAPTAIN AMERICA SAYS THAT. FILLS ME WITH CONFIDENCE. YOU, NOT SO MUCH. YOU NEED A HAND?
WE'LL TALK. I'LL BUY YOU A DRINK SOMETIME. WE'LL TOAST.
TO?
TO SECOND CHANCES.
LATER, PAL.

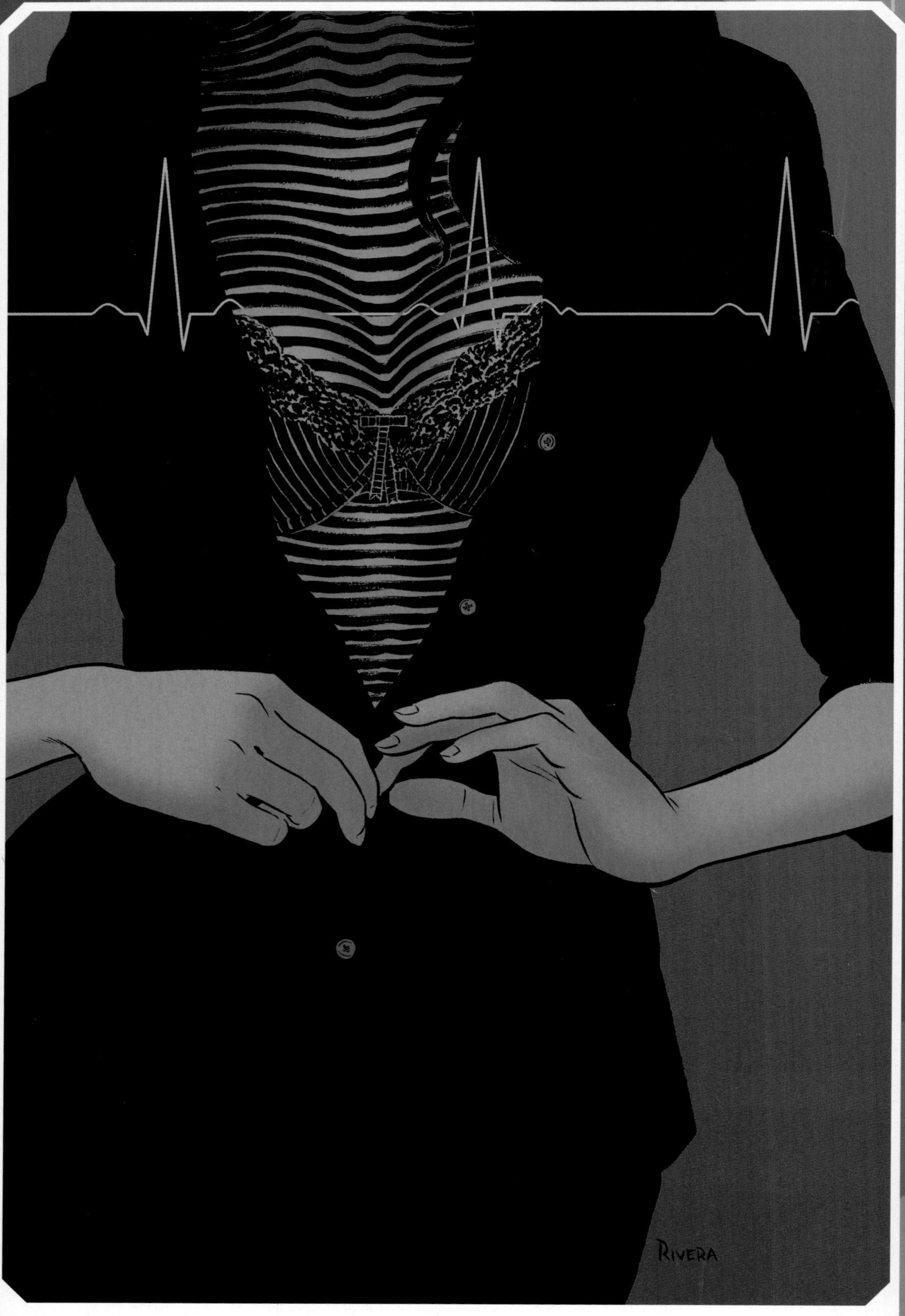
RIVERA

DAREDEVIL #12

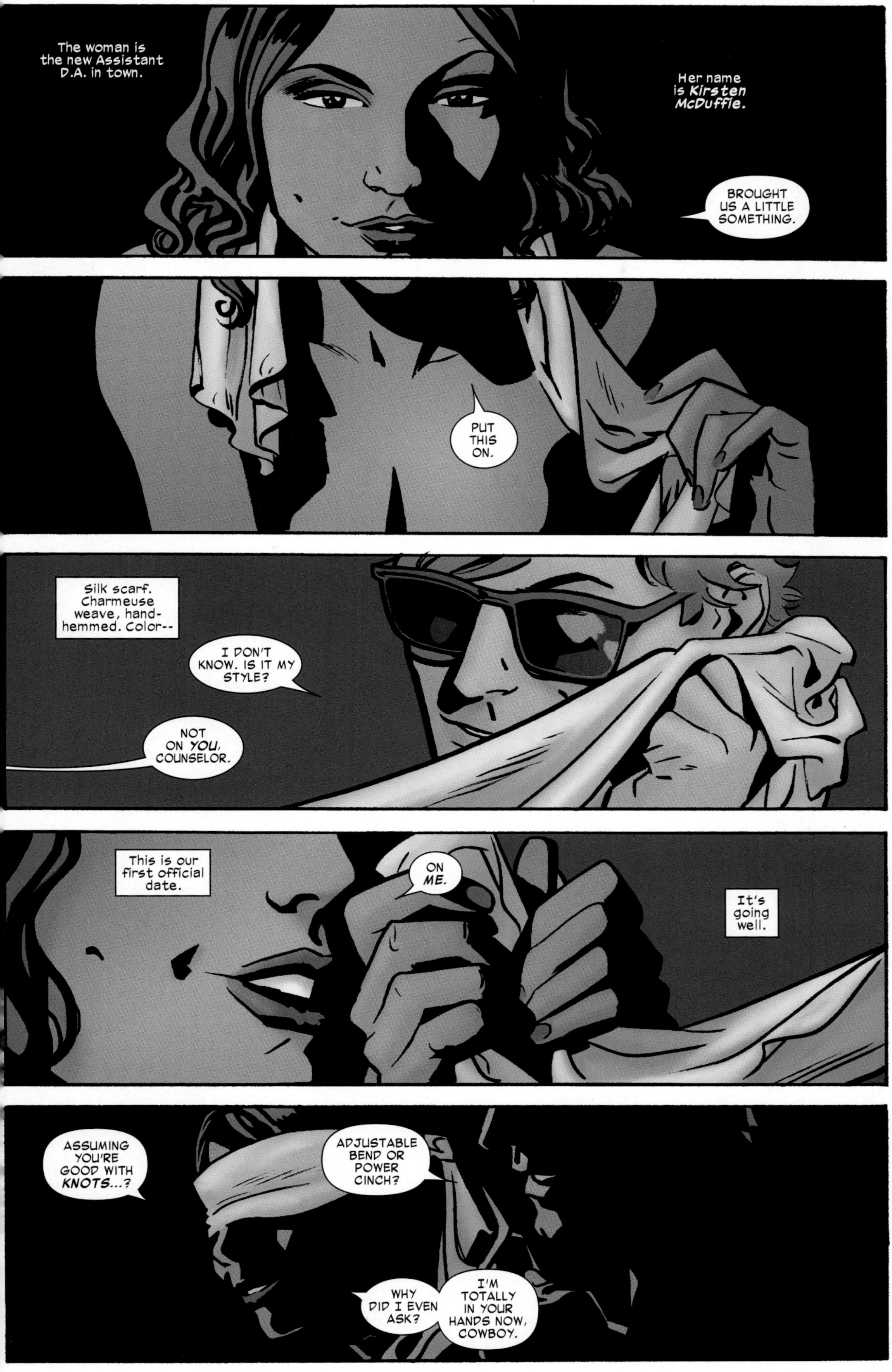
The woman is the new Assistant D.A. in town.
Her name is Kirsten McDuffie.
BROUGHT US A LITTLE SOMETHING.
PUT THIS ON.
Silk scarf. Charmeuse weave, hand-hemmed. Color--
I DON'T KNOW. IS IT MY STYLE?
NOT ON YOU, COUNSELOR.
This is our first official date.
ON ME.
It's going well.
ASSUMING YOU'RE GOOD WITH KNOTS...?
ADJUSTABLE BEND OR POWER CINCH?
WHY DID I EVEN ASK?
I'M TOTALLY IN YOUR HANDS NOW, COWBOY.

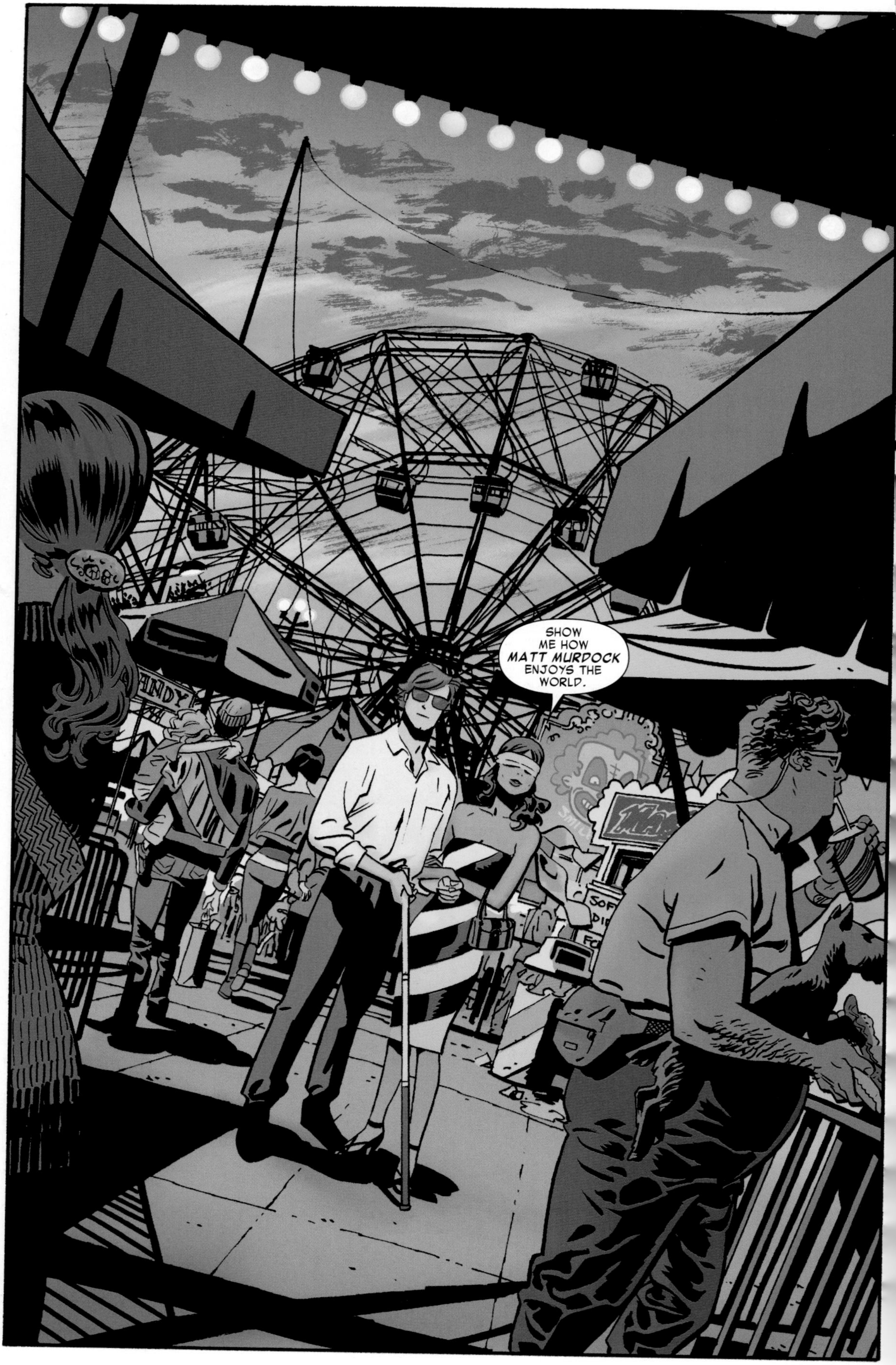
SHOW ME HOW MATT MURDOCK ENJOYS THE WORLD.

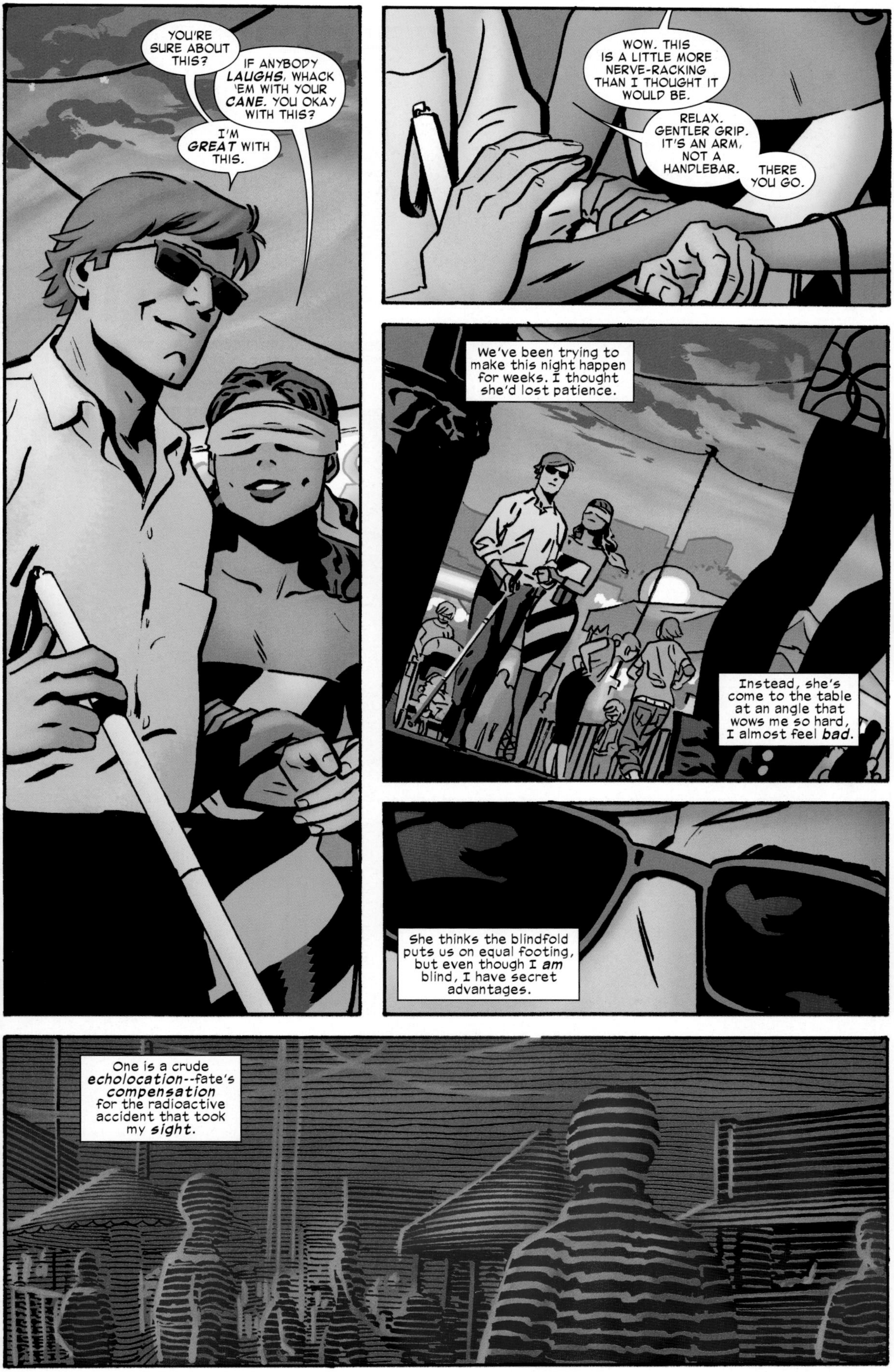
YOU'RE SURE ABOUT THIS?
IF ANYBODY LAUGHS, WHACK 'EM WITH YOUR CANE. YOU OKAY WITH THIS?
I'M GREAT WITH THIS.
WOW. THIS IS A LITTLE MORE NERVE-RACKING THAN I THOUGHT IT WOULD BE.
RELAX. GENTLER GRIP. IT'S AN ARM, NOT A HANDLEBAR.
THERE YOU GO.
We've been trying to make this night happen for weeks. I thought she'd lost patience.
Instead, she's come to the table at an angle that wows me so hard, I almost feel bad.
She thinks the blindfold puts us on equal footing, but even though I am blind, I have secret advantages.
One is a crude echolocation--fate's compensation for the radioactive accident that took my sight.

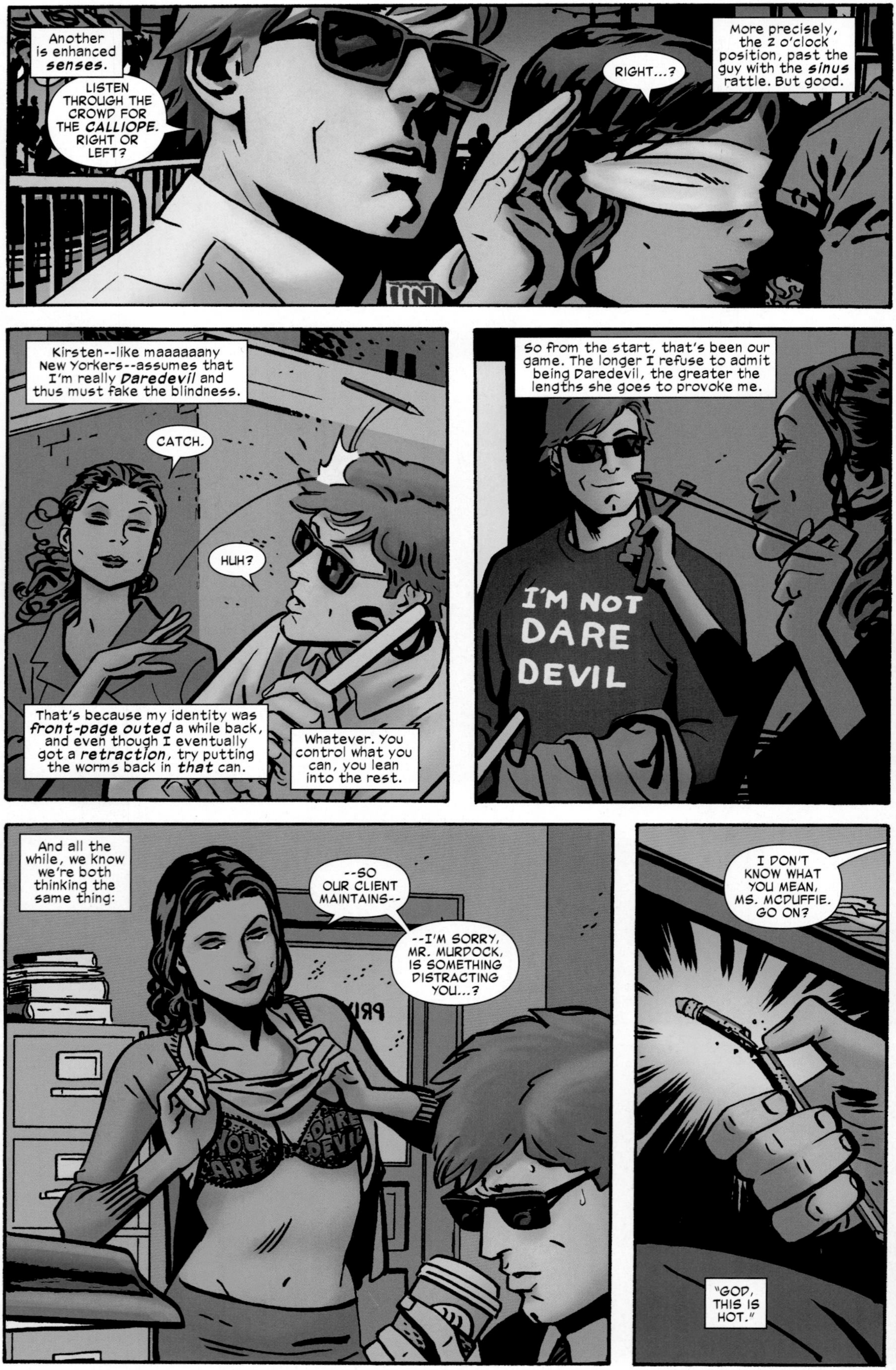

Another is enhanced *senses*.
LISTEN THROUGH THE CROWD FOR THE *CALLIOPE*. RIGHT OR LEFT?
RIGHT...?
More precisely, the 2 o'clock position, past the guy with the *sinus* rattle. But good.
Kirsten--like maaaaaany New Yorkers--assumes that I'm really *Daredevil* and thus must fake the blindness.
CATCH.
HUH?
That's because my identity was *front-page outed* a while back, and even though I eventually got a *retraction*, try putting the worms back in *that* can.
Whatever. You control what you can, you lean into the rest.
So from the start, that's been our game. The longer I refuse to admit being Daredevil, the greater the lengths she goes to provoke me.
I'M NOT DARE DEVIL
And all the while, we know we're both thinking the same thing:
--SO OUR CLIENT MAINTAINS--
--I'M SORRY, MR. MURDOCK, IS SOMETHING DISTRACTING YOU...?
YOU ARE DARE DEVIL
I DON'T KNOW WHAT YOU MEAN, MS. MCDUFFIE. GO ON?
"GOD, THIS IS HOT."

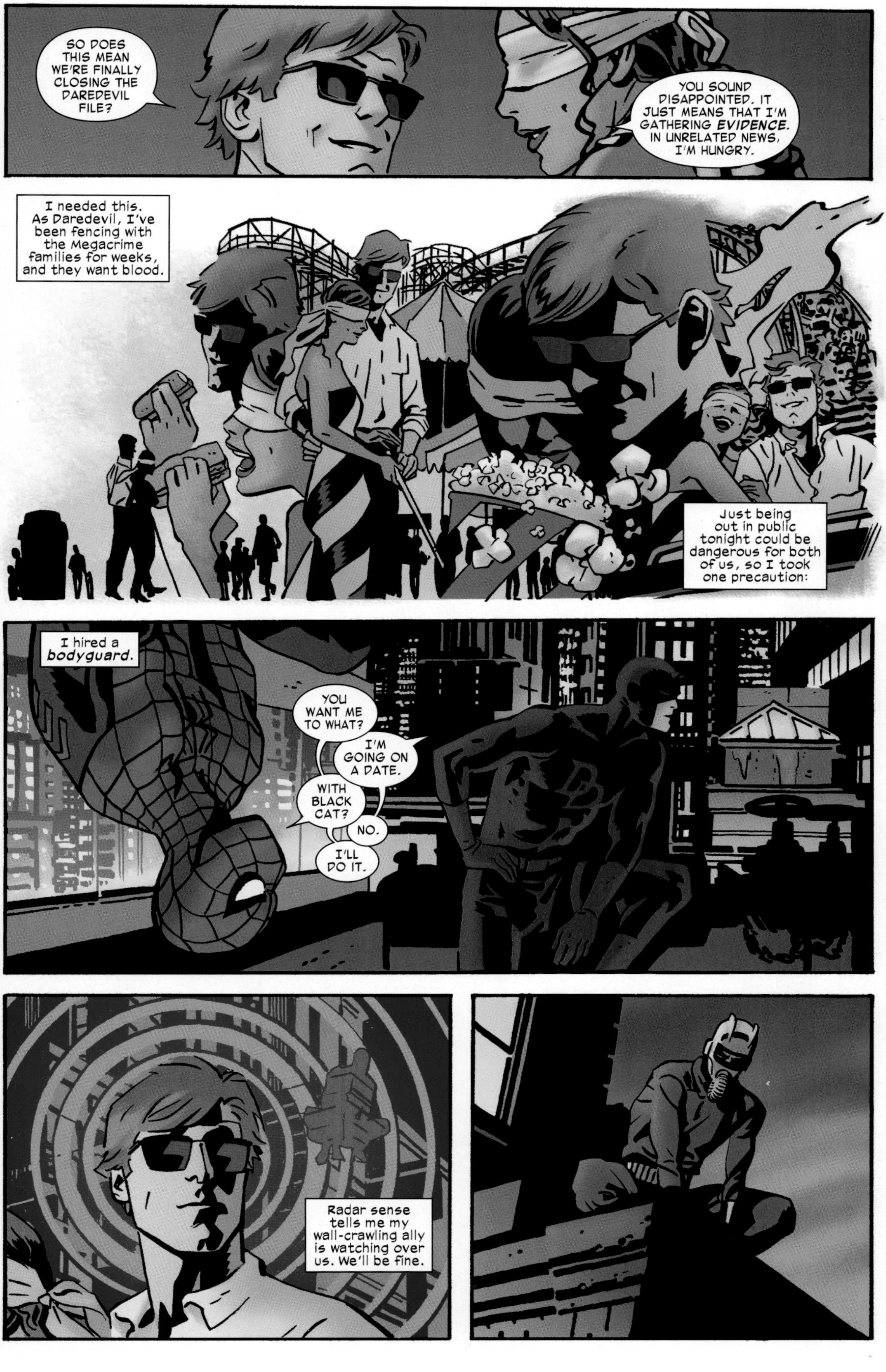

SO DOES THIS MEAN WE'RE FINALLY CLOSING THE DAREDEVIL FILE?
YOU SOUND DISAPPOINTED. IT JUST MEANS THAT I'M GATHERING EVIDENCE. IN UNRELATED NEWS, I'M HUNGRY.
I needed this. As Daredevil, I've been fencing with the Megacrime families for weeks, and they want blood.
Just being out in public tonight could be dangerous for both of us, so I took one precaution:
I hired a bodyguard.
YOU WANT ME TO WHAT?
I'M GOING ON A DATE.
WITH BLACK CAT?
NO.
I'LL DO IT.
Radar sense tells me my wall-crawling ally is watching over us. We'll be fine.

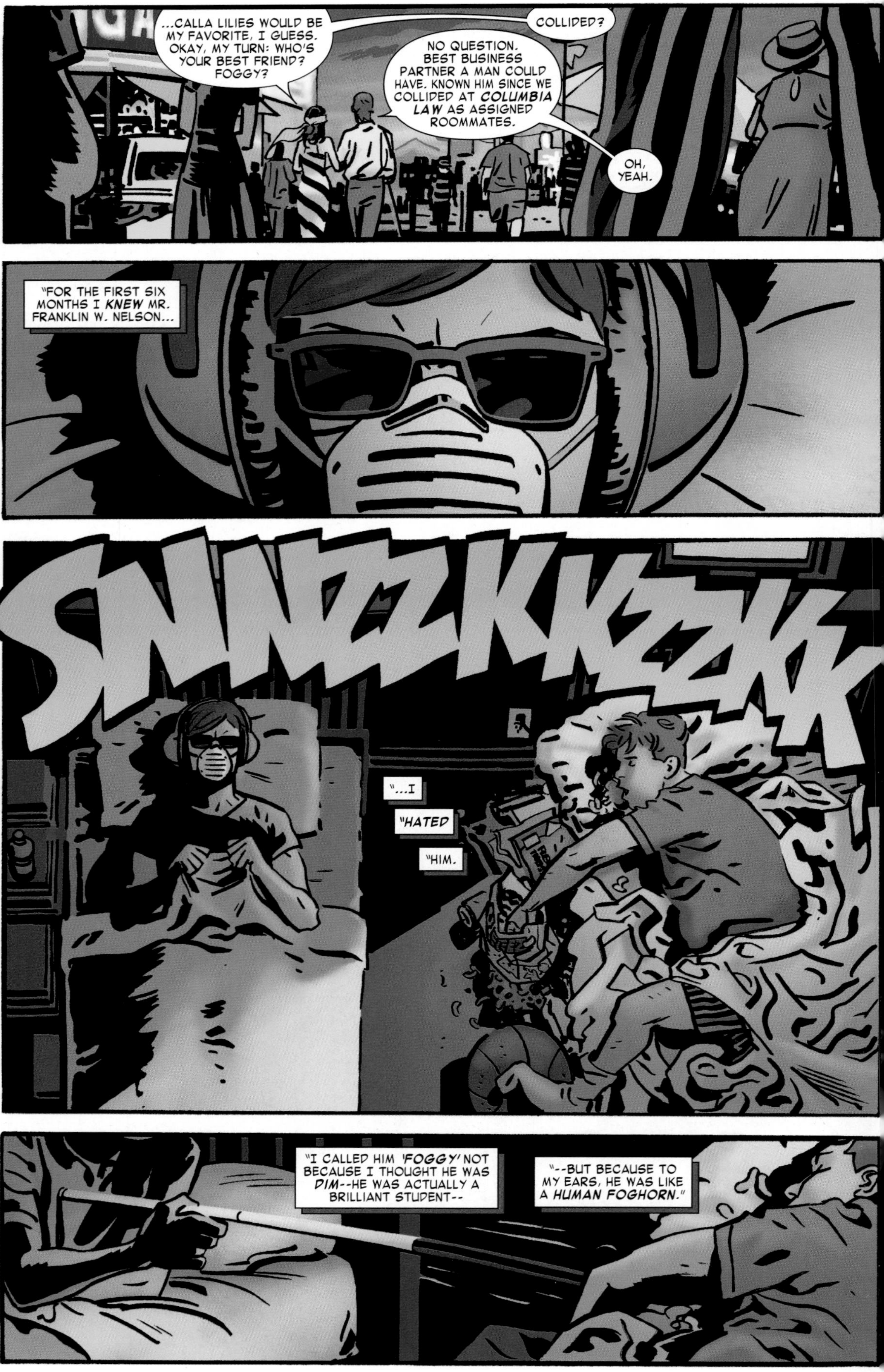

...CALLA LILIES WOULD BE MY FAVORITE, I GUESS. OKAY, MY TURN: WHO'S YOUR BEST FRIEND? FOGGY?
NO QUESTION. BEST BUSINESS PARTNER A MAN COULD HAVE. KNOWN HIM SINCE WE COLLIDED AT COLUMBIA LAW AS ASSIGNED ROOMMATES.
COLLIDED?
OH, YEAH.
"FOR THE FIRST SIX MONTHS I KNEW MR. FRANKLIN W. NELSON...
SNNZKKZKK
"...I
"HATED
"HIM.
"I CALLED HIM 'FOGGY' NOT BECAUSE I THOUGHT HE WAS DIM--HE WAS ACTUALLY A BRILLIANT STUDENT--
"--BUT BECAUSE TO MY EARS, HE WAS LIKE A HUMAN FOGHORN."

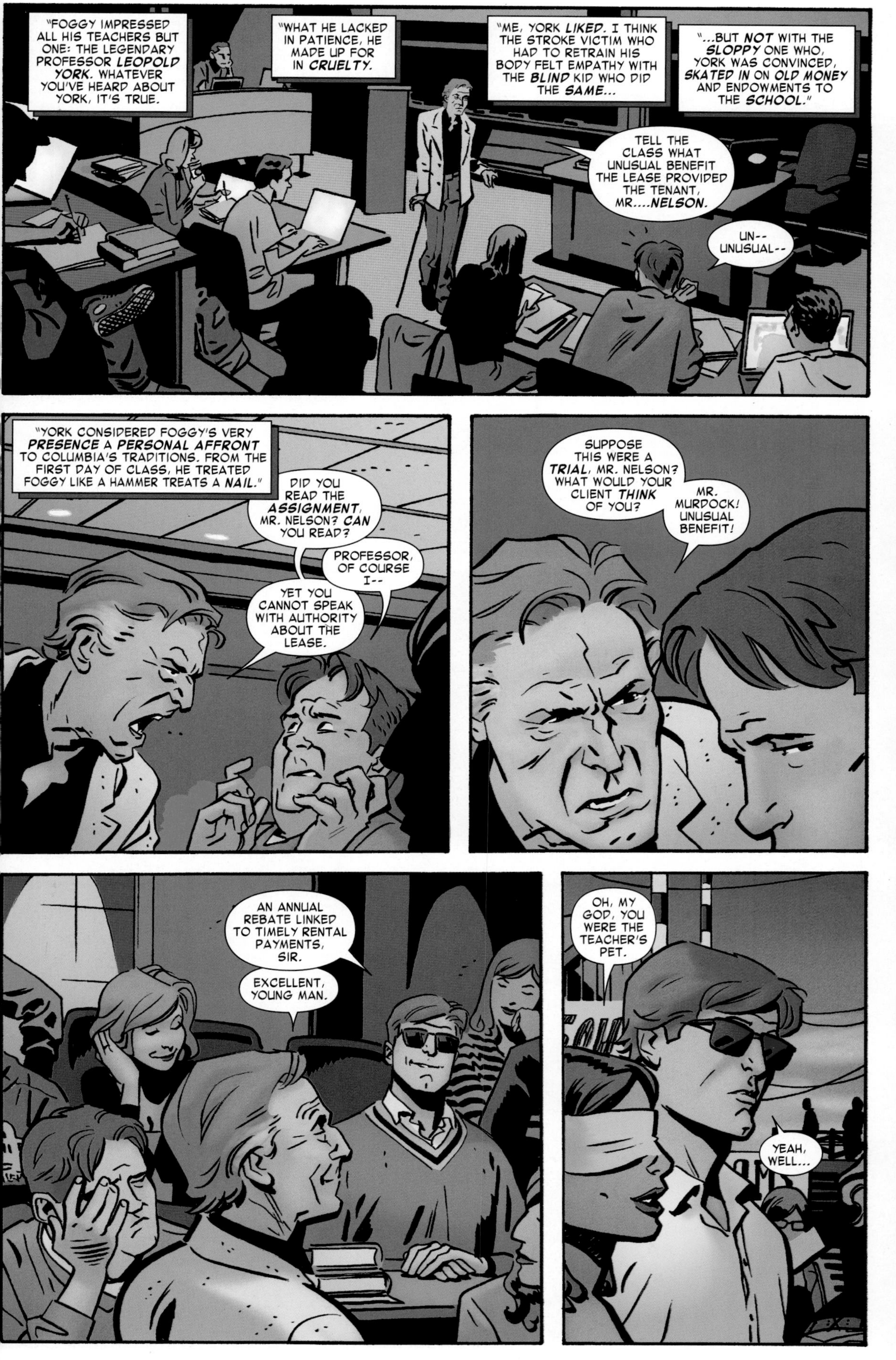
"FOGGY IMPRESSED ALL HIS TEACHERS BUT ONE: THE LEGENDARY PROFESSOR LEOPOLD YORK. WHATEVER YOU'VE HEARD ABOUT YORK, IT'S TRUE.
"WHAT HE LACKED IN PATIENCE, HE MADE UP FOR IN CRUELTY.
"ME, YORK LIKED. I THINK THE STROKE VICTIM WHO HAD TO RETRAIN HIS BODY FELT EMPATHY WITH THE BLIND KID WHO DID THE SAME...
"...BUT NOT WITH THE SLOPPY ONE WHO, YORK WAS CONVINCED, SKATED IN ON OLD MONEY AND ENDOWMENTS TO THE SCHOOL."
TELL THE CLASS WHAT UNUSUAL BENEFIT THE LEASE PROVIDED THE TENANT, MR....NELSON.
UN-- UNUSUAL--
"YORK CONSIDERED FOGGY'S VERY PRESENCE A PERSONAL AFFRONT TO COLUMBIA'S TRADITIONS. FROM THE FIRST DAY OF CLASS, HE TREATED FOGGY LIKE A HAMMER TREATS A NAIL."
DID YOU READ THE ASSIGNMENT, MR. NELSON? CAN YOU READ?
PROFESSOR, OF COURSE I--
YET YOU CANNOT SPEAK WITH AUTHORITY ABOUT THE LEASE.
SUPPOSE THIS WERE A TRIAL, MR. NELSON? WHAT WOULD YOUR CLIENT THINK OF YOU?
MR. MURDOCK! UNUSUAL BENEFIT!
AN ANNUAL REBATE LINKED TO TIMELY RENTAL PAYMENTS, SIR.
EXCELLENT, YOUNG MAN.
OH, MY GOD, YOU WERE THE TEACHER'S PET.
YEAH, WELL...

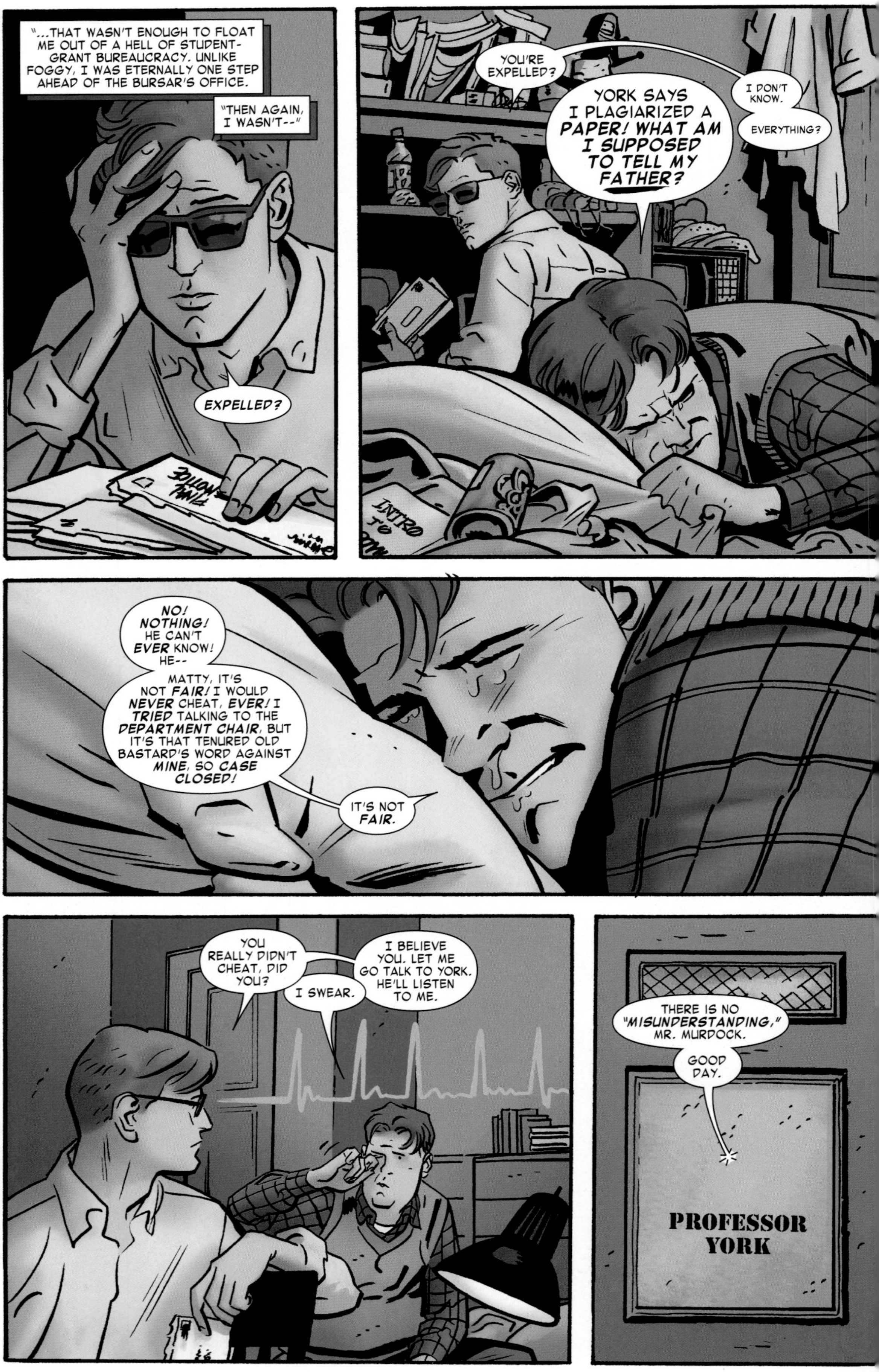
"...THAT WASN'T ENOUGH TO FLOAT ME OUT OF A HELL OF STUDENT-GRANT BUREAUCRACY. UNLIKE FOGGY, I WAS ETERNALLY ONE STEP AHEAD OF THE BURSAR'S OFFICE.
"THEN AGAIN, I WASN'T--"
EXPELLED?
YOU'RE EXPELLED?
YORK SAYS I PLAGIARIZED A PAPER! WHAT AM I SUPPOSED TO TELL MY FATHER?
I DON'T KNOW.
EVERYTHING?
NO! NOTHING! HE CAN'T EVER KNOW! HE--
MATTY, IT'S NOT FAIR! I WOULD NEVER CHEAT, EVER! I TRIED TALKING TO THE DEPARTMENT CHAIR, BUT IT'S THAT TENURED OLD BASTARD'S WORD AGAINST MINE, SO CASE CLOSED!
IT'S NOT FAIR.
YOU REALLY DIDN'T CHEAT, DID YOU?
I SWEAR.
I BELIEVE YOU. LET ME GO TALK TO YORK. HE'LL LISTEN TO ME.
THERE IS NO "MISUNDERSTANDING," MR. MURDOCK.
GOOD DAY.
PROFESSOR YORK

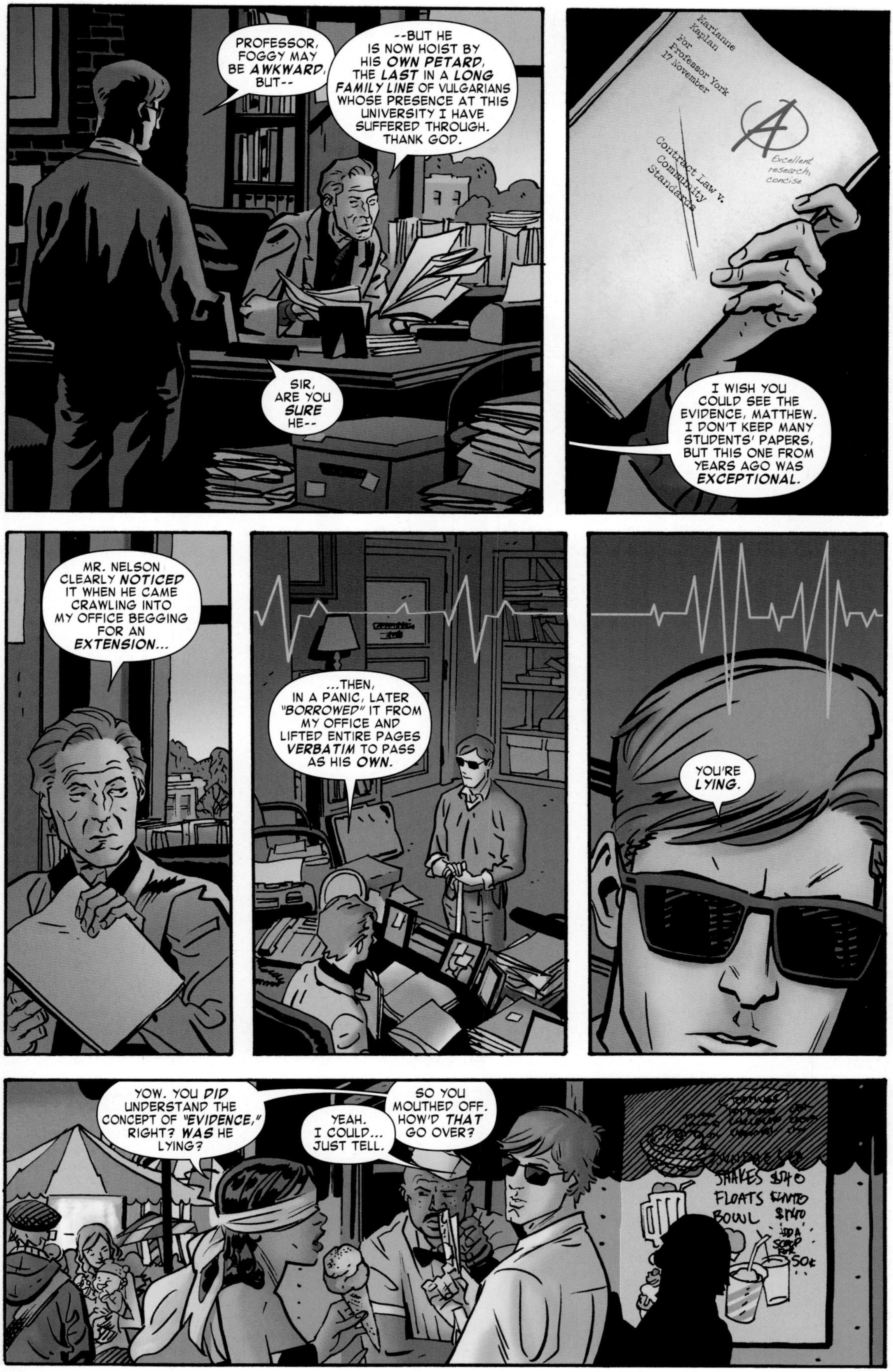
PROFESSOR, FOGGY MAY BE AWKWARD, BUT--
--BUT HE IS NOW HOIST BY HIS OWN PETARD, THE LAST IN A LONG FAMILY LINE OF VULGARIANS WHOSE PRESENCE AT THIS UNIVERSITY I HAVE SUFFERED THROUGH. THANK GOD.
SIR, ARE YOU SURE HE--
Marianne Kaplan
For Professor York
17 November
Contract Law v. Community Standards
A
Excellent research, concise
I WISH YOU COULD SEE THE EVIDENCE, MATTHEW. I DON'T KEEP MANY STUDENTS' PAPERS, BUT THIS ONE FROM YEARS AGO WAS EXCEPTIONAL.
MR. NELSON CLEARLY NOTICED IT WHEN HE CAME CRAWLING INTO MY OFFICE BEGGING FOR AN EXTENSION...
...THEN, IN A PANIC, LATER "BORROWED" IT FROM MY OFFICE AND LIFTED ENTIRE PAGES VERBATIM TO PASS AS HIS OWN.
YOU'RE LYING.
YOW. YOU DID UNDERSTAND THE CONCEPT OF "EVIDENCE," RIGHT? WAS HE LYING?
YEAH. I COULD... JUST TELL.
SO YOU MOUTHED OFF. HOW'D THAT GO OVER?
SHAKES
FLOATS
BOWL

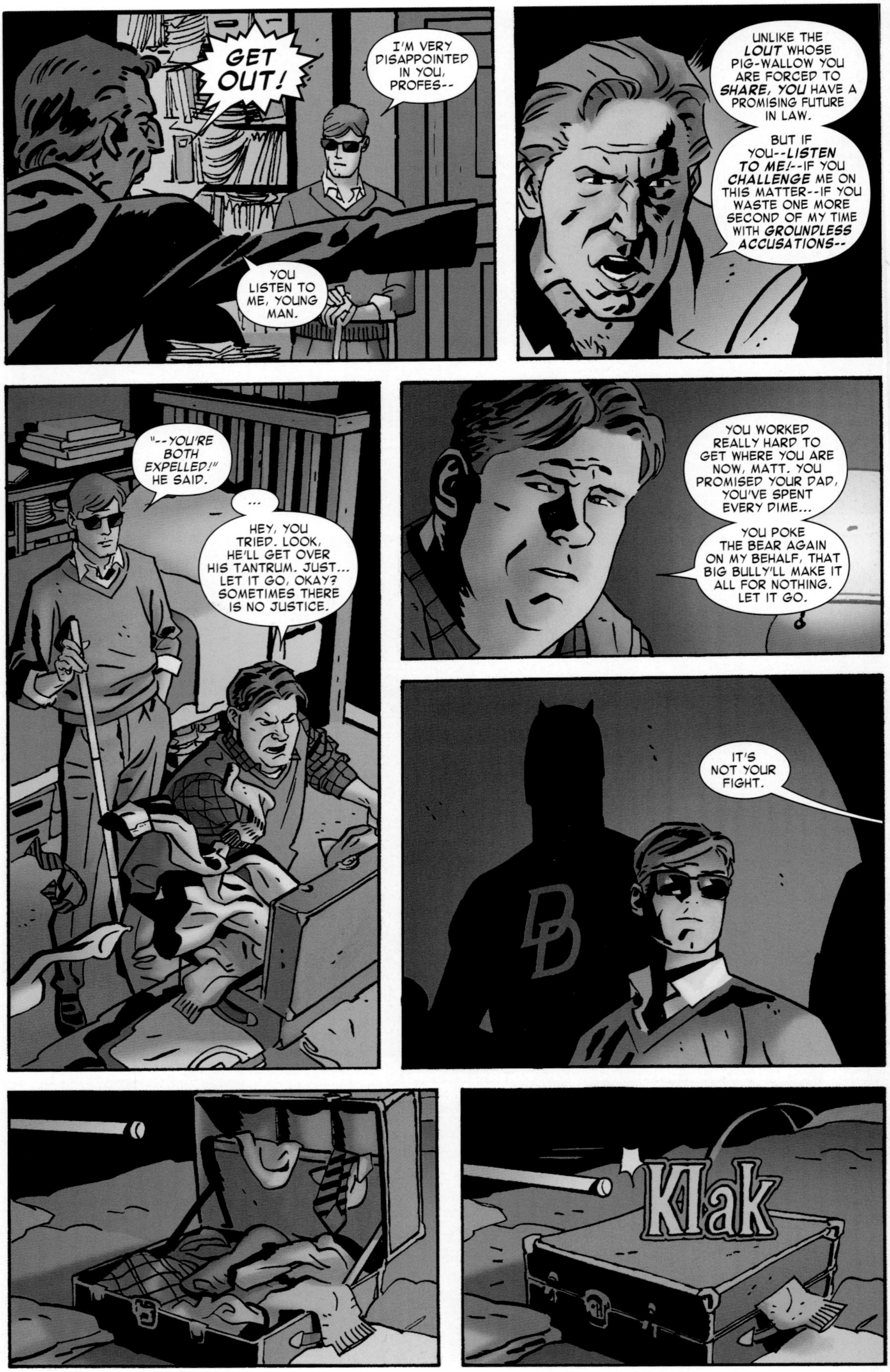
GET OUT!
I'M VERY DISAPPOINTED IN YOU, PROFES--
YOU LISTEN TO ME, YOUNG MAN.
UNLIKE THE LOUT WHOSE PIG-WALLOW YOU ARE FORCED TO SHARE, YOU HAVE A PROMISING FUTURE IN LAW.
BUT IF YOU--LISTEN TO ME!--IF YOU CHALLENGE ME ON THIS MATTER--IF YOU WASTE ONE MORE SECOND OF MY TIME WITH GROUNDLESS ACCUSATIONS--
"--YOU'RE BOTH EXPELLED!" HE SAID.
...
HEY, YOU TRIED. LOOK, HE'LL GET OVER HIS TANTRUM. JUST... LET IT GO, OKAY? SOMETIMES THERE IS NO JUSTICE.
YOU WORKED REALLY HARD TO GET WHERE YOU ARE NOW, MATT. YOU PROMISED YOUR DAD, YOU'VE SPENT EVERY DIME...
YOU POKE THE BEAR AGAIN ON MY BEHALF, THAT BIG BULLY'LL MAKE IT ALL FOR NOTHING. LET IT GO.
IT'S NOT YOUR FIGHT.
KLAK

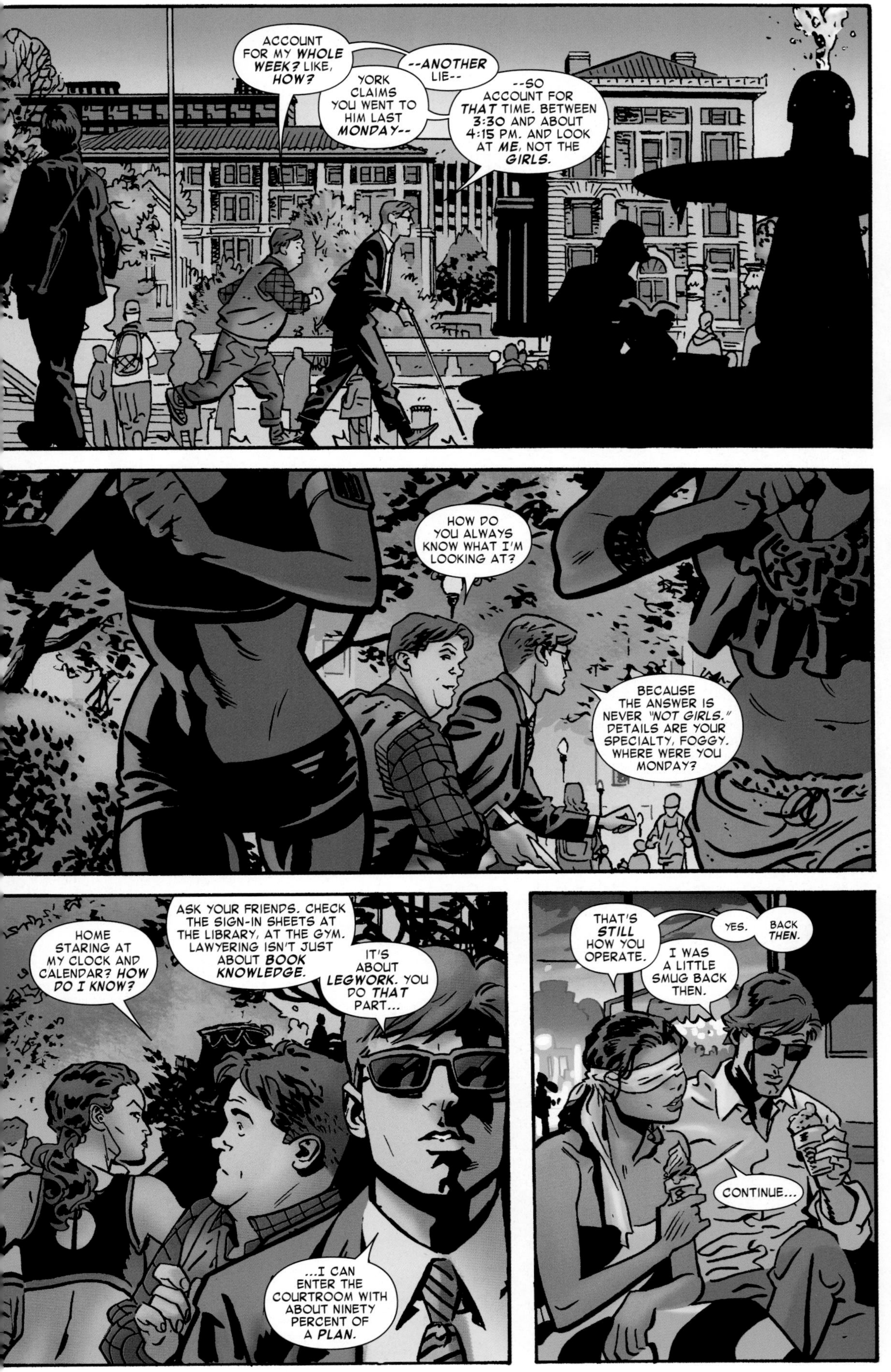
ACCOUNT FOR MY WHOLE WEEK? LIKE, HOW?
--ANOTHER LIE--
YORK CLAIMS YOU WENT TO HIM LAST MONDAY--
--SO ACCOUNT FOR THAT TIME. BETWEEN 3:30 AND ABOUT 4:15 PM. AND LOOK AT ME, NOT THE GIRLS.
HOW DO YOU ALWAYS KNOW WHAT I'M LOOKING AT?
BECAUSE THE ANSWER IS NEVER "NOT GIRLS." DETAILS ARE YOUR SPECIALTY, FOGGY. WHERE WERE YOU MONDAY?
HOME STARING AT MY CLOCK AND CALENDAR? HOW DO I KNOW?
ASK YOUR FRIENDS. CHECK THE SIGN-IN SHEETS AT THE LIBRARY, AT THE GYM. LAWYERING ISN'T JUST ABOUT BOOK KNOWLEDGE.
IT'S ABOUT LEGWORK. YOU DO THAT PART...
...I CAN ENTER THE COURTROOM WITH ABOUT NINETY PERCENT OF A PLAN.
THAT'S STILL HOW YOU OPERATE.
YES.
BACK THEN.
I WAS A LITTLE SMUG BACK THEN.
CONTINUE...

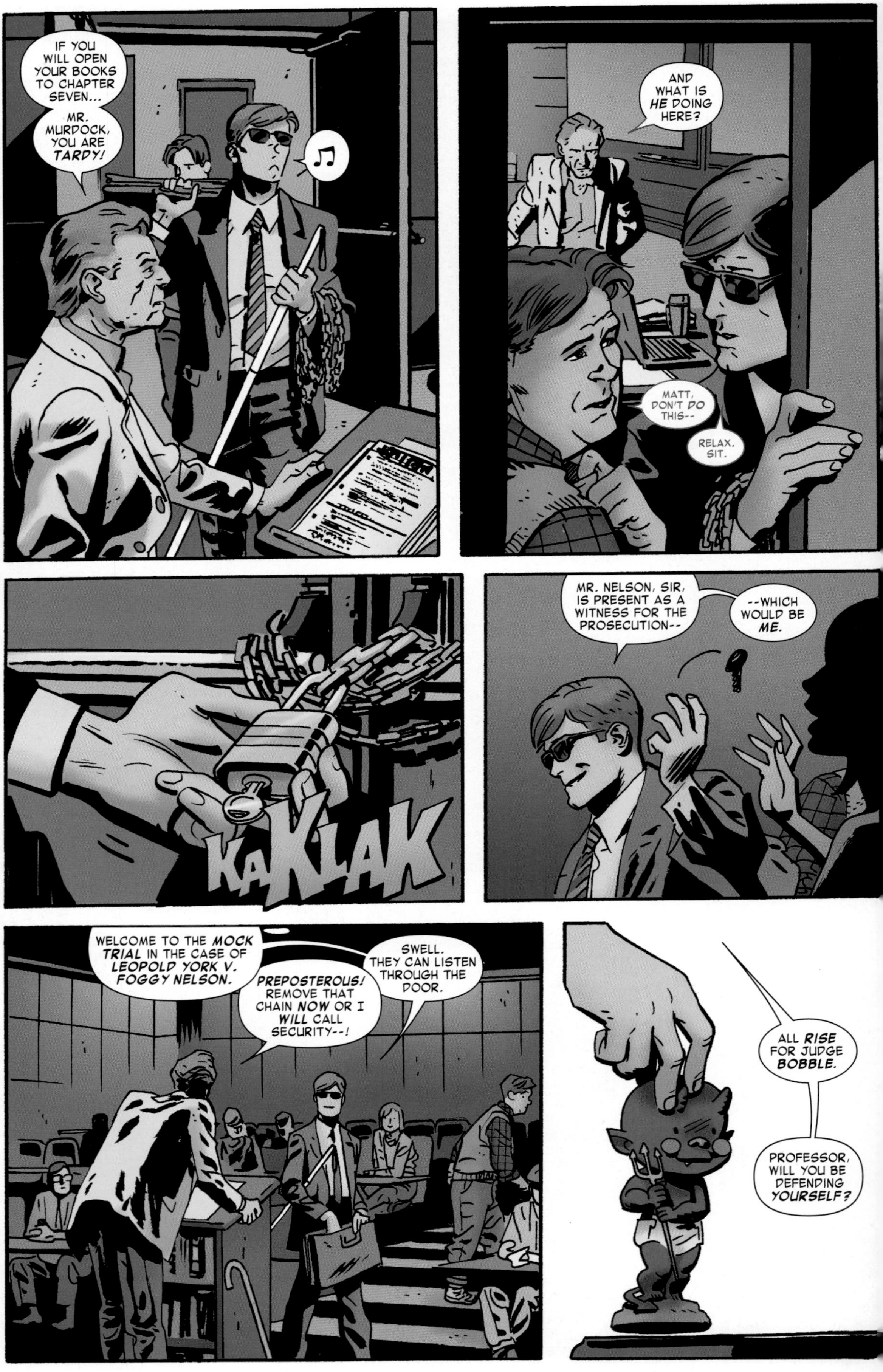

IF YOU WILL OPEN YOUR BOOKS TO CHAPTER SEVEN...
MR. MURDOCK, YOU ARE *TARDY!*
♫
AND WHAT IS *HE* DOING HERE?
MATT, DON'T *DO* THIS--
RELAX. SIT.
KAKLAK
MR. NELSON, SIR, IS PRESENT AS A WITNESS FOR THE PROSECUTION--
--WHICH WOULD BE *ME.*
WELCOME TO THE *MOCK TRIAL* IN THE CASE OF *LEOPOLD YORK V. FOGGY NELSON.*
PREPOSTEROUS! REMOVE THAT CHAIN *NOW* OR I *WILL* CALL SECURITY--!
SWELL. THEY CAN LISTEN THROUGH THE DOOR.
ALL *RISE* FOR JUDGE *BOBBLE.*
PROFESSOR, WILL YOU BE DEFENDING *YOURSELF?*

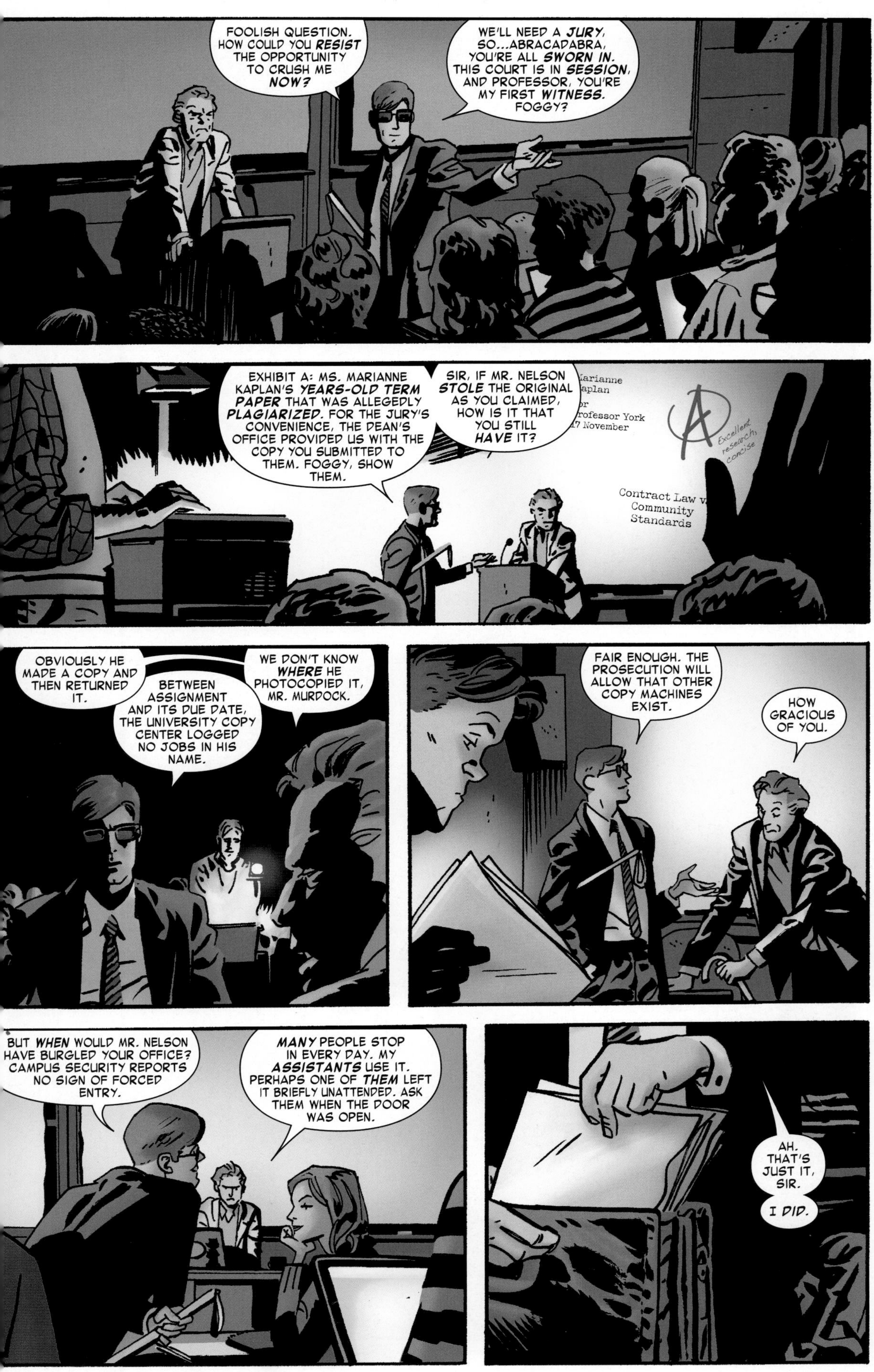

FOOLISH QUESTION. HOW COULD YOU RESIST THE OPPORTUNITY TO CRUSH ME NOW?
WE'LL NEED A JURY, SO...ABRACADABRA, YOU'RE ALL SWORN IN. THIS COURT IS IN SESSION, AND PROFESSOR, YOU'RE MY FIRST WITNESS. FOGGY?
EXHIBIT A: MS. MARIANNE KAPLAN'S YEARS-OLD TERM PAPER THAT WAS ALLEGEDLY PLAGIARIZED. FOR THE JURY'S CONVENIENCE, THE DEAN'S OFFICE PROVIDED US WITH THE COPY YOU SUBMITTED TO THEM. FOGGY, SHOW THEM.
SIR, IF MR. NELSON STOLE THE ORIGINAL AS YOU CLAIMED, HOW IS IT THAT YOU STILL HAVE IT?
Contract Law v Community Standards
Excellent research concise
OBVIOUSLY HE MADE A COPY AND THEN RETURNED IT.
WE DON'T KNOW WHERE HE PHOTOCOPIED IT, MR. MURDOCK.
BETWEEN ASSIGNMENT AND ITS DUE DATE, THE UNIVERSITY COPY CENTER LOGGED NO JOBS IN HIS NAME.
FAIR ENOUGH. THE PROSECUTION WILL ALLOW THAT OTHER COPY MACHINES EXIST.
HOW GRACIOUS OF YOU.
BUT WHEN WOULD MR. NELSON HAVE BURGLED YOUR OFFICE? CAMPUS SECURITY REPORTS NO SIGN OF FORCED ENTRY.
MANY PEOPLE STOP IN EVERY DAY. MY ASSISTANTS USE IT. PERHAPS ONE OF THEM LEFT IT BRIEFLY UNATTENDED. ASK THEM WHEN THE DOOR WAS OPEN.
AH. THAT'S JUST IT, SIR.
I DID.

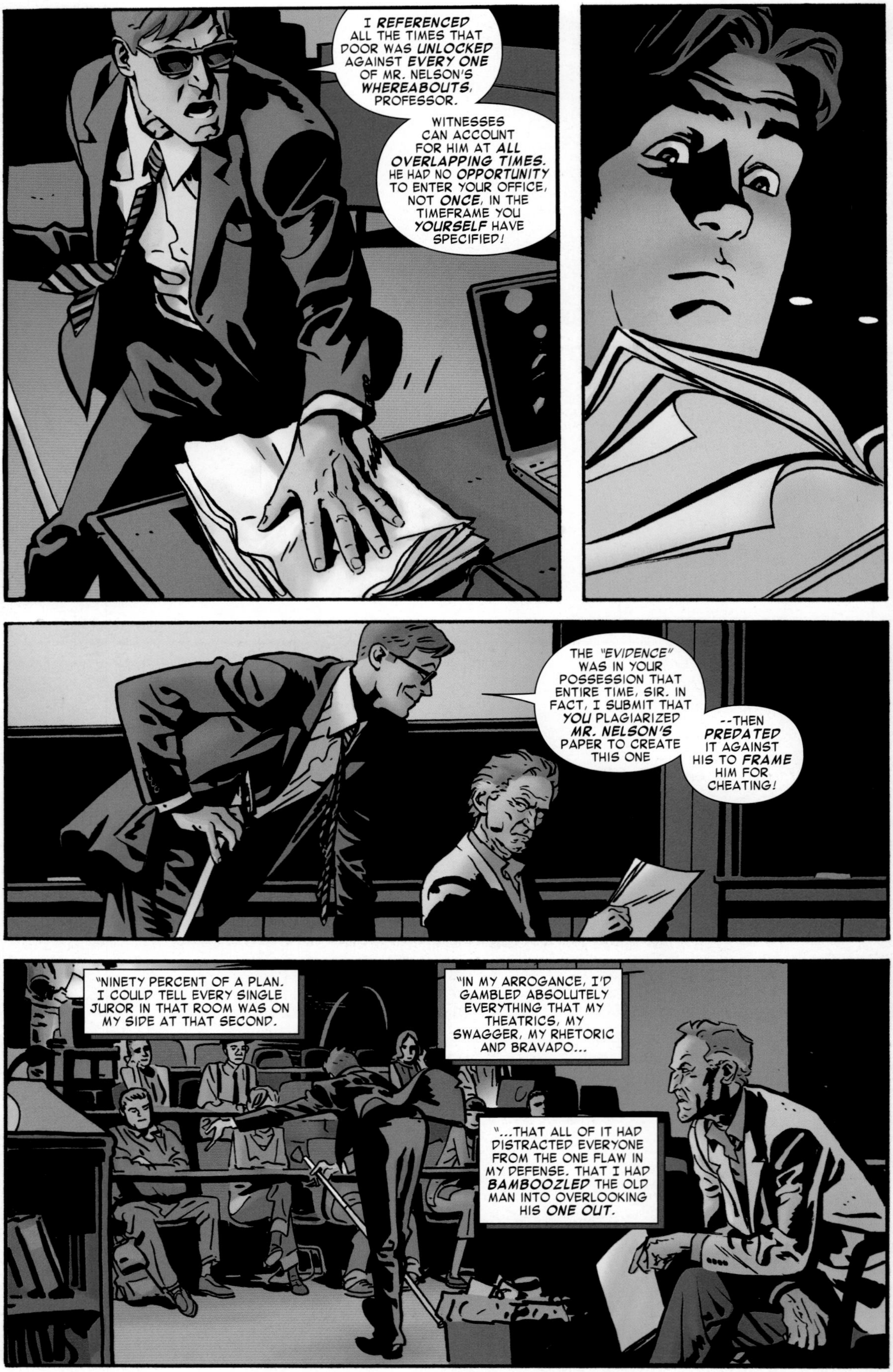
I REFERENCED ALL THE TIMES THAT DOOR WAS UNLOCKED AGAINST EVERY ONE OF MR. NELSON'S WHEREABOUTS, PROFESSOR.
WITNESSES CAN ACCOUNT FOR HIM AT ALL OVERLAPPING TIMES. HE HAD NO OPPORTUNITY TO ENTER YOUR OFFICE, NOT ONCE, IN THE TIMEFRAME YOU YOURSELF HAVE SPECIFIED!
THE "EVIDENCE" WAS IN YOUR POSSESSION THAT ENTIRE TIME, SIR. IN FACT, I SUBMIT THAT YOU PLAGIARIZED MR. NELSON'S PAPER TO CREATE THIS ONE
--THEN PREDATED IT AGAINST HIS TO FRAME HIM FOR CHEATING!
"NINETY PERCENT OF A PLAN. I COULD TELL EVERY SINGLE JUROR IN THAT ROOM WAS ON MY SIDE AT THAT SECOND.
"IN MY ARROGANCE, I'D GAMBLED ABSOLUTELY EVERYTHING THAT MY THEATRICS, MY SWAGGER, MY RHETORIC AND BRAVADO...
"...THAT ALL OF IT HAD DISTRACTED EVERYONE FROM THE ONE FLAW IN MY DEFENSE. THAT I HAD BAMBOOZLED THE OLD MAN INTO OVERLOOKING HIS ONE OUT.

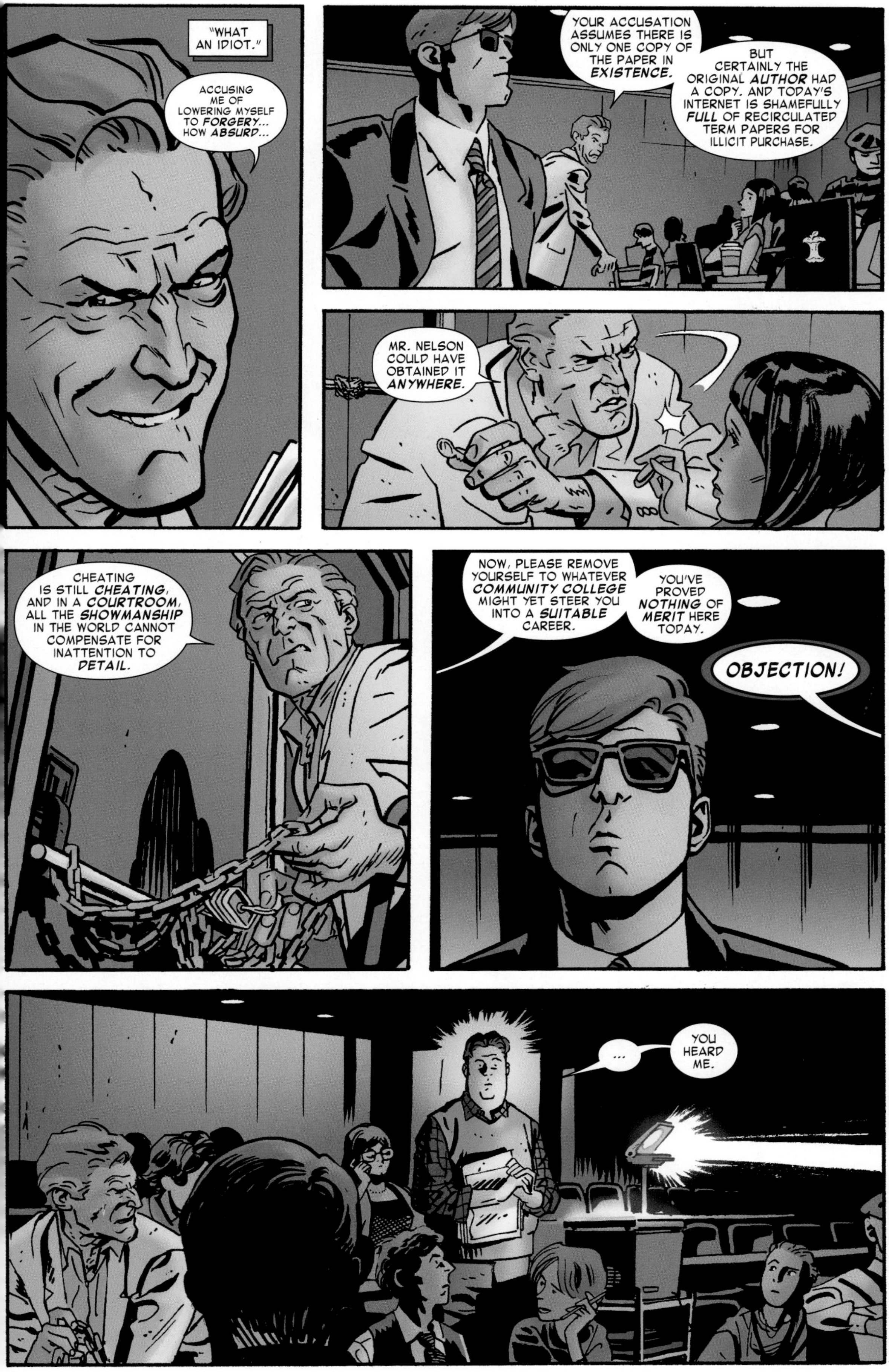
"WHAT AN IDIOT."
ACCUSING ME OF LOWERING MYSELF TO FORGERY... HOW ABSURD...
YOUR ACCUSATION ASSUMES THERE IS ONLY ONE COPY OF THE PAPER IN EXISTENCE.
BUT CERTAINLY THE ORIGINAL AUTHOR HAD A COPY. AND TODAY'S INTERNET IS SHAMEFULLY FULL OF RECIRCULATED TERM PAPERS FOR ILLICIT PURCHASE.
MR. NELSON COULD HAVE OBTAINED IT ANYWHERE.
CHEATING IS STILL CHEATING, AND IN A COURTROOM, ALL THE SHOWMANSHIP IN THE WORLD CANNOT COMPENSATE FOR INATTENTION TO DETAIL.
NOW, PLEASE REMOVE YOURSELF TO WHATEVER COMMUNITY COLLEGE MIGHT YET STEER YOU INTO A SUITABLE CAREER.
YOU'VE PROVED NOTHING OF MERIT HERE TODAY.
OBJECTION!
...
YOU HEARD ME.

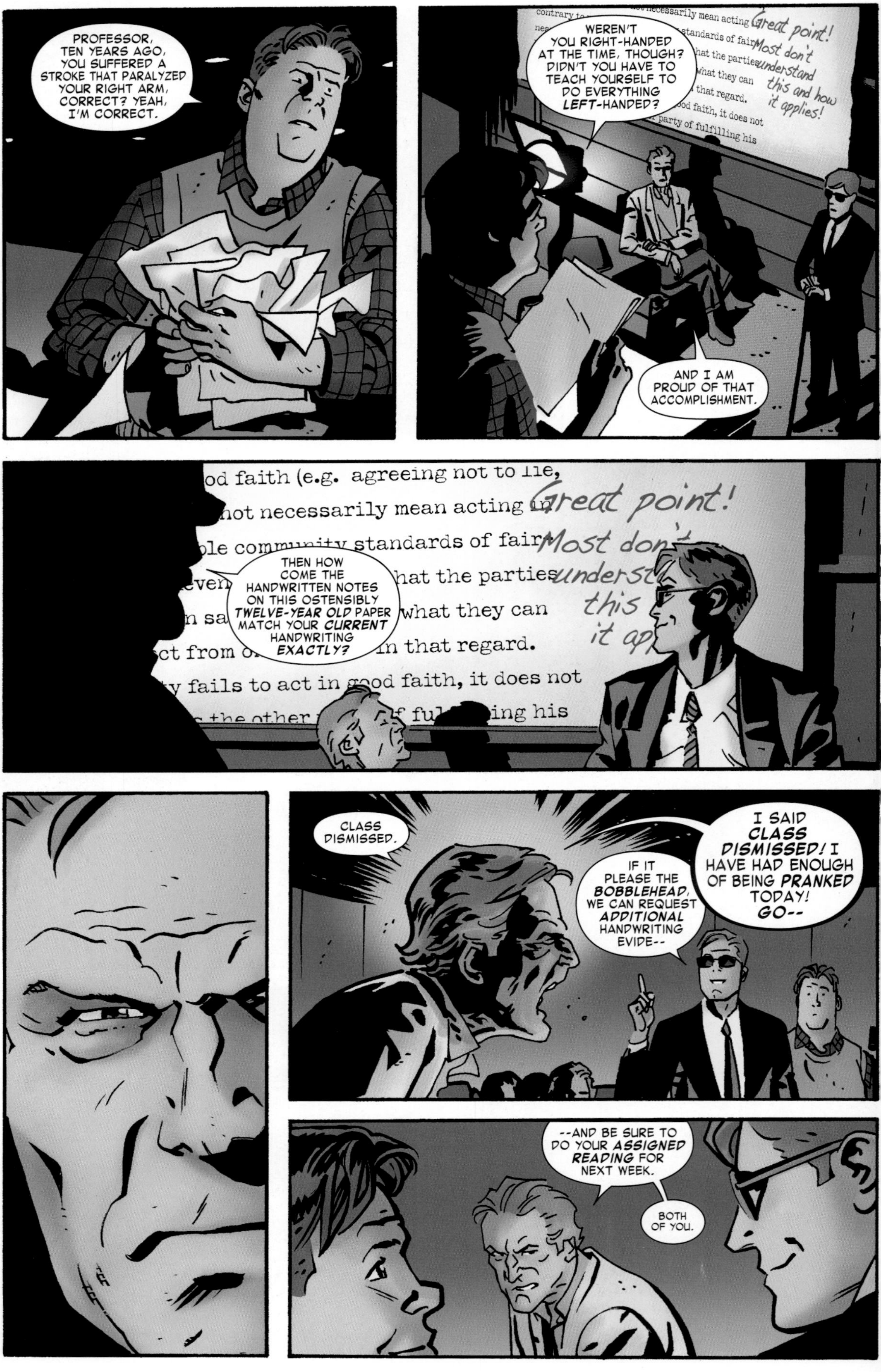
PROFESSOR, TEN YEARS AGO, YOU SUFFERED A STROKE THAT PARALYZED YOUR RIGHT ARM, CORRECT? YEAH, I'M CORRECT.
WEREN'T YOU RIGHT-HANDED AT THE TIME, THOUGH? DIDN'T YOU HAVE TO TEACH YOURSELF TO DO EVERYTHING LEFT-HANDED?
Great point! Most don't understand this and how it applies!
AND I AM PROUD OF THAT ACCOMPLISHMENT.
THEN HOW COME THE HANDWRITTEN NOTES ON THIS OSTENSIBLY TWELVE-YEAR OLD PAPER MATCH YOUR CURRENT HANDWRITING EXACTLY?
CLASS DISMISSED.
IF IT PLEASE THE BOBBLEHEAD, WE CAN REQUEST ADDITIONAL HANDWRITING EVIDE--
I SAID CLASS DISMISSED! I HAVE HAD ENOUGH OF BEING PRANKED TODAY! GO--
--AND BE SURE TO DO YOUR ASSIGNED READING FOR NEXT WEEK.
BOTH OF YOU.

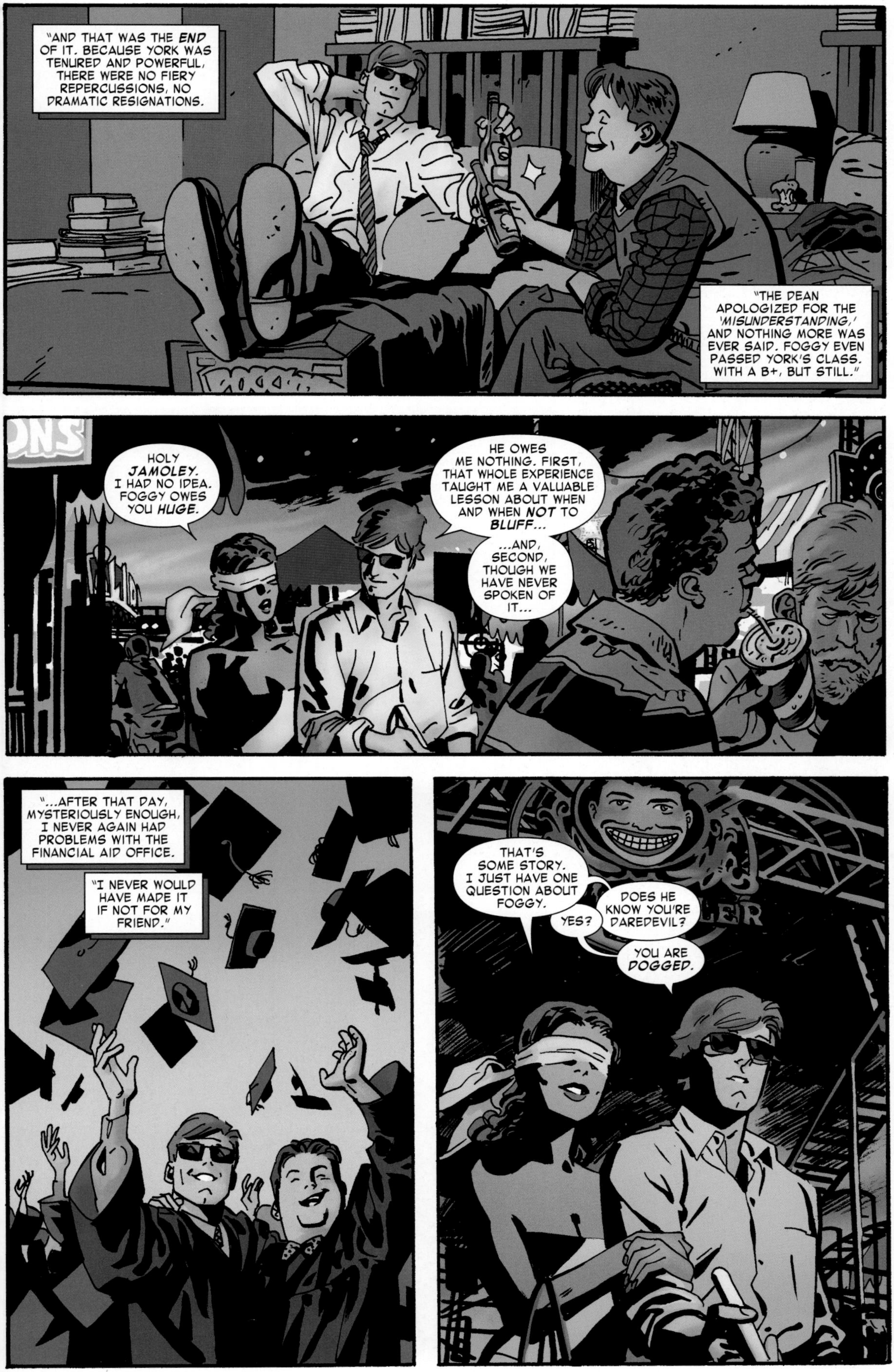
"AND THAT WAS THE END OF IT. BECAUSE YORK WAS TENURED AND POWERFUL, THERE WERE NO FIERY REPERCUSSIONS, NO DRAMATIC RESIGNATIONS.
"THE DEAN APOLOGIZED FOR THE 'MISUNDERSTANDING,' AND NOTHING MORE WAS EVER SAID. FOGGY EVEN PASSED YORK'S CLASS. WITH A B+, BUT STILL."
HOLY JAMOLEY. I HAD NO IDEA. FOGGY OWES YOU HUGE.
HE OWES ME NOTHING. FIRST, THAT WHOLE EXPERIENCE TAUGHT ME A VALUABLE LESSON ABOUT WHEN AND WHEN NOT TO BLUFF...
...AND, SECOND, THOUGH WE HAVE NEVER SPOKEN OF IT...
"...AFTER THAT DAY, MYSTERIOUSLY ENOUGH, I NEVER AGAIN HAD PROBLEMS WITH THE FINANCIAL AID OFFICE.
"I NEVER WOULD HAVE MADE IT IF NOT FOR MY FRIEND."
THAT'S SOME STORY. I JUST HAVE ONE QUESTION ABOUT FOGGY.
YES?
DOES HE KNOW YOU'RE DAREDEVIL?
YOU ARE DOGGED.

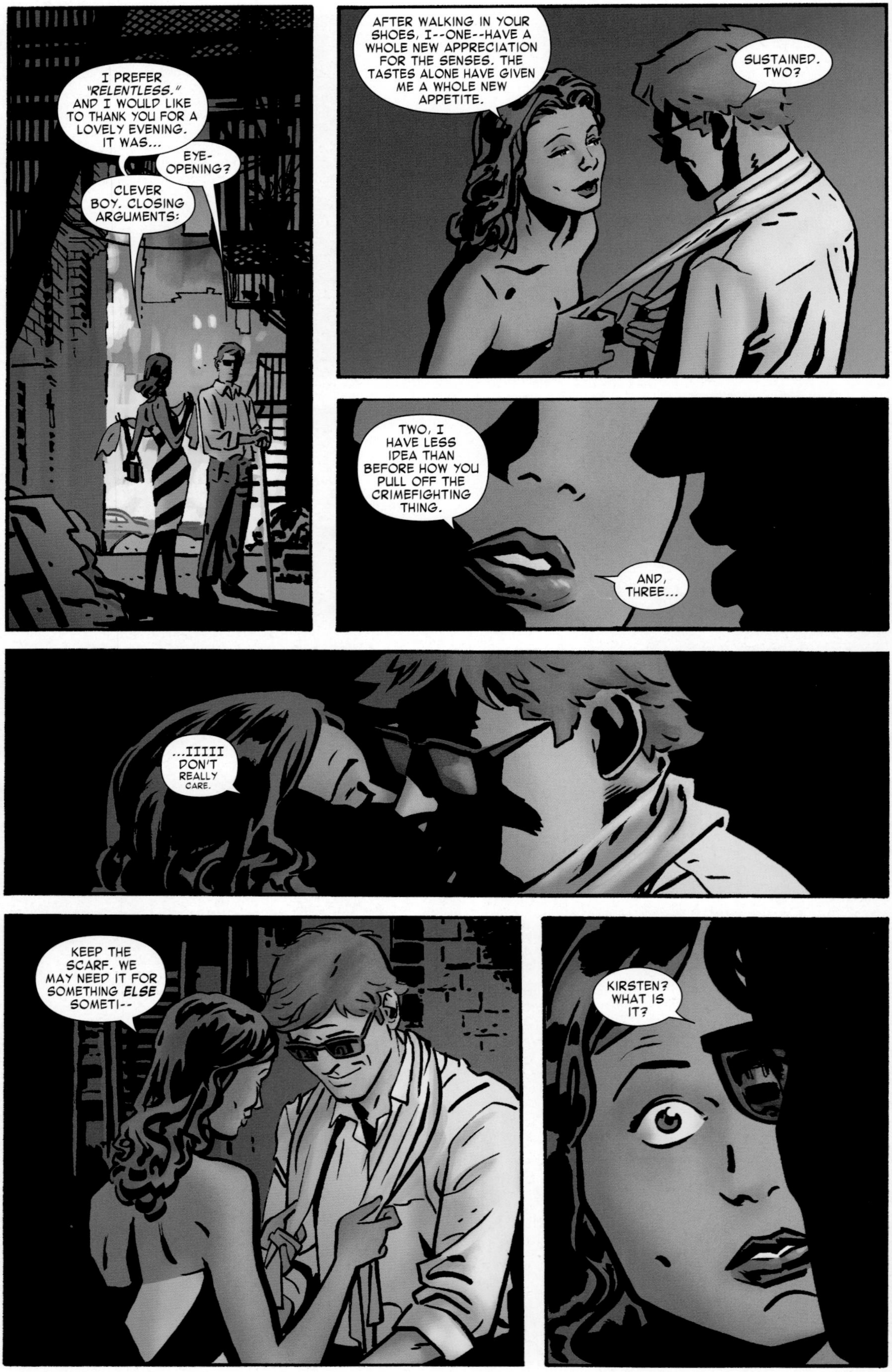
I PREFER "RELENTLESS." AND I WOULD LIKE TO THANK YOU FOR A LOVELY EVENING. IT WAS...
EYE-OPENING?
CLEVER BOY. CLOSING ARGUMENTS:
AFTER WALKING IN YOUR SHOES, I--ONE--HAVE A WHOLE NEW APPRECIATION FOR THE SENSES. THE TASTES ALONE HAVE GIVEN ME A WHOLE NEW APPETITE.
SUSTAINED. TWO?
TWO, I HAVE LESS IDEA THAN BEFORE HOW YOU PULL OFF THE CRIMEFIGHTING THING.
AND, THREE...
...IIIII DON'T REALLY CARE.
KEEP THE SCARF. WE MAY NEED IT FOR SOMETHING ELSE SOMETI--
KIRSTEN? WHAT IS IT?

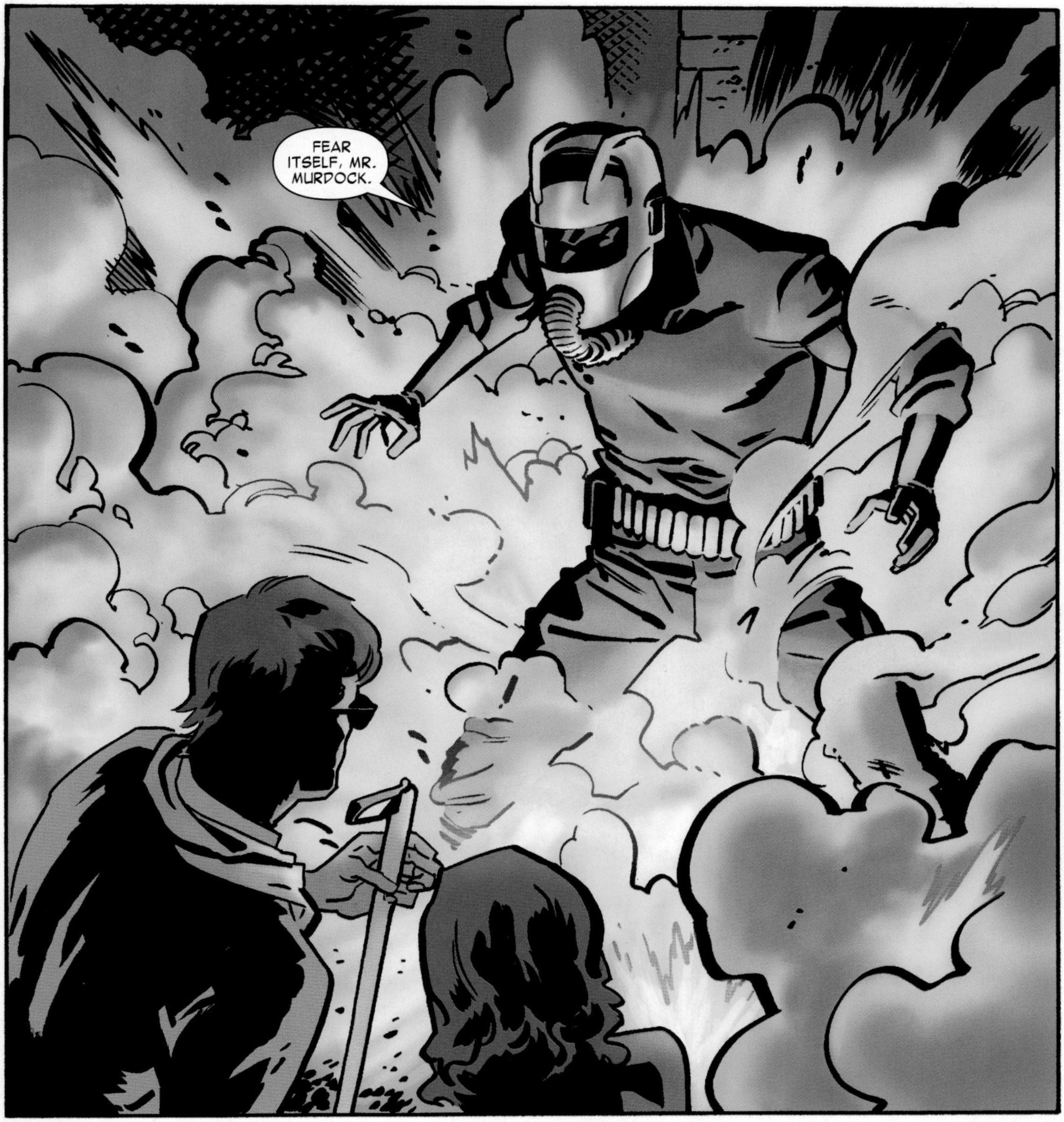
FEAR ITSELF, MR. MURDOCK.

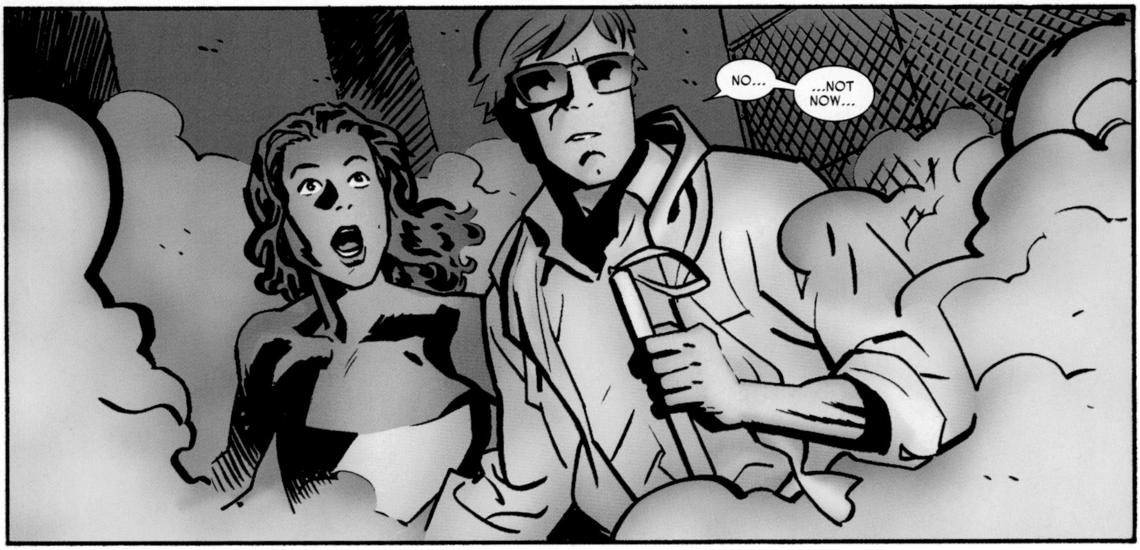
NO...
...NOT NOW...

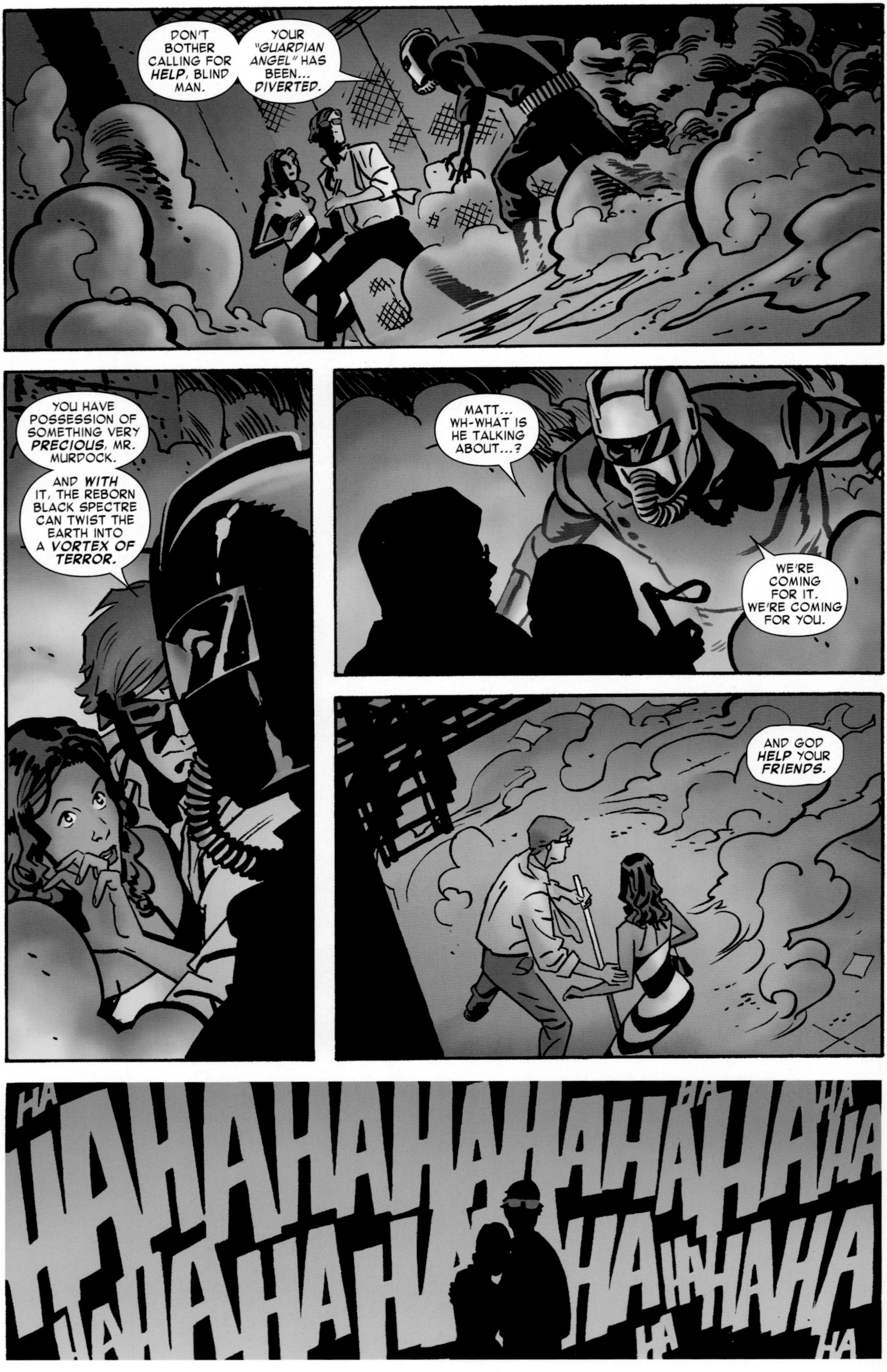
DON'T BOTHER CALLING FOR HELP, BLIND MAN.
YOUR "GUARDIAN ANGEL" HAS BEEN... DIVERTED.
YOU HAVE POSSESSION OF SOMETHING VERY PRECIOUS, MR. MURDOCK.
AND WITH IT, THE REBORN BLACK SPECTRE CAN TWIST THE EARTH INTO A VORTEX OF TERROR.
MATT... WH-WHAT IS HE TALKING ABOUT...?
WE'RE COMING FOR IT. WE'RE COMING FOR YOU.
AND GOD HELP YOUR FRIENDS.
HA HAHAHAHAHAHAHAHAHA HA HA HAHAHAHAHAHA HA HAHA HA HA

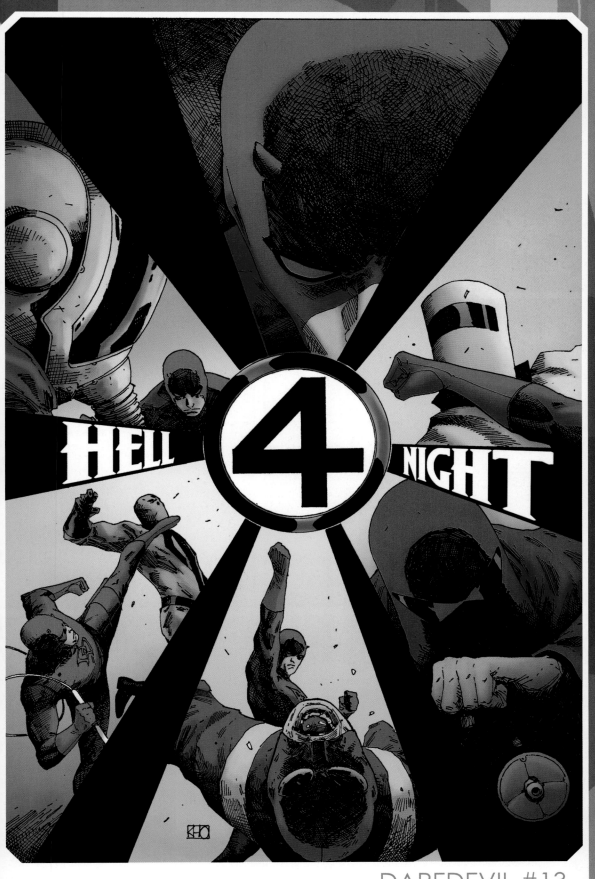

HELL 4 NIGHT

DAREDEVIL #13

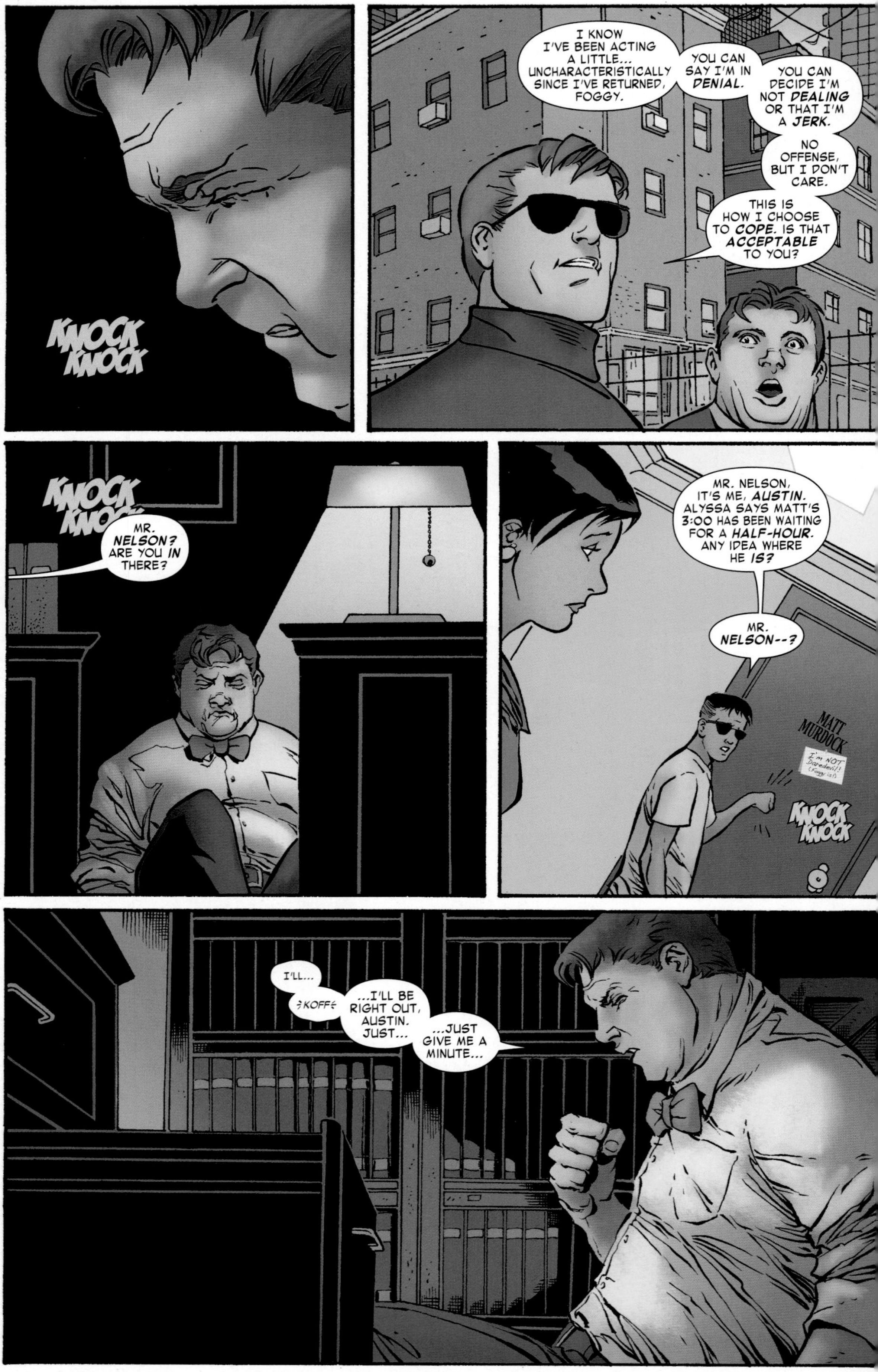
KNOCK KNOCK
I KNOW I'VE BEEN ACTING A LITTLE... UNCHARACTERISTICALLY SINCE I'VE RETURNED, FOGGY.
YOU CAN SAY I'M IN DENIAL.
YOU CAN DECIDE I'M NOT DEALING OR THAT I'M A JERK.
NO OFFENSE, BUT I DON'T CARE.
THIS IS HOW I CHOOSE TO COPE. IS THAT ACCEPTABLE TO YOU?
KNOCK KNOCK
MR. NELSON? ARE YOU IN THERE?
MR. NELSON, IT'S ME, AUSTIN. ALYSSA SAYS MATT'S 3:00 HAS BEEN WAITING FOR A HALF-HOUR. ANY IDEA WHERE HE IS?
MR. NELSON--?
MATT MURDOCK
I'm NOT Daredevil! (Foggy is!)
KNOCK KNOCK
I'LL...
KOFF
...I'LL BE RIGHT OUT, AUSTIN. JUST...
...JUST GIVE ME A MINUTE...

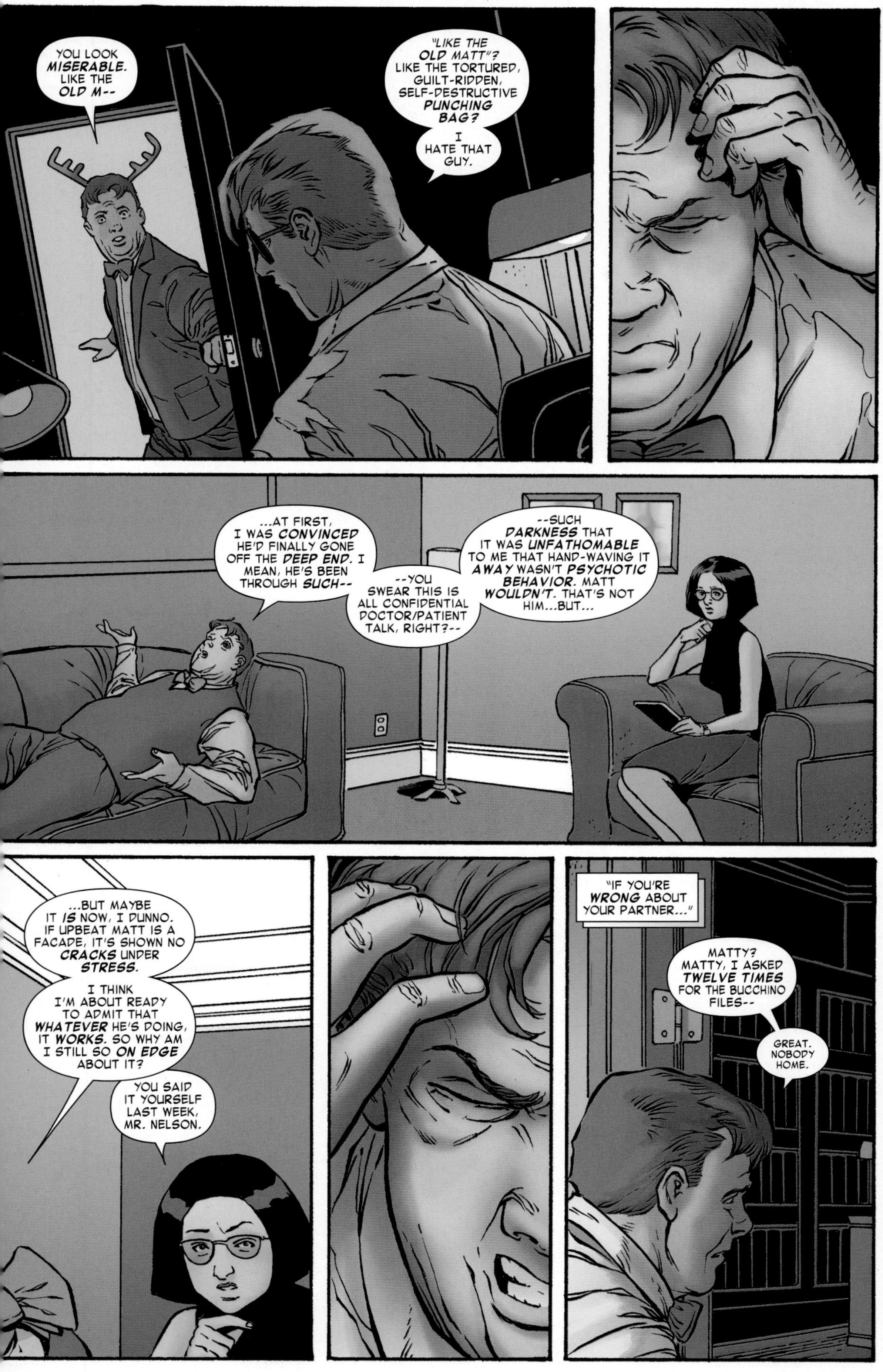
YOU LOOK MISERABLE. LIKE THE OLD M--
"LIKE THE OLD MATT"? LIKE THE TORTURED, GUILT-RIDDEN, SELF-DESTRUCTIVE PUNCHING BAG?
I HATE THAT GUY.
...AT FIRST, I WAS CONVINCED HE'D FINALLY GONE OFF THE DEEP END. I MEAN, HE'S BEEN THROUGH SUCH--
--YOU SWEAR THIS IS ALL CONFIDENTIAL DOCTOR/PATIENT TALK, RIGHT?--
--SUCH DARKNESS THAT IT WAS UNFATHOMABLE TO ME THAT HAND-WAVING IT AWAY WASN'T PSYCHOTIC BEHAVIOR. MATT WOULDN'T. THAT'S NOT HIM...BUT...
...BUT MAYBE IT IS NOW, I DUNNO. IF UPBEAT MATT IS A FACADE, IT'S SHOWN NO CRACKS UNDER STRESS.
I THINK I'M ABOUT READY TO ADMIT THAT WHATEVER HE'S DOING, IT WORKS. SO WHY AM I STILL SO ON EDGE ABOUT IT?
YOU SAID IT YOURSELF LAST WEEK, MR. NELSON.
"IF YOU'RE WRONG ABOUT YOUR PARTNER..."
MATTY? MATTY, I ASKED TWELVE TIMES FOR THE BUCCHINO FILES--
GREAT. NOBODY HOME.

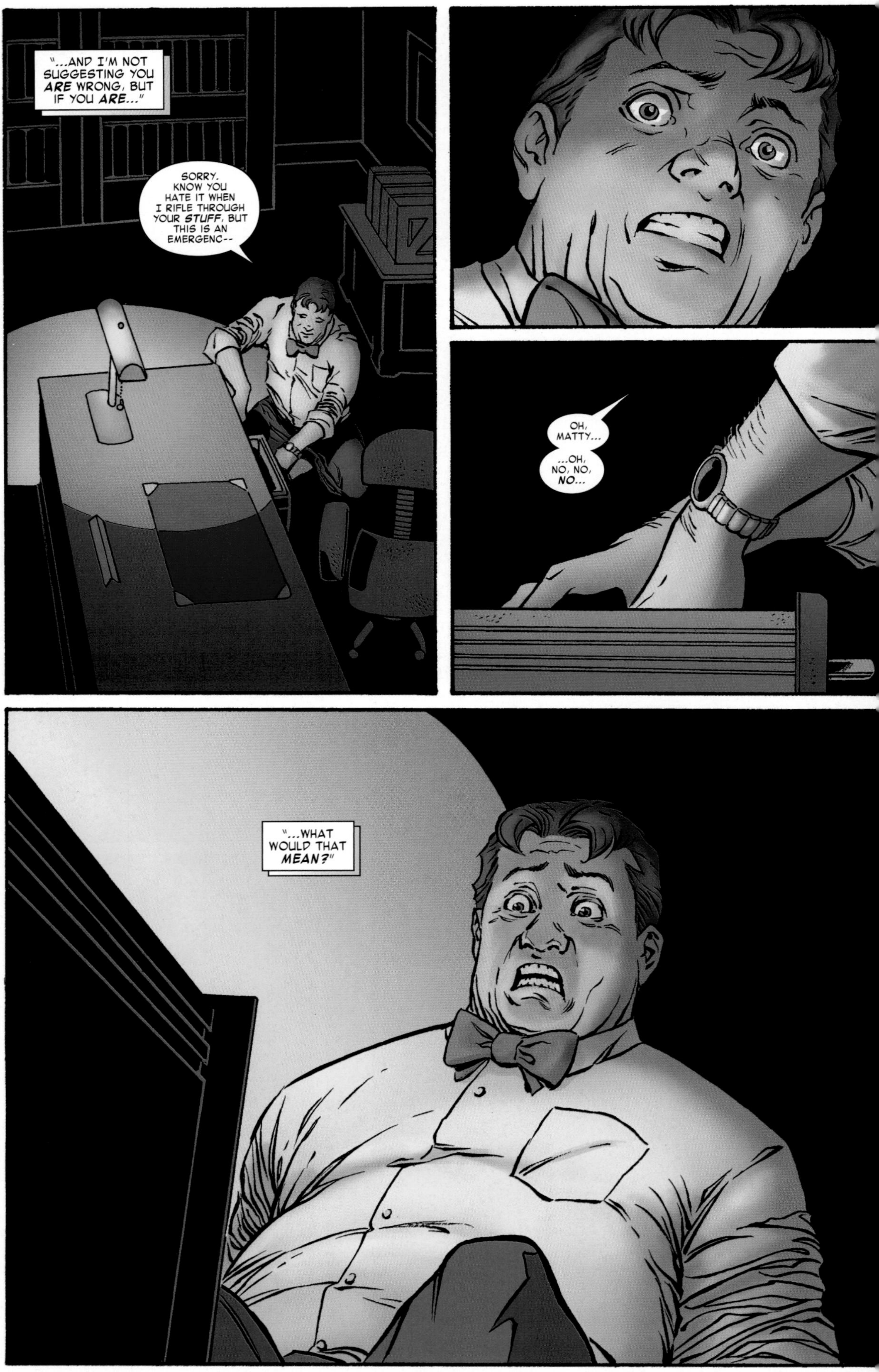
"...AND I'M NOT SUGGESTING YOU ARE WRONG, BUT IF YOU ARE..."
SORRY. KNOW YOU HATE IT WHEN I RIFLE THROUGH YOUR STUFF, BUT THIS IS AN EMERGENC--
OH, MATTY...
...OH, NO, NO, NO...
"...WHAT WOULD THAT MEAN?"

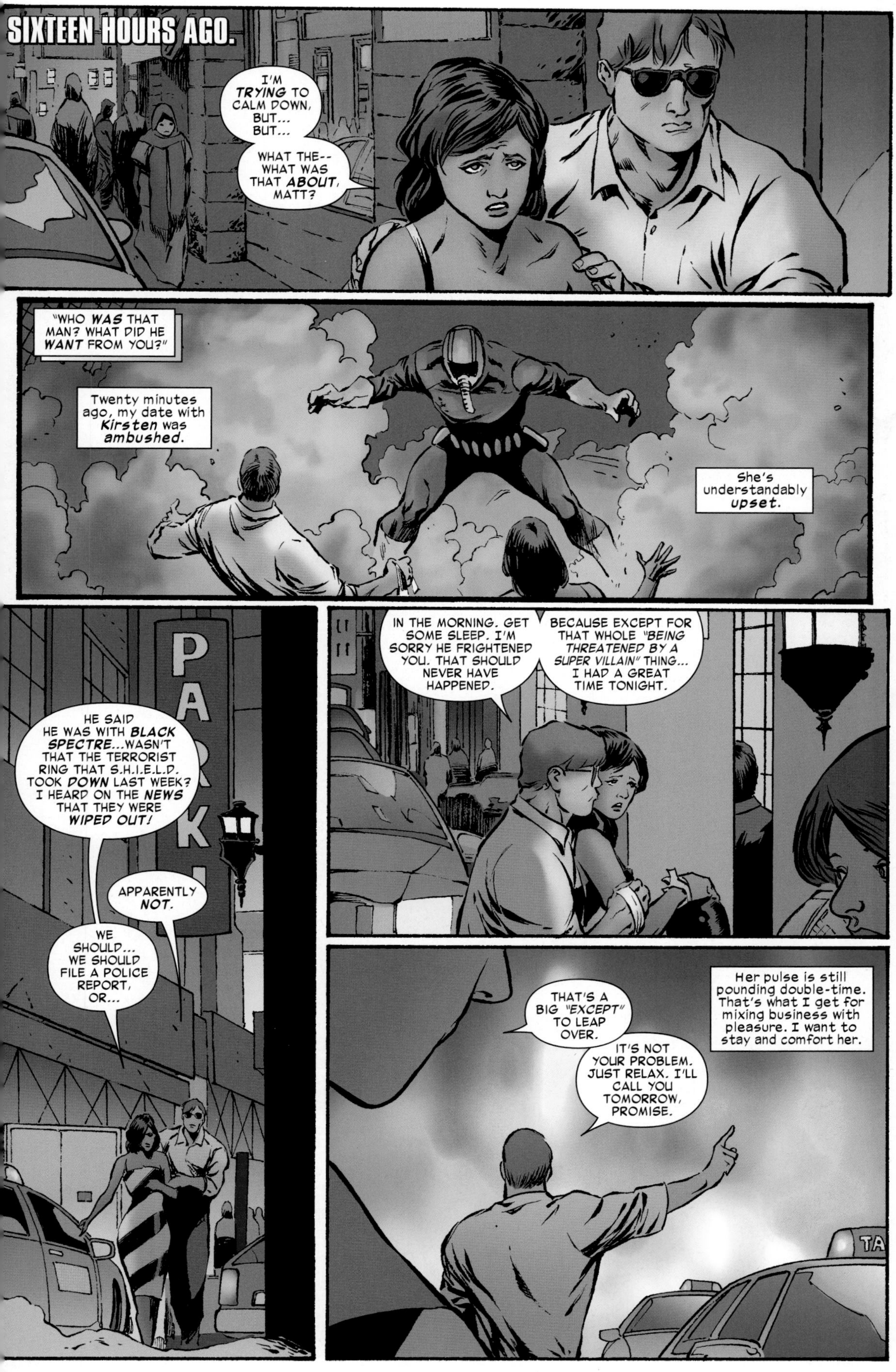
SIXTEEN HOURS AGO.
I'M TRYING TO CALM DOWN, BUT... BUT...
WHAT THE-- WHAT WAS THAT ABOUT, MATT?
"WHO WAS THAT MAN? WHAT DID HE WANT FROM YOU?"
Twenty minutes ago, my date with Kirsten was ambushed.
She's understandably upset.
HE SAID HE WAS WITH BLACK SPECTRE...WASN'T THAT THE TERRORIST RING THAT S.H.I.E.L.D. TOOK DOWN LAST WEEK? I HEARD ON THE NEWS THAT THEY WERE WIPED OUT!
APPARENTLY NOT.
WE SHOULD... WE SHOULD FILE A POLICE REPORT, OR...
PARK
BECAUSE EXCEPT FOR THAT WHOLE "BEING THREATENED BY A SUPER VILLAIN" THING... I HAD A GREAT TIME TONIGHT.
IN THE MORNING. GET SOME SLEEP. I'M SORRY HE FRIGHTENED YOU. THAT SHOULD NEVER HAVE HAPPENED.
Her pulse is still pounding double-time. That's what I get for mixing business with pleasure. I want to stay and comfort her.
THAT'S A BIG "EXCEPT" TO LEAP OVER.
IT'S NOT YOUR PROBLEM. JUST RELAX. I'LL CALL YOU TOMORROW, PROMISE.
TA

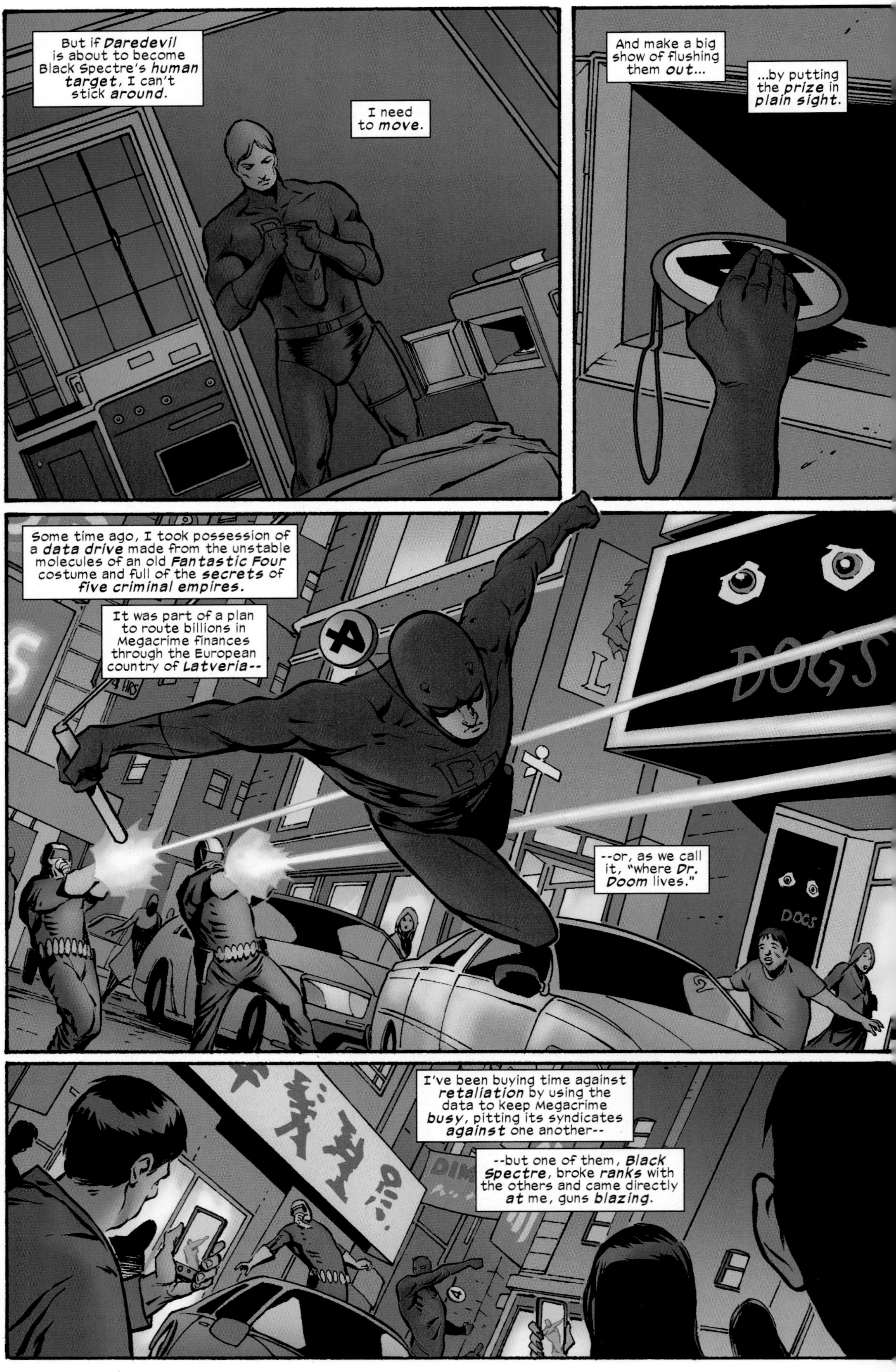
But if Daredevil is about to become Black Spectre's human target, I can't stick around.
I need to move.
And make a big show of flushing them out...
...by putting the prize in plain sight.
Some time ago, I took possession of a data drive made from the unstable molecules of an old Fantastic Four costume and full of the secrets of five criminal empires.
It was part of a plan to route billions in Megacrime finances through the European country of Latveria--
--or, as we call it, "where Dr. Doom lives."
DOGS
I've been buying time against retaliation by using the data to keep Megacrime busy, pitting its syndicates against one another--
--but one of them, Black Spectre, broke ranks with the others and came directly at me, guns blazing.

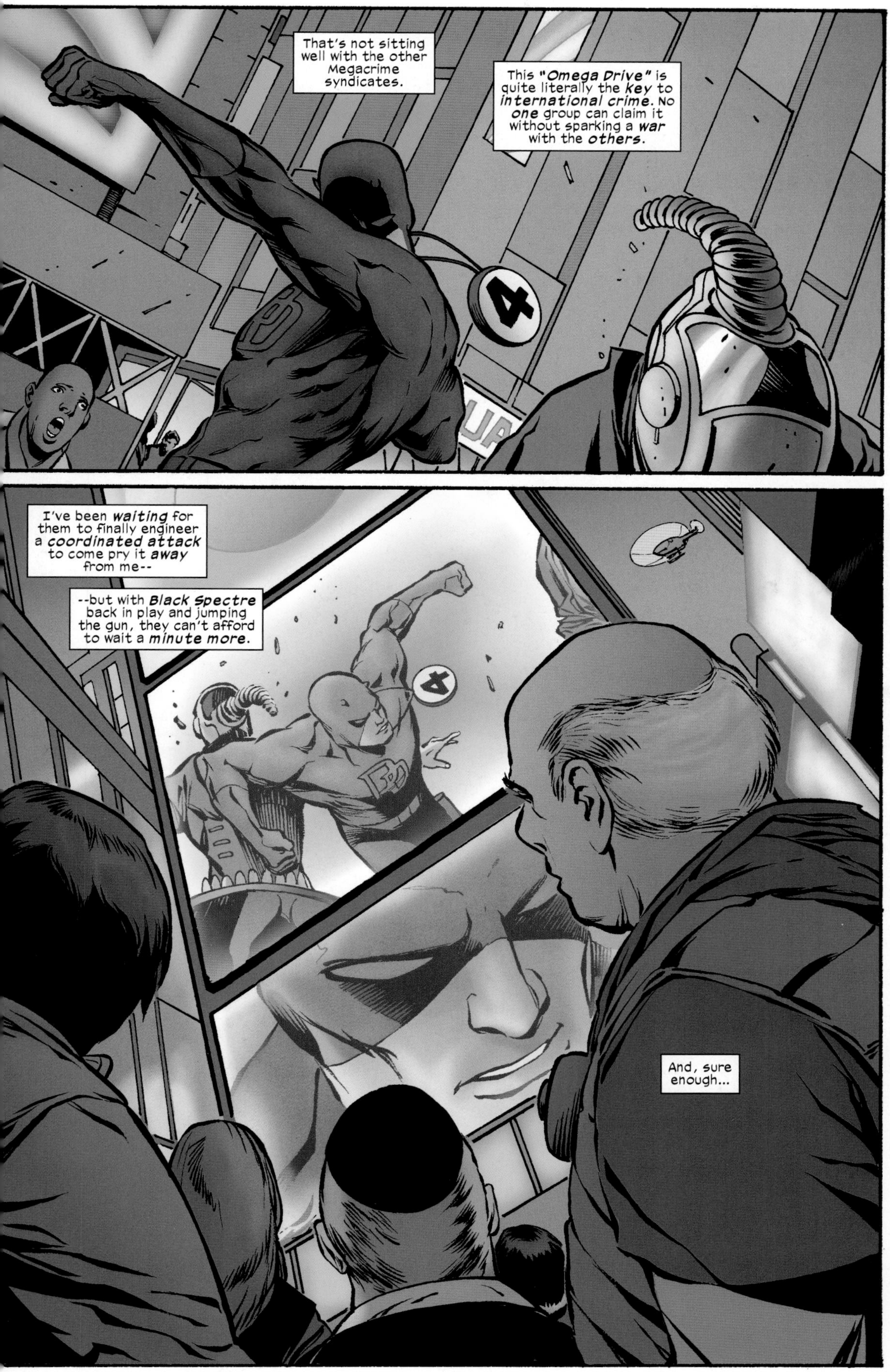

That's not sitting well with the other Megacrime syndicates.
This "*Omega Drive*" is quite literally the *key* to *international crime*. No *one* group can claim it without sparking a *war* with the *others*.
UA
I've been *waiting* for them to finally engineer a *coordinated attack* to come pry it *away* from me--
--but with *Black Spectre* back in play and jumping the gun, they can't afford to wait a *minute more*.
And, sure enough...

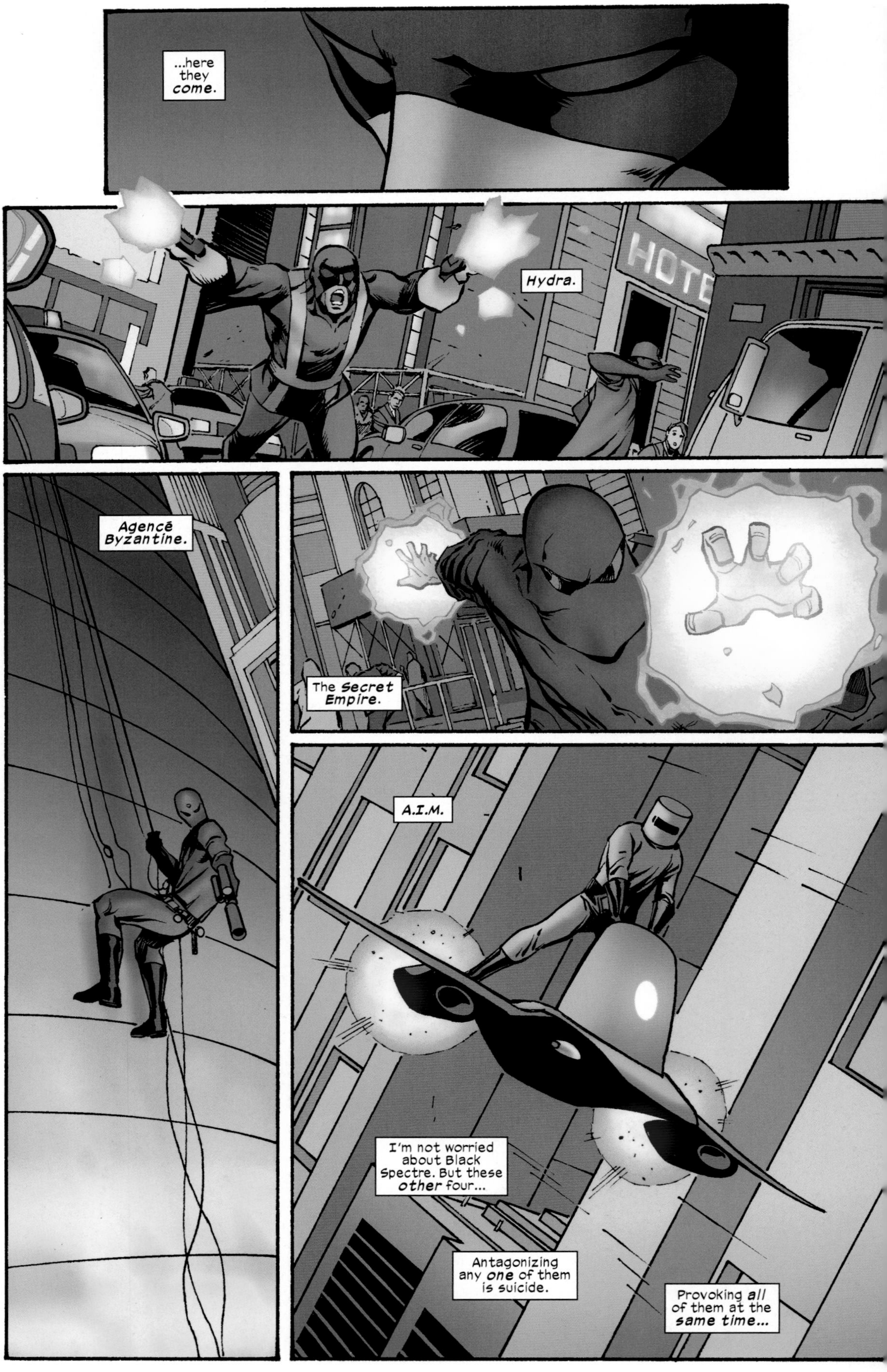
...here they come.
Hydra.
HOTE
Agencē Byzantine.
The Secret Empire.
A.I.M.
I'm not worried about Black Spectre. But these other four...
Antagonizing any one of them is suicide.
Provoking all of them at the same time...

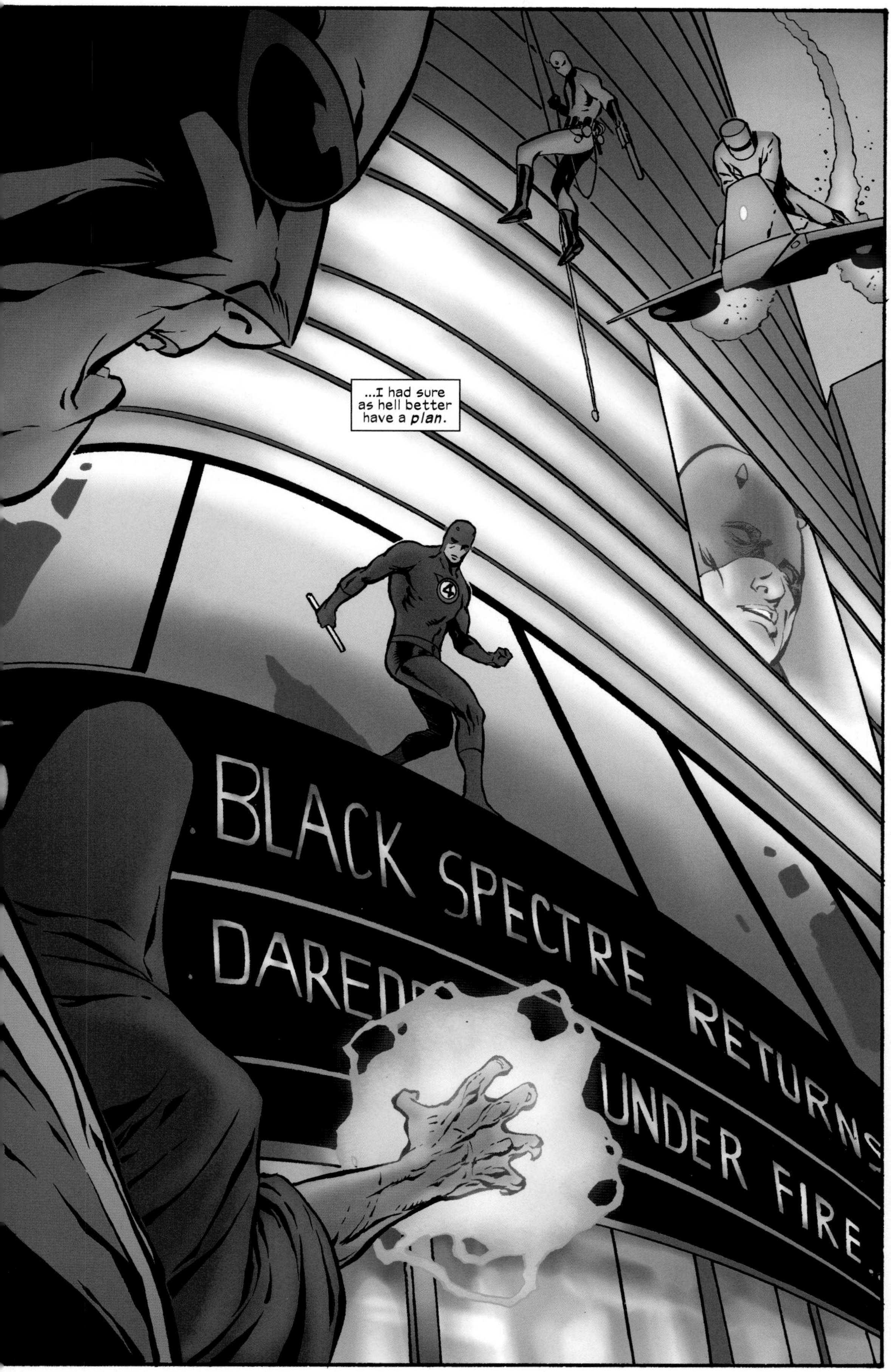
...I had sure as hell better have a *plan*.
BLACK SPECTRE RETURNS
UNDER FIRE

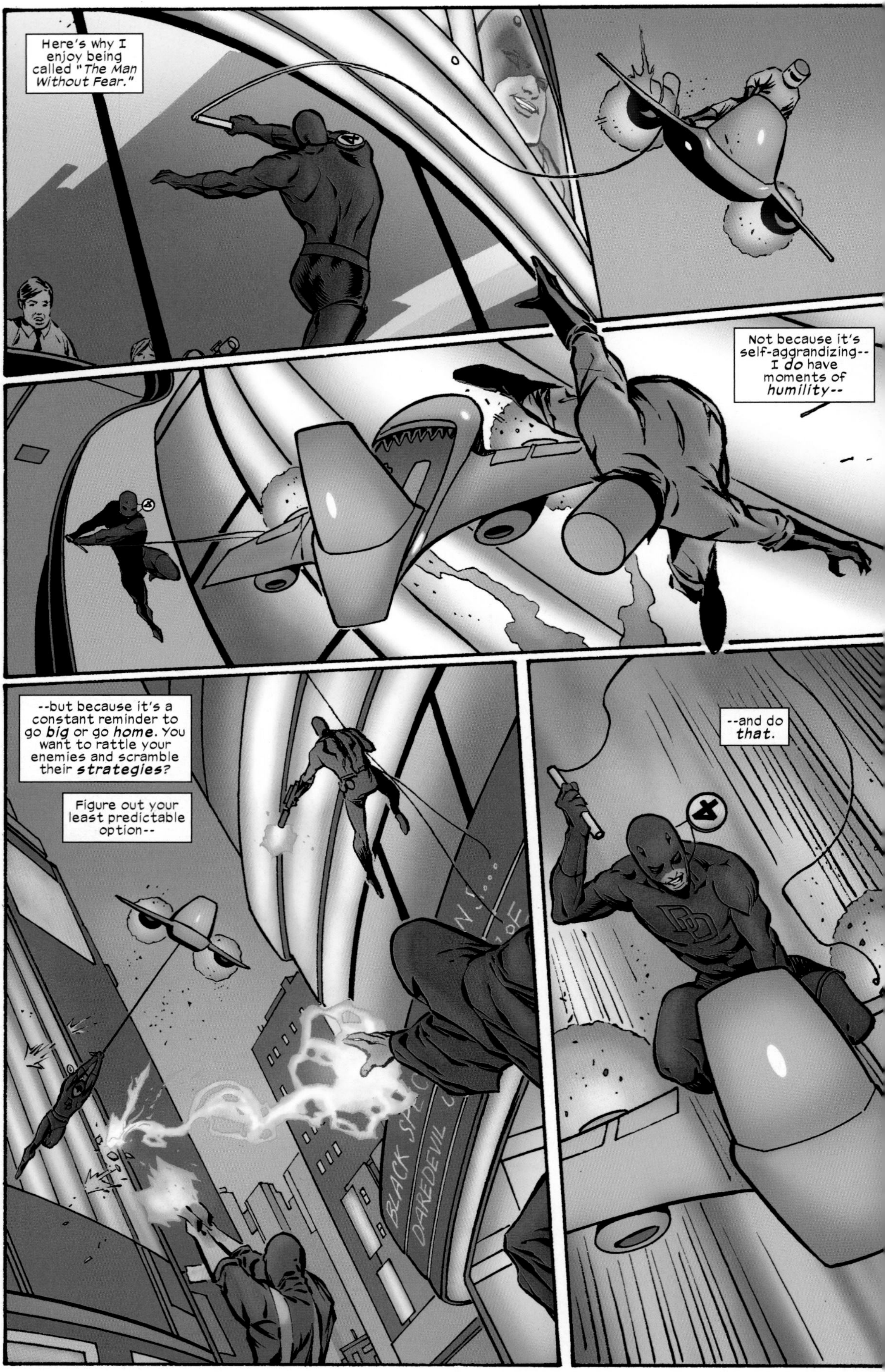
Here's why I enjoy being called "The Man Without Fear."
Not because it's self-aggrandizing-- I do have moments of humility--
--but because it's a constant reminder to go big or go home. You want to rattle your enemies and scramble their strategies?
Figure out your least predictable option--
--and do that.
BLACK SPEC
DAREDEVIL

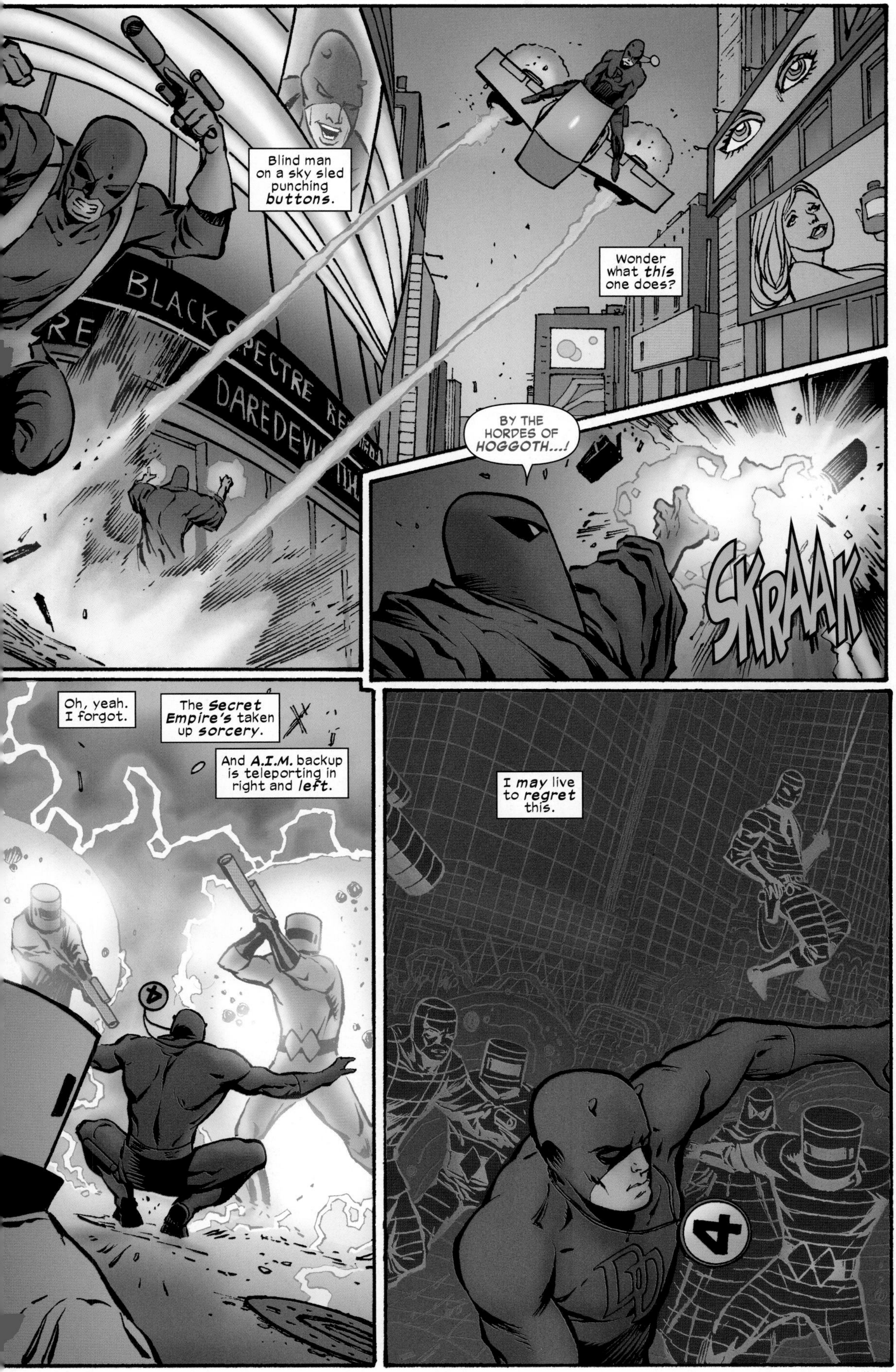

Blind man on a sky sled punching buttons.
Wonder what this one does?
BY THE HORDES OF HOGGOTH...!
SKRAAK
Oh, yeah. I forgot.
The Secret Empire's taken up sorcery.
And A.I.M. backup is teleporting in right and left.
I may live to regret this.

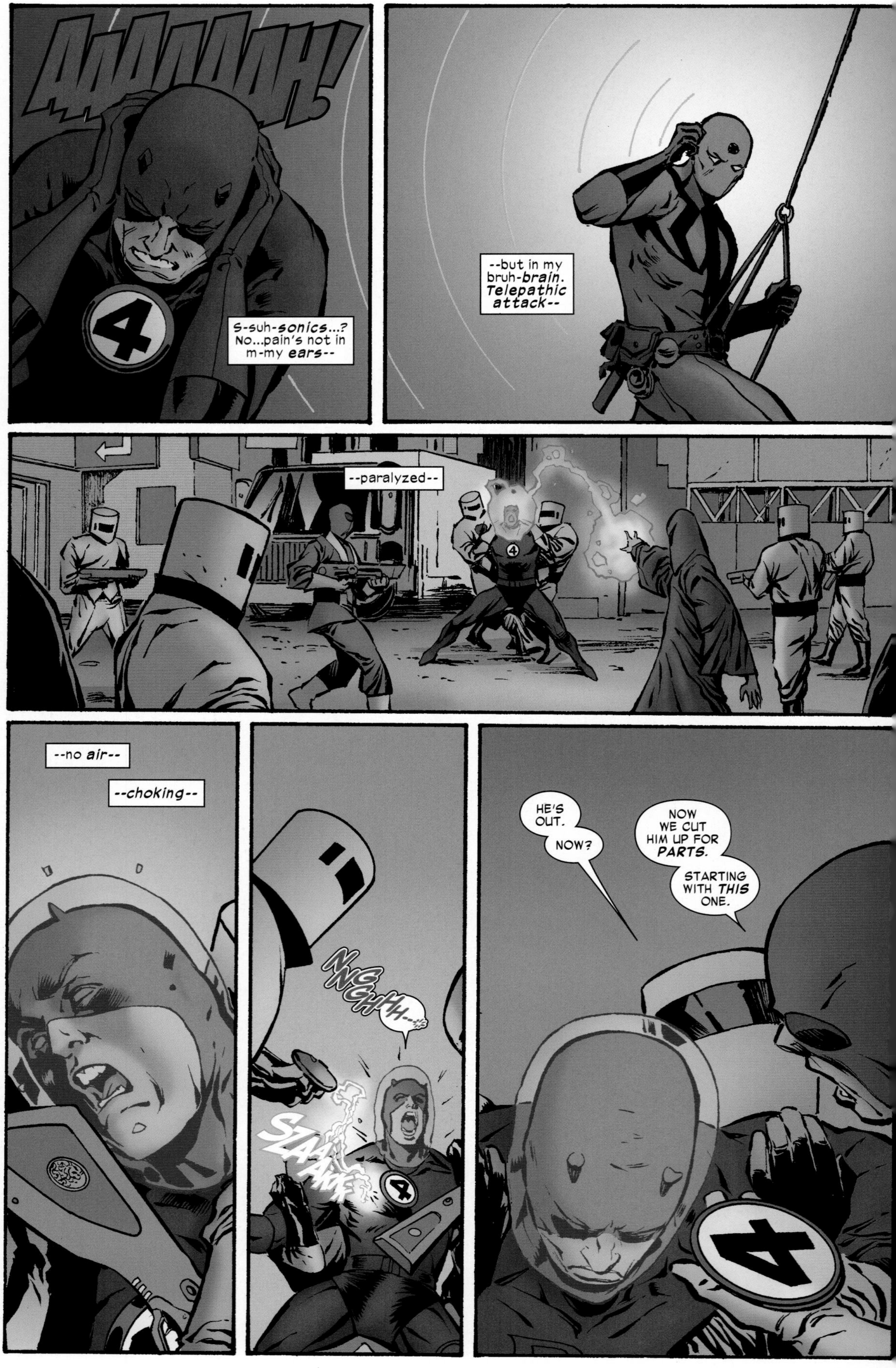
AAAAAAH!
S-suh-sonics...? No...pain's not in m-my ears--
--but in my bruh-brain. Telepathic attack--
--paralyzed--
--no air--
--choking--
NNGH NGHHH--
SZAAAKK
HE'S OUT.
NOW?
NOW WE CUT HIM UP FOR PARTS.
STARTING WITH THIS ONE.

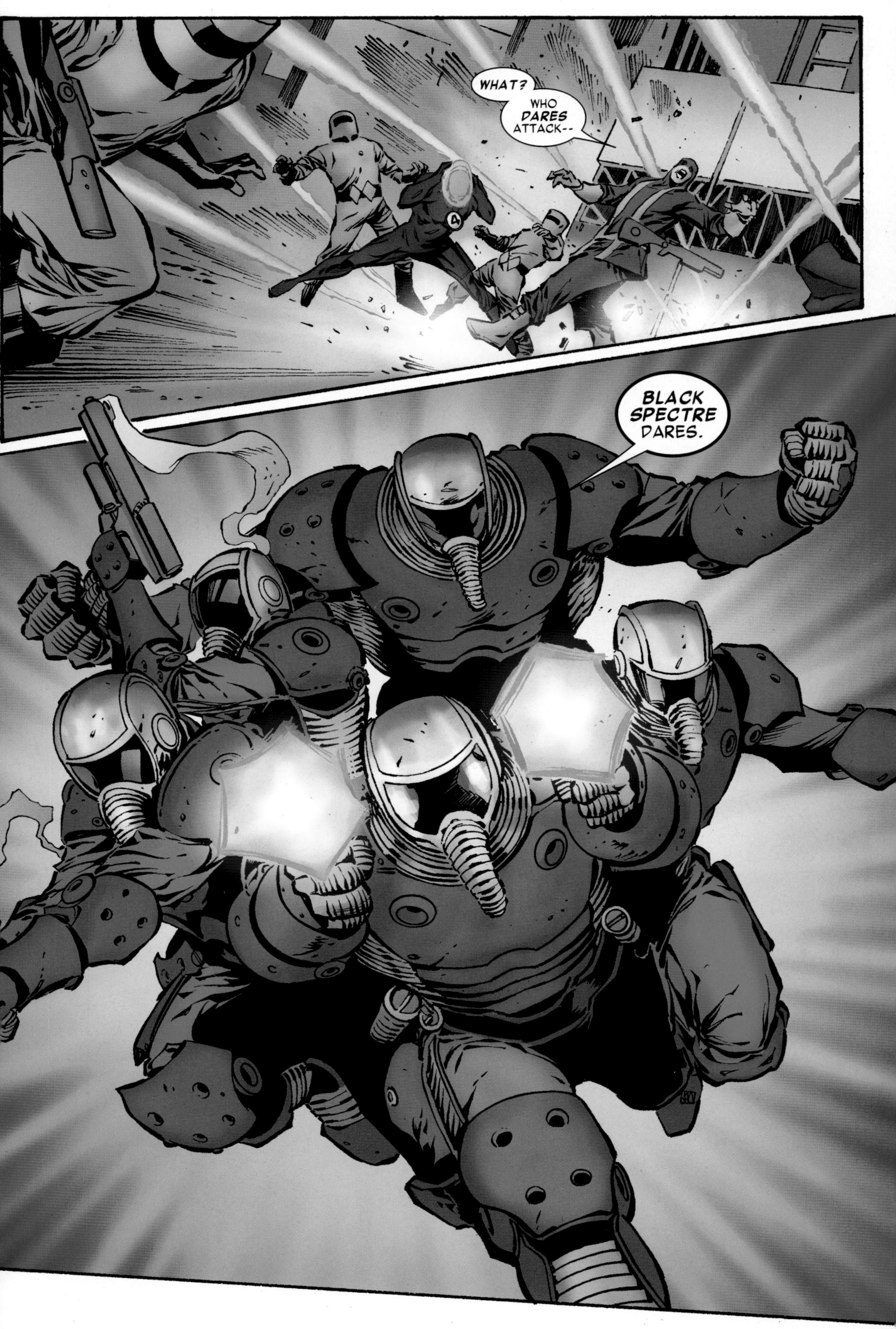
WHAT?
WHO DARES ATTACK--
BLACK SPECTRE DARES.

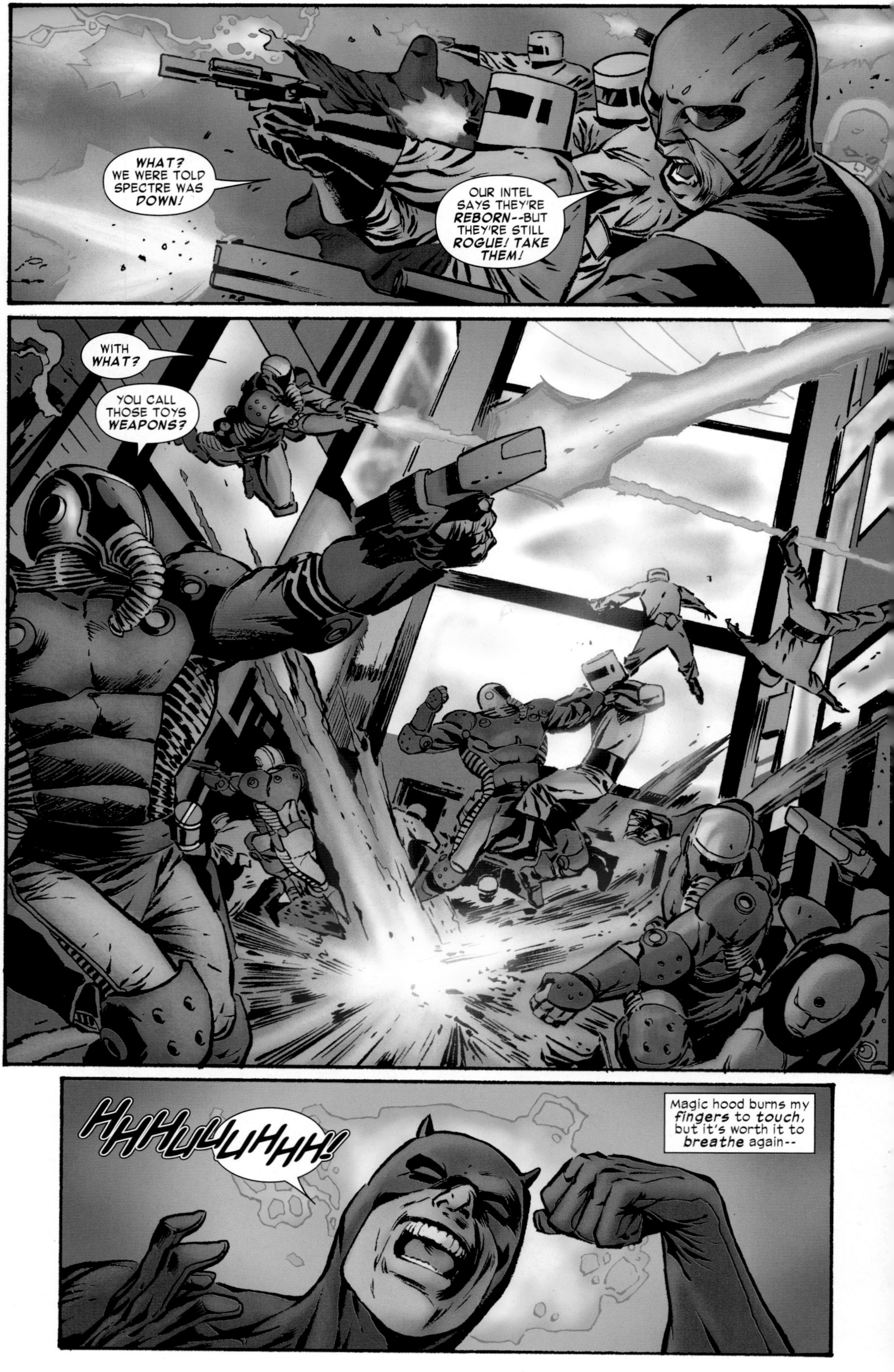
WHAT? WE WERE TOLD SPECTRE WAS DOWN!
OUR INTEL SAYS THEY'RE REBORN--BUT THEY'RE STILL ROGUE! TAKE THEM!
WITH WHAT?
YOU CALL THOSE TOYS WEAPONS?
HHHUUUUHHH!
Magic hood burns my fingers to touch, but it's worth it to breathe again--

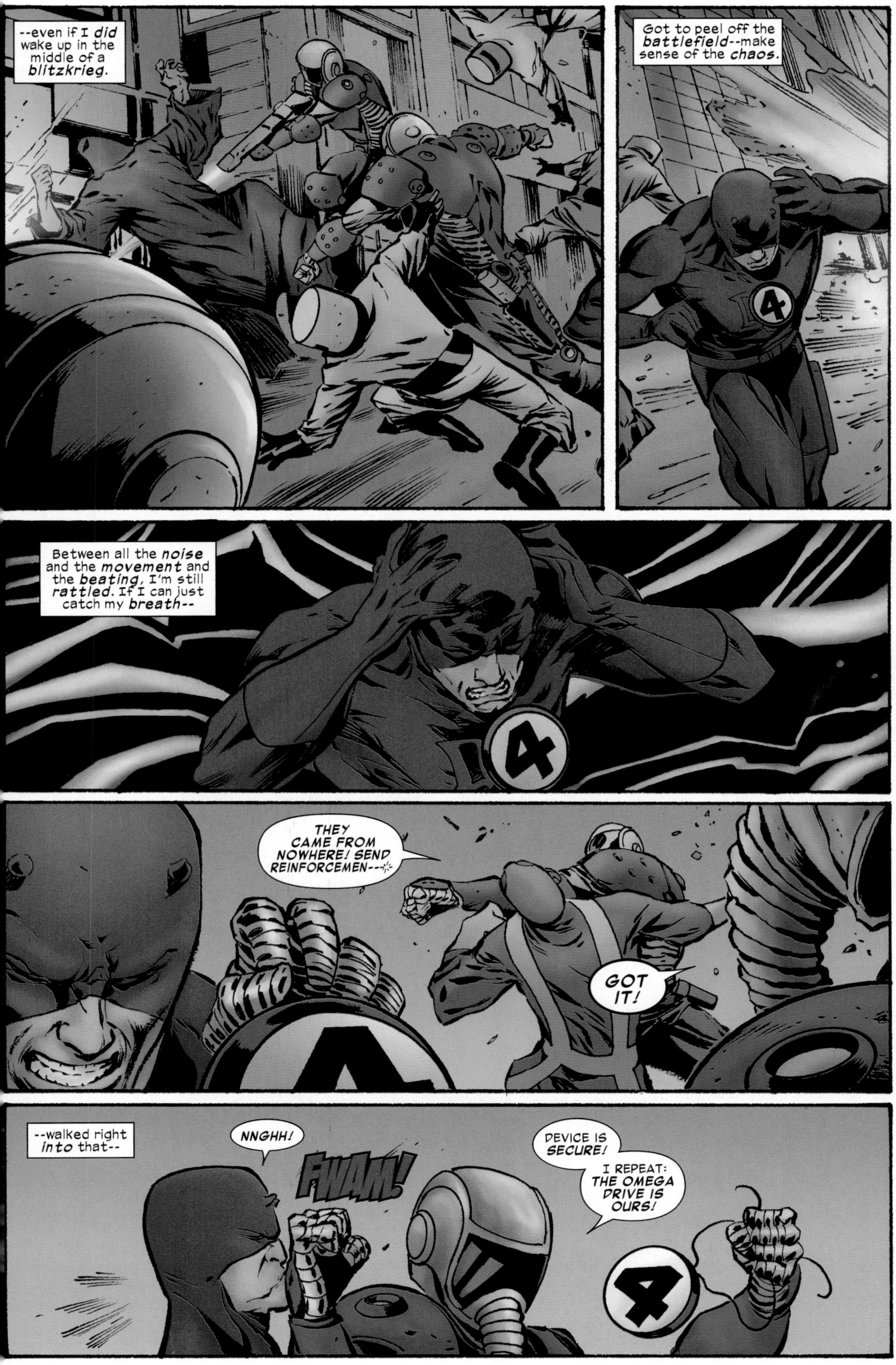
--even if I did wake up in the middle of a blitzkrieg.
Got to peel off the battlefield--make sense of the chaos.
Between all the noise and the movement and the beating, I'm still rattled. If I can just catch my breath--
THEY CAME FROM NOWHERE! SEND REINFORCEMEN---
GOT IT!
--walked right into that--
NNGHH!
FWAM!
DEVICE IS SECURE!
I REPEAT: THE OMEGA DRIVE IS OURS!

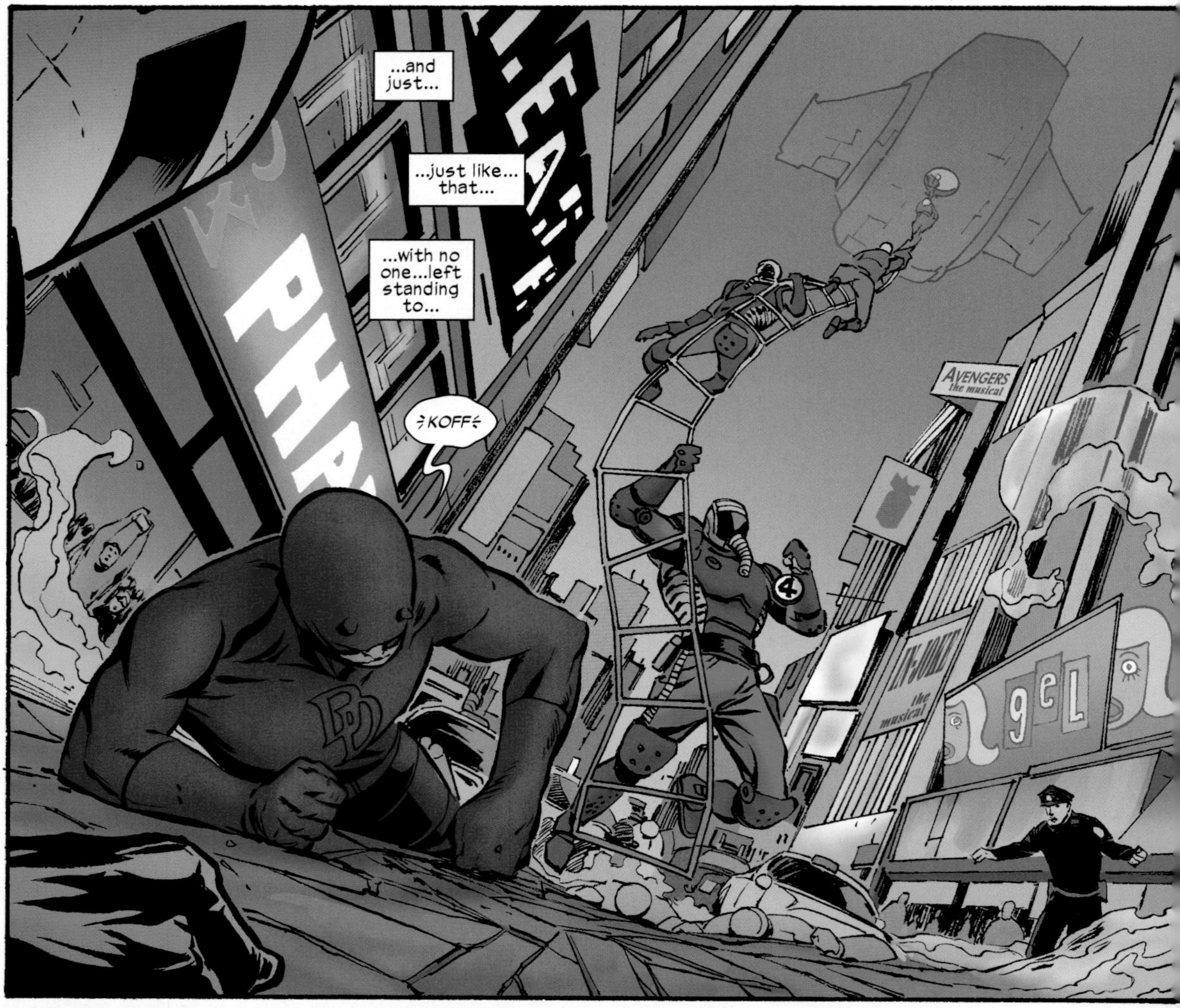
...and just...
...just like... that...
...with no one...left standing to...
KOFF
AVENGERS the musical

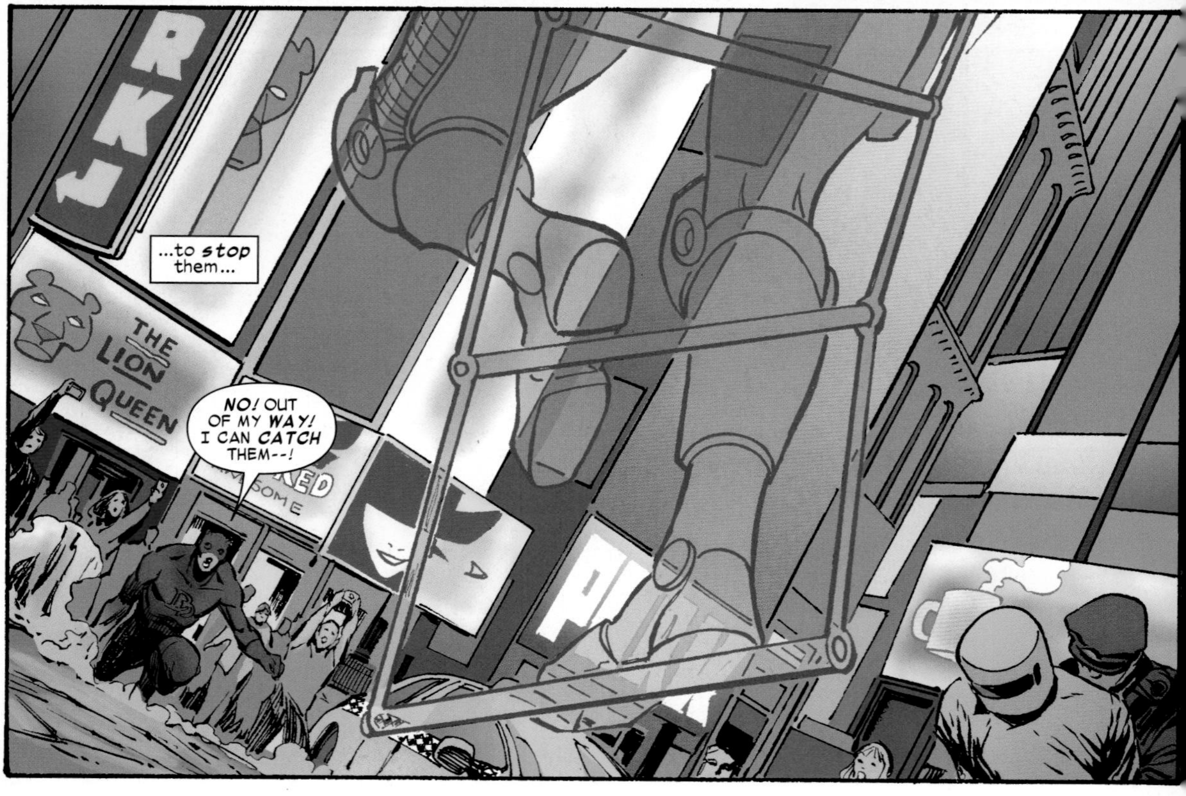
...to stop them...
THE LION QUEEN
NO! OUT OF MY WAY! I CAN CATCH THEM--!

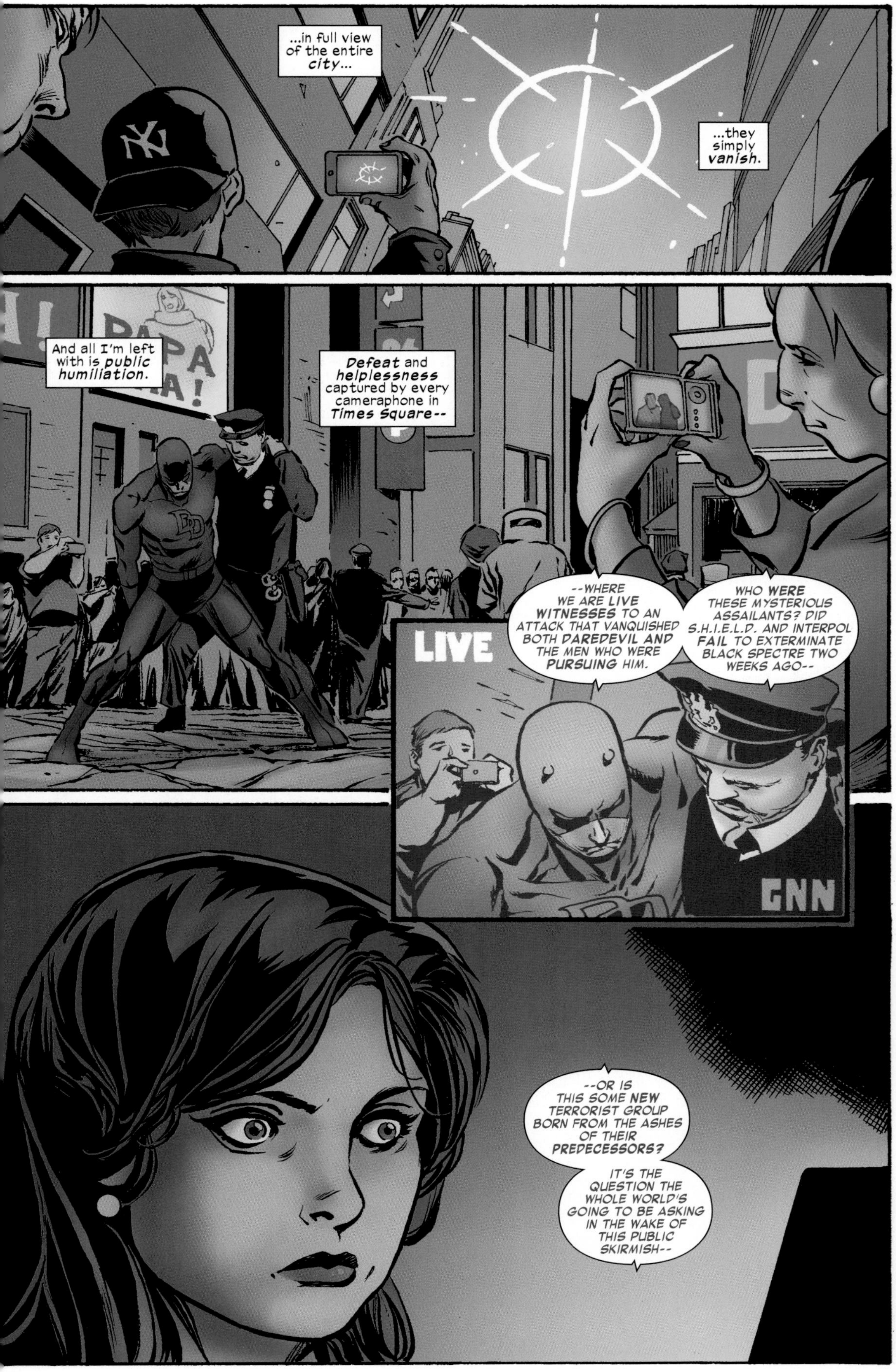

...in full view of the entire city...
...they simply vanish.
And all I'm left with is public humiliation.
Defeat and helplessness captured by every cameraphone in Times Square--
LIVE
--WHERE WE ARE LIVE WITNESSES TO AN ATTACK THAT VANQUISHED BOTH DAREDEVIL AND THE MEN WHO WERE PURSUING HIM.
WHO WERE THESE MYSTERIOUS ASSAILANTS? DID S.H.I.E.L.D. AND INTERPOL FAIL TO EXTERMINATE BLACK SPECTRE TWO WEEKS AGO--
GNN
--OR IS THIS SOME NEW TERRORIST GROUP BORN FROM THE ASHES OF THEIR PREDECESSORS?
IT'S THE QUESTION THE WHOLE WORLD'S GOING TO BE ASKING IN THE WAKE OF THIS PUBLIC SKIRMISH--

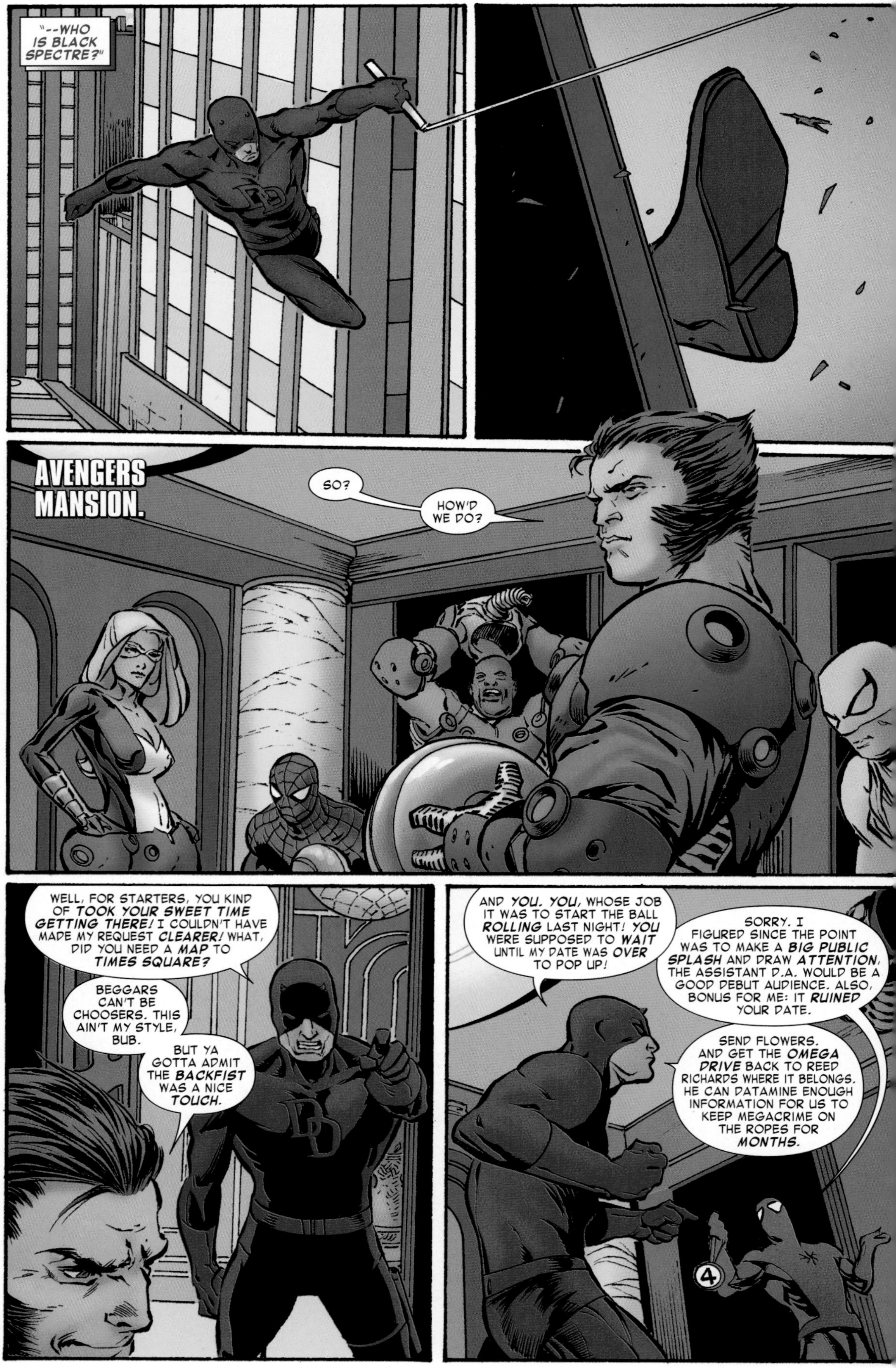
"--WHO IS BLACK SPECTRE?"
AVENGERS MANSION.
SO?
HOW'D WE DO?
WELL, FOR STARTERS, YOU KIND OF TOOK YOUR SWEET TIME GETTING THERE! I COULDN'T HAVE MADE MY REQUEST CLEARER! WHAT, DID YOU NEED A MAP TO TIMES SQUARE?
BEGGARS CAN'T BE CHOOSERS. THIS AIN'T MY STYLE, BUB.
BUT YA GOTTA ADMIT THE BACKFIST WAS A NICE TOUCH.
AND YOU. YOU, WHOSE JOB IT WAS TO START THE BALL ROLLING LAST NIGHT! YOU WERE SUPPOSED TO WAIT UNTIL MY DATE WAS OVER TO POP UP!
SORRY. I FIGURED SINCE THE POINT WAS TO MAKE A BIG PUBLIC SPLASH AND DRAW ATTENTION, THE ASSISTANT D.A. WOULD BE A GOOD DEBUT AUDIENCE. ALSO, BONUS FOR ME: IT RUINED YOUR DATE.
SEND FLOWERS. AND GET THE OMEGA DRIVE BACK TO REED RICHARDS WHERE IT BELONGS. HE CAN DATAMINE ENOUGH INFORMATION FOR US TO KEEP MEGACRIME ON THE ROPES FOR MONTHS.

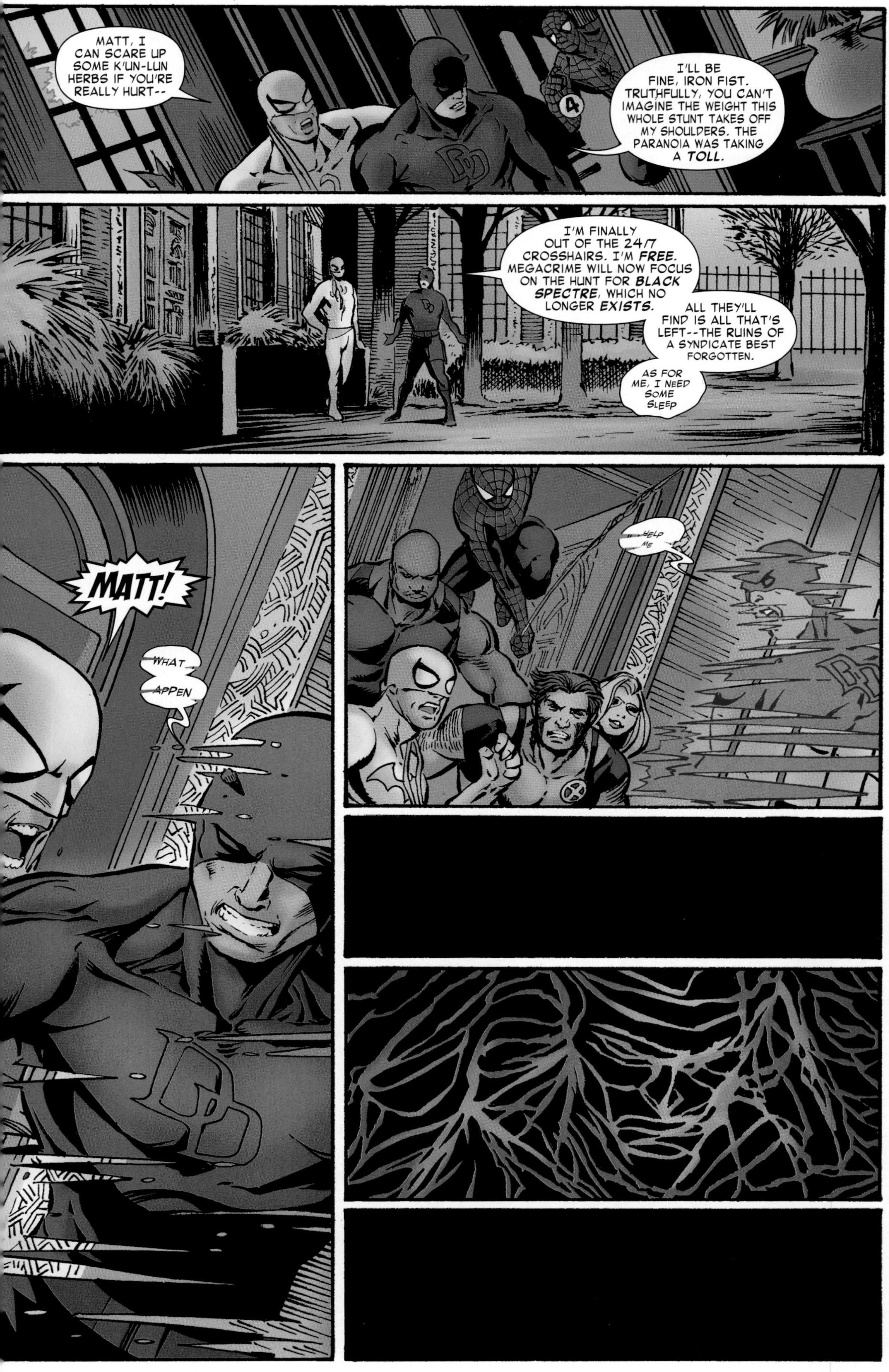
MATT, I CAN SCARE UP SOME K'UN-LUN HERBS IF YOU'RE REALLY HURT--
I'LL BE FINE, IRON FIST. TRUTHFULLY, YOU CAN'T IMAGINE THE WEIGHT THIS WHOLE STUNT TAKES OFF MY SHOULDERS. THE PARANOIA WAS TAKING A TOLL.
I'M FINALLY OUT OF THE 24/7 CROSSHAIRS. I'M FREE. MEGACRIME WILL NOW FOCUS ON THE HUNT FOR BLACK SPECTRE, WHICH NO LONGER EXISTS.
ALL THEY'LL FIND IS ALL THAT'S LEFT--THE RUINS OF A SYNDICATE BEST FORGOTTEN.
AS FOR ME, I NEED SOME SLEEP
MATT!
WHAT
APPEN
HELP
ME

[redacted]

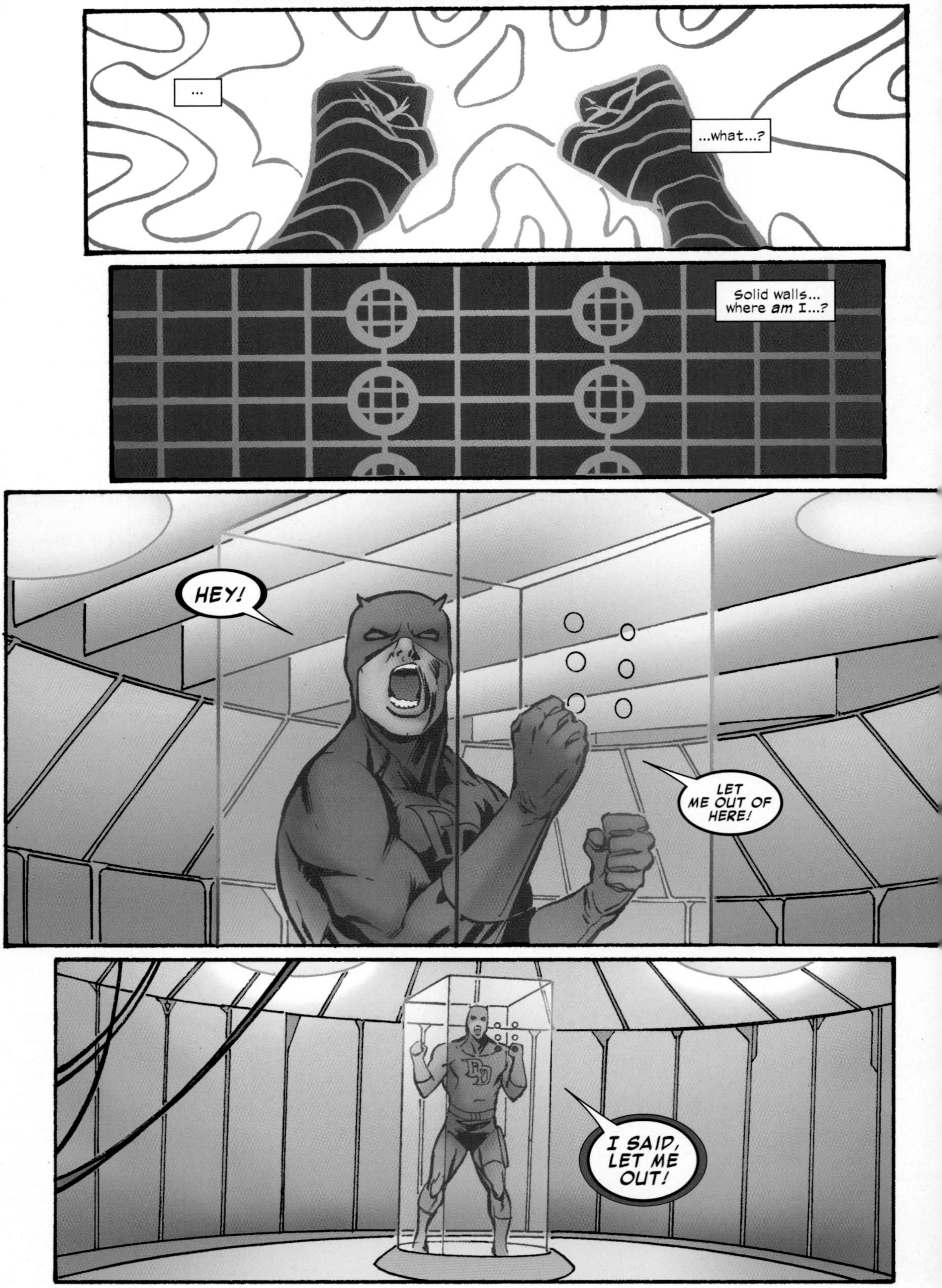
...
...what...?
Solid walls... where am I...?
HEY!
LET ME OUT OF HERE!
I SAID, LET ME OUT!

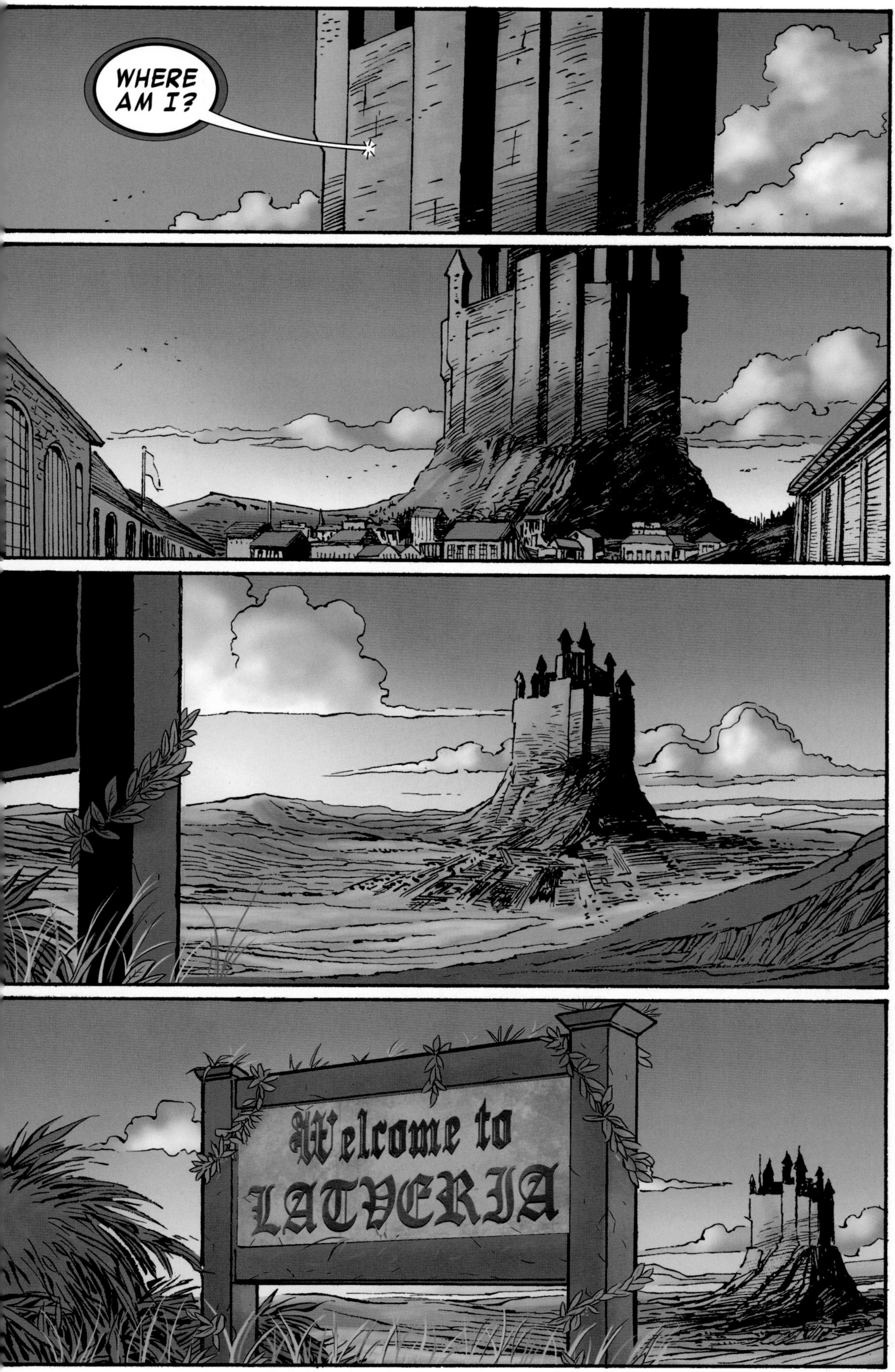
WHERE AM I?
Welcome to LATVERIA

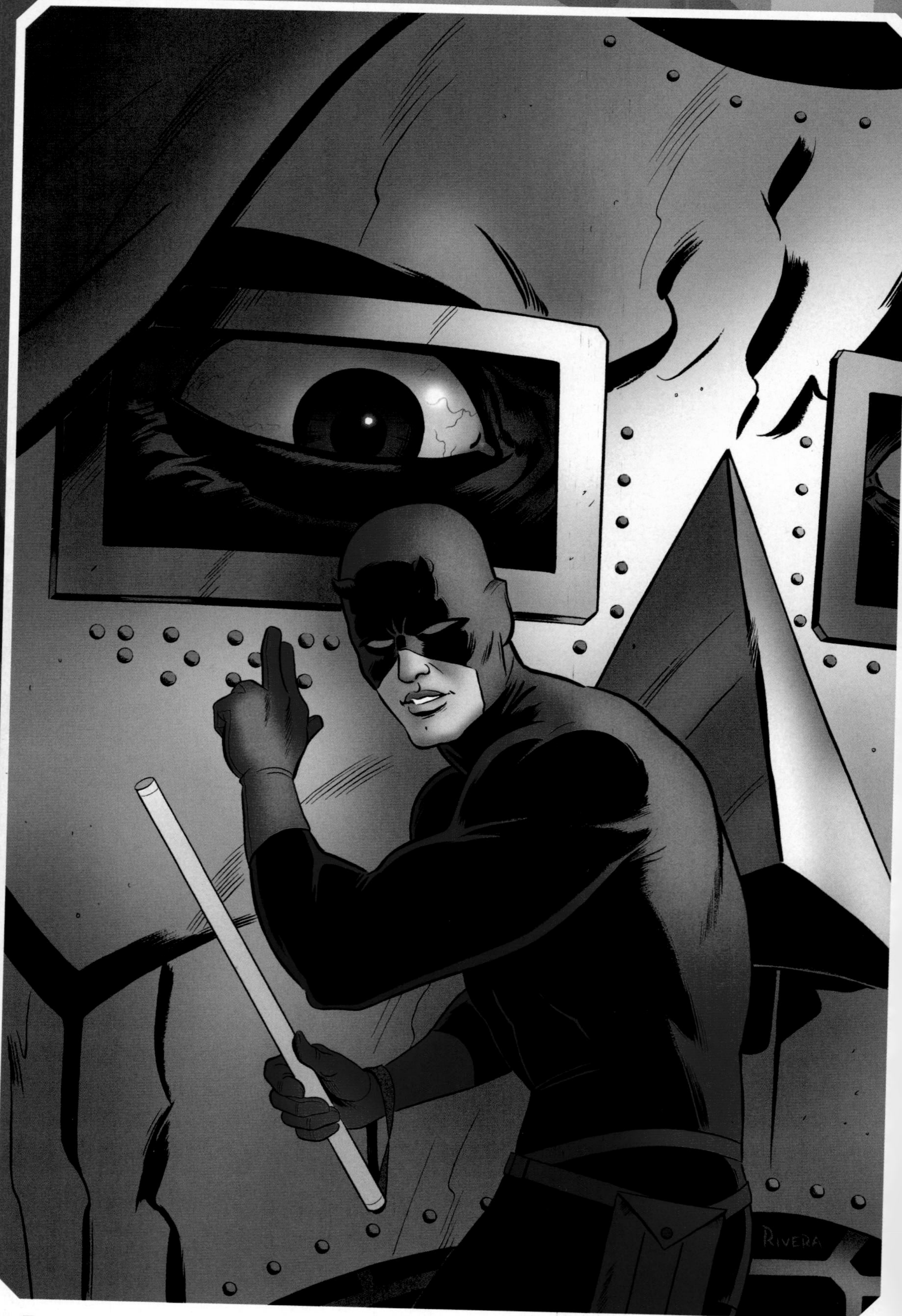
RIVERA

DAREDEVIL #14

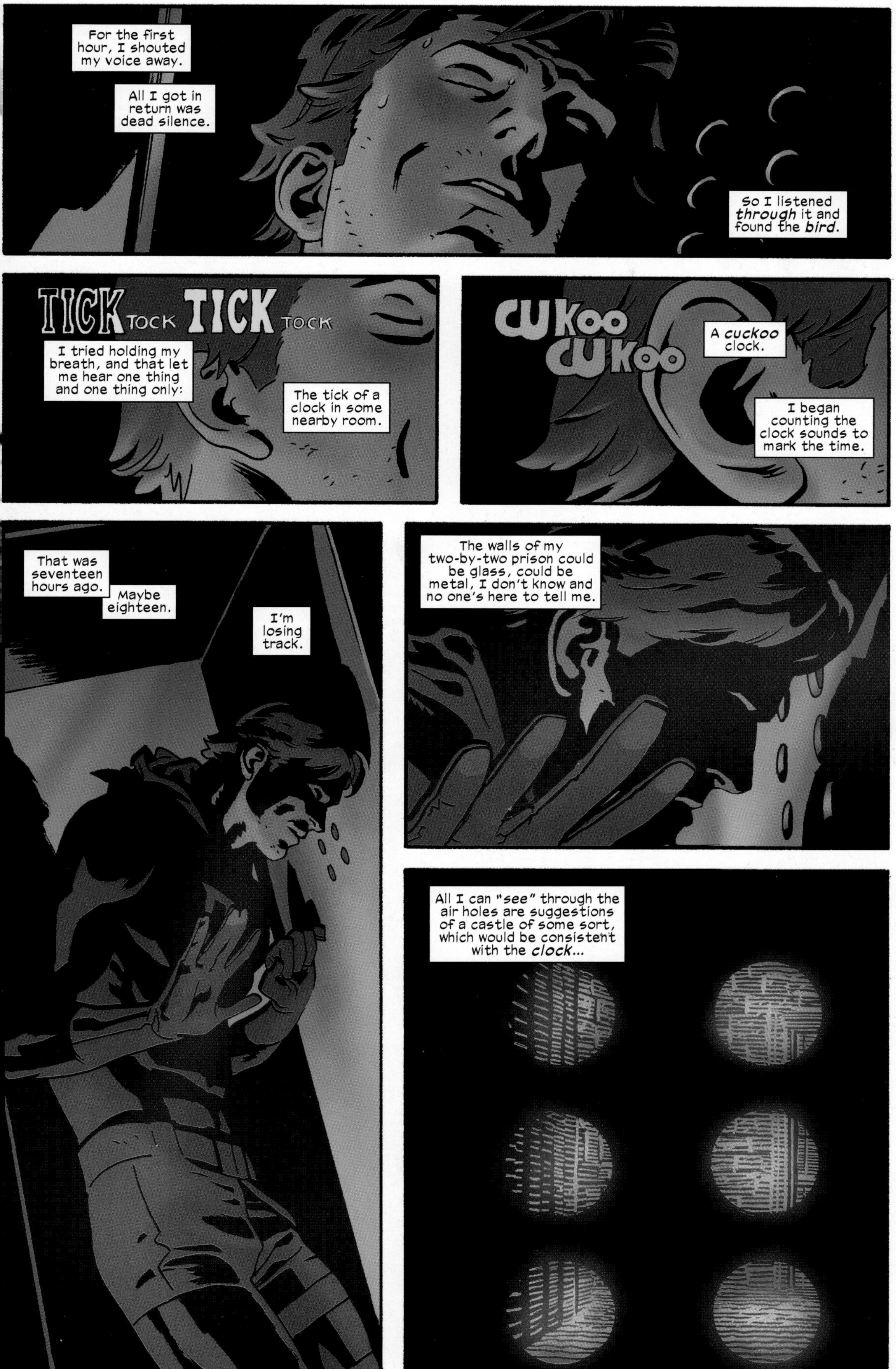
For the first hour, I shouted my voice away.
All I got in return was dead silence.
So I listened *through* it and found the *bird*.
TICK TOCK TICK TOCK
I tried holding my breath, and that let me hear one thing and one thing only:
The tick of a clock in some nearby room.
CUKOO CUKOO
A *cuckoo* clock.
I began counting the clock sounds to mark the time.
That was seventeen hours ago.
Maybe eighteen.
I'm losing track.
The walls of my two-by-two prison could be glass, could be metal, I don't know and no one's here to tell me.
All I can "*see*" through the air holes are suggestions of a castle of some sort, which would be consistent with the *clock*...

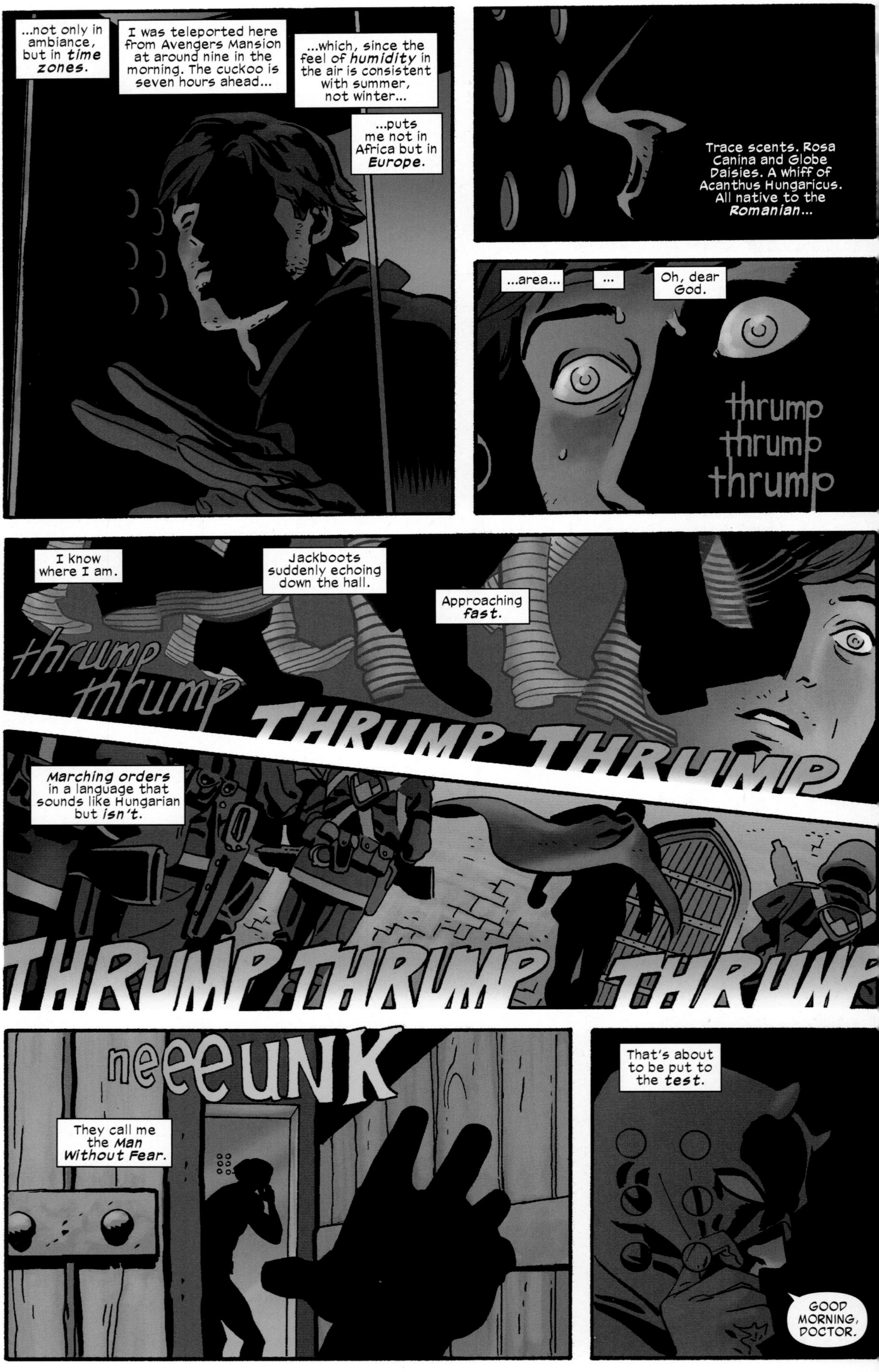
...not only in ambiance, but in *time zones*.
I was teleported here from Avengers Mansion at around nine in the morning. The cuckoo is seven hours ahead...
...which, since the feel of *humidity* in the air is consistent with summer, not winter...
...puts me not in Africa but in *Europe*.
Trace scents. Rosa Canina and Globe Daisies. A whiff of Acanthus Hungaricus. All native to the *Romanian*...
...area...
...
Oh, dear God.
thrump thrump thrump
I know where I am.
Jackboots suddenly echoing down the hall.
Approaching *fast*.
thrump thrump
THRUMP THRUMP
Marching orders in a language that sounds like Hungarian but *isn't*.
THRUMP THRUMP THRUMP
neeeeUNK
They call me the *Man Without Fear*.
That's about to be put to the *test*.
GOOD MORNING, DOCTOR.

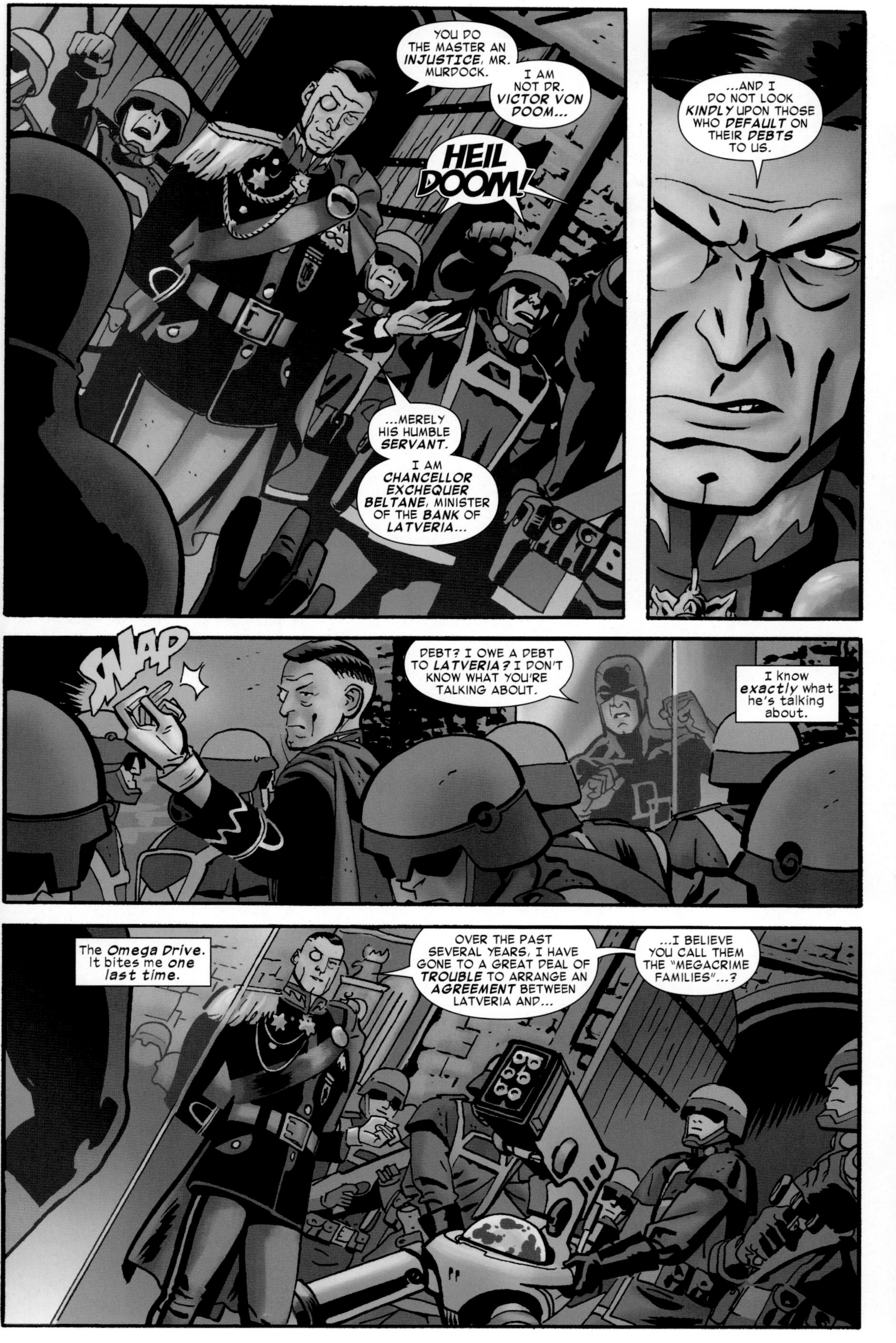
YOU DO THE MASTER AN INJUSTICE, MR. MURDOCK.
I AM NOT DR. VICTOR VON DOOM...
HEIL DOOM!
...MERELY HIS HUMBLE SERVANT.
I AM CHANCELLOR EXCHEQUER BELTANE, MINISTER OF THE BANK OF LATVERIA...
...AND I DO NOT LOOK KINDLY UPON THOSE WHO DEFAULT ON THEIR DEBTS TO US.
SNAP
DEBT? I OWE A DEBT TO LATVERIA? I DON'T KNOW WHAT YOU'RE TALKING ABOUT.
I know exactly what he's talking about.
The Omega Drive. It bites me one last time.
OVER THE PAST SEVERAL YEARS, I HAVE GONE TO A GREAT DEAL OF TROUBLE TO ARRANGE AN AGREEMENT BETWEEN LATVERIA AND...
...I BELIEVE YOU CALL THEM THE "MEGACRIME FAMILIES"...?

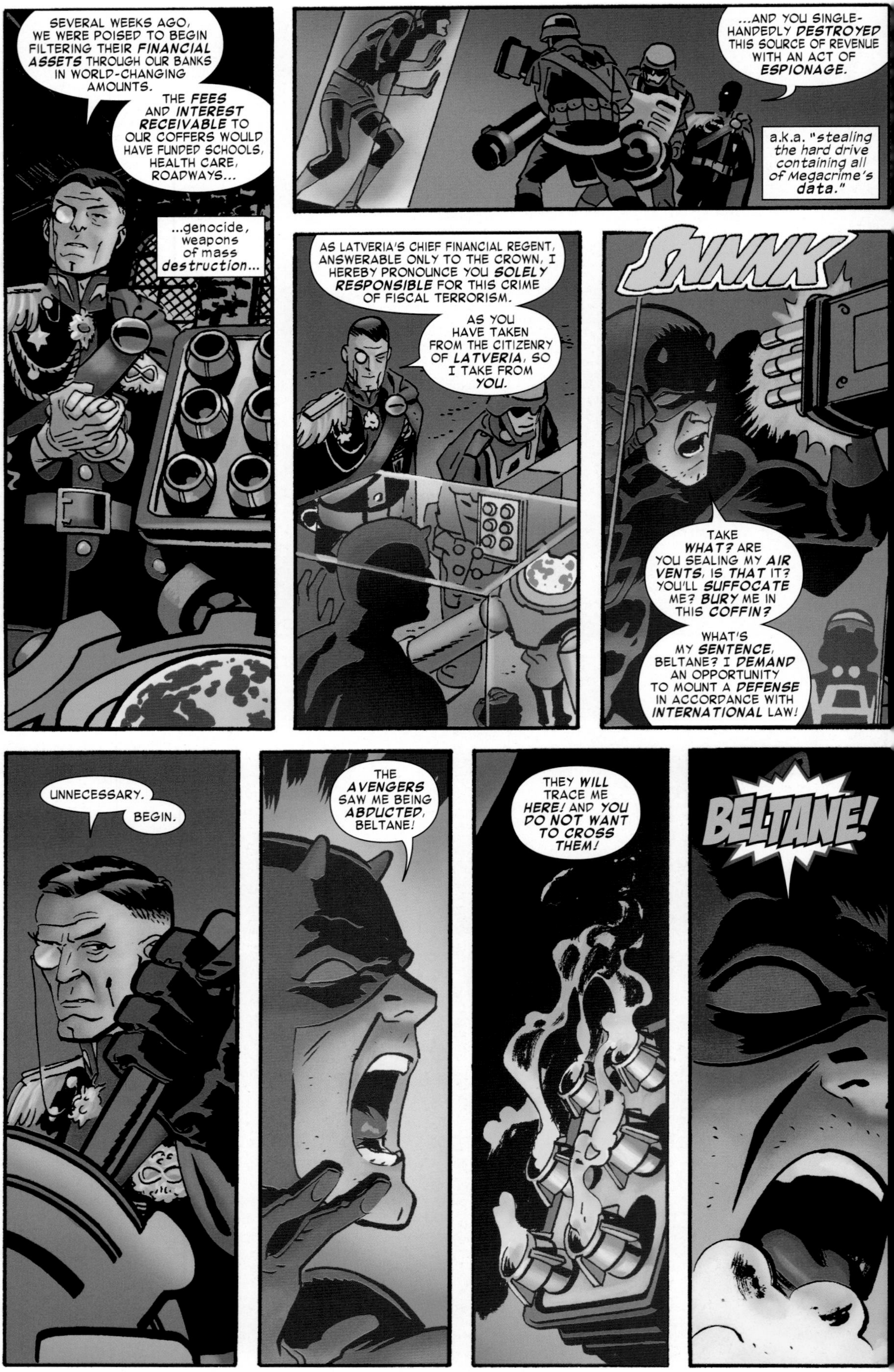
SEVERAL WEEKS AGO, WE WERE POISED TO BEGIN FILTERING THEIR FINANCIAL ASSETS THROUGH OUR BANKS IN WORLD-CHANGING AMOUNTS.
THE FEES AND INTEREST RECEIVABLE TO OUR COFFERS WOULD HAVE FUNDED SCHOOLS, HEALTH CARE, ROADWAYS...
...genocide, weapons of mass destruction...
...AND YOU SINGLE-HANDEDLY DESTROYED THIS SOURCE OF REVENUE WITH AN ACT OF ESPIONAGE.
a.k.a. "stealing the hard drive containing all of Megacrime's data."
AS LATVERIA'S CHIEF FINANCIAL REGENT, ANSWERABLE ONLY TO THE CROWN, I HEREBY PRONOUNCE YOU SOLELY RESPONSIBLE FOR THIS CRIME OF FISCAL TERRORISM.
AS YOU HAVE TAKEN FROM THE CITIZENRY OF LATVERIA, SO I TAKE FROM YOU.
SNNNK
TAKE WHAT? ARE YOU SEALING MY AIR VENTS, IS THAT IT? YOU'LL SUFFOCATE ME? BURY ME IN THIS COFFIN?
WHAT'S MY SENTENCE, BELTANE? I DEMAND AN OPPORTUNITY TO MOUNT A DEFENSE IN ACCORDANCE WITH INTERNATIONAL LAW!
UNNECESSARY.
BEGIN.
THE AVENGERS SAW ME BEING ABDUCTED, BELTANE!
THEY WILL TRACE ME HERE! AND YOU DO NOT WANT TO CROSS THEM!
BELTANE!

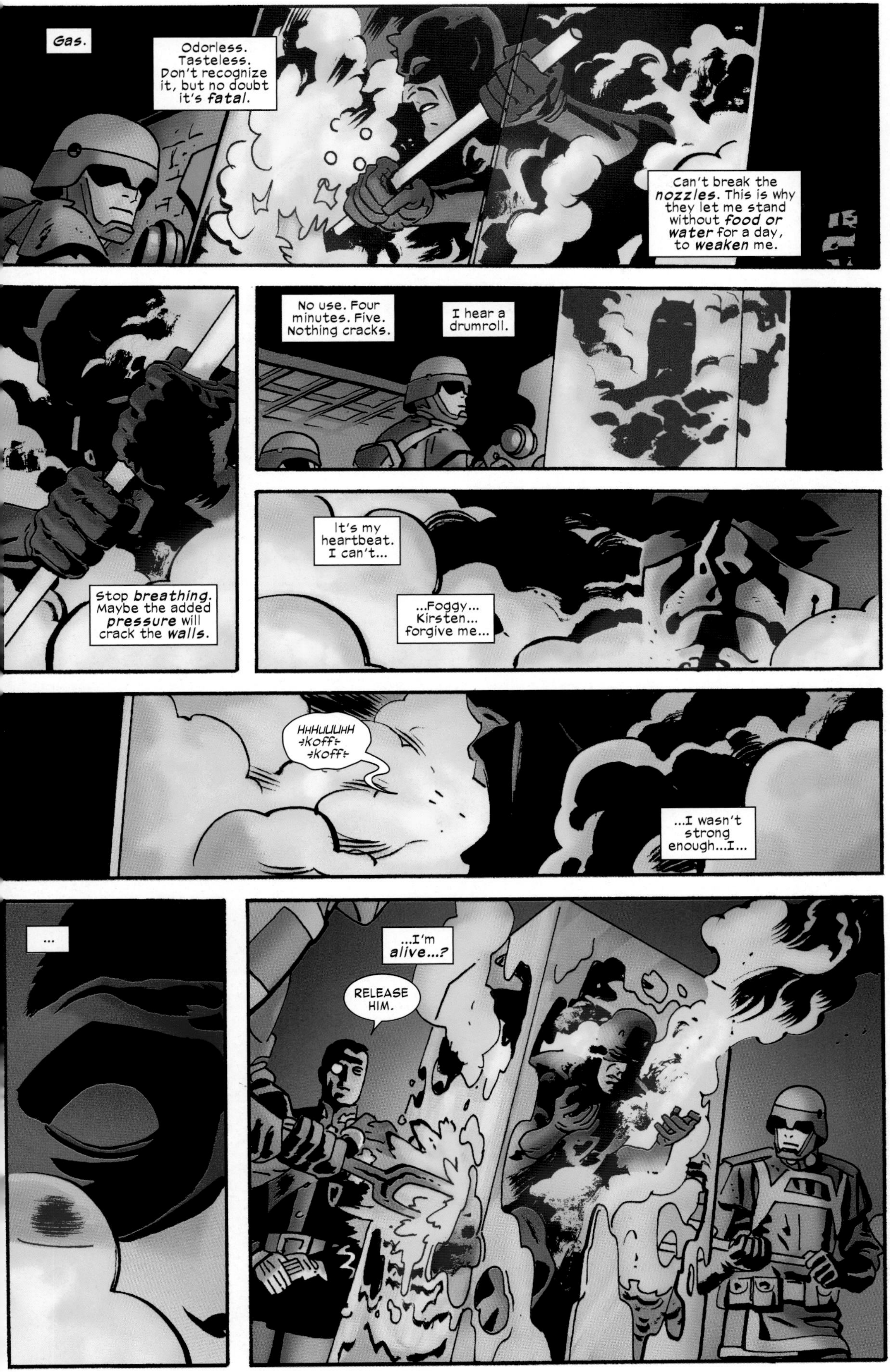
Gas.
Odorless. Tasteless. Don't recognize it, but no doubt it's *fatal*.
Can't break the *nozzles*. This is why they let me stand without *food or water* for a day, to *weaken* me.
Stop *breathing*. Maybe the added *pressure* will crack the *walls*.
No use. Four minutes. Five. Nothing cracks.
I hear a drumroll.
It's my heartbeat. I can't...
...Foggy... Kirsten... forgive me...
HHHUUUHH *koff* *koff*
...I wasn't strong enough...I...
...
...I'm *alive*...?
RELEASE HIM.

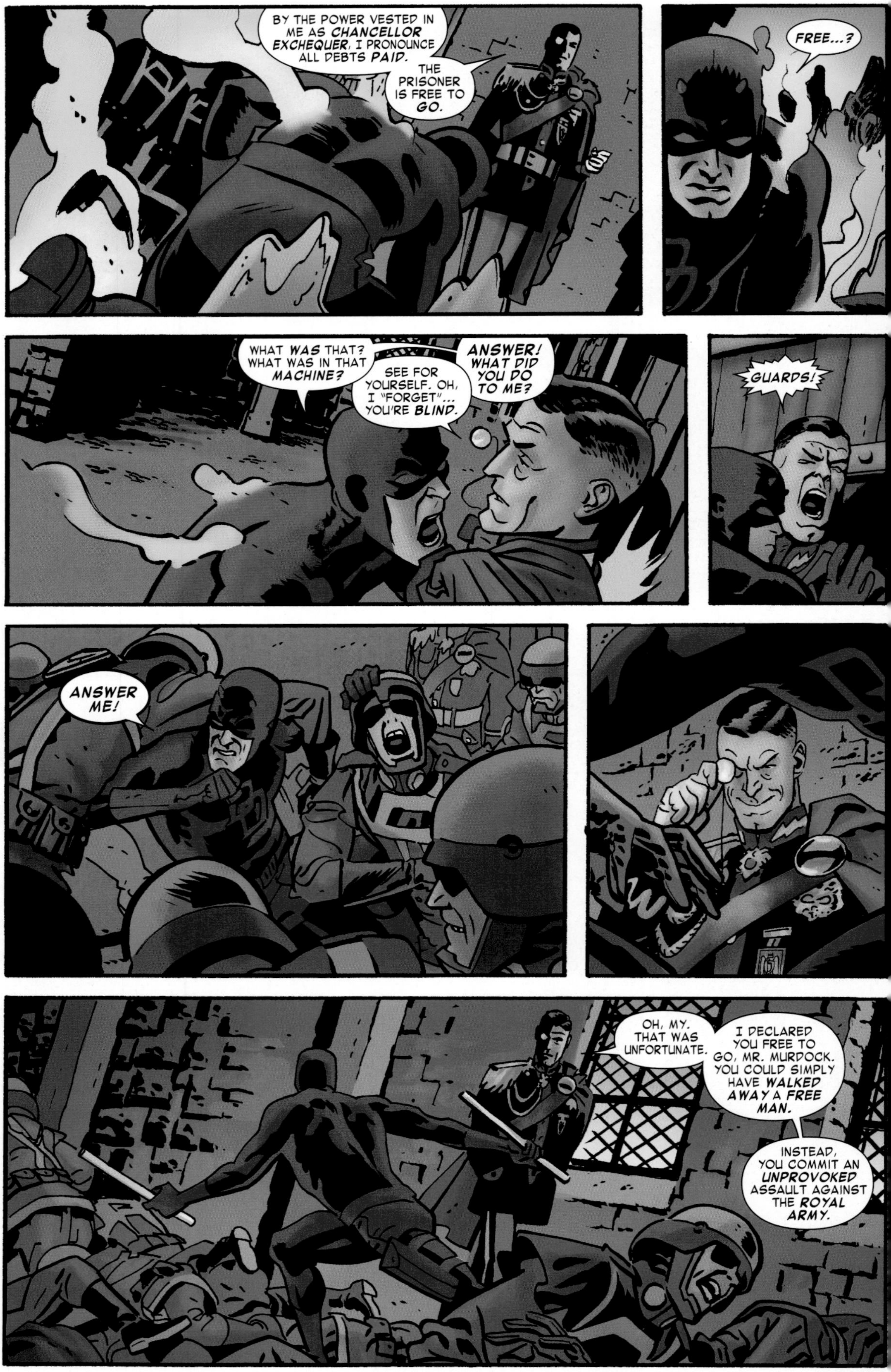
BY THE POWER VESTED IN ME AS CHANCELLOR EXCHEQUER, I PRONOUNCE ALL DEBTS PAID.
THE PRISONER IS FREE TO GO.
FREE...?
WHAT WAS THAT? WHAT WAS IN THAT MACHINE?
SEE FOR YOURSELF. OH, I "FORGET"... YOU'RE BLIND.
ANSWER! WHAT DID YOU DO TO ME?
GUARDS!
ANSWER ME!
OH, MY. THAT WAS UNFORTUNATE.
I DECLARED YOU FREE TO GO, MR. MURDOCK. YOU COULD SIMPLY HAVE WALKED AWAY A FREE MAN.
INSTEAD, YOU COMMIT AN UNPROVOKED ASSAULT AGAINST THE ROYAL ARMY.

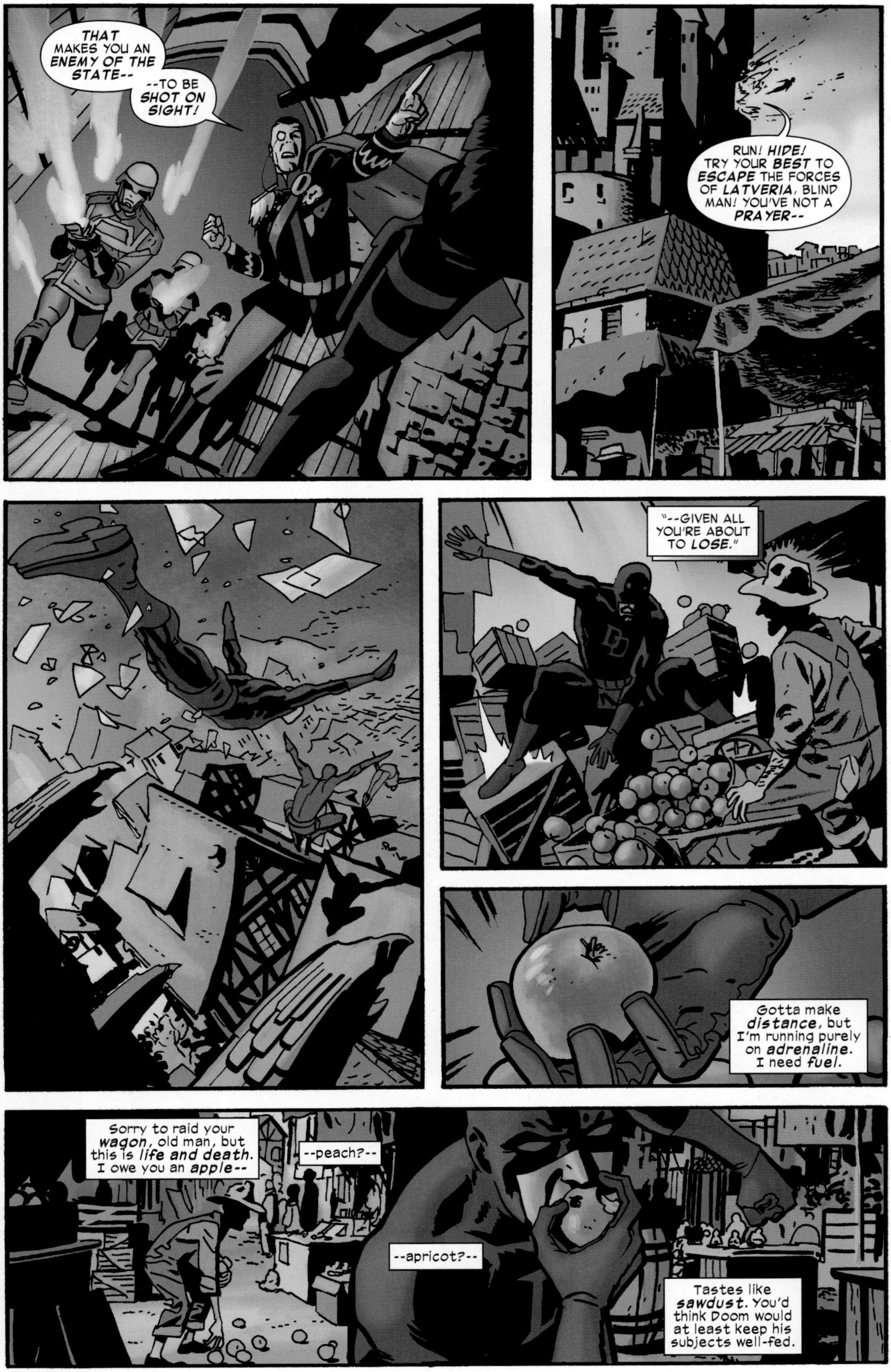
THAT MAKES YOU AN ENEMY OF THE STATE--
--TO BE SHOT ON SIGHT!
RUN! HIDE! TRY YOUR BEST TO ESCAPE THE FORCES OF LATVERIA, BLIND MAN! YOU'VE NOT A PRAYER--
"--GIVEN ALL YOU'RE ABOUT TO LOSE."
Gotta make distance, but I'm running purely on adrenaline. I need fuel.
Sorry to raid your wagon, old man, but this is life and death. I owe you an apple--
--peach?--
--apricot?--
Tastes like sawdust. You'd think Doom would at least keep his subjects well-fed.

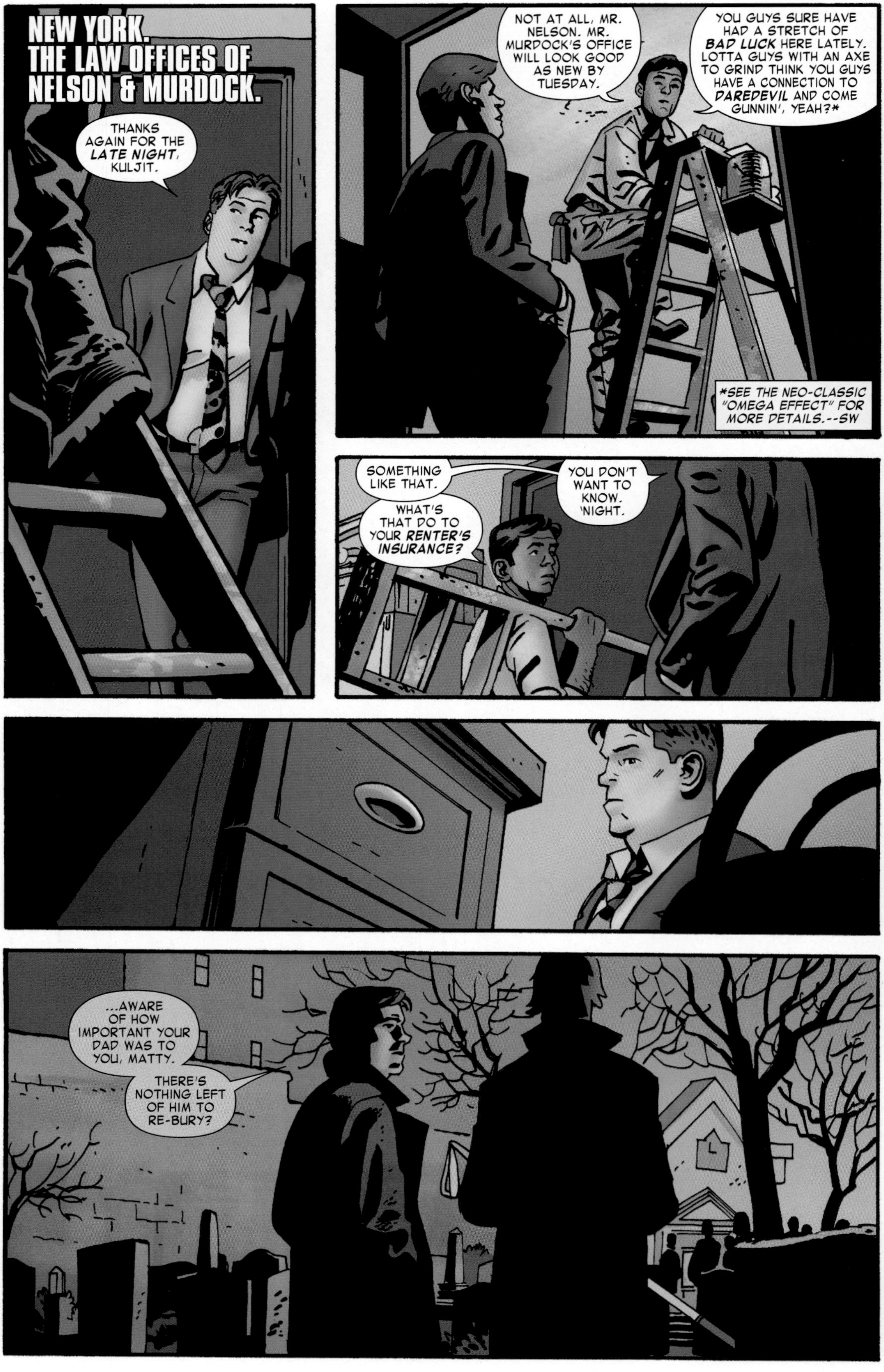
NEW YORK. THE LAW OFFICES OF NELSON & MURDOCK.
THANKS AGAIN FOR THE LATE NIGHT, KULJIT.
NOT AT ALL, MR. NELSON. MR. MURDOCK'S OFFICE WILL LOOK GOOD AS NEW BY TUESDAY.
YOU GUYS SURE HAVE HAD A STRETCH OF BAD LUCK HERE LATELY. LOTTA GUYS WITH AN AXE TO GRIND THINK YOU GUYS HAVE A CONNECTION TO DAREDEVIL AND COME GUNNIN', YEAH?*
*SEE THE NEO-CLASSIC "OMEGA EFFECT" FOR MORE DETAILS.--SW
SOMETHING LIKE THAT.
WHAT'S THAT DO TO YOUR RENTER'S INSURANCE?
YOU DON'T WANT TO KNOW. 'NIGHT.
...AWARE OF HOW IMPORTANT YOUR DAD WAS TO YOU, MATTY.
THERE'S NOTHING LEFT OF HIM TO RE-BURY?

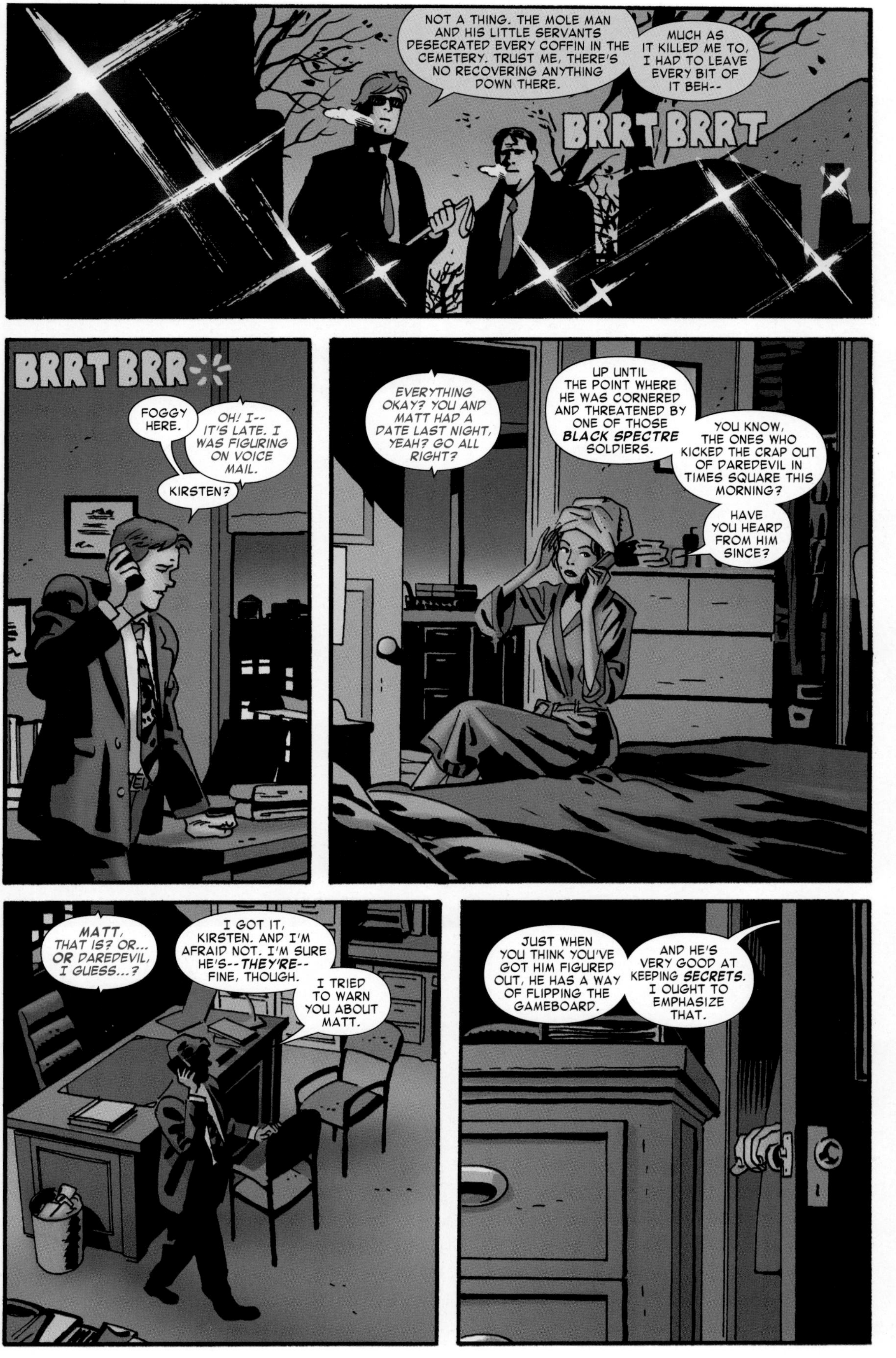
NOT A THING. THE MOLE MAN AND HIS LITTLE SERVANTS DESECRATED EVERY COFFIN IN THE CEMETERY. TRUST ME, THERE'S NO RECOVERING ANYTHING DOWN THERE.
MUCH AS IT KILLED ME TO, I HAD TO LEAVE EVERY BIT OF IT BEH--
BRRT BRRT
BRRT BRR
FOGGY HERE.
OH! I-- IT'S LATE. I WAS FIGURING ON VOICE MAIL.
KIRSTEN?
EVERYTHING OKAY? YOU AND MATT HAD A DATE LAST NIGHT, YEAH? GO ALL RIGHT?
UP UNTIL THE POINT WHERE HE WAS CORNERED AND THREATENED BY ONE OF THOSE BLACK SPECTRE SOLDIERS.
YOU KNOW, THE ONES WHO KICKED THE CRAP OUT OF DAREDEVIL IN TIMES SQUARE THIS MORNING?
HAVE YOU HEARD FROM HIM SINCE?
MATT, THAT IS? OR... OR DAREDEVIL, I GUESS...?
I GOT IT, KIRSTEN. AND I'M AFRAID NOT. I'M SURE HE'S--THEY'RE-- FINE, THOUGH.
I TRIED TO WARN YOU ABOUT MATT.
JUST WHEN YOU THINK YOU'VE GOT HIM FIGURED OUT, HE HAS A WAY OF FLIPPING THE GAMEBOARD.
AND HE'S VERY GOOD AT KEEPING SECRETS. I OUGHT TO EMPHASIZE THAT.

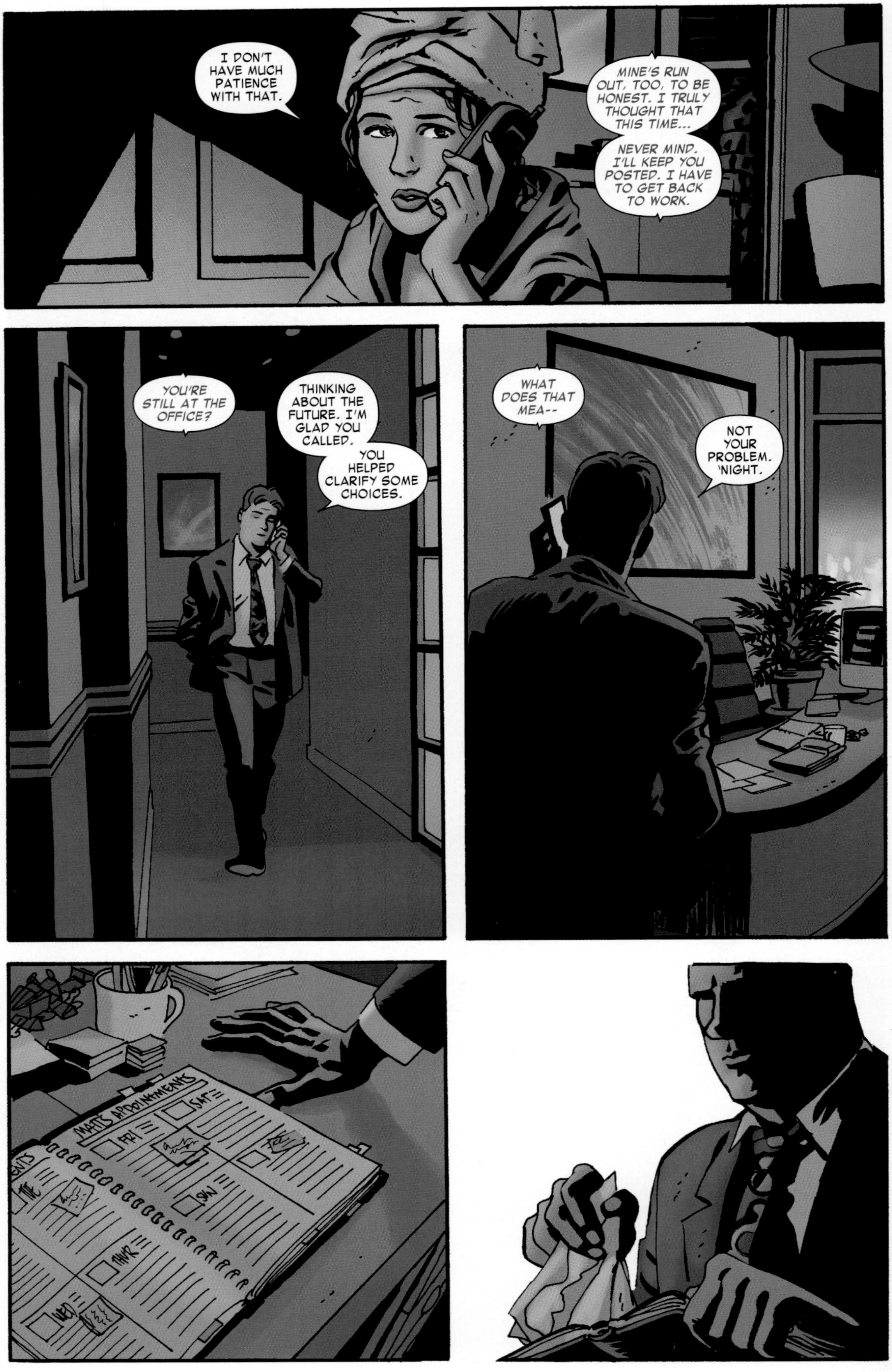

I DON'T HAVE MUCH PATIENCE WITH THAT.
MINE'S RUN OUT, TOO, TO BE HONEST. I TRULY THOUGHT THAT THIS TIME...
NEVER MIND. I'LL KEEP YOU POSTED. I HAVE TO GET BACK TO WORK.
YOU'RE STILL AT THE OFFICE?
THINKING ABOUT THE FUTURE. I'M GLAD YOU CALLED.
YOU HELPED CLARIFY SOME CHOICES.
WHAT DOES THAT MEA--
NOT YOUR PROBLEM. 'NIGHT.
MATT'S APPOINTMENTS

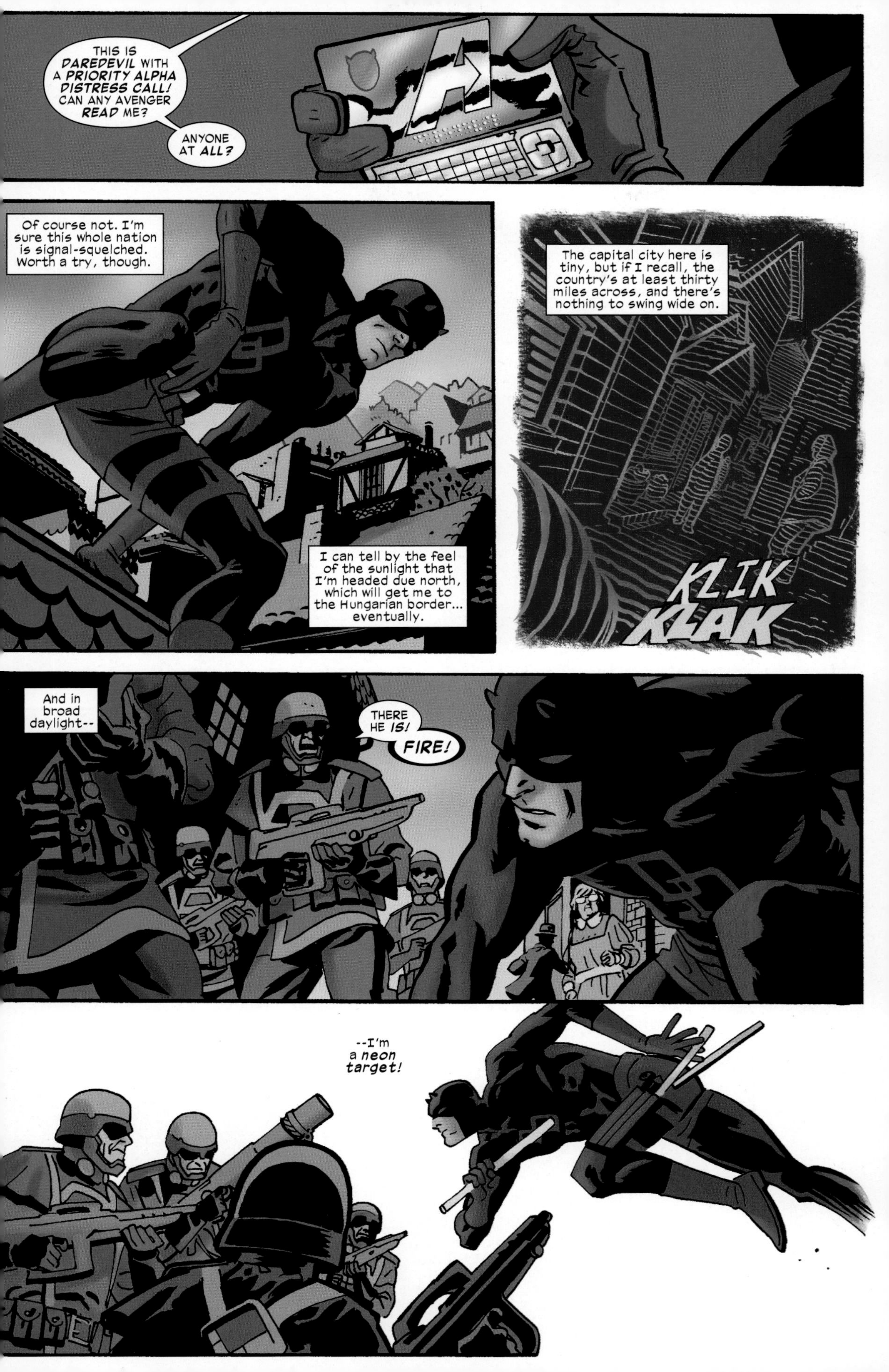
THIS IS *DAREDEVIL* WITH A *PRIORITY ALPHA DISTRESS CALL!* CAN ANY AVENGER *READ* ME?
ANYONE AT *ALL?*
Of course not. I'm sure this whole nation is signal-squelched. Worth a try, though.
I can tell by the feel of the sunlight that I'm headed due north, which will get me to the Hungarian border... eventually.
The capital city here is tiny, but if I recall, the country's at least thirty miles across, and there's nothing to swing wide on.
KLIK
KLAK
And in broad daylight--
THERE HE *IS!*
FIRE!
--I'm a *neon target!*

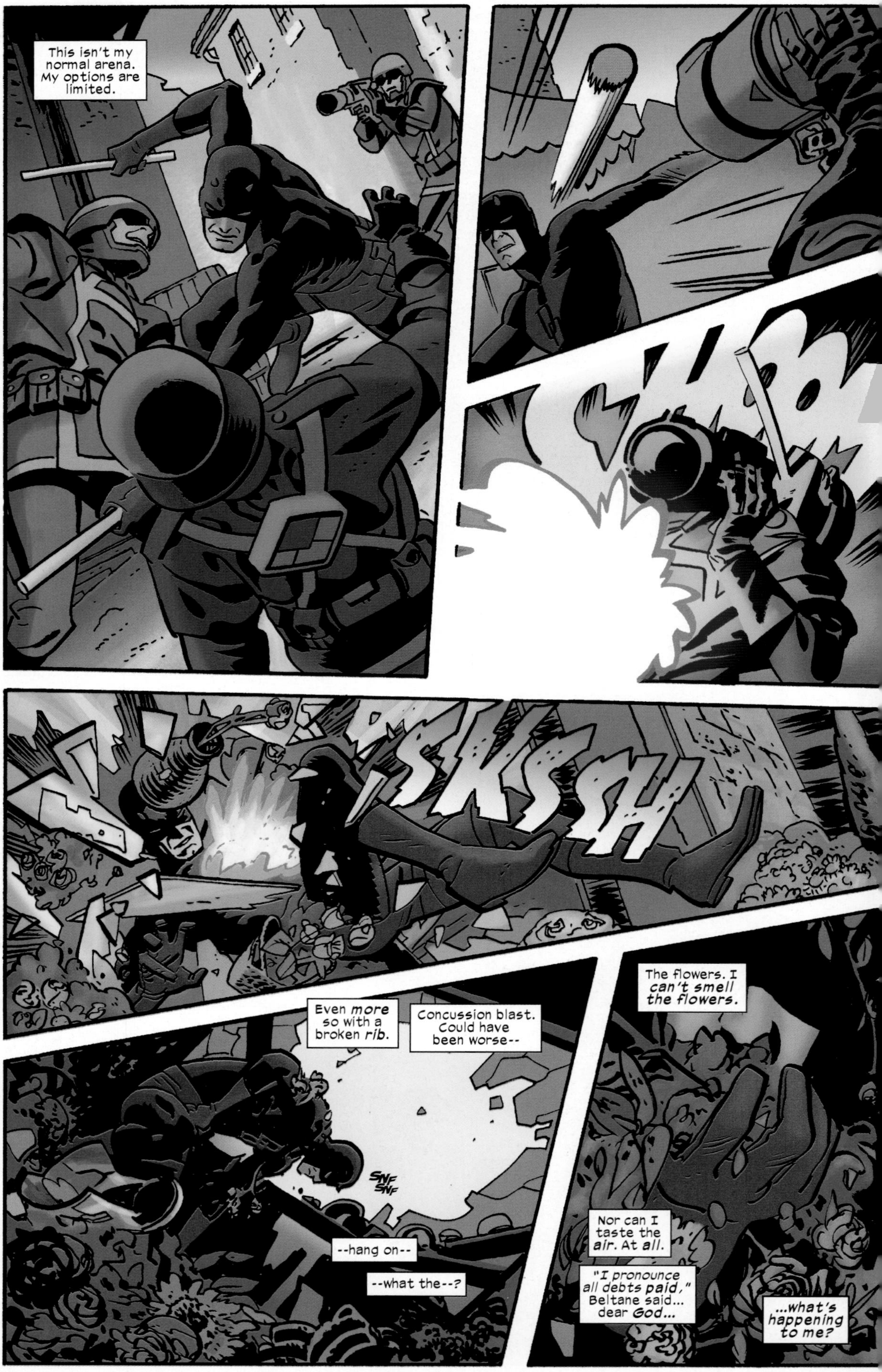
This isn't my normal arena. My options are limited.
SKSSH
Even more so with a broken rib.
Concussion blast. Could have been worse--
SNF SNF
--hang on--
--what the--?
The flowers. I can't smell the flowers.
Nor can I taste the air. At all.
"I pronounce all debts paid," Beltane said... dear God...
...what's happening to me?

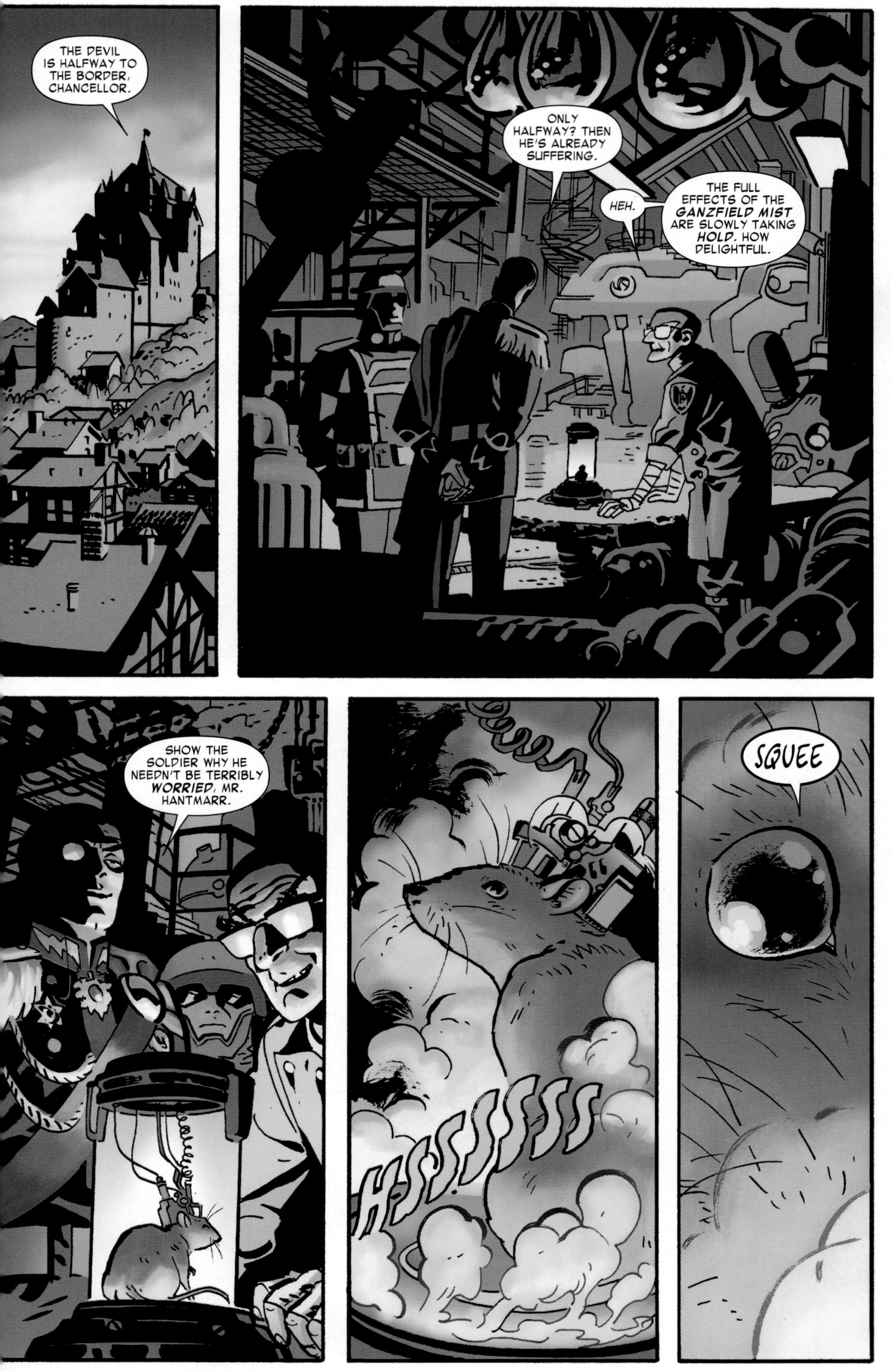
THE DEVIL IS HALFWAY TO THE BORDER, CHANCELLOR.
ONLY HALFWAY? THEN HE'S ALREADY SUFFERING.
HEH.
THE FULL EFFECTS OF THE *GANZFIELD MIST* ARE SLOWLY TAKING *HOLD*. HOW DELIGHTFUL.
SHOW THE SOLDIER WHY HE NEEDN'T BE TERRIBLY *WORRIED*, MR. HANTMARR.
HSSSSSSS
SQUEE

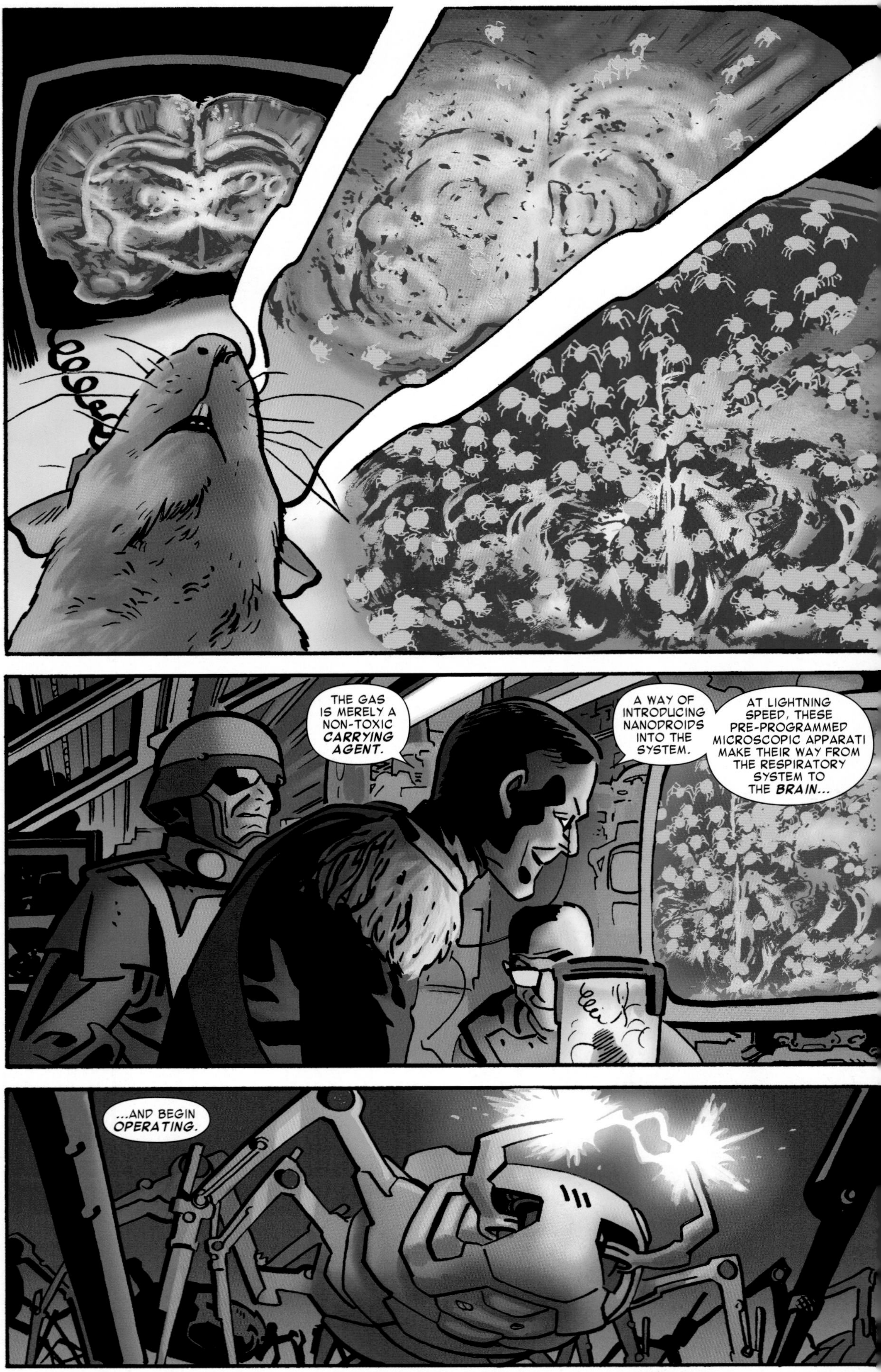
THE GAS IS MERELY A NON-TOXIC CARRYING AGENT.
A WAY OF INTRODUCING NANODROIDS INTO THE SYSTEM.
AT LIGHTNING SPEED, THESE PRE-PROGRAMMED MICROSCOPIC APPARATI MAKE THEIR WAY FROM THE RESPIRATORY SYSTEM TO THE BRAIN...
...AND BEGIN OPERATING.

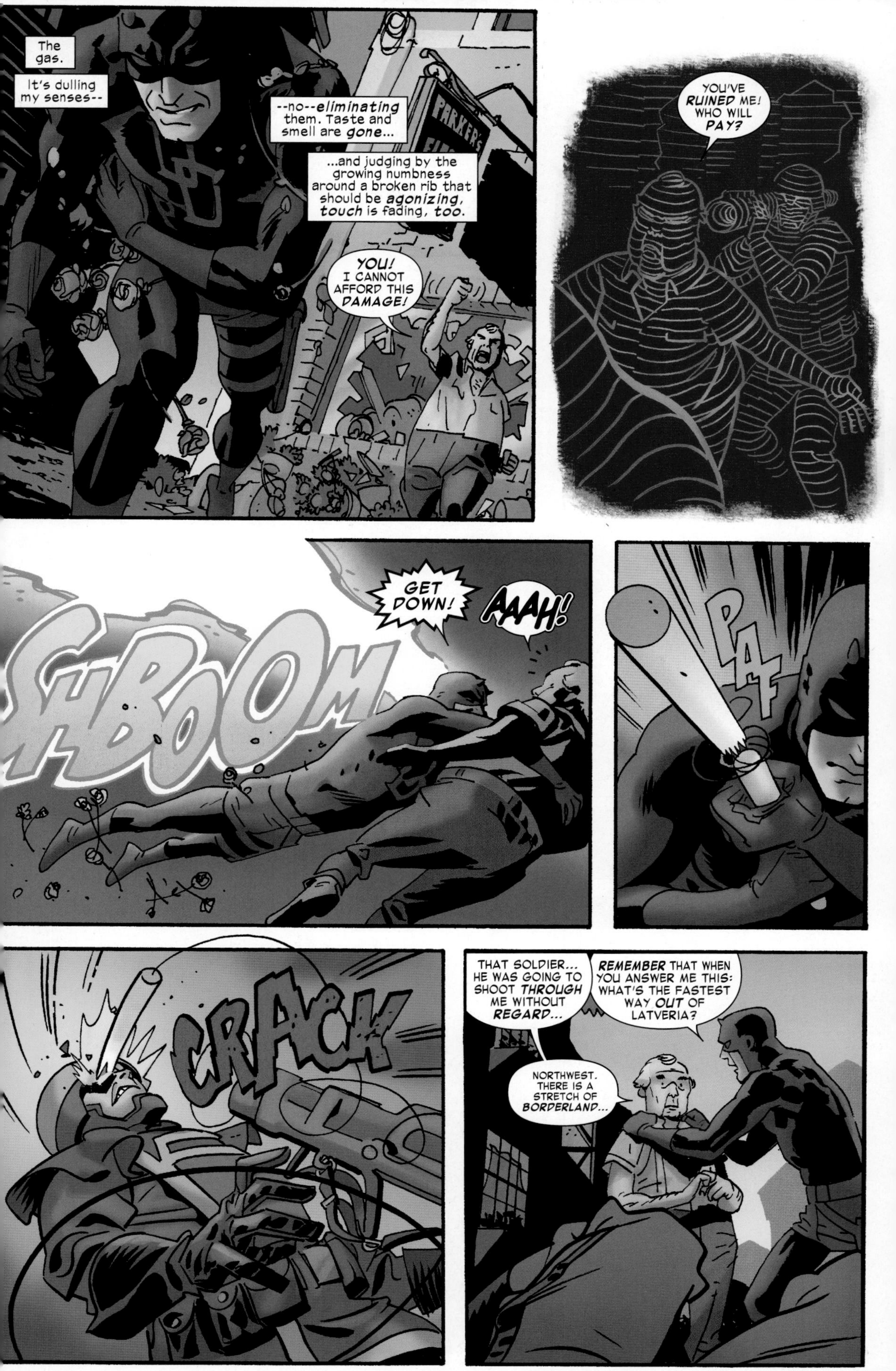
The gas.
It's dulling my senses--
--no--eliminating them. Taste and smell are gone...
...and judging by the growing numbness around a broken rib that should be agonizing, touch is fading, too.
PARKERS
YOU! I CANNOT AFFORD THIS DAMAGE!
YOU'VE RUINED ME! WHO WILL PAY?
SHBOOM
GET DOWN!
AAAH!
PAF
CRACK
THAT SOLDIER... HE WAS GOING TO SHOOT THROUGH ME WITHOUT REGARD...
REMEMBER THAT WHEN YOU ANSWER ME THIS: WHAT'S THE FASTEST WAY OUT OF LATVERIA?
NORTHWEST. THERE IS A STRETCH OF BORDERLAND...

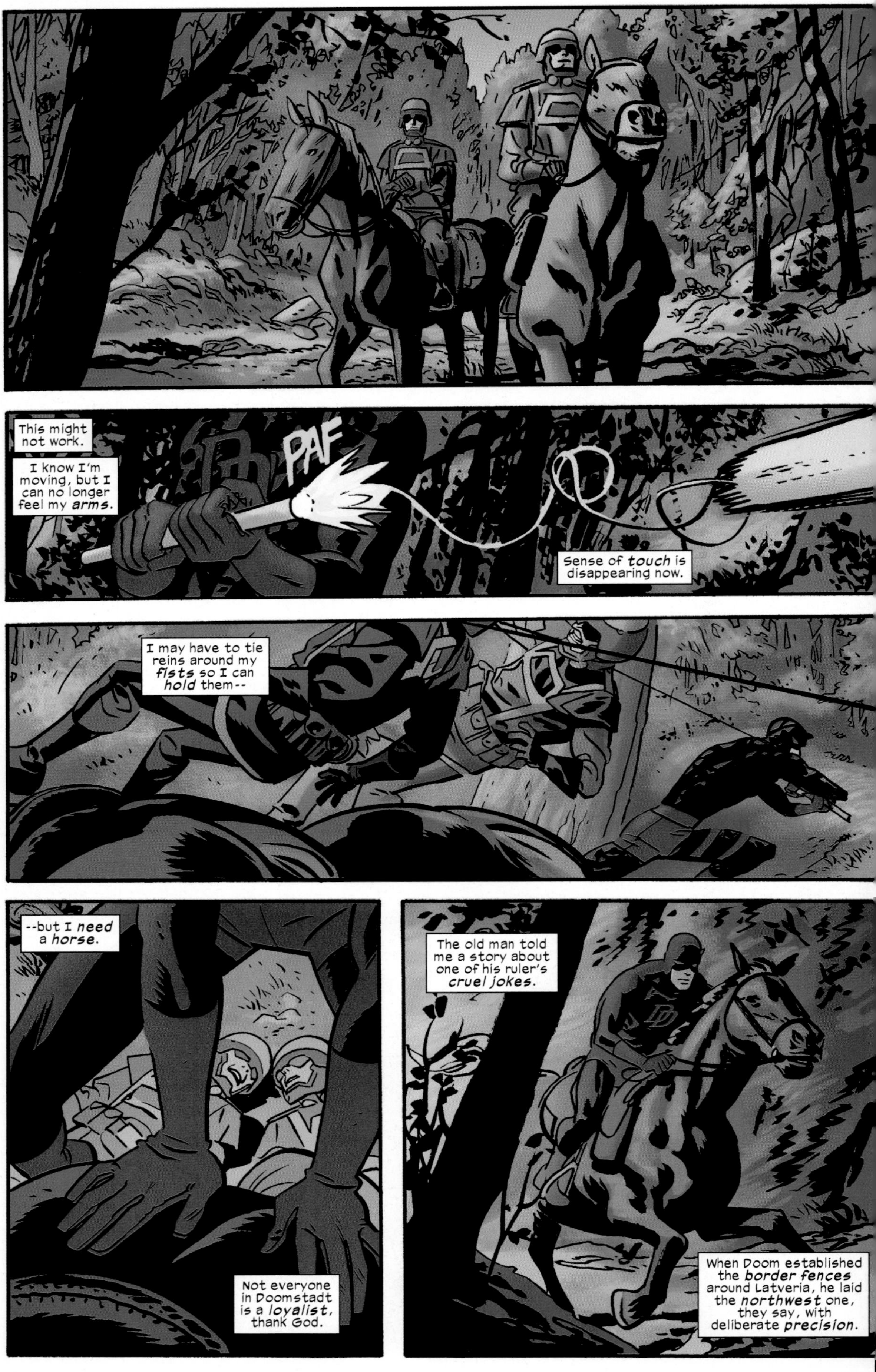
This might not work.
I know I'm moving, but I can no longer feel my *arms*.
PAF
Sense of *touch* is disappearing now.
I may have to tie reins around my *fists* so I can *hold* them--
--but I *need* a *horse*.
Not everyone in Doomstadt is a *loyalist*, thank God.
The old man told me a story about one of his ruler's *cruel jokes*.
When Doom established the *border fences* around Latveria, he laid the *northwest* one, they say, with deliberate *precision*.

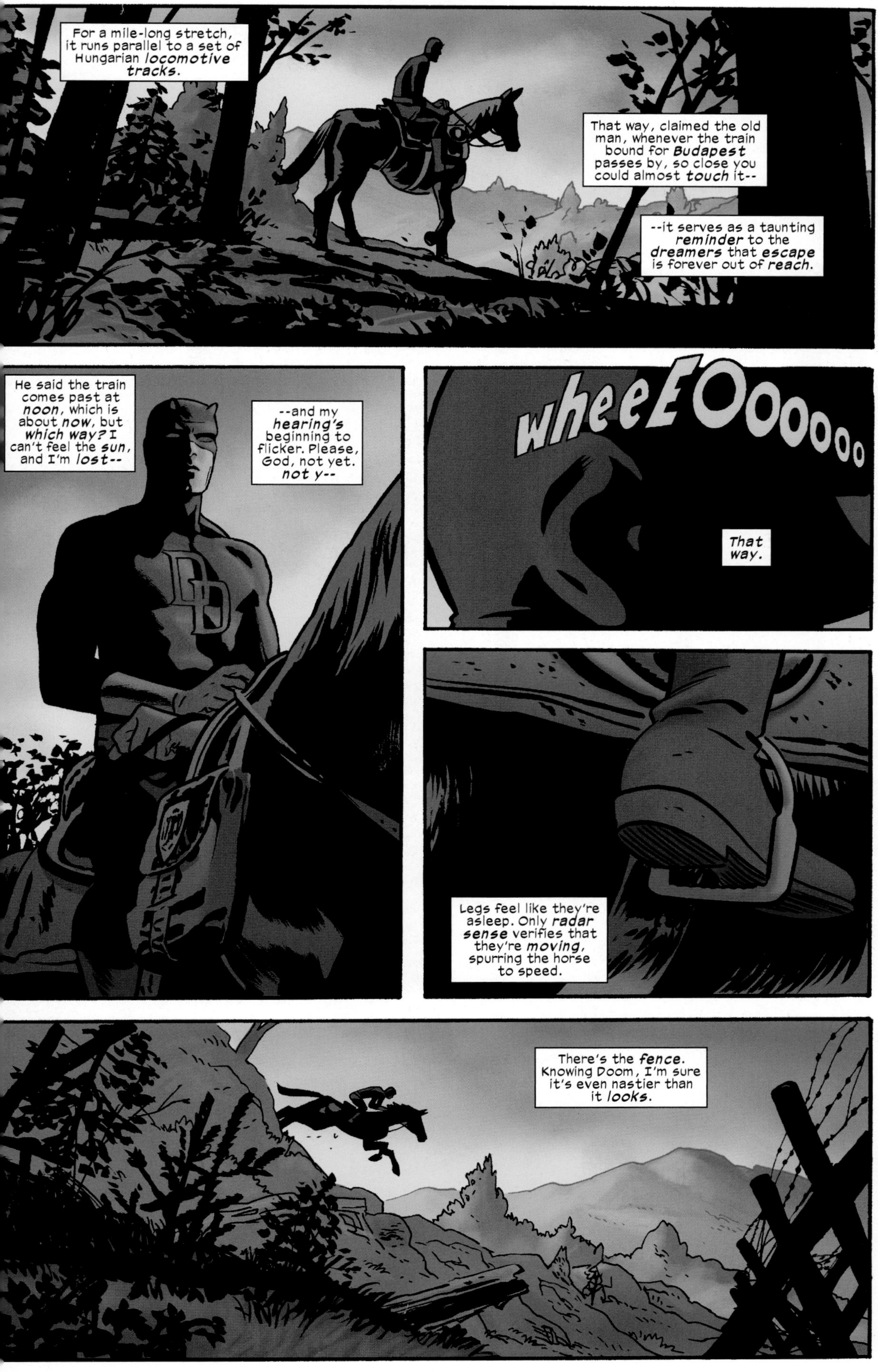

For a mile-long stretch, it runs parallel to a set of Hungarian *locomotive tracks*.
That way, claimed the old man, whenever the train bound for *Budapest* passes by, so close you could almost *touch* it--
--it serves as a taunting *reminder* to the *dreamers* that *escape* is forever out of *reach*.
He said the train comes past at *noon*, which is about *now*, but *which way?* I can't feel the *sun*, and I'm *lost*--
--and my *hearing's* beginning to flicker. Please, God, not yet. *not y*--
wheeEOooooo
That way.
Legs feel like they're asleep. Only *radar sense* verifies that they're *moving*, spurring the horse to speed.
There's the *fence*. Knowing Doom, I'm sure it's even nastier than it *looks*.

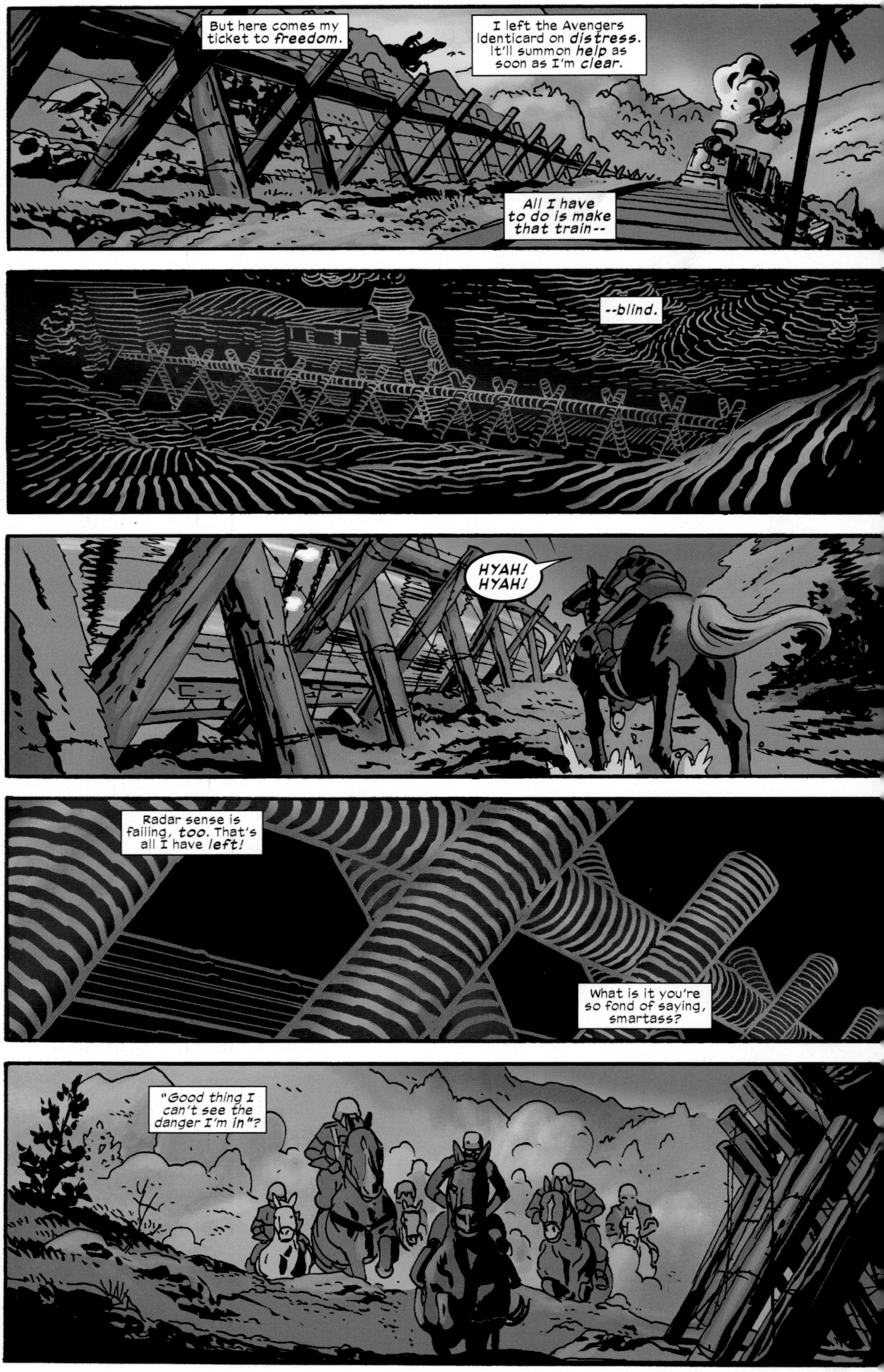

But here comes my ticket to *freedom*.
I left the Avengers Identicard on *distress*. It'll summon *help* as soon as I'm *clear*.
All I have to do is make that train--
--blind.
HYAH! HYAH!
Radar sense is failing, *too*. That's all I have *left!*
What is it you're so fond of saying, smartass?
"Good thing I can't see the danger I'm *in*"?

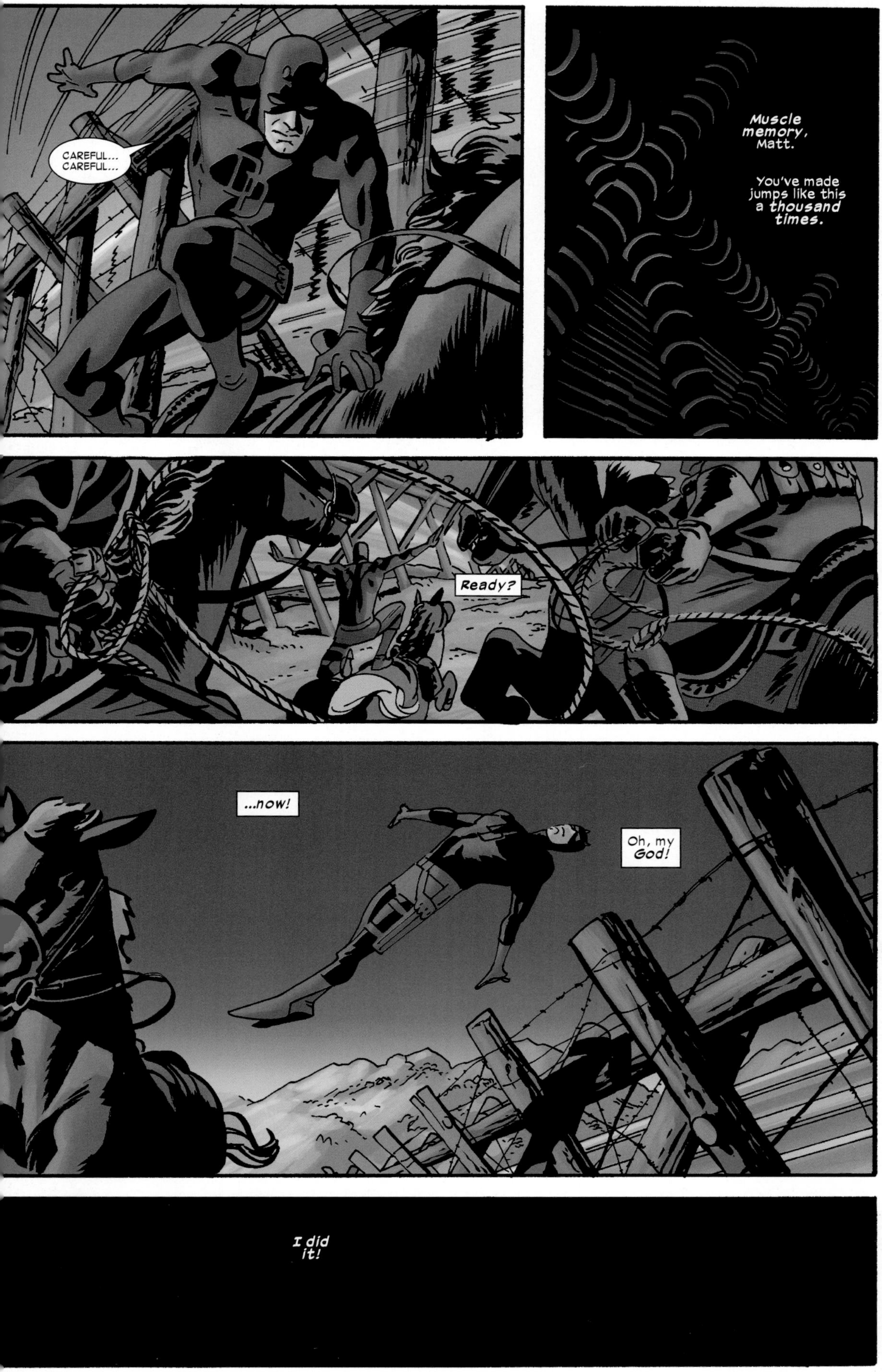
CAREFUL... CAREFUL...
Muscle memory, Matt.
You've made jumps like this a thousand times.
Ready?
...now!
Oh, my God!
I did it!

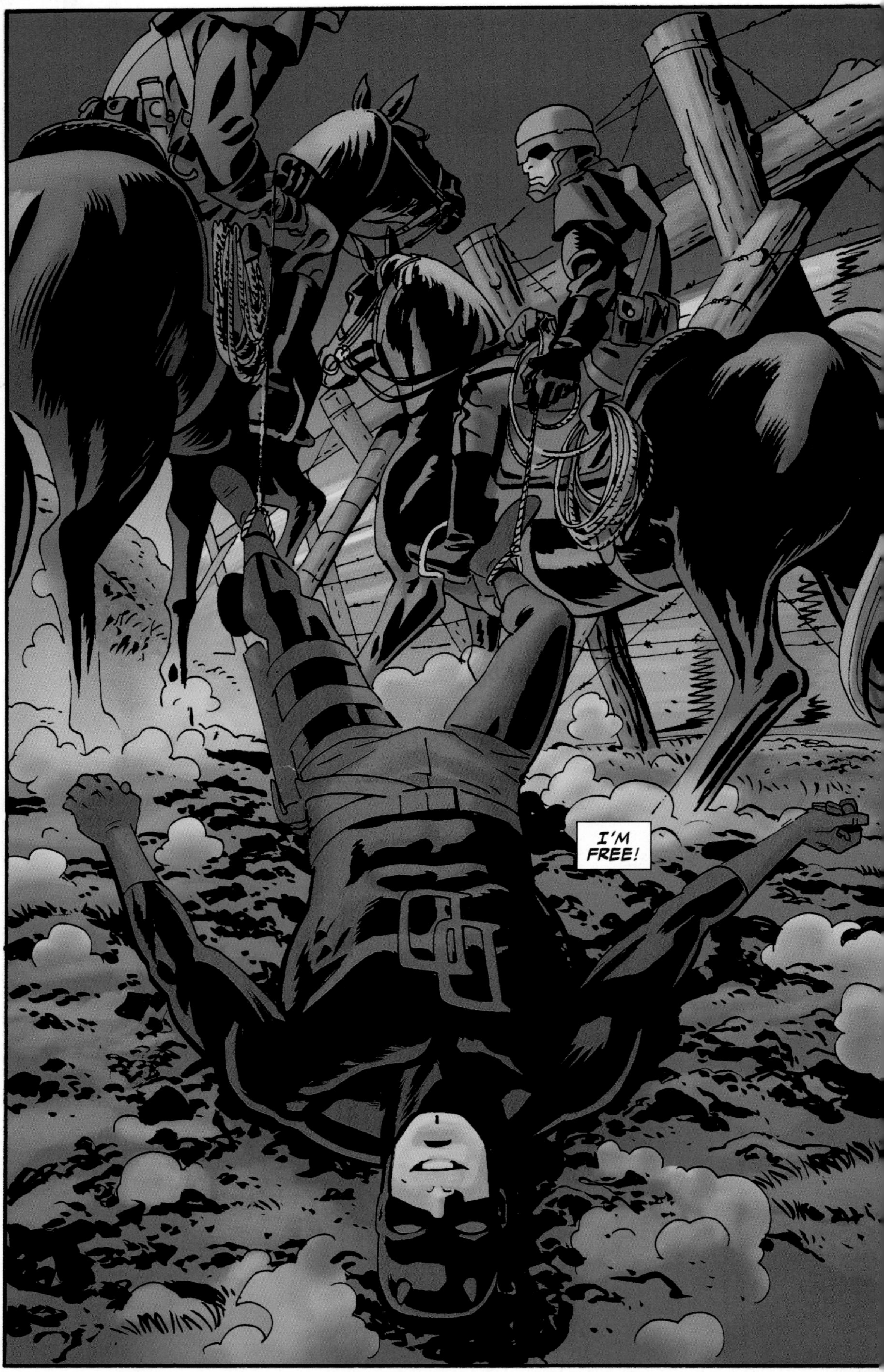
I'M FREE!

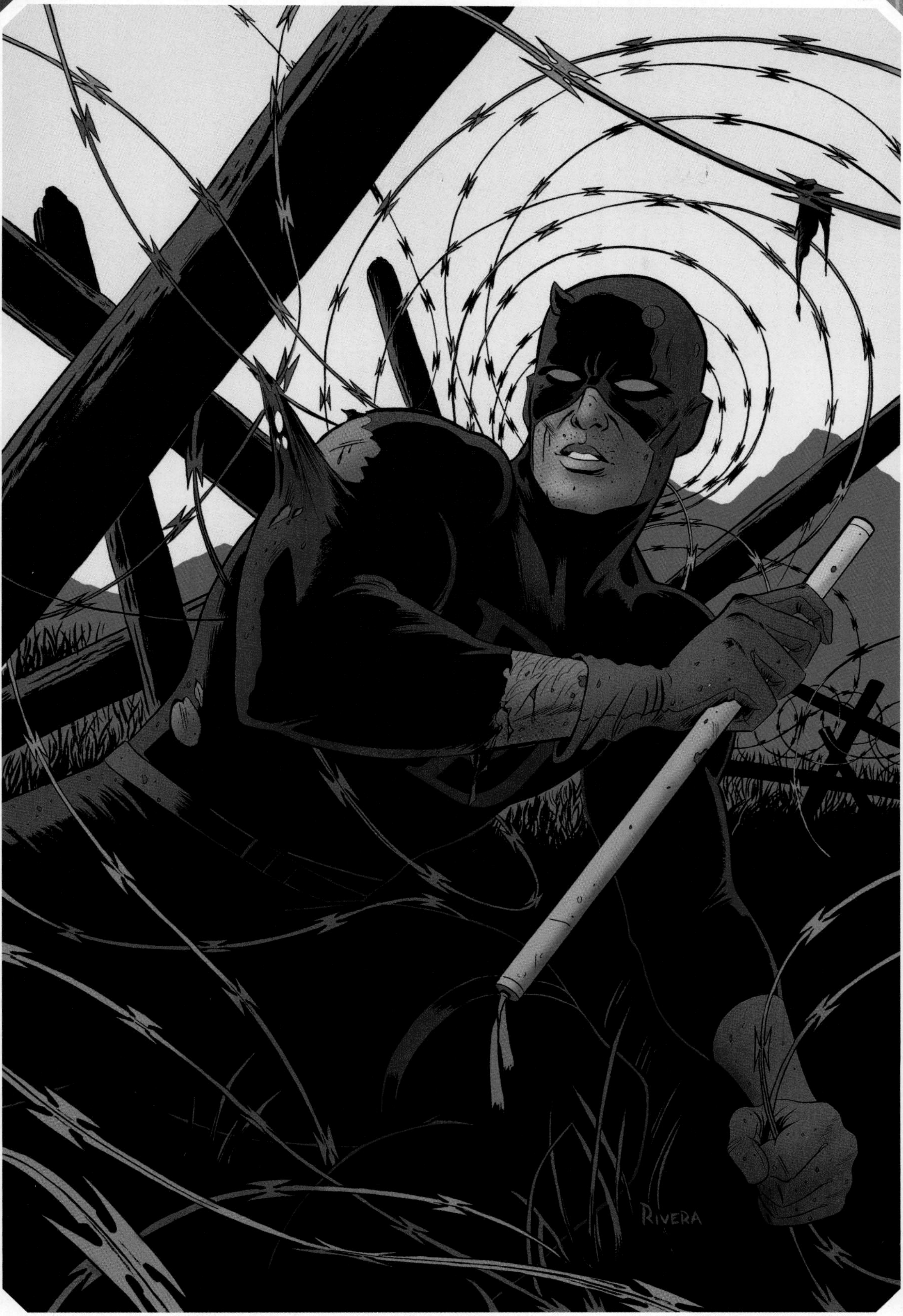
RIVERA

DAREDEVIL #15

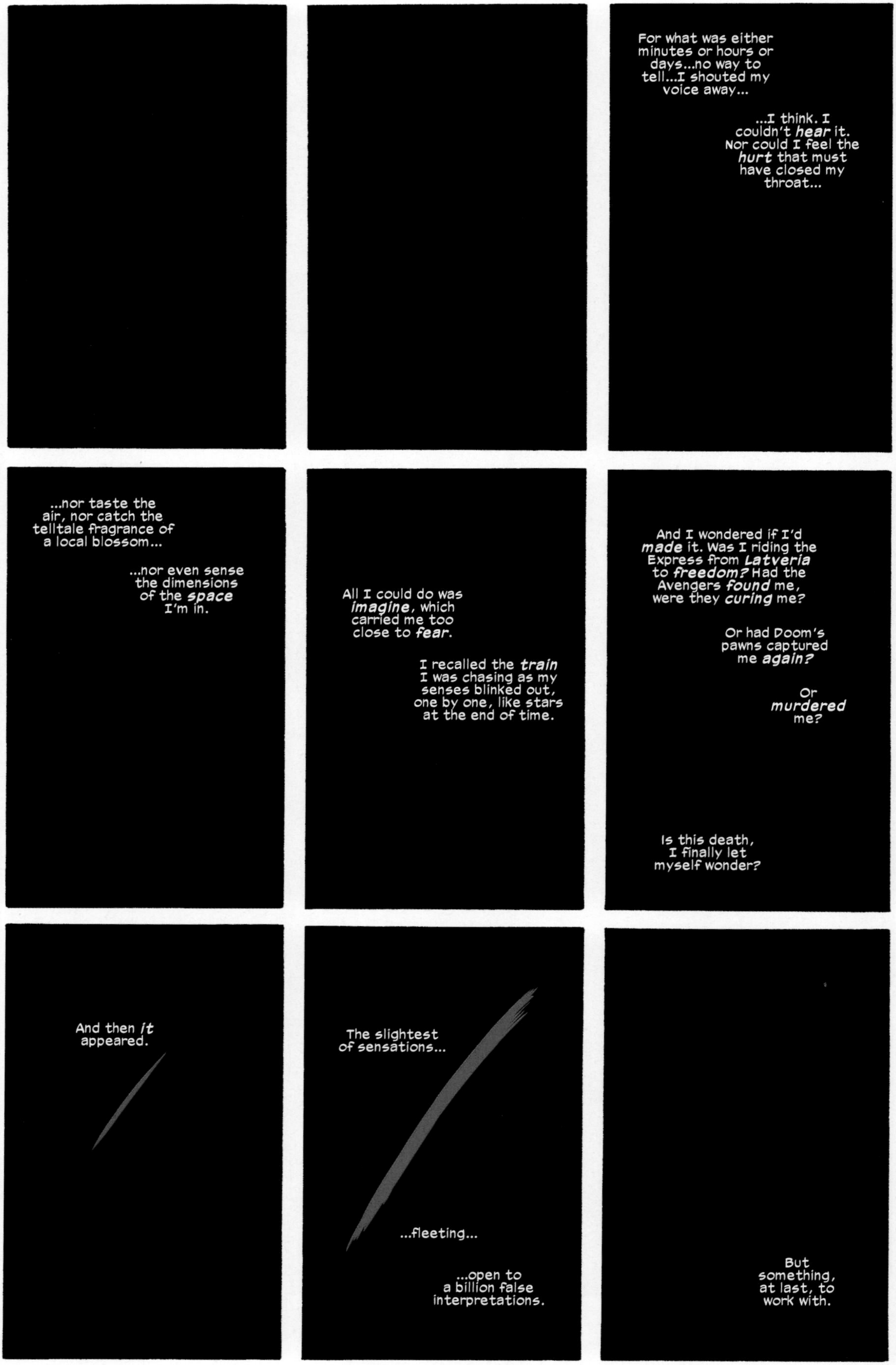
For what was either minutes or hours or days...no way to tell...I shouted my voice away...
...I think. I couldn't hear it. Nor could I feel the hurt that must have closed my throat...
...nor taste the air, nor catch the telltale fragrance of a local blossom...
...nor even sense the dimensions of the space I'm in.
All I could do was imagine, which carried me too close to fear.
I recalled the train I was chasing as my senses blinked out, one by one, like stars at the end of time.
And I wondered if I'd made it. Was I riding the Express from Latveria to freedom? Had the Avengers found me, were they curing me?
Or had Doom's pawns captured me again?
Or murdered me?
Is this death, I finally let myself wonder?
And then it appeared.
The slightest of sensations...
...fleeting...
...open to a billion false interpretations.
But something, at last, to work with.

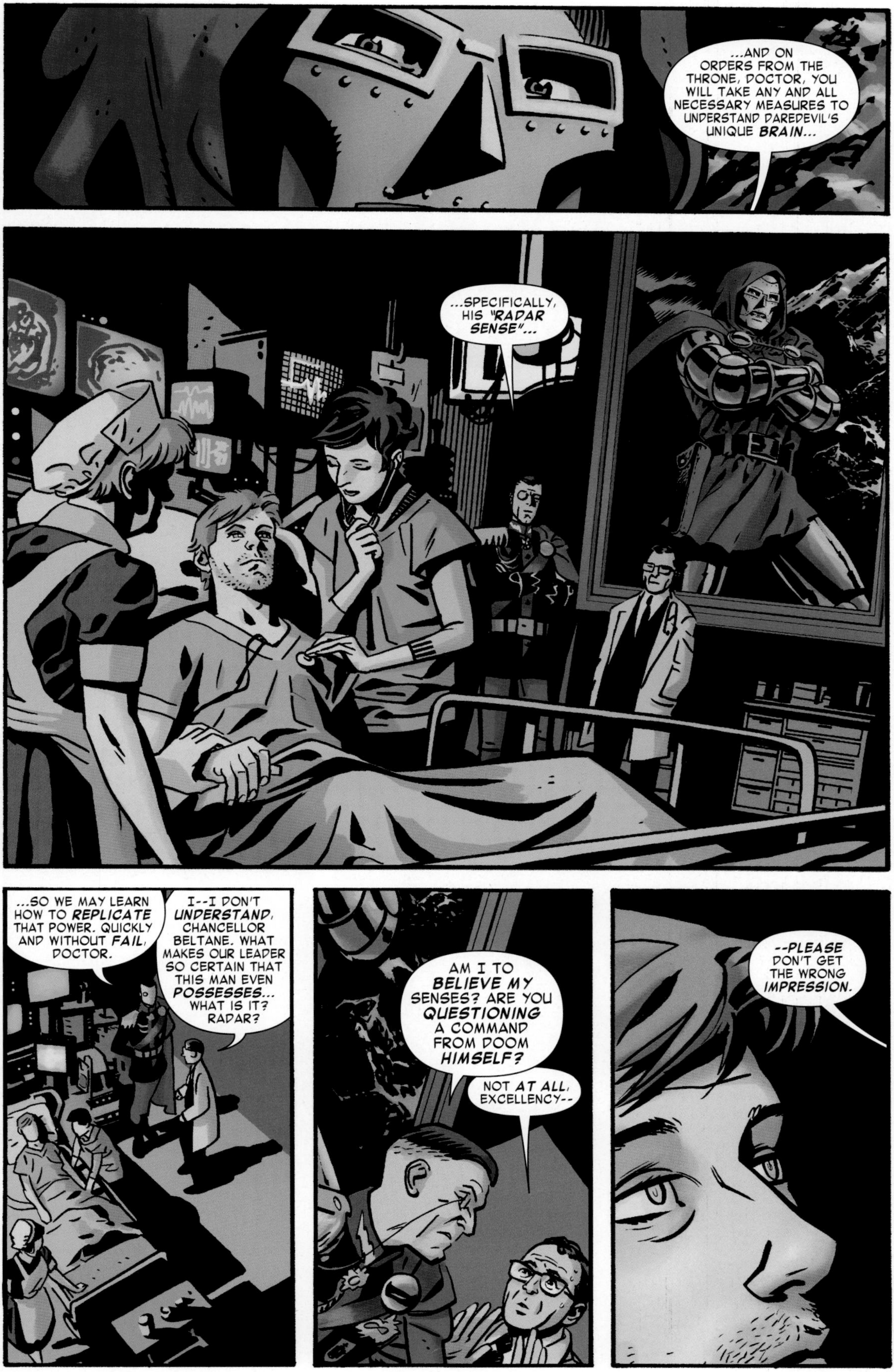

...AND ON ORDERS FROM THE THRONE, DOCTOR, YOU WILL TAKE ANY AND ALL NECESSARY MEASURES TO UNDERSTAND DAREDEVIL'S UNIQUE BRAIN...
...SPECIFICALLY, HIS "RADAR SENSE"...
...SO WE MAY LEARN HOW TO REPLICATE THAT POWER. QUICKLY AND WITHOUT FAIL, DOCTOR.
I--I DON'T UNDERSTAND, CHANCELLOR BELTANE. WHAT MAKES OUR LEADER SO CERTAIN THAT THIS MAN EVEN POSSESSES... WHAT IS IT? RADAR?
AM I TO BELIEVE MY SENSES? ARE YOU QUESTIONING A COMMAND FROM DOOM HIMSELF?
NOT AT ALL, EXCELLENCY--
--PLEASE DON'T GET THE WRONG IMPRESSION.

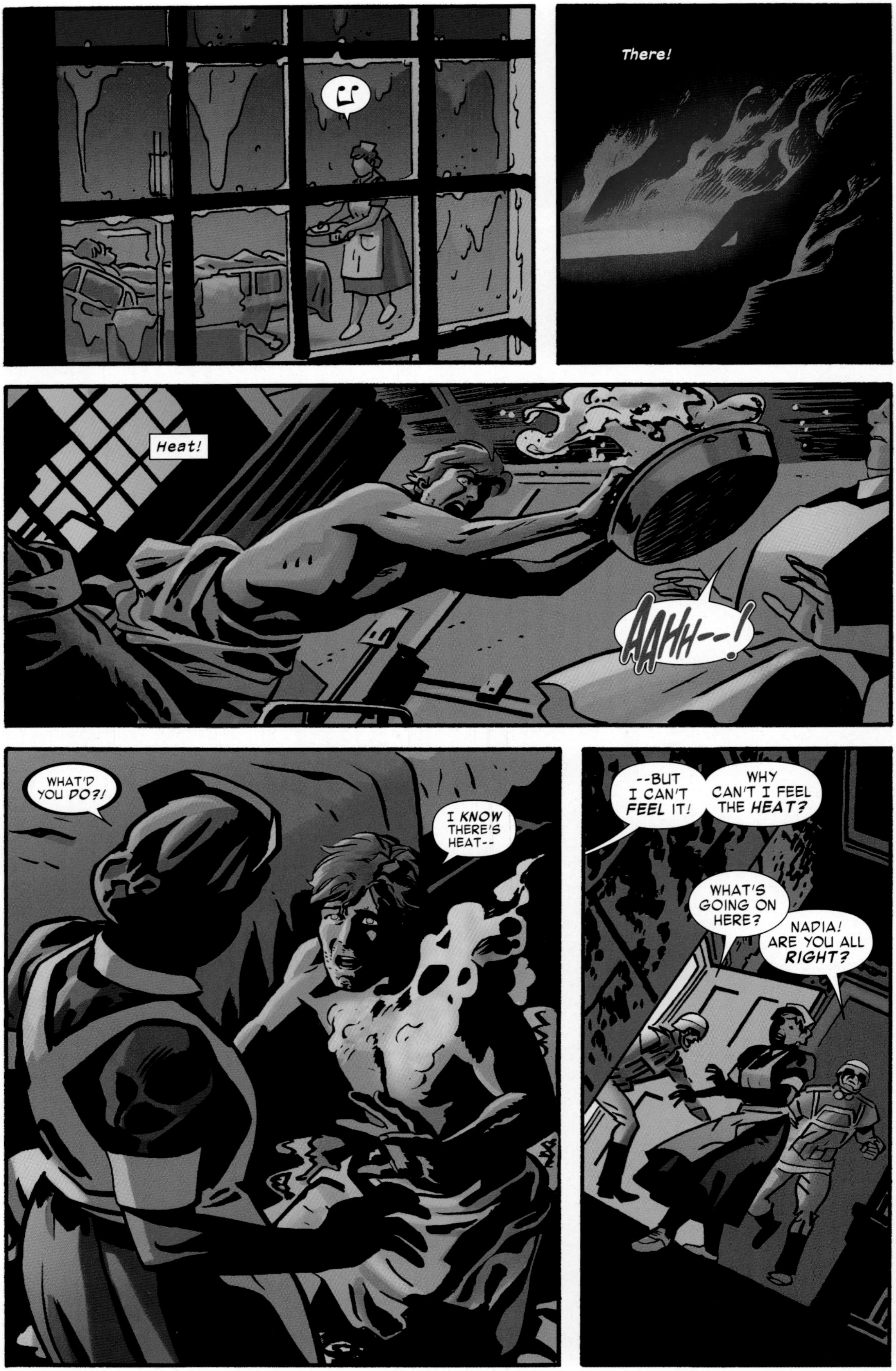

There!
Heat!
AAHH--!
WHAT'D YOU DO?!
I KNOW THERE'S HEAT--
--BUT I CAN'T FEEL IT!
WHY CAN'T I FEEL THE HEAT?
WHAT'S GOING ON HERE?
NADIA! ARE YOU ALL RIGHT?

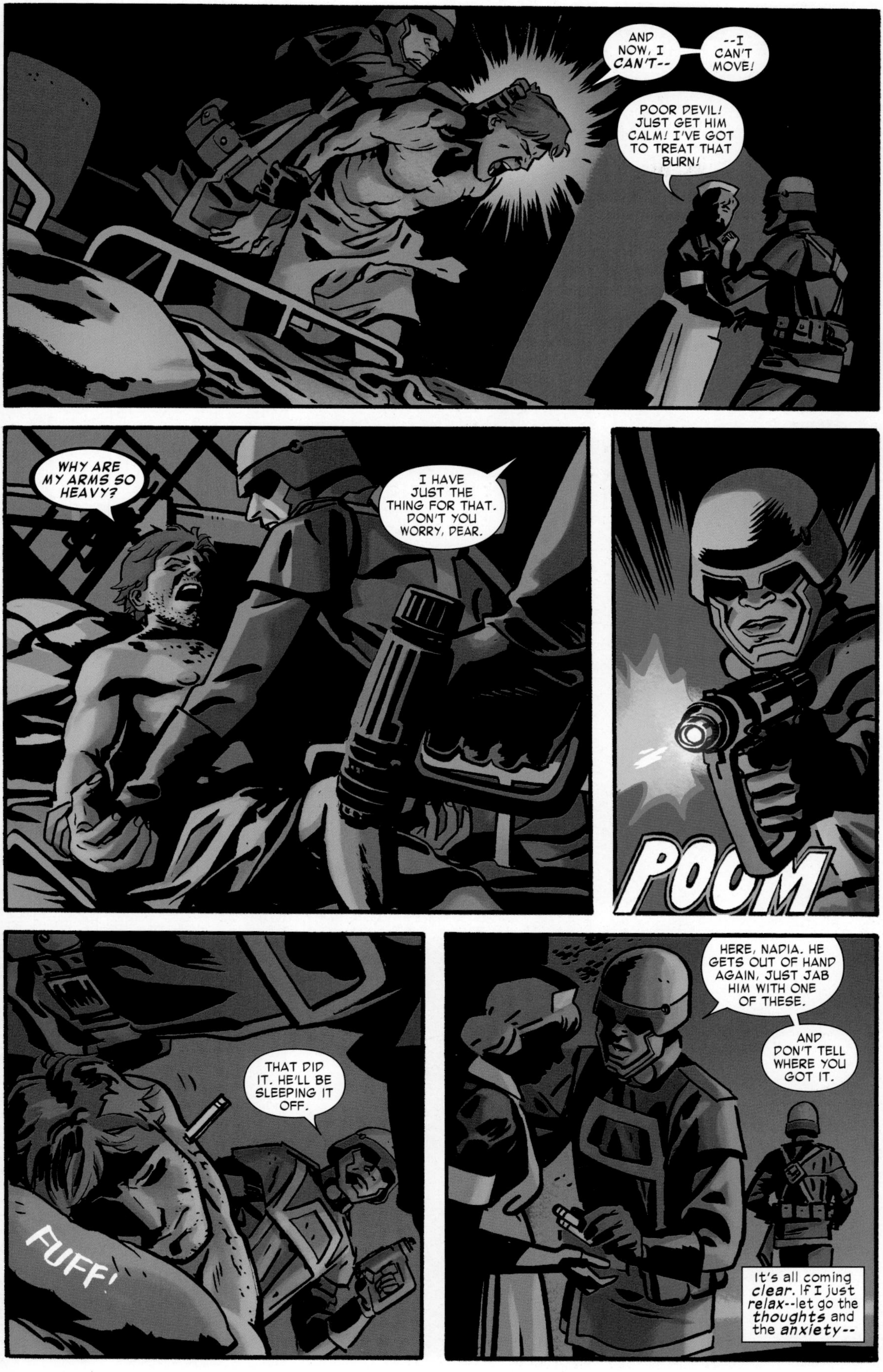
AND NOW, I CAN'T--
--I CAN'T MOVE!
POOR DEVIL! JUST GET HIM CALM! I'VE GOT TO TREAT THAT BURN!
WHY ARE MY ARMS SO HEAVY?
I HAVE JUST THE THING FOR THAT. DON'T YOU WORRY, DEAR.
POOM
THAT DID IT. HE'LL BE SLEEPING IT OFF.
FUFF!
HERE, NADIA. HE GETS OUT OF HAND AGAIN, JUST JAB HIM WITH ONE OF THESE.
AND DON'T TELL WHERE YOU GOT IT.
It's all coming clear. If I just relax--let go the thoughts and the anxiety--

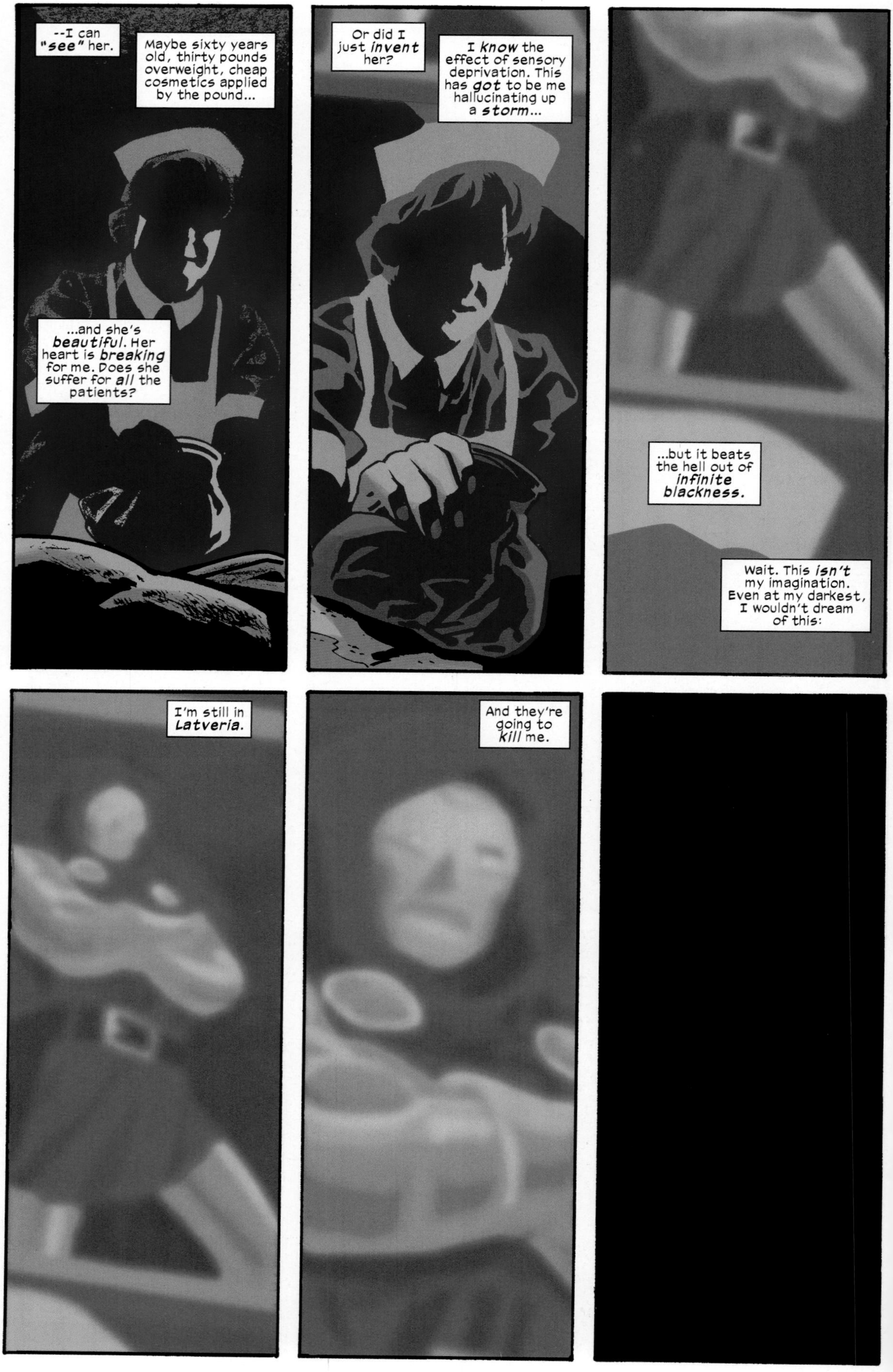
--I can "*see*" her.
Maybe sixty years old, thirty pounds overweight, cheap cosmetics applied by the pound...
...and she's *beautiful*. Her heart is *breaking* for me. Does she suffer for *all* the patients?
Or did I just *invent* her?
I *know* the effect of sensory deprivation. This has *got* to be me hallucinating up a *storm*...
...but it beats the hell out of *infinite blackness.*
Wait. This *isn't* my imagination. Even at my darkest, I wouldn't dream of this:
I'm still in *Latveria*.
And they're going to *kill* me.

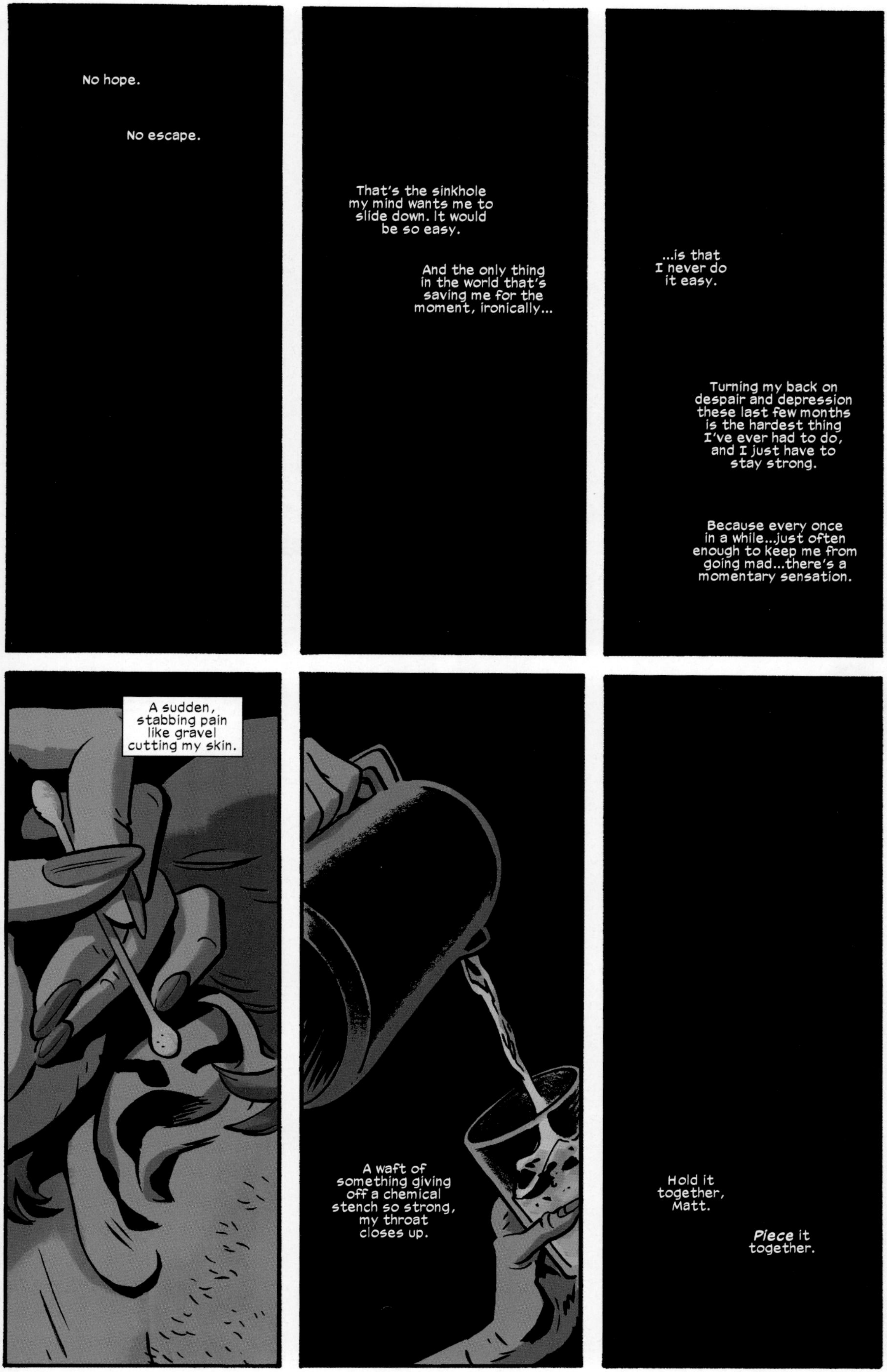
No hope.
No escape.
That's the sinkhole my mind wants me to slide down. It would be so easy.
And the only thing in the world that's saving me for the moment, ironically...
...is that I never do it easy.
Turning my back on despair and depression these last few months is the hardest thing I've ever had to do, and I just have to stay strong.
Because every once in a while...just often enough to keep me from going mad...there's a momentary sensation.
A sudden, stabbing pain like gravel cutting my skin.
A waft of something giving off a chemical stench so strong, my throat closes up.
Hold it together, Matt.
Piece it together.

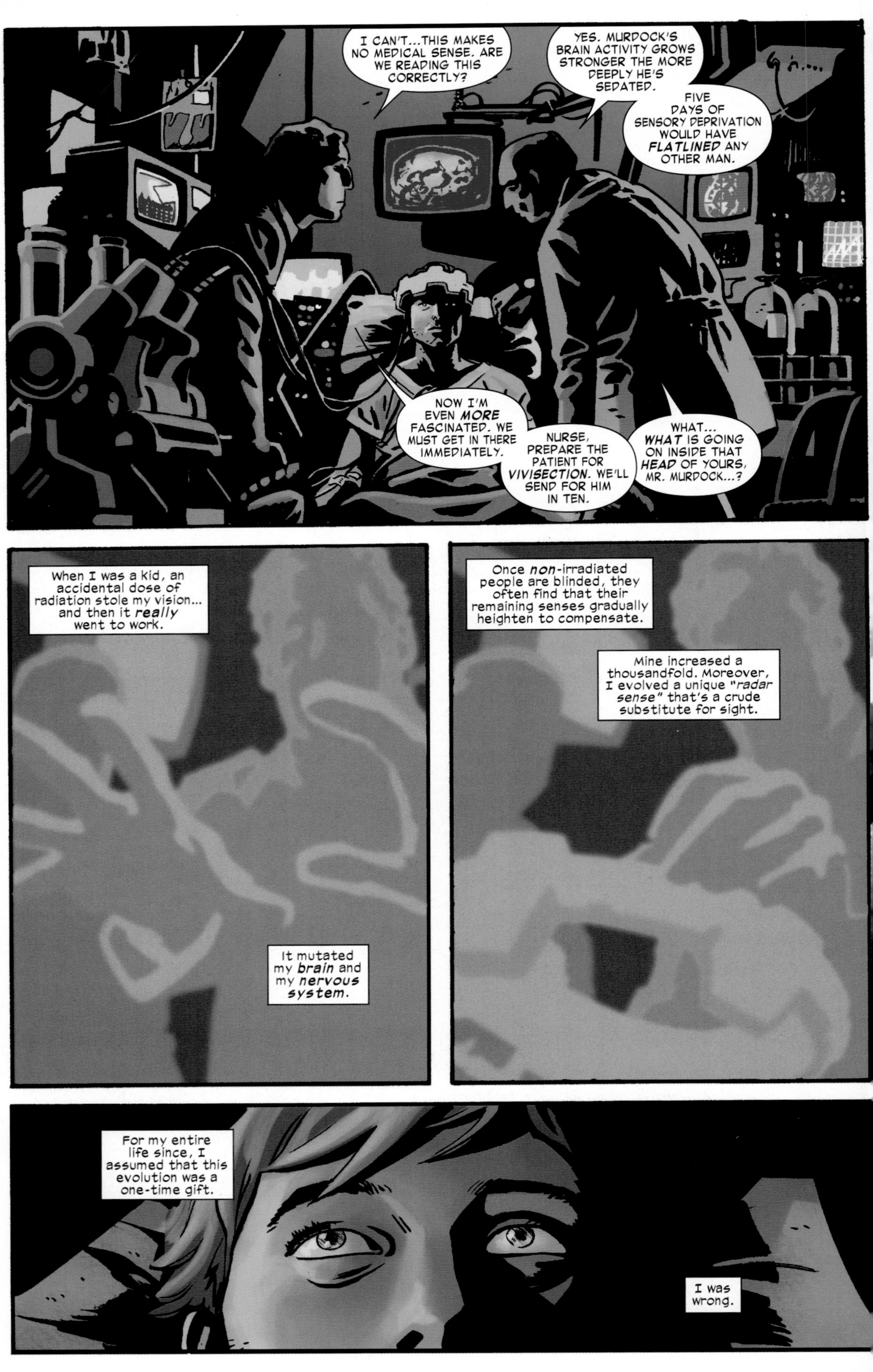
I CAN'T...THIS MAKES NO MEDICAL SENSE. ARE WE READING THIS CORRECTLY?
YES. MURDOCK'S BRAIN ACTIVITY GROWS STRONGER THE MORE DEEPLY HE'S SEDATED.
FIVE DAYS OF SENSORY DEPRIVATION WOULD HAVE *FLATLINED* ANY OTHER MAN.
NOW I'M EVEN *MORE* FASCINATED. WE MUST GET IN THERE IMMEDIATELY.
NURSE, PREPARE THE PATIENT FOR *VIVISECTION*. WE'LL SEND FOR HIM IN TEN.
WHAT... *WHAT* IS GOING ON INSIDE THAT *HEAD* OF YOURS, MR. MURDOCK...?
When I was a kid, an accidental dose of radiation stole my vision... and then it *really* went to work.
It mutated my *brain* and my *nervous system*.
Once *non*-irradiated people are blinded, they often find that their remaining senses gradually heighten to compensate.
Mine increased a thousandfold. Moreover, I evolved a unique "*radar sense*" that's a crude substitute for sight.
For my entire life since, I assumed that this evolution was a one-time gift.
I was wrong.

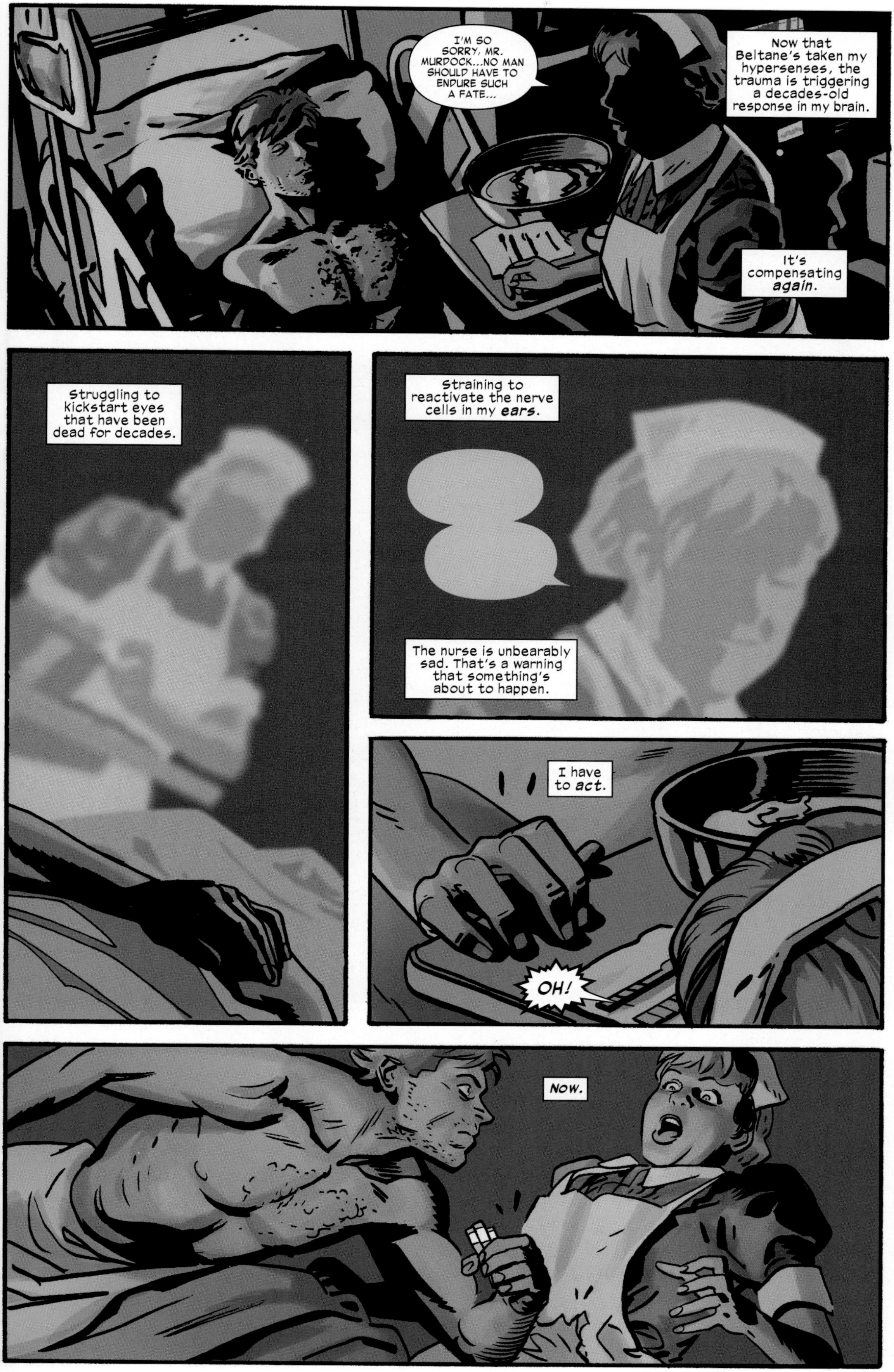
I'M SO SORRY, MR. MURDOCK...NO MAN SHOULD HAVE TO ENDURE SUCH A FATE...
Now that Beltane's taken my hypersenses, the trauma is triggering a decades-old response in my brain.
It's compensating *again*.
Struggling to kickstart eyes that have been dead for decades.
Straining to reactivate the nerve cells in my *ears*.
The nurse is unbearably sad. That's a warning that something's about to happen.
I have to *act*.
OH!
NOW.

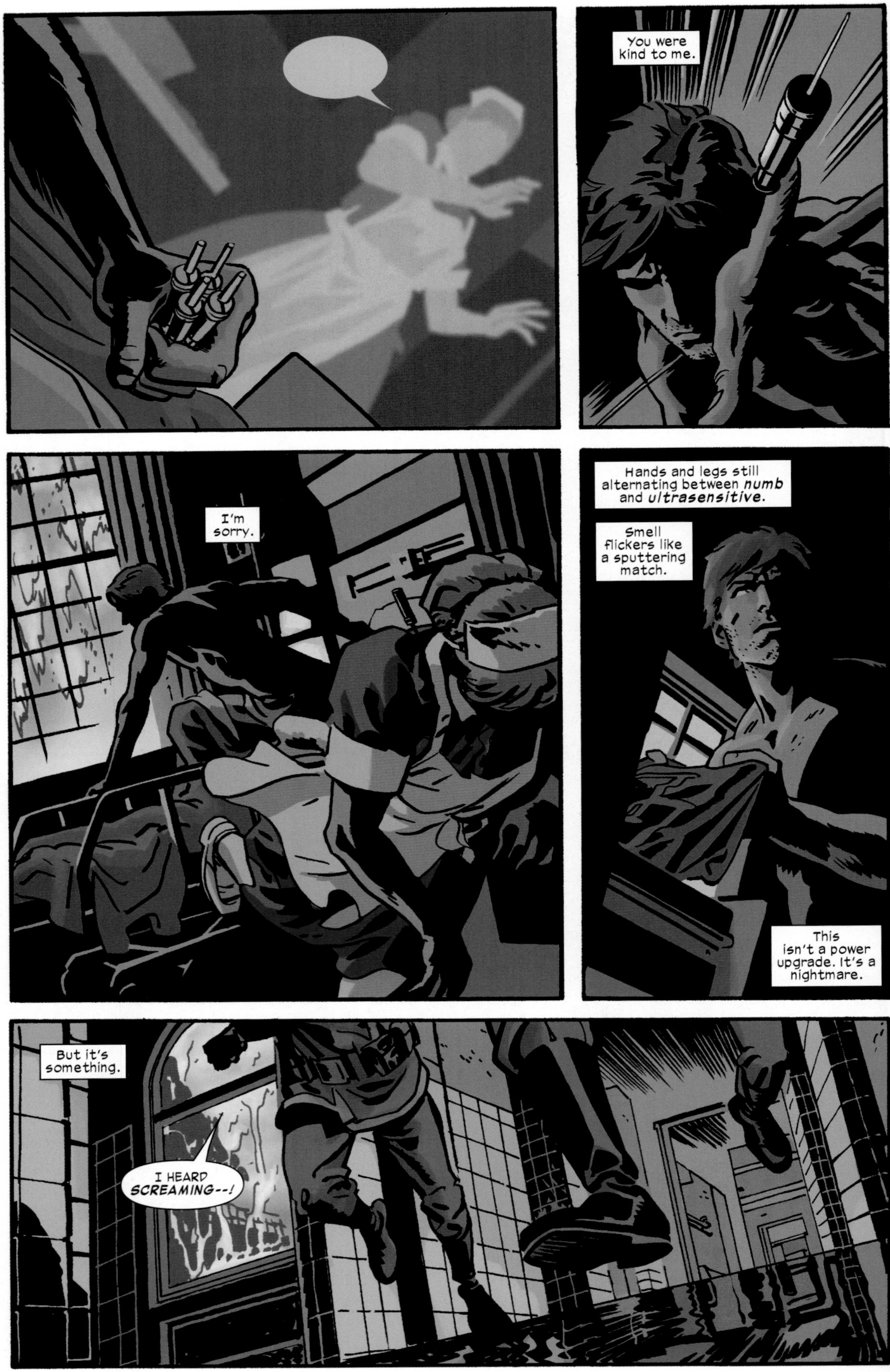
You were kind to me.
I'm sorry.
Hands and legs still alternating between *numb* and *ultrasensitive*.
Smell flickers like a sputtering match.
This isn't a power upgrade. It's a nightmare.
But it's something.
I HEARD *SCREAMING--!*

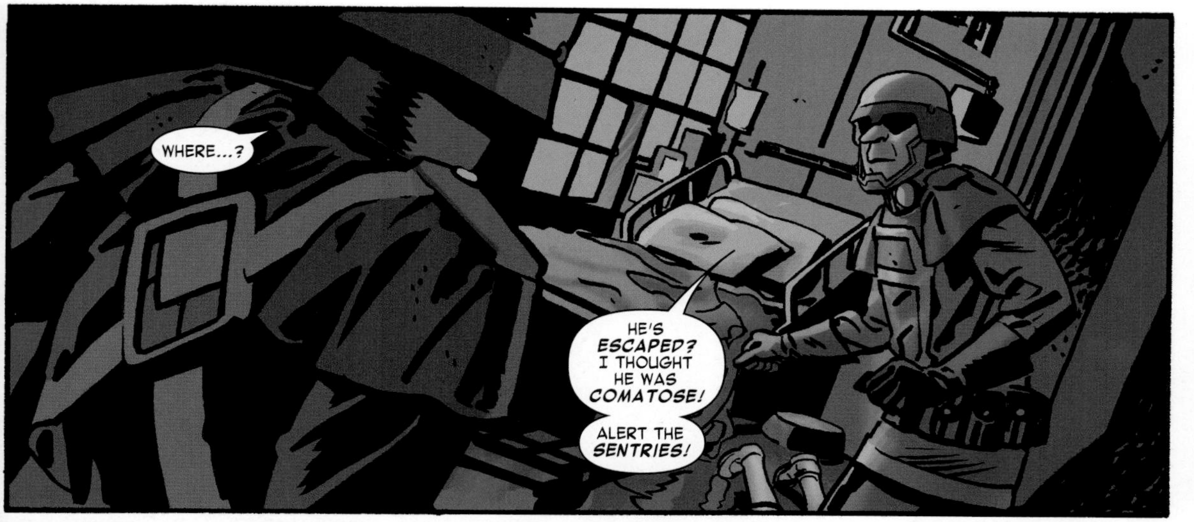
WHERE...?
HE'S ESCAPED? I THOUGHT HE WAS COMATOSE!
ALERT THE SENTRIES!

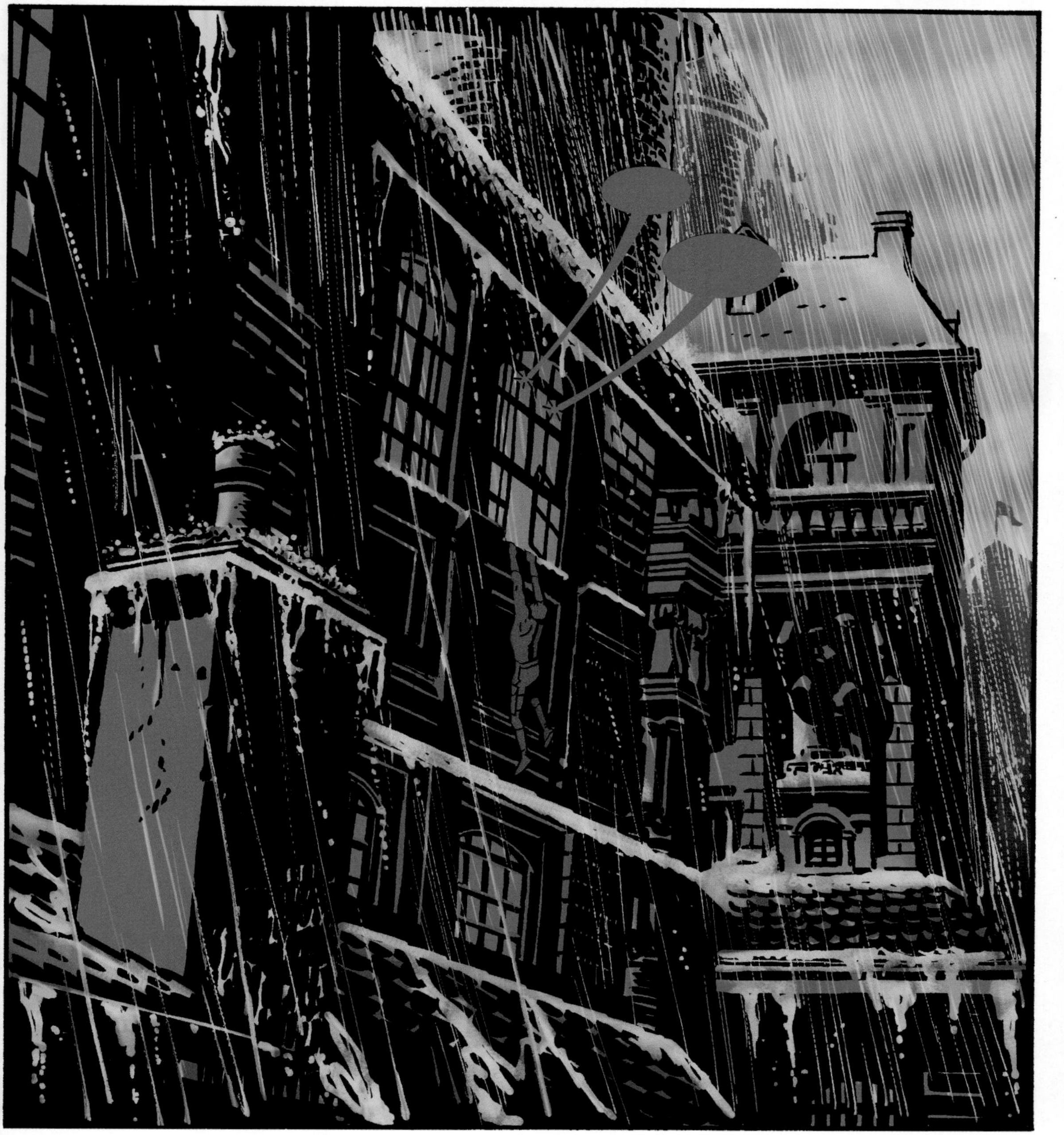

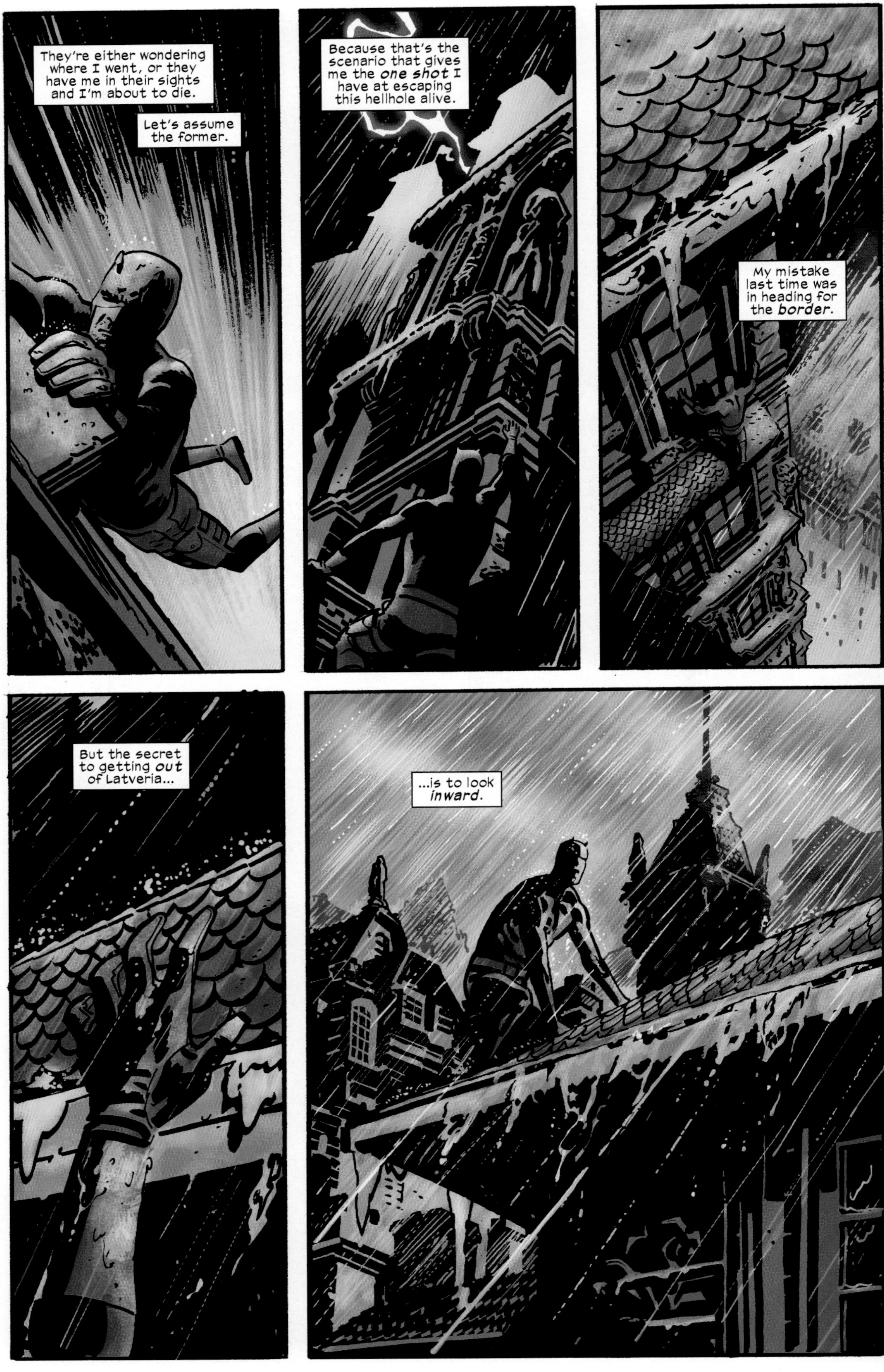
They're either wondering where I went, or they have me in their sights and I'm about to die.
Let's assume the former.
Because that's the scenario that gives me the *one shot* I have at escaping this hellhole alive.
My mistake last time was in heading for the *border*.
But the secret to getting *out* of Latveria...
...is to look *inward*.

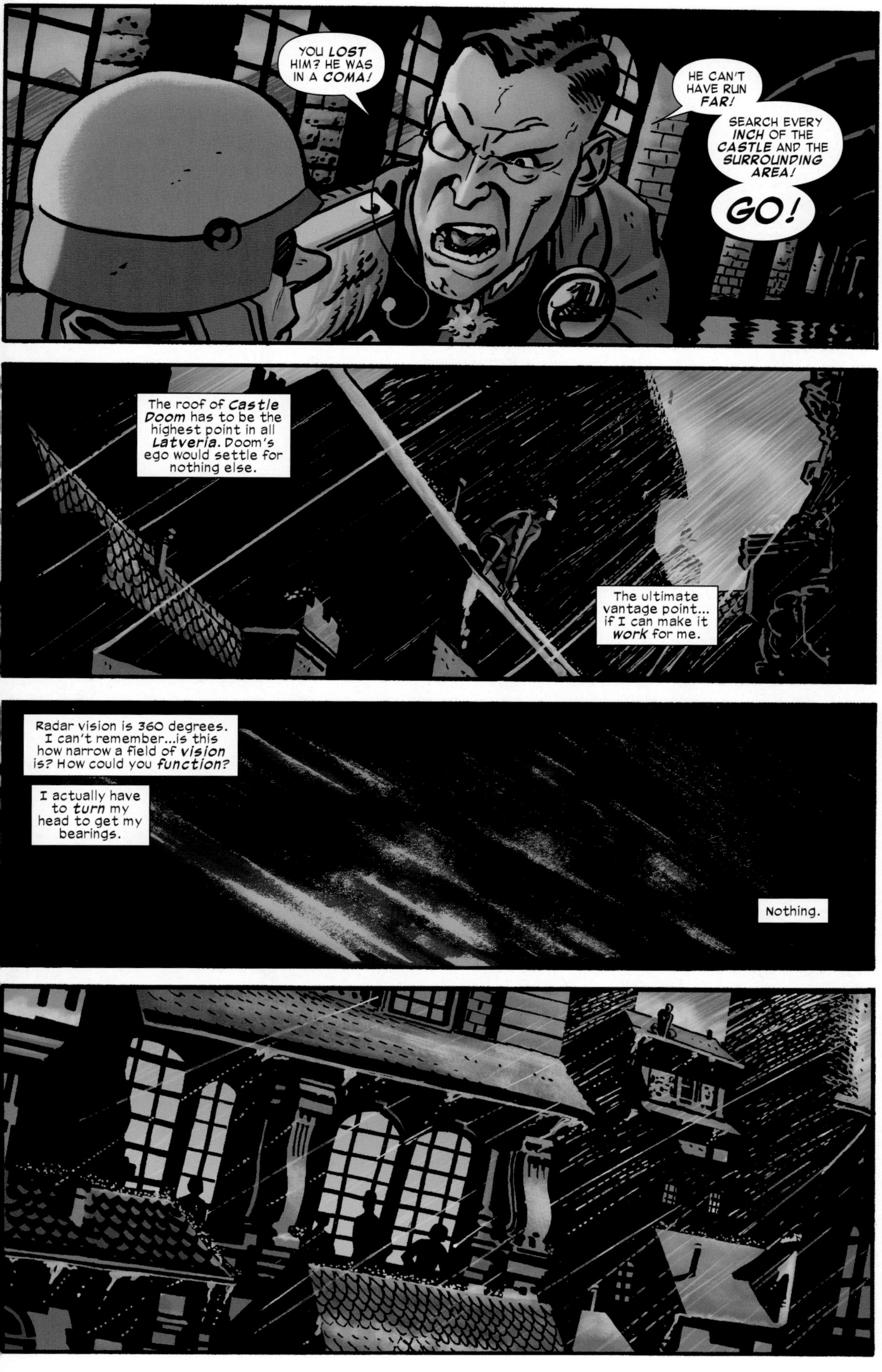
YOU LOST HIM? HE WAS IN A COMA!
HE CAN'T HAVE RUN FAR!
SEARCH EVERY INCH OF THE CASTLE AND THE SURROUNDING AREA!
GO!
The roof of Castle Doom has to be the highest point in all Latveria. Doom's ego would settle for nothing else.
The ultimate vantage point... if I can make it work for me.
Radar vision is 360 degrees. I can't remember...is this how narrow a field of vision is? How could you function?
I actually have to turn my head to get my bearings.
Nothing.

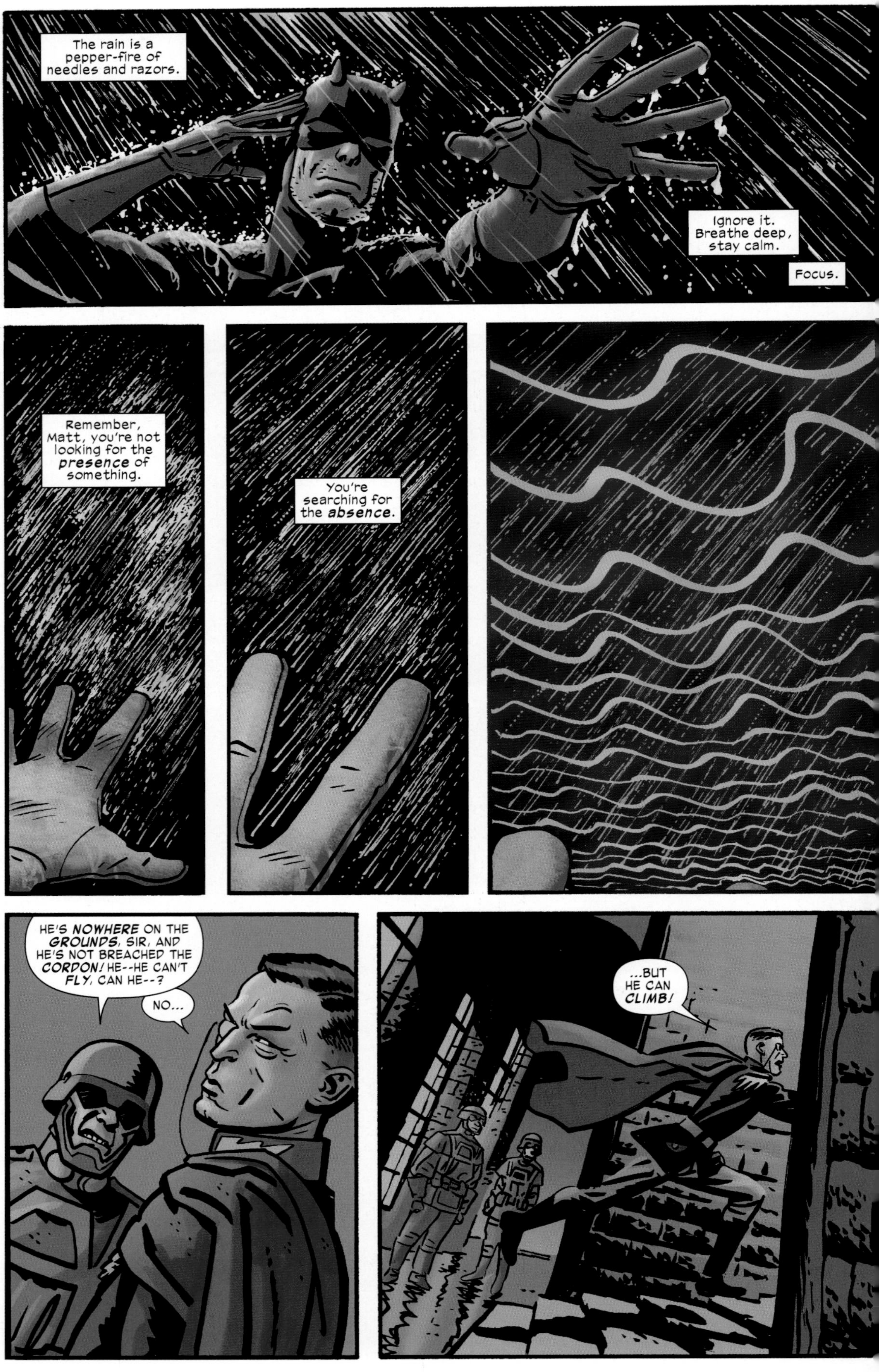
The rain is a pepper-fire of needles and razors.
Ignore it. Breathe deep, stay calm.
Focus.
Remember, Matt, you're not looking for the *presence* of something.
You're searching for the *absence*.
HE'S *NOWHERE* ON THE *GROUNDS*, SIR, AND HE'S NOT BREACHED THE *CORDON!* HE--HE CAN'T *FLY*, CAN HE--?
NO...
...BUT HE CAN *CLIMB!*

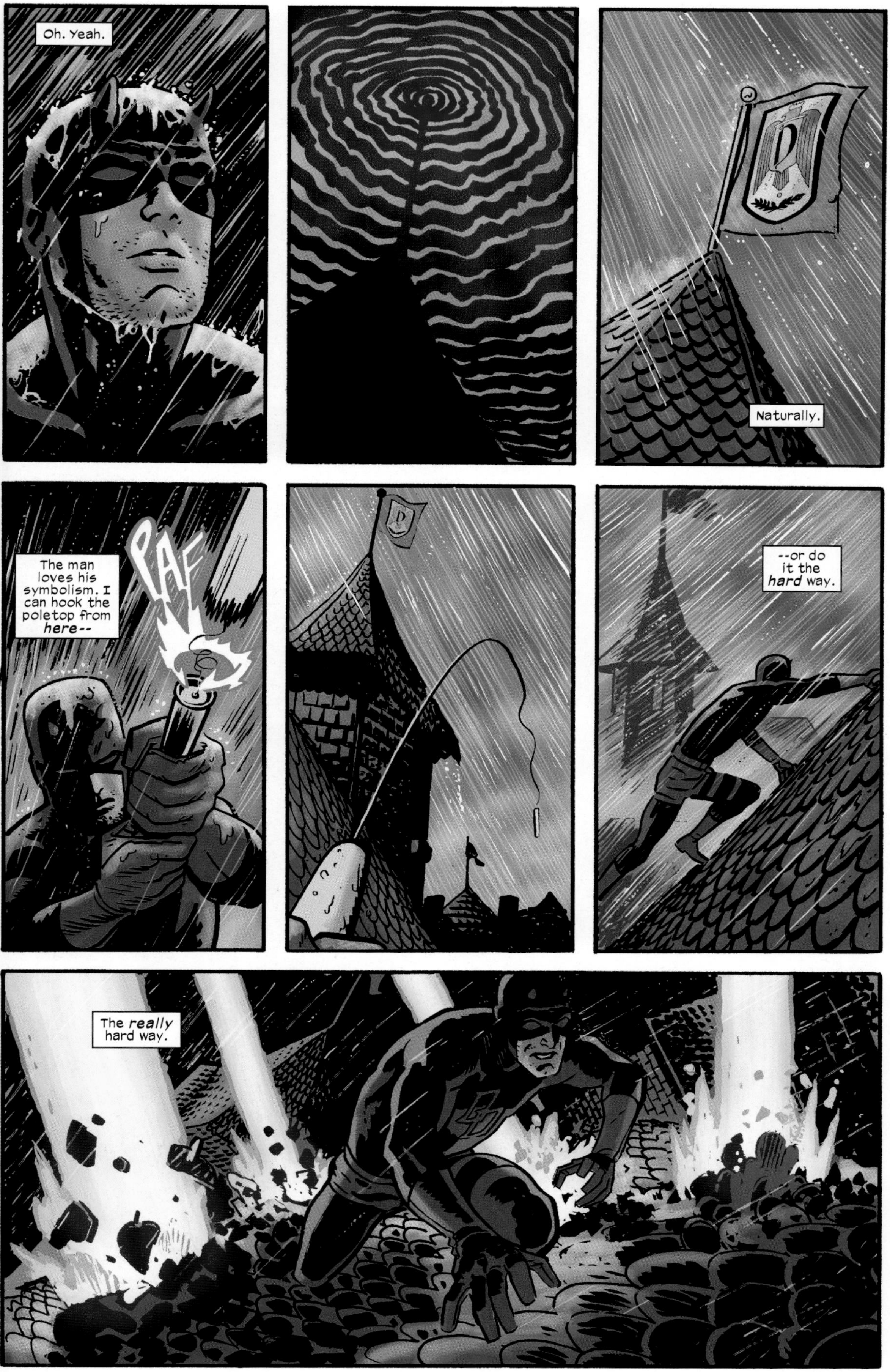

Oh. Yeah.
Naturally.
The man loves his symbolism. I can hook the poletop from *here*--
PAF
--or do it the *hard* way.
The *really* hard way.

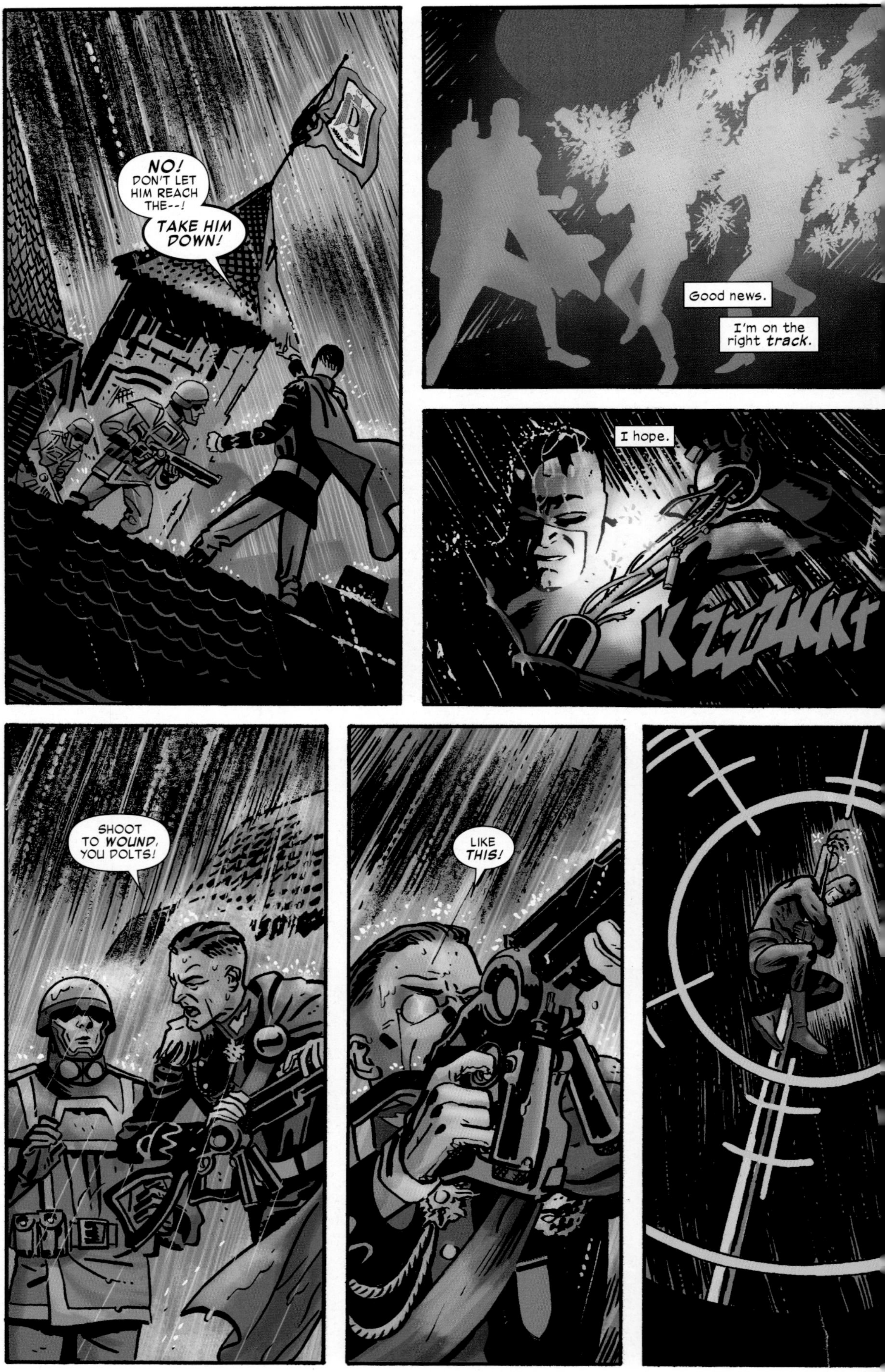
NO! DON'T LET HIM REACH THE--!
TAKE HIM DOWN!
Good news.
I'm on the right track.
I hope.
KZZZKKT
SHOOT TO WOUND, YOU DOLTS!
LIKE THIS!

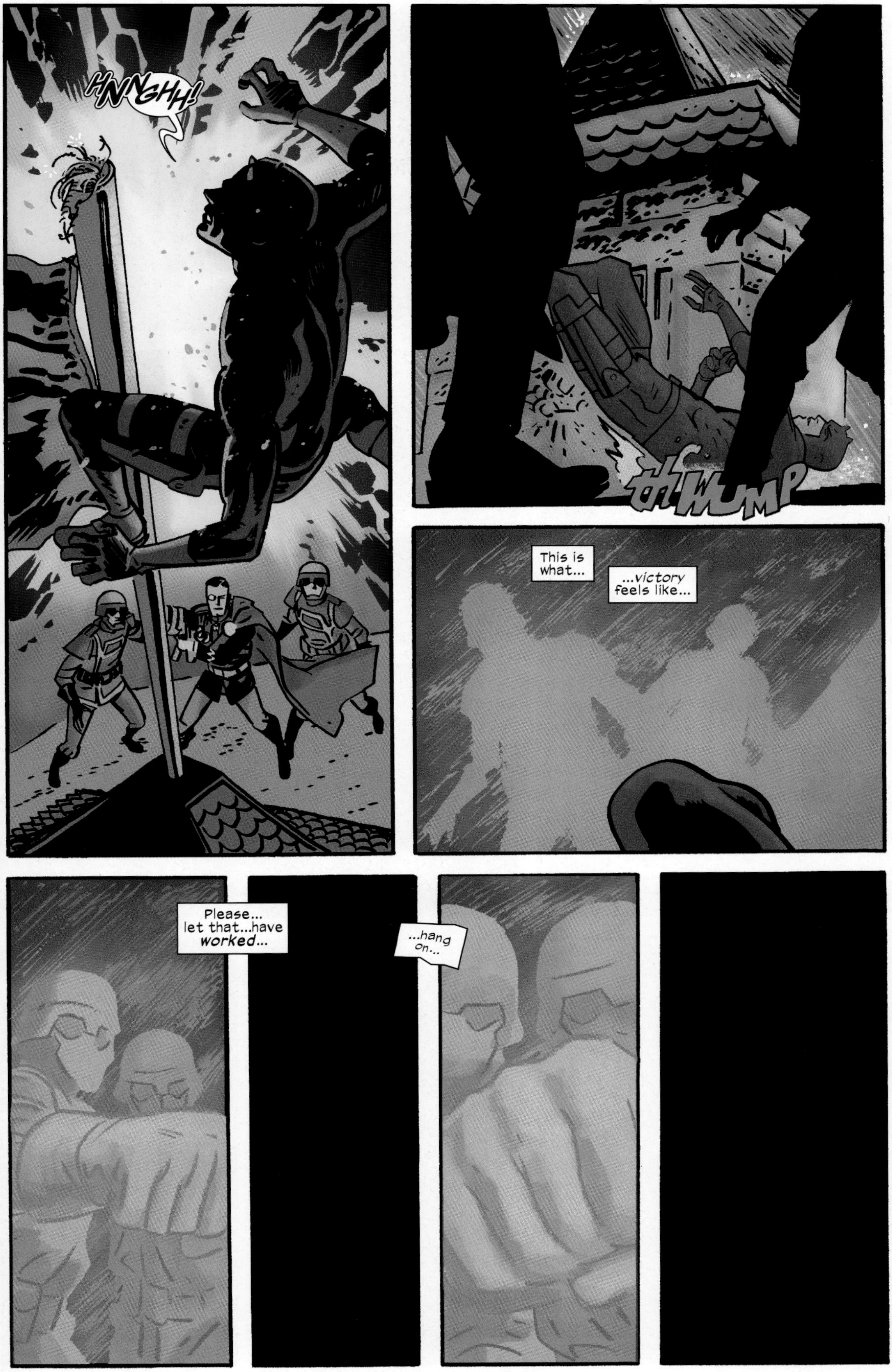
HNNGHH!
thWUMP
This is what...
...victory feels like...
Please... let that...have worked...
...hang on...

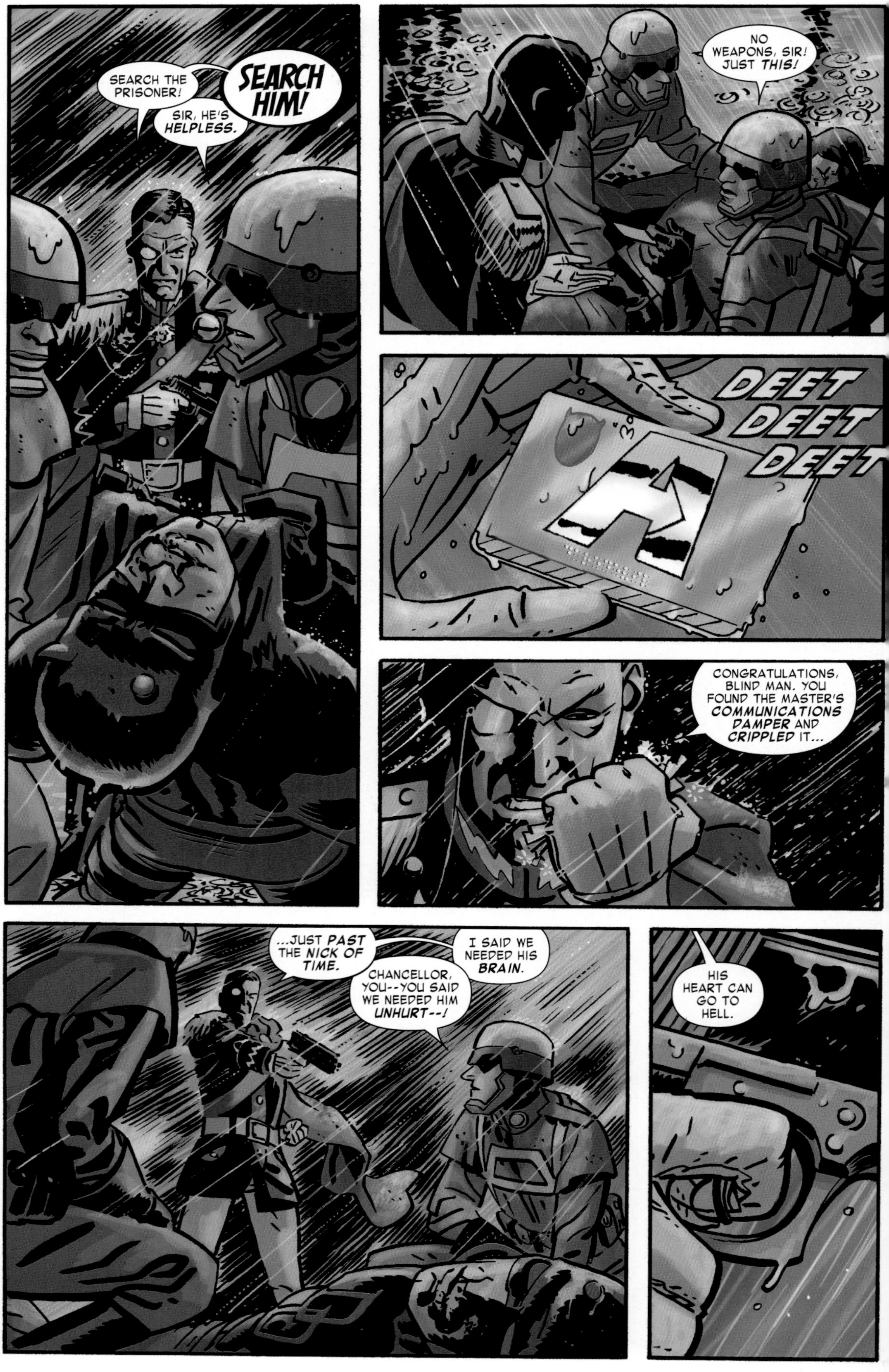
SEARCH THE PRISONER!
SEARCH HIM!
SIR, HE'S HELPLESS.
NO WEAPONS, SIR! JUST THIS!
DEET DEET DEET
CONGRATULATIONS, BLIND MAN. YOU FOUND THE MASTER'S COMMUNICATIONS DAMPER AND CRIPPLED IT...
...JUST PAST THE NICK OF TIME.
CHANCELLOR, YOU--YOU SAID WE NEEDED HIM UNHURT--!
I SAID WE NEEDED HIS BRAIN.
HIS HEART CAN GO TO HELL.

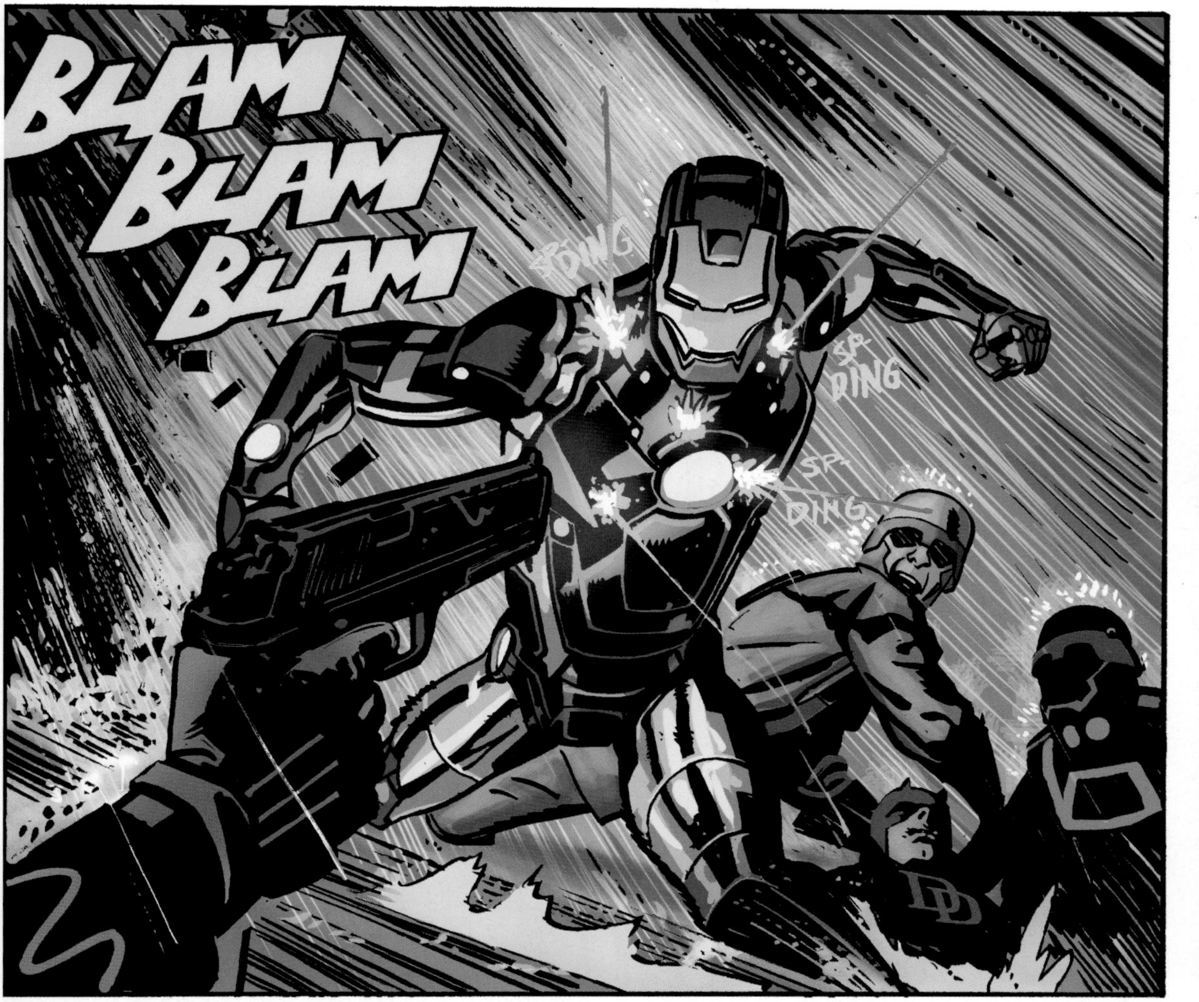
BLAM
BLAM
BLAM
SPDING
SP-DING
SP-DING

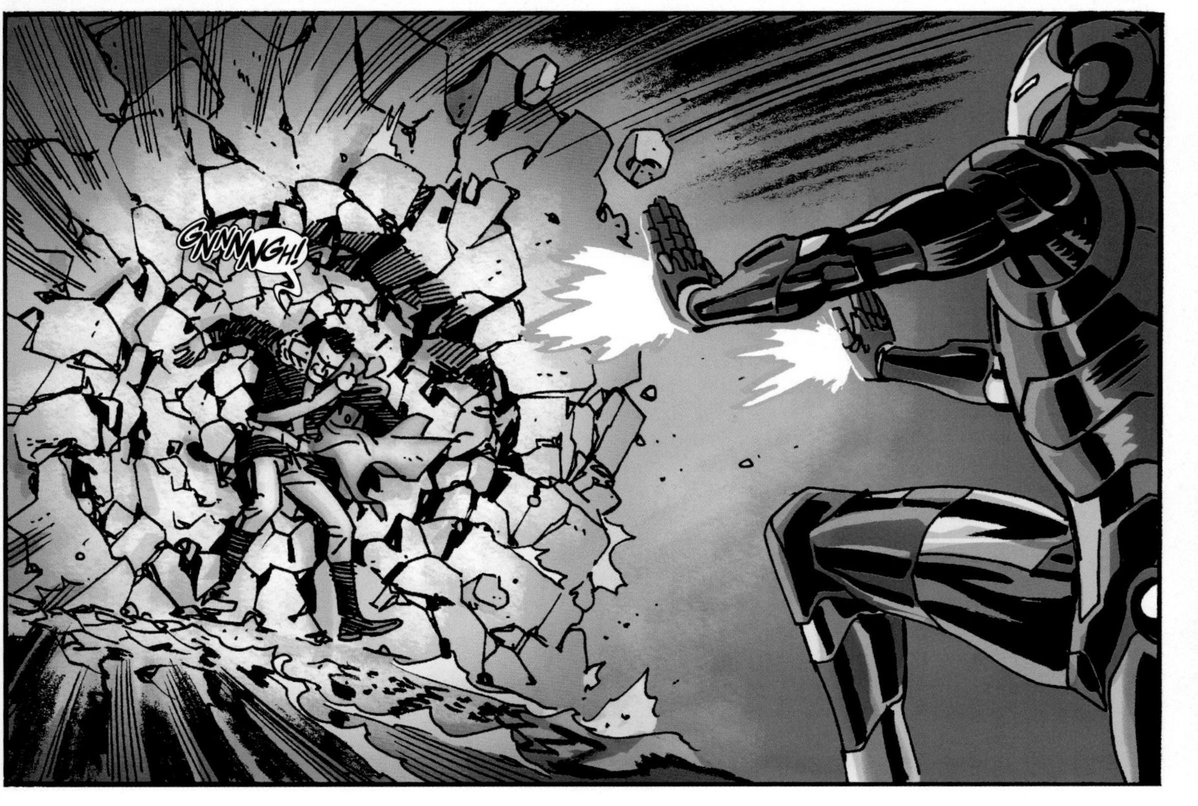
GNNNNGH!

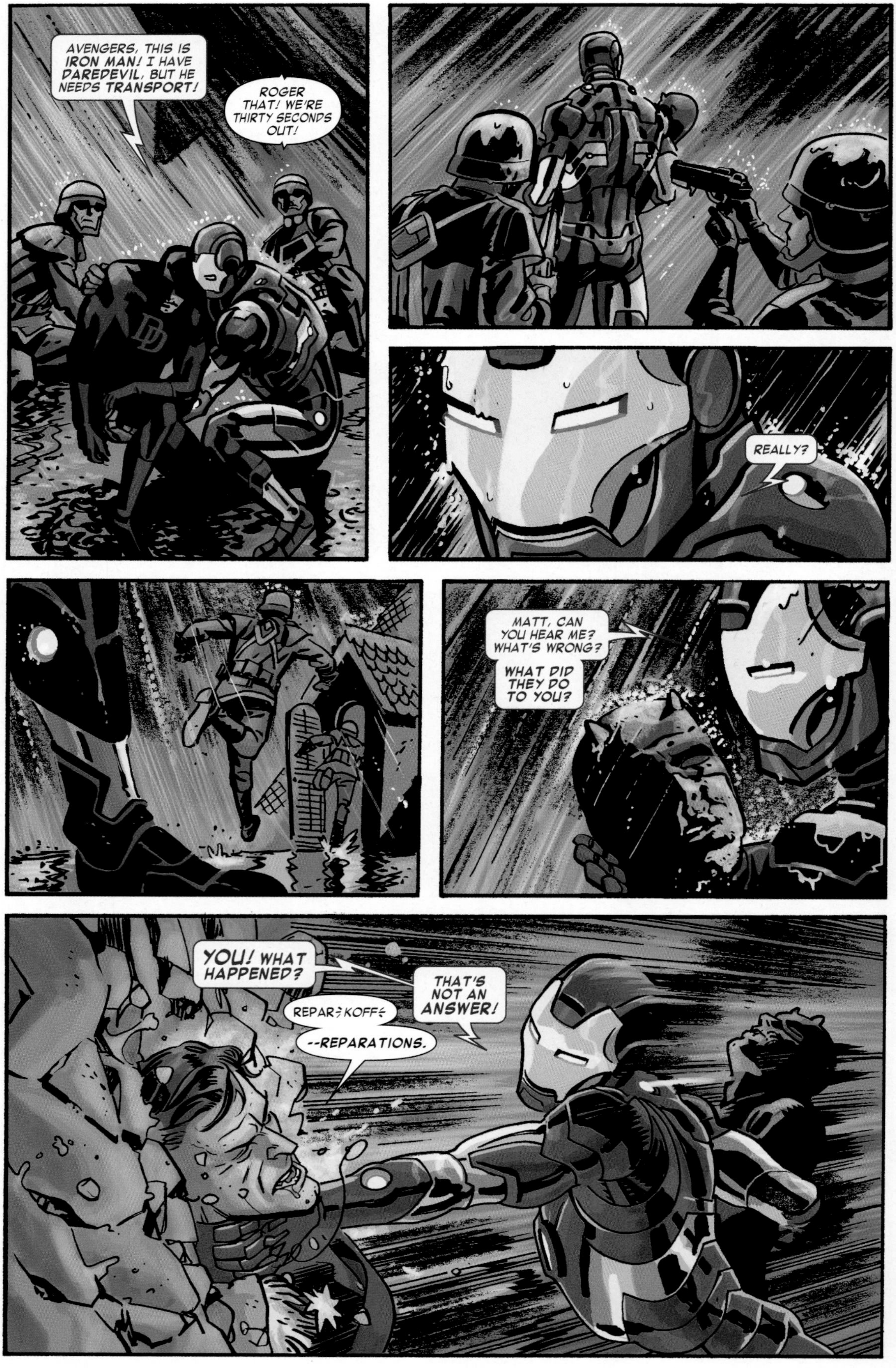
AVENGERS, THIS IS IRON MAN! I HAVE DAREDEVIL, BUT HE NEEDS TRANSPORT!
ROGER THAT! WE'RE THIRTY SECONDS OUT!
REALLY?
MATT, CAN YOU HEAR ME? WHAT'S WRONG?
WHAT DID THEY DO TO YOU?
YOU! WHAT HAPPENED?
REPAR-KOFF-
--REPARATIONS.
THAT'S NOT AN ANSWER!

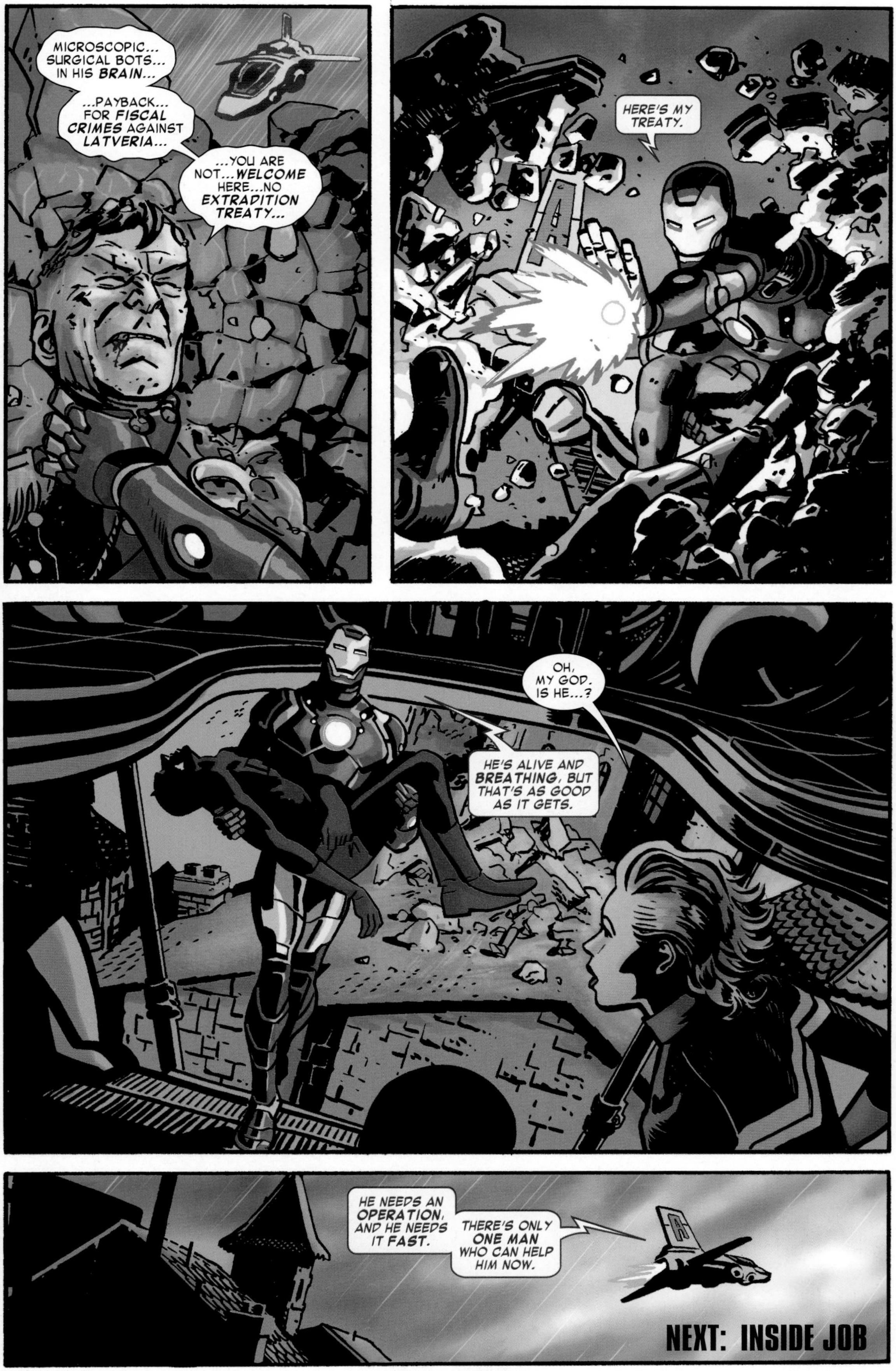
MICROSCOPIC... SURGICAL BOTS... IN HIS BRAIN...
...PAYBACK... FOR FISCAL CRIMES AGAINST LATVERIA...
...YOU ARE NOT...WELCOME HERE...NO EXTRADITION TREATY...
HERE'S MY TREATY.
OH, MY GOD. IS HE...?
HE'S ALIVE AND BREATHING, BUT THAT'S AS GOOD AS IT GETS.
HE NEEDS AN OPERATION, AND HE NEEDS IT FAST.
THERE'S ONLY ONE MAN WHO CAN HELP HIM NOW.
NEXT: INSIDE JOB

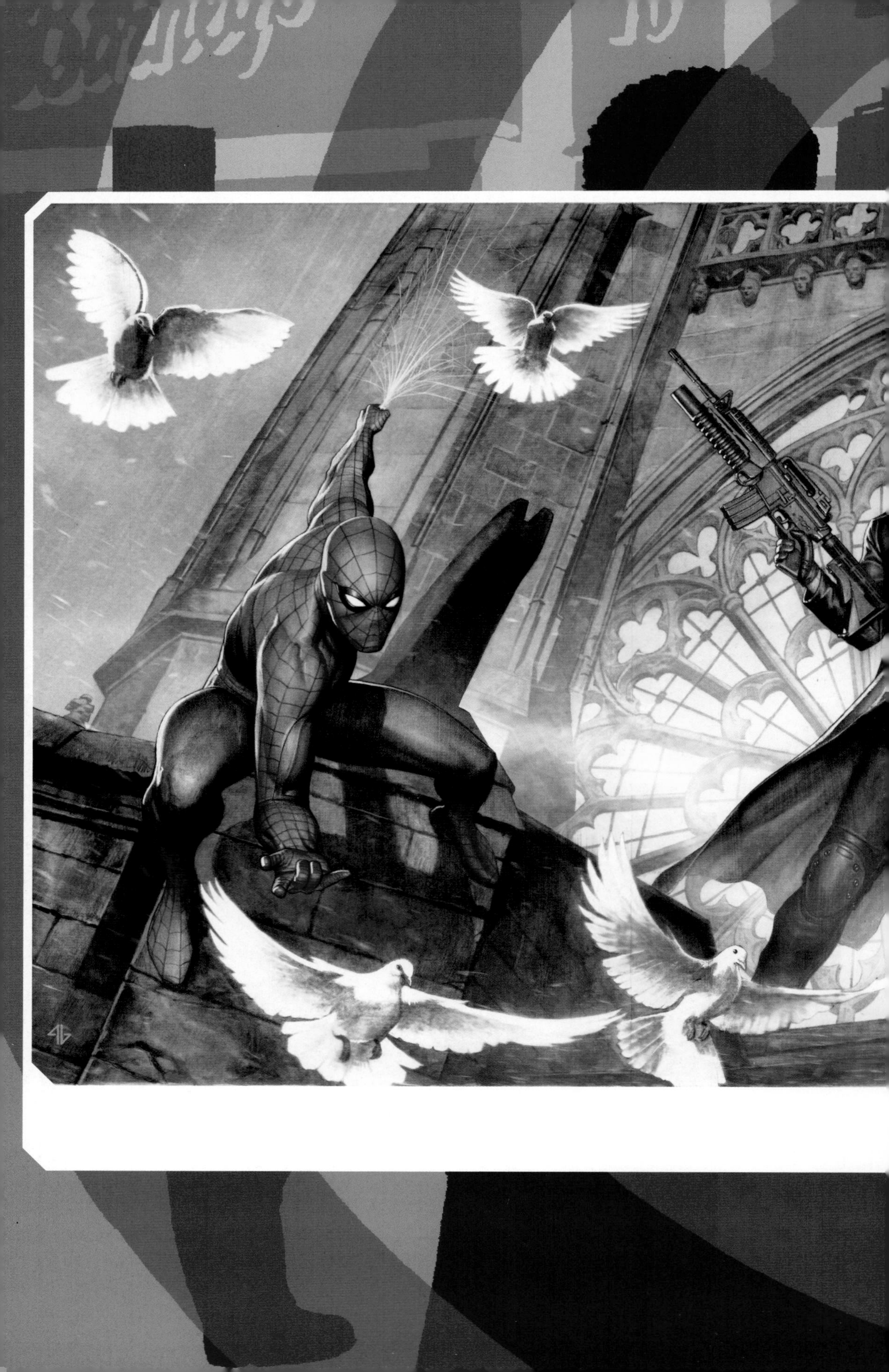

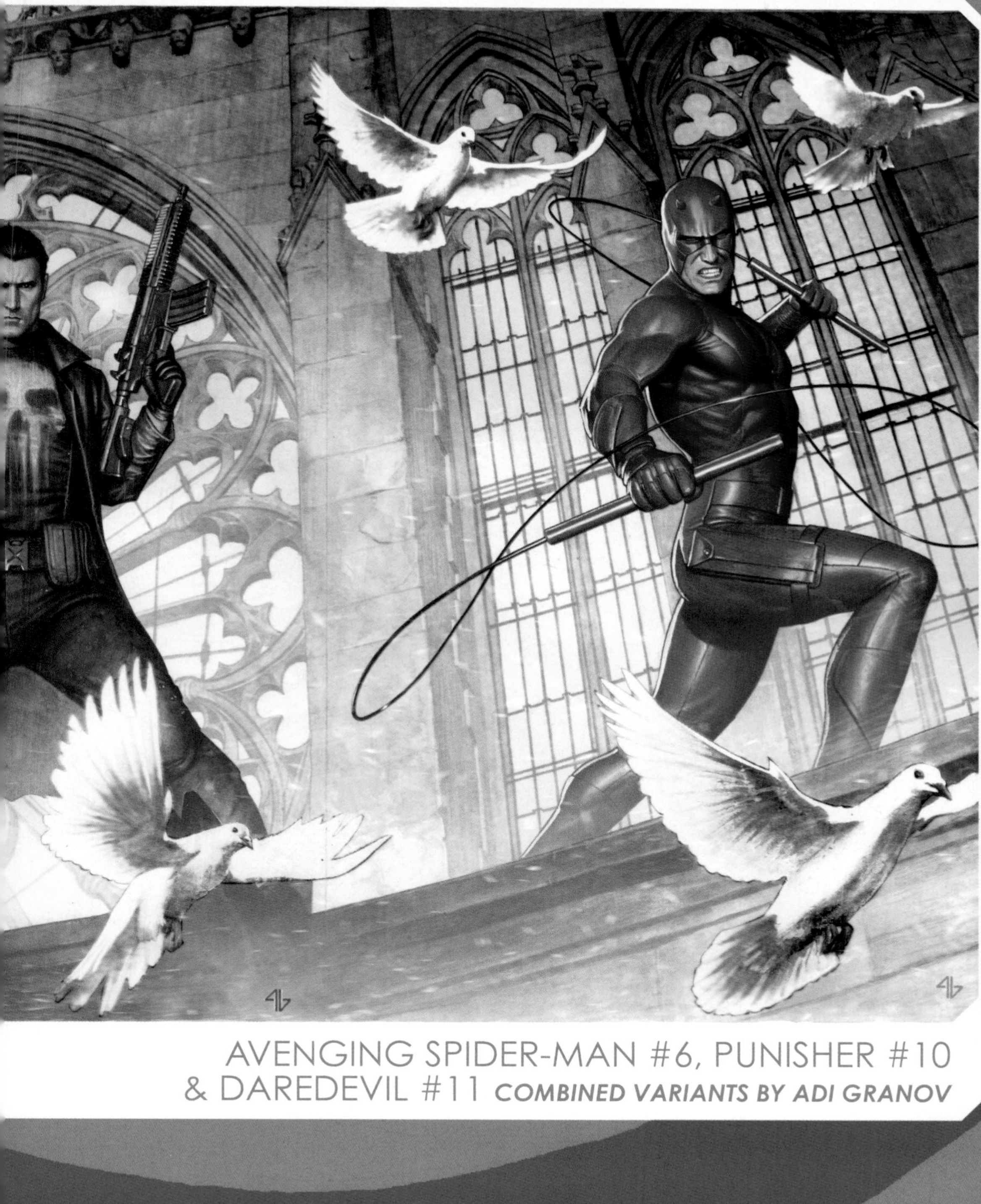

AVENGING SPIDER-MAN #6, PUNISHER #10
& DAREDEVIL #11 **COMBINED VARIANTS BY ADI GRANOV**

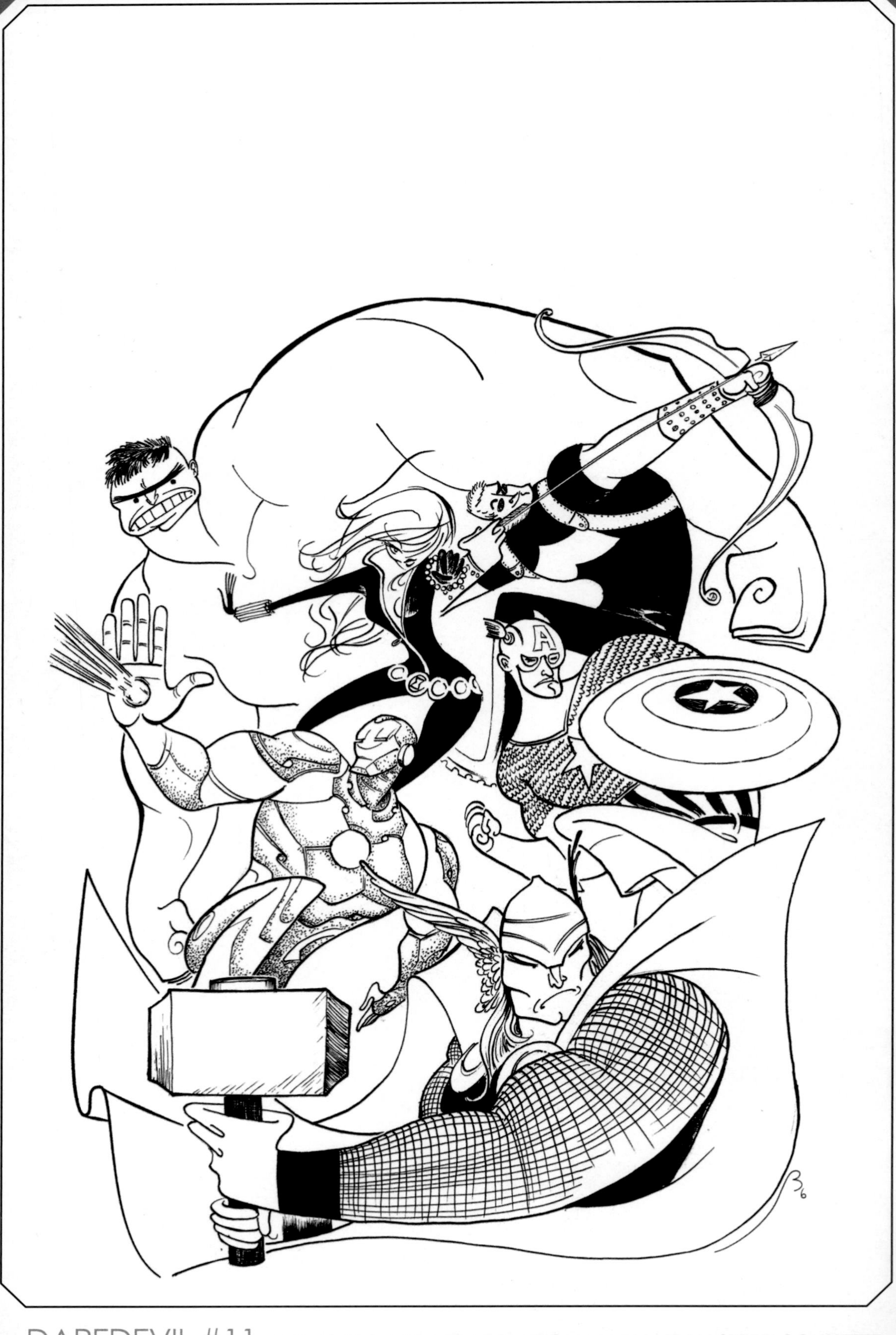

DAREDEVIL #11 ***AVENGERS ART APPRECIATION VARIANT BY STEFFI SCHUETZE***

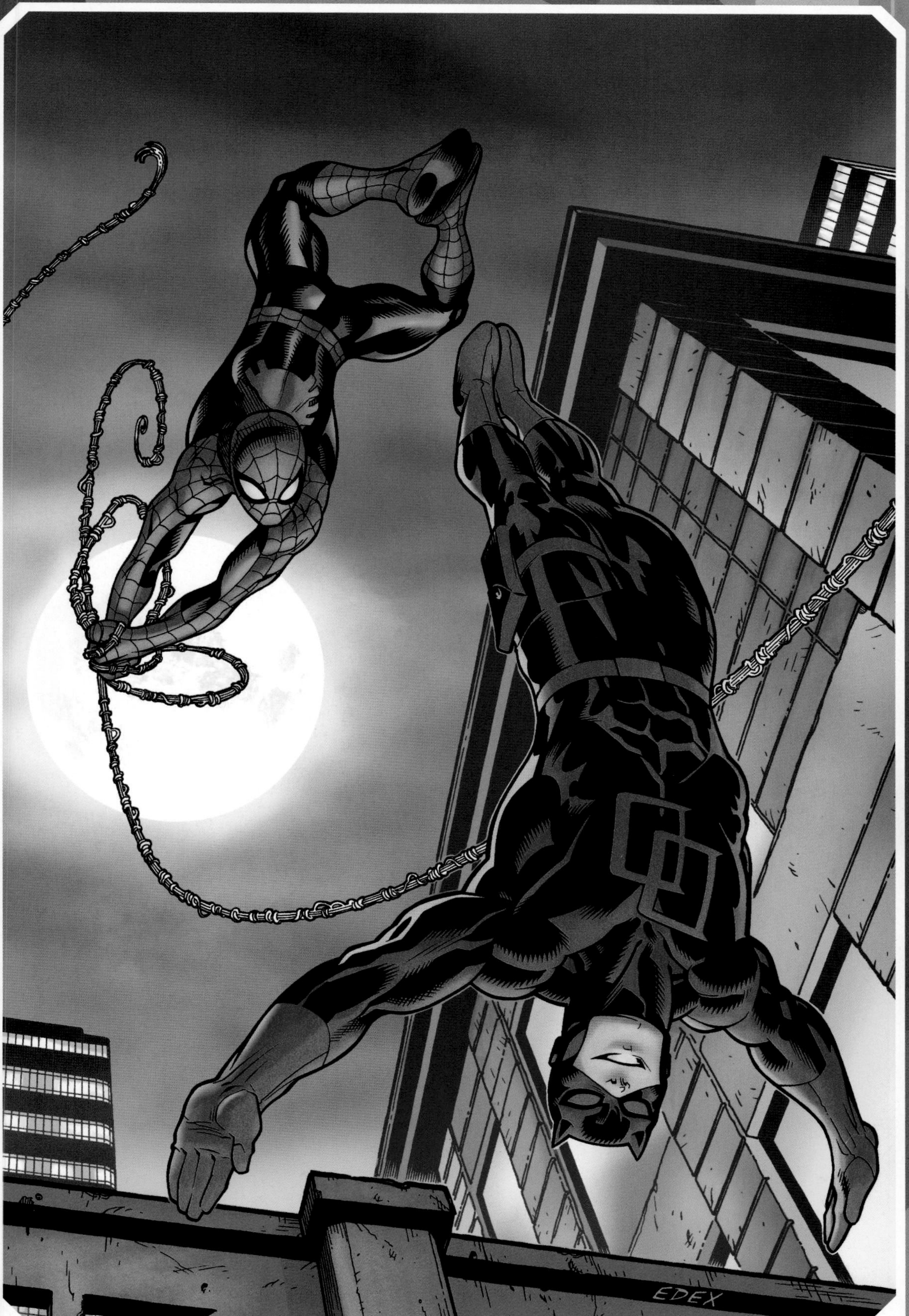
EDEX

DAREDEVIL #14 *AMAZING SPIDER-MAN 50TH ANNIVERSARY VARIANT*
BY ED McGUINNESS, DEXTER VINES & JAVIER RODRIGUEZ

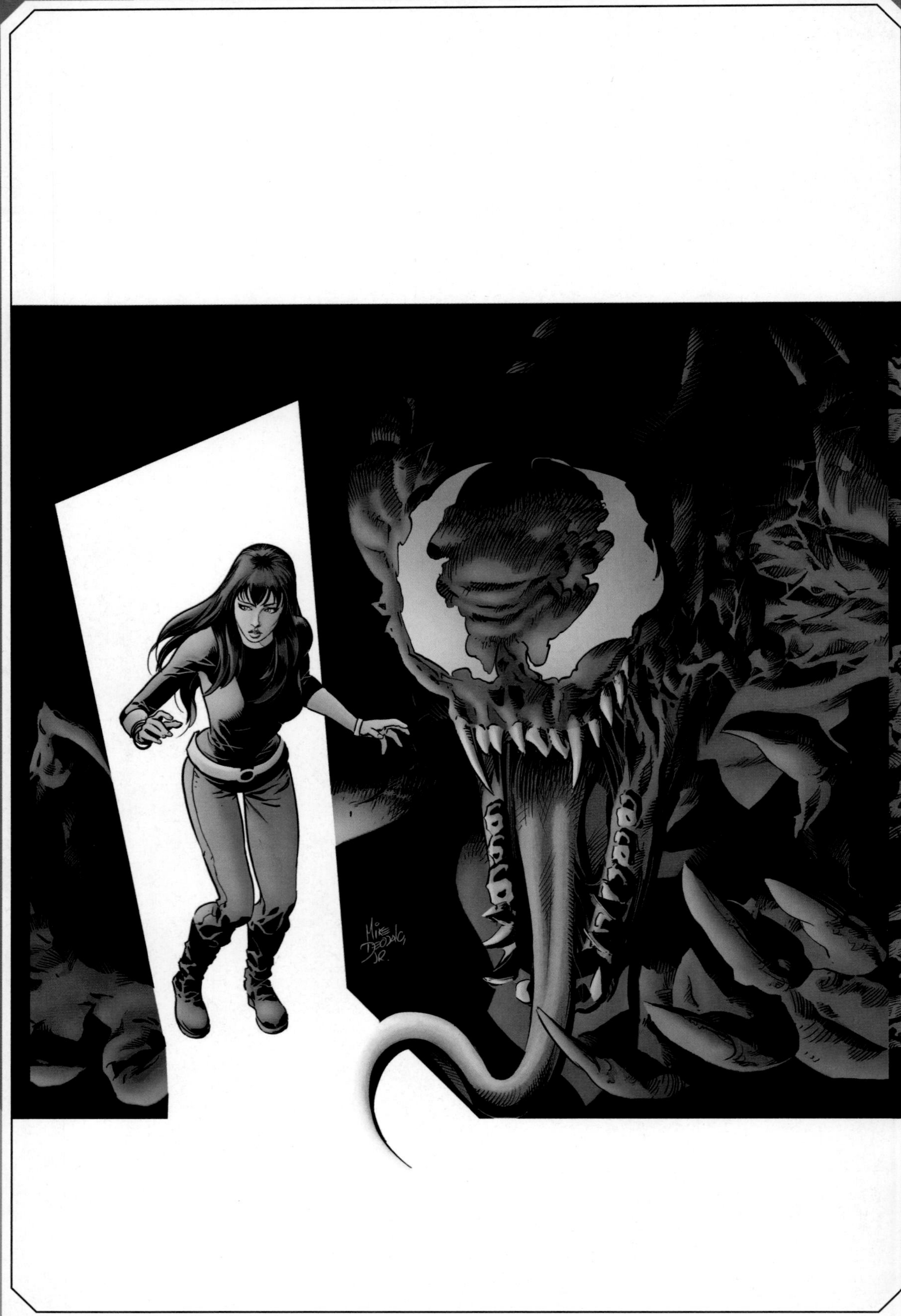
MIKE DEODATO JR.

DAREDEVIL #14 ***ASM IN MOTION VARIANT***
BY MIKE DEODATO JR. & MATT HOLLINGSWORTH

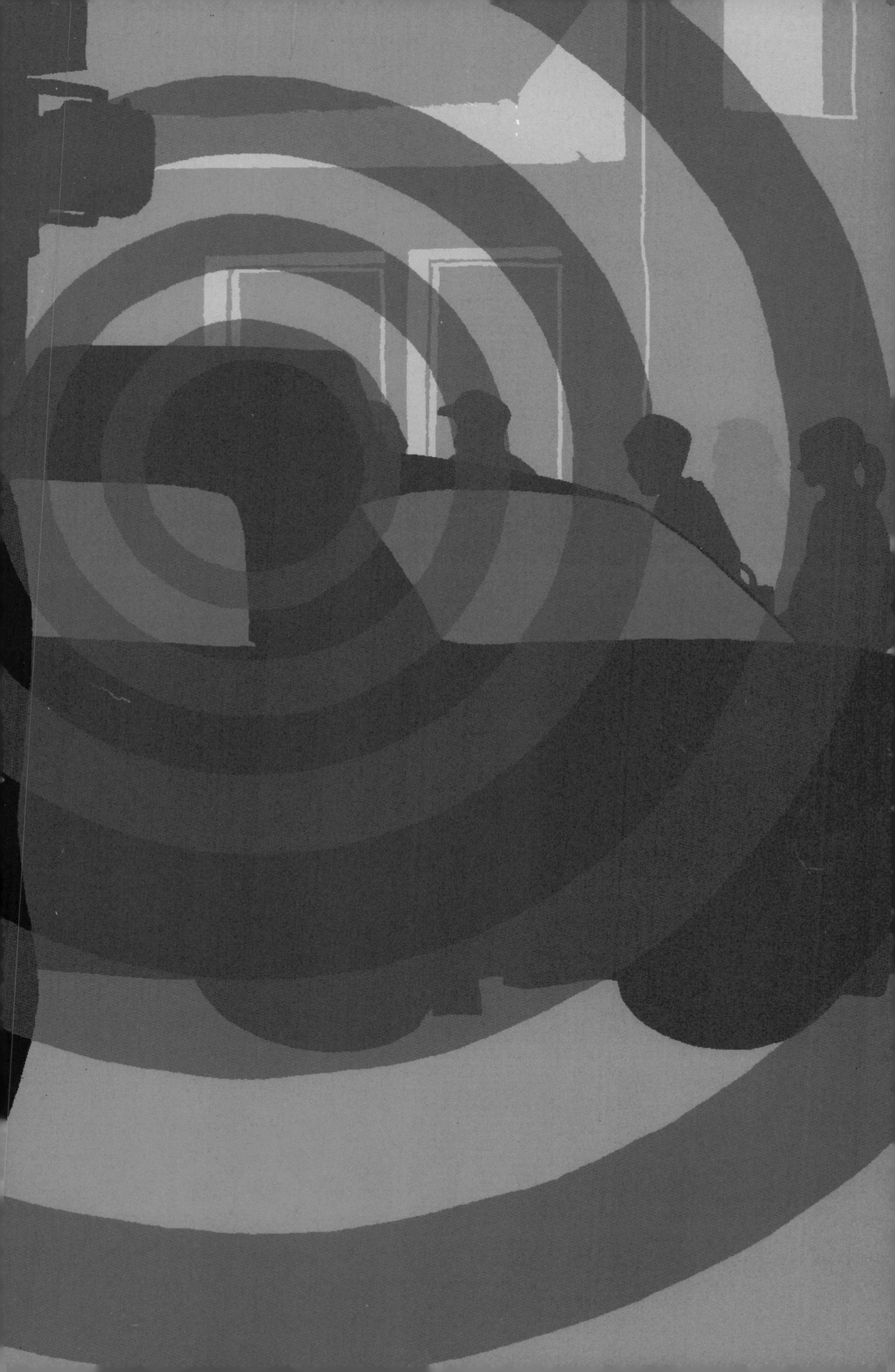